Arata
THE LEGEND

20

We are Man, born of Heaven and Earth,
Moon and Sun and everything under them.

Eyes, Ears, Nose, Tongue, Body, Mind...

Purity will pierce evil and
open up the world of darkness.

All life will be reborn and invigorated.

Appear now.

STORY & ART BY
Yuu Watase

Arata THE LEGEND

CHARACTERS

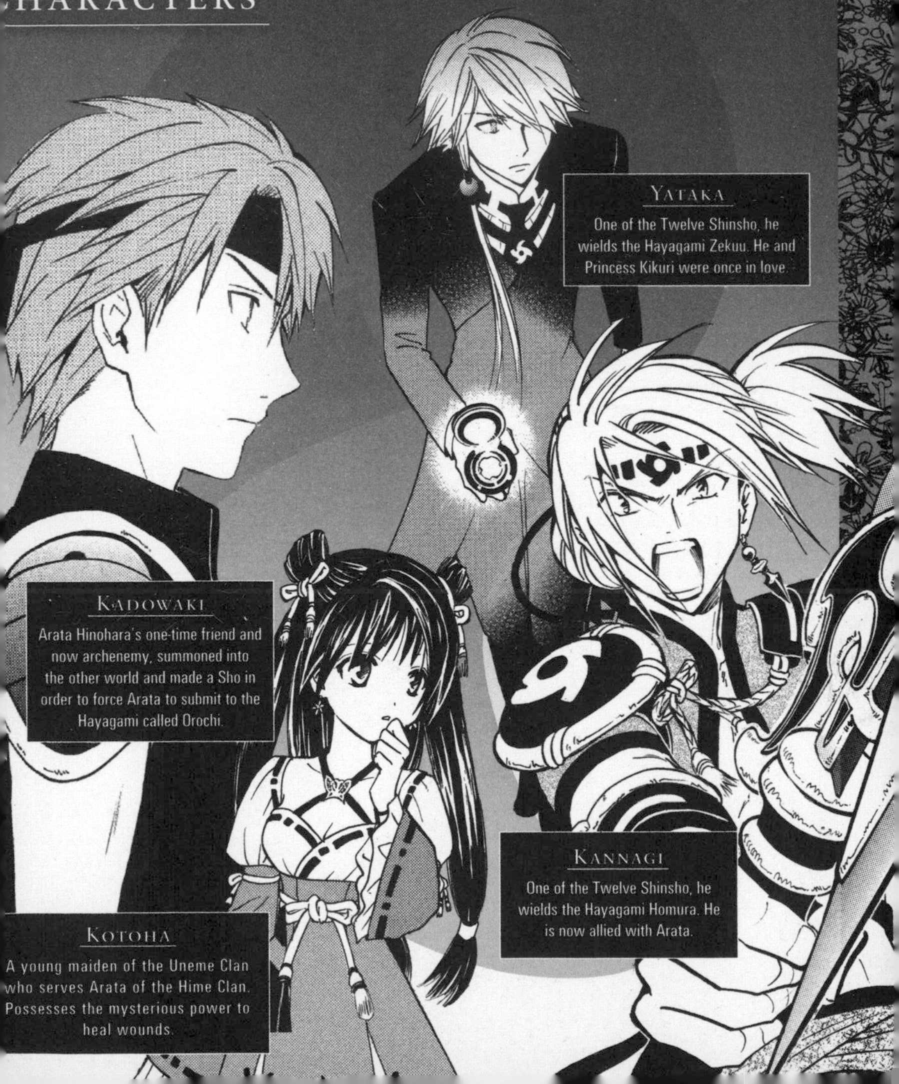

Yataka
One of the Twelve Shinsho, he wields the Hayagami Zekuu. He and Princess Kikuri were once in love.

Kadowaki
Arata Hinohara's one-time friend and now archenemy, summoned into the other world and made a Sho in order to force Arata to submit to the Hayagami called Orochi.

Kannagi
One of the Twelve Shinsho, he wields the Hayagami Homura. He is now allied with Arata.

Kotoha
A young maiden of the Uneme Clan who serves Arata of the Hime Clan. Possesses the mysterious power to heal wounds.

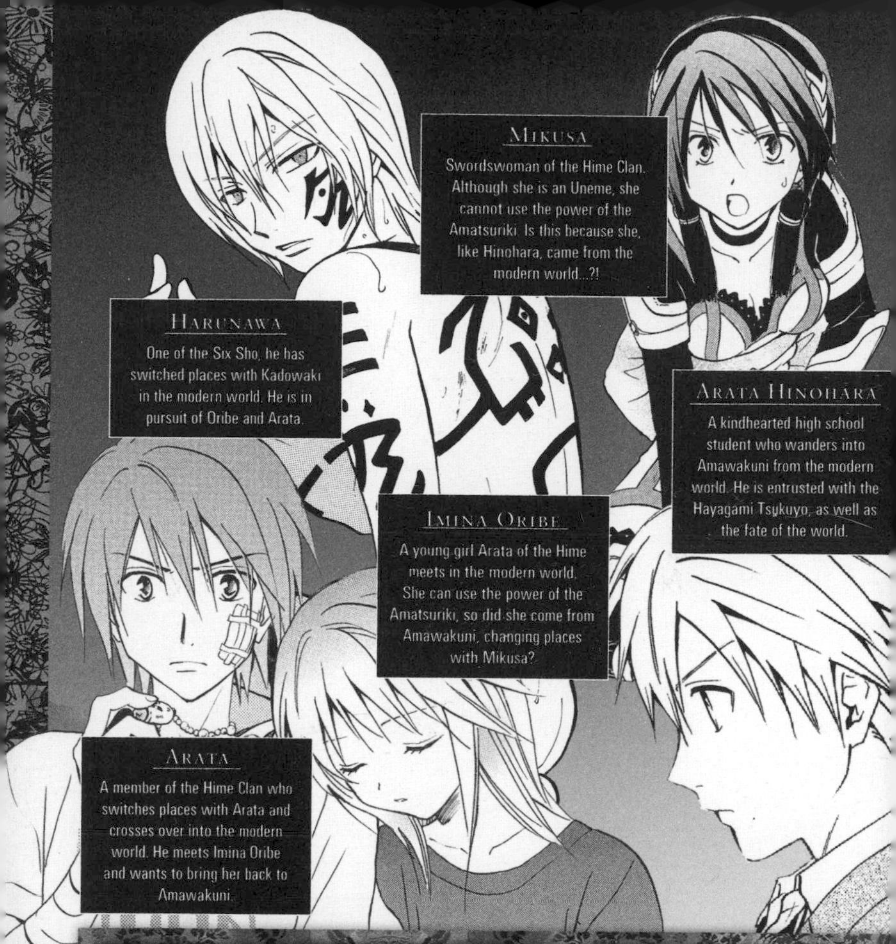
MIKUSA
Swordswoman of the Hime Clan. Although she is an Uneme, she cannot use the power of the Amatsuriki. Is this because she, like Hinohara, came from the modern world...?!
HARUNAWA
One of the Six Sho, he has switched places with Kadowaki in the modern world. He is in pursuit of Oribe and Arata.
ARATA HINOHARA
A kindhearted high school student who wanders into Amawakuni from the modern world. He is entrusted with the Hayagami Tsukuyo, as well as the fate of the world.
IMINA ORIBE
A young girl Arata of the Hime meets in the modern world. She can use the power of the Amatsuriki, so did she come from Amawakuni, changing places with Mikusa?
ARATA
A member of the Hime Clan who switches places with Arata and crosses over into the modern world. He meets Imina Oribe and wants to bring her back to Amawakuni.

THE STORY THUS FAR

Arata Hinohara, a modern Japanese high school student, finds himself in Amawakuni, a land in another dimension. There he is chosen as the new wielder of the legendary Hayagami Tsukuyo and embarks on a quest to save Princess Hime, who has kept the powers of the various Hayagami in check but now hovers precariously near death.

Isora, one of the Six Sho, has abducted Mikusa, and while in pursuit Arata Hinohara encounters Kadowaki. But is Kadowaki a friend or foe? That's the question Isora puts to Arata, and it's not an easy one to answer. Kadowaki attacks Isora and winds up captured, yet Arata manages to save both him and Mikusa. Combining their powers, Arata and Kadowaki free Isora from his demonization, leaving the defeated Sho to submit to one or the other. In the end, he chooses to submit to Kadowaki!

Meanwhile, in modern-day Japan, Arata of the Hime and Oribe continue their efforts to elude Harunawa, who is out to slay them both.

20
Arata
THE LEGEND

CONTENTS

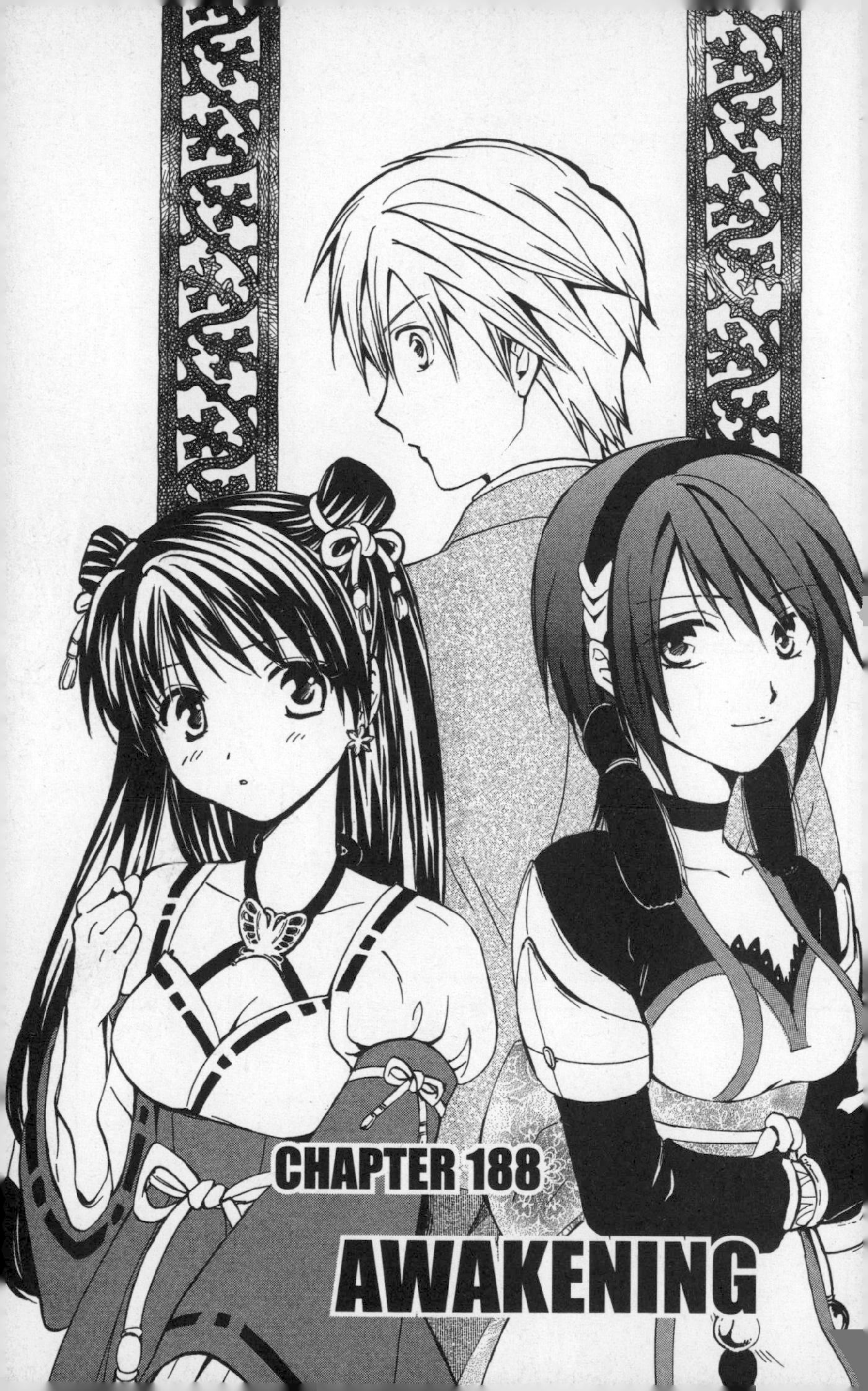
CHAPTER 188
AWAKENING

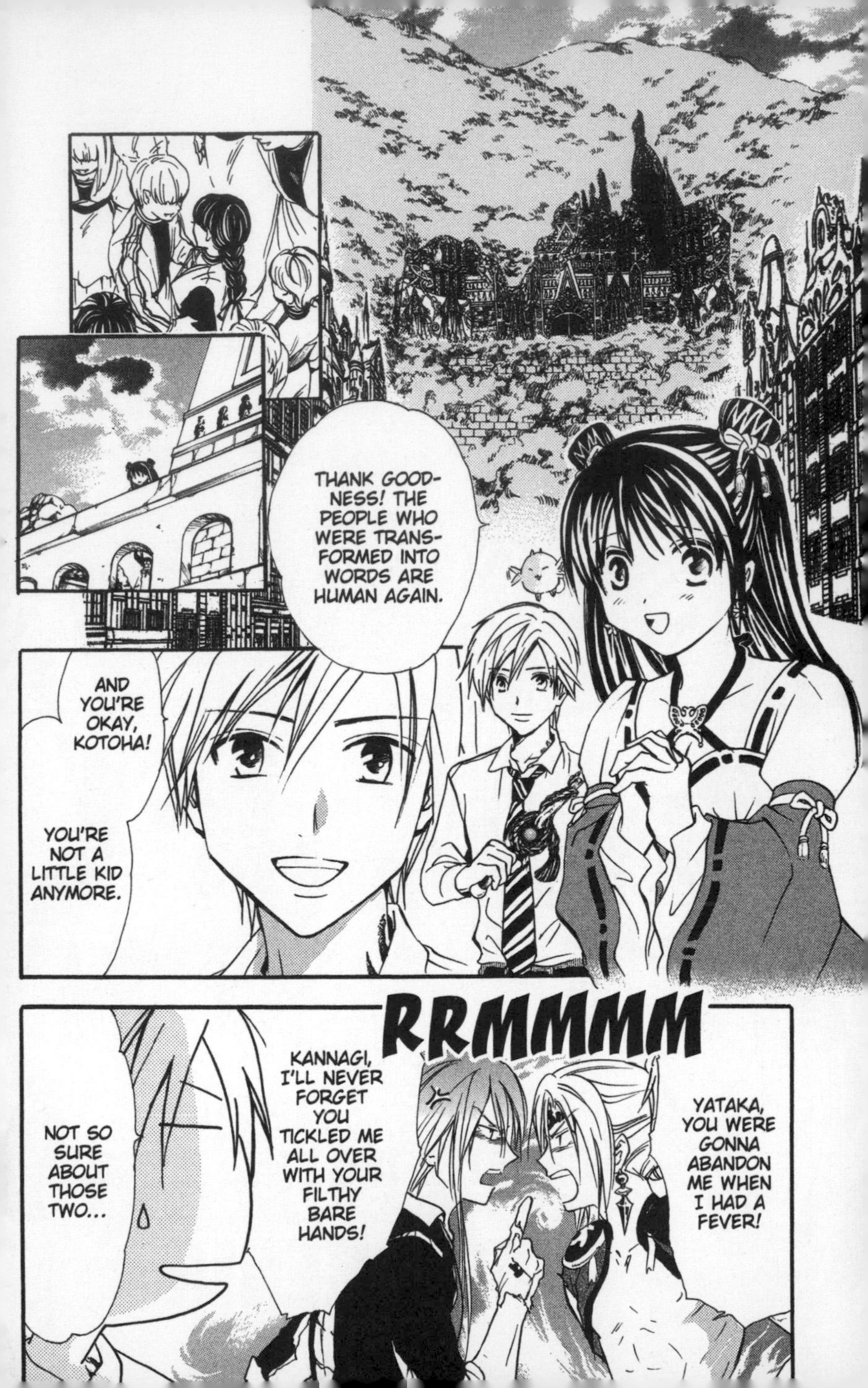
THANK GOOD-NESS! THE PEOPLE WHO WERE TRANS-FORMED INTO WORDS ARE HUMAN AGAIN.
AND YOU'RE OKAY, KOTOHA!
YOU'RE NOT A LITTLE KID ANYMORE.
RRMMMMM
YATAKA, YOU WERE GONNA ABANDON ME WHEN I HAD A FEVER!
KANNAGI, I'LL NEVER FORGET YOU TICKLED ME ALL OVER WITH YOUR FILTHY BARE HANDS!
NOT SO SURE ABOUT THOSE TWO...

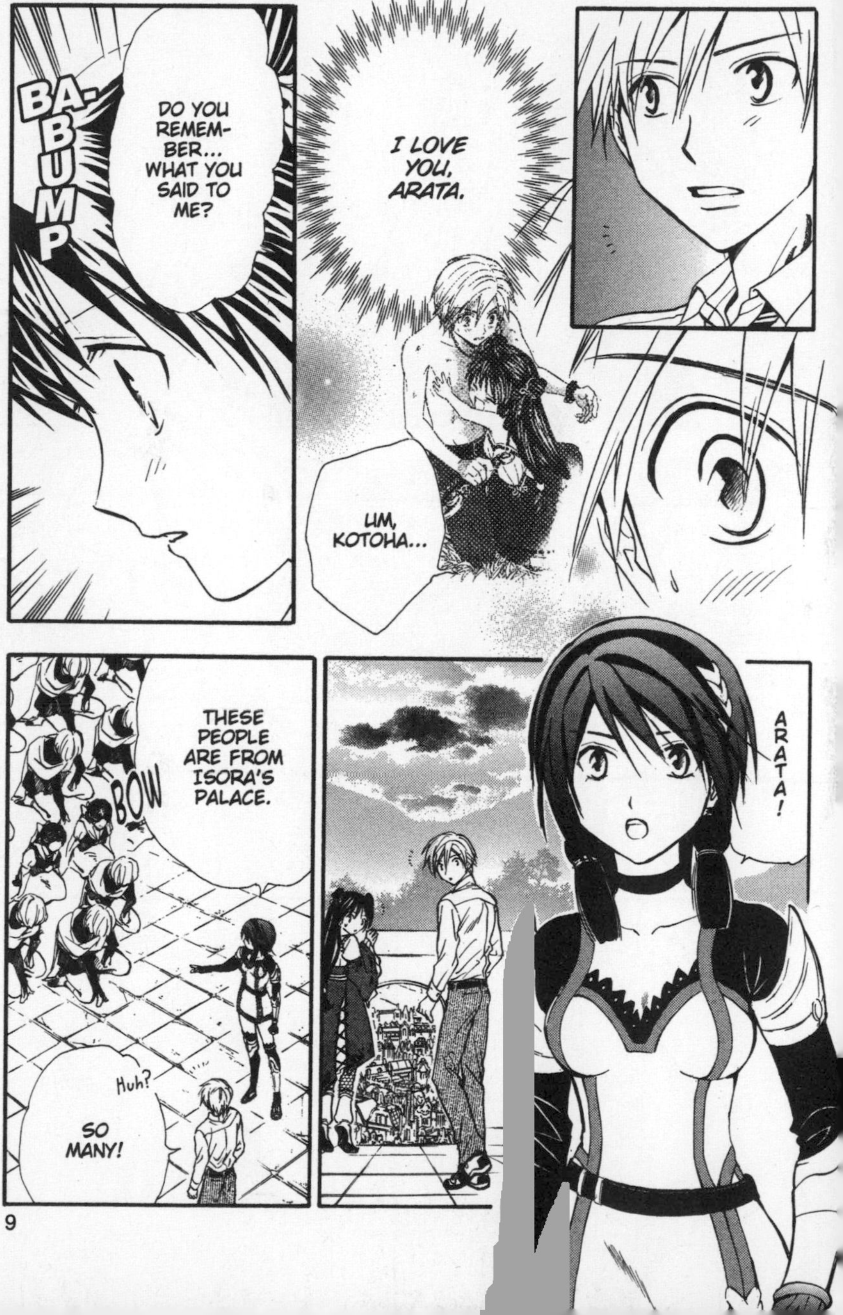
I LOVE YOU, ARATA.
UM, KOTOHA...
DO YOU REMEMBER... WHAT YOU SAID TO ME?
BA-BUMP
ARATA!
THESE PEOPLE ARE FROM ISORA'S PALACE.
BOW
Huh?
SO MANY!

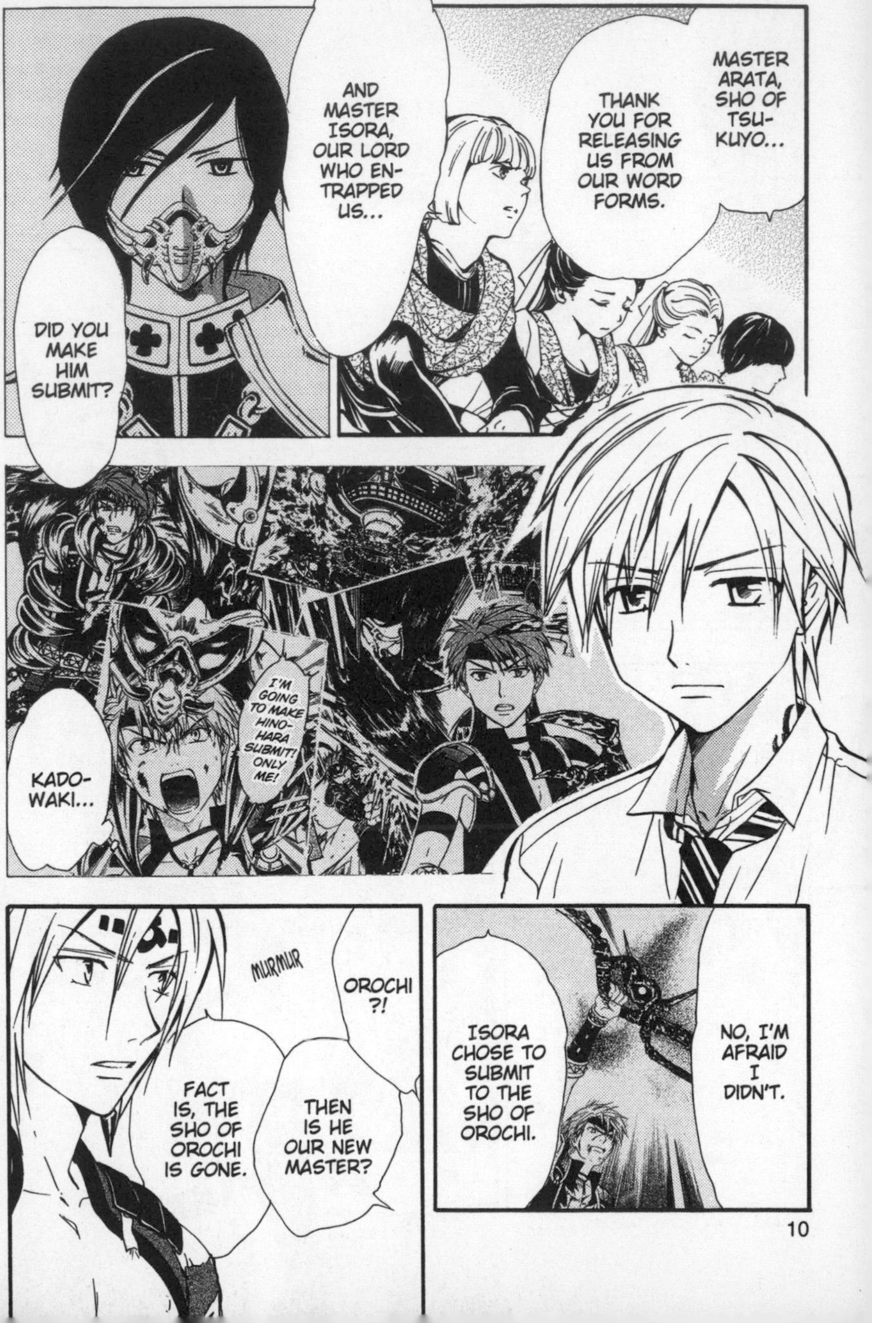
MASTER ARATA, SHO OF TSU-KUYO...
THANK YOU FOR RELEASING US FROM OUR WORD FORMS.
AND MASTER ISORA, OUR LORD WHO EN-TRAPPED US...
DID YOU MAKE HIM SUBMIT?
I'M GOING TO MAKE HINO-HARA SUBMIT! ONLY ME!
KADO-WAKI...
NO, I'M AFRAID I DIDN'T.
ISORA CHOSE TO SUBMIT TO THE SHO OF OROCHI.
OROCHI ?!
MURMUR
THEN IS HE OUR NEW MASTER?
FACT IS, THE SHO OF OROCHI IS GONE.

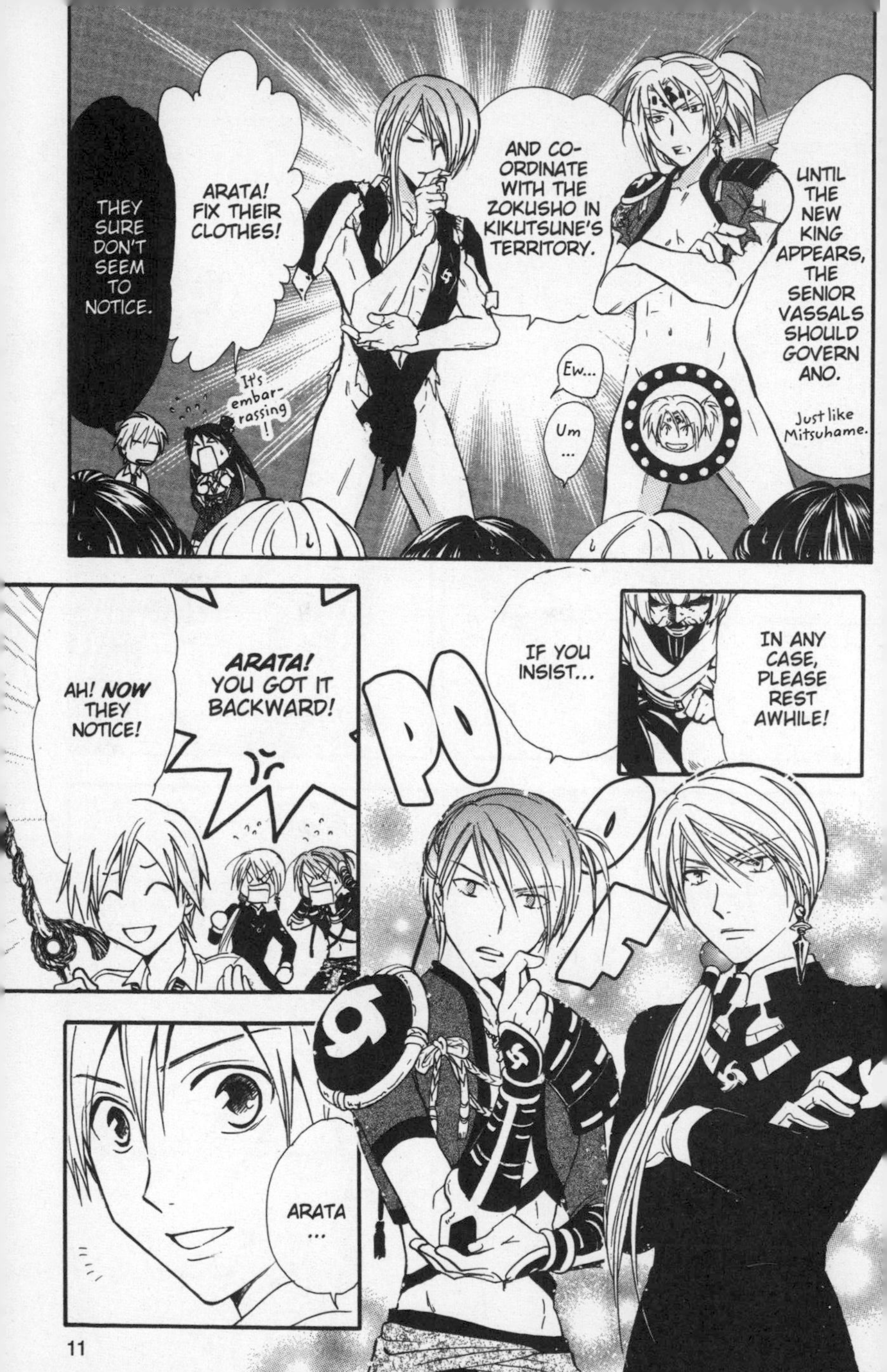
UNTIL THE NEW KING APPEARS, THE SENIOR VASSALS SHOULD GOVERN ANO.
Just like Mitsuhame.
AND CO-ORDINATE WITH THE ZOKUSHO IN KIKUTSUNE'S TERRITORY.
Ew...
Um ...
ARATA! FIX THEIR CLOTHES!
It's embarrassing!
THEY SURE DON'T SEEM TO NOTICE.
IN ANY CASE, PLEASE REST AWHILE!
IF YOU INSIST...
POOF
ARATA! YOU GOT IT BACKWARD!
AH! ***NOW*** THEY NOTICE!
ARATA ...

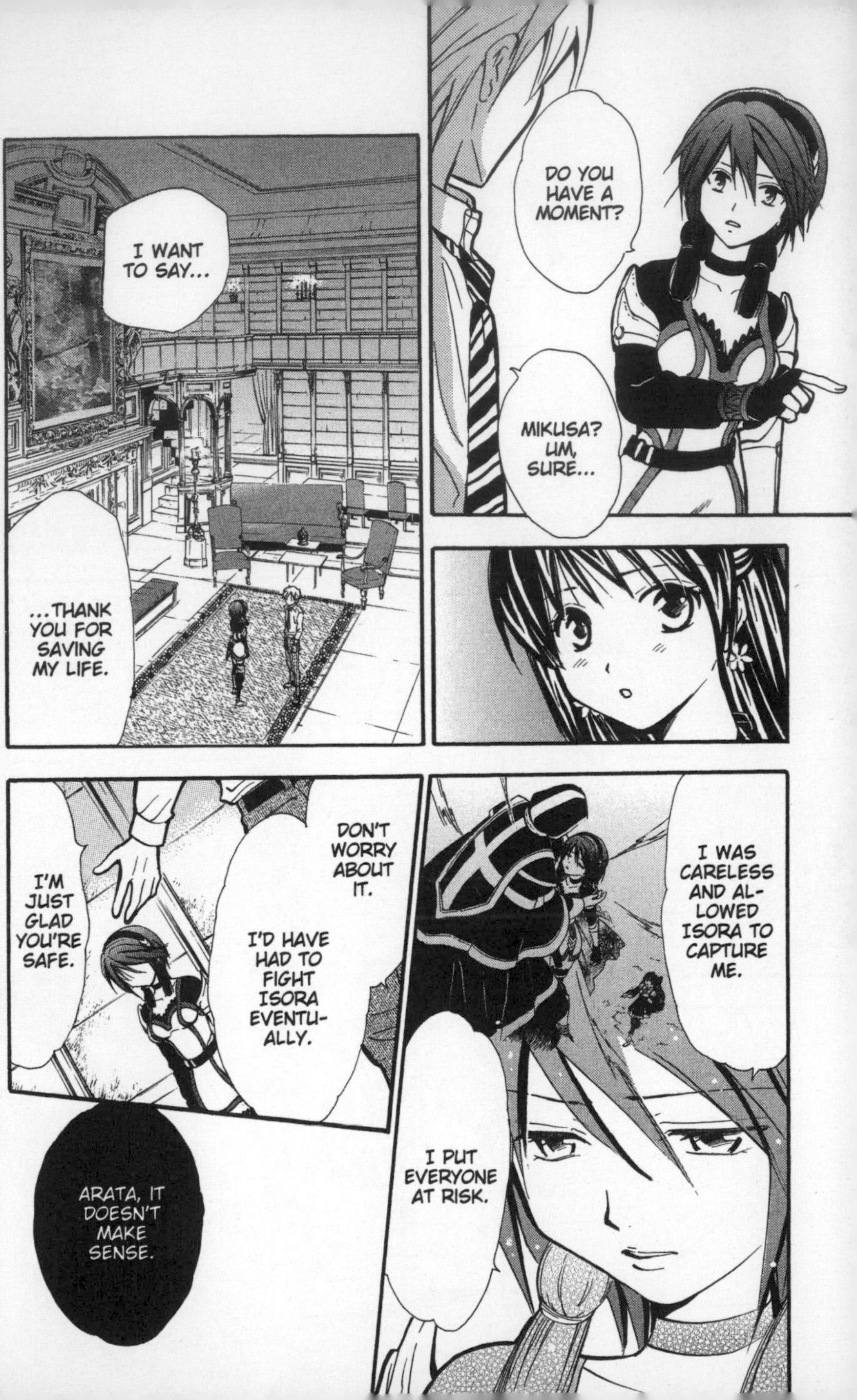
DO YOU HAVE A MOMENT?
MIKUSA? UM, SURE...
I WANT TO SAY...
...THANK YOU FOR SAVING MY LIFE.
I WAS CARELESS AND AL-LOWED ISORA TO CAPTURE ME.
I PUT EVERYONE AT RISK.
DON'T WORRY ABOUT IT.
I'D HAVE HAD TO FIGHT ISORA EVENTU-ALLY.
I'M JUST GLAD YOU'RE SAFE.
ARATA, IT DOESN'T MAKE SENSE.

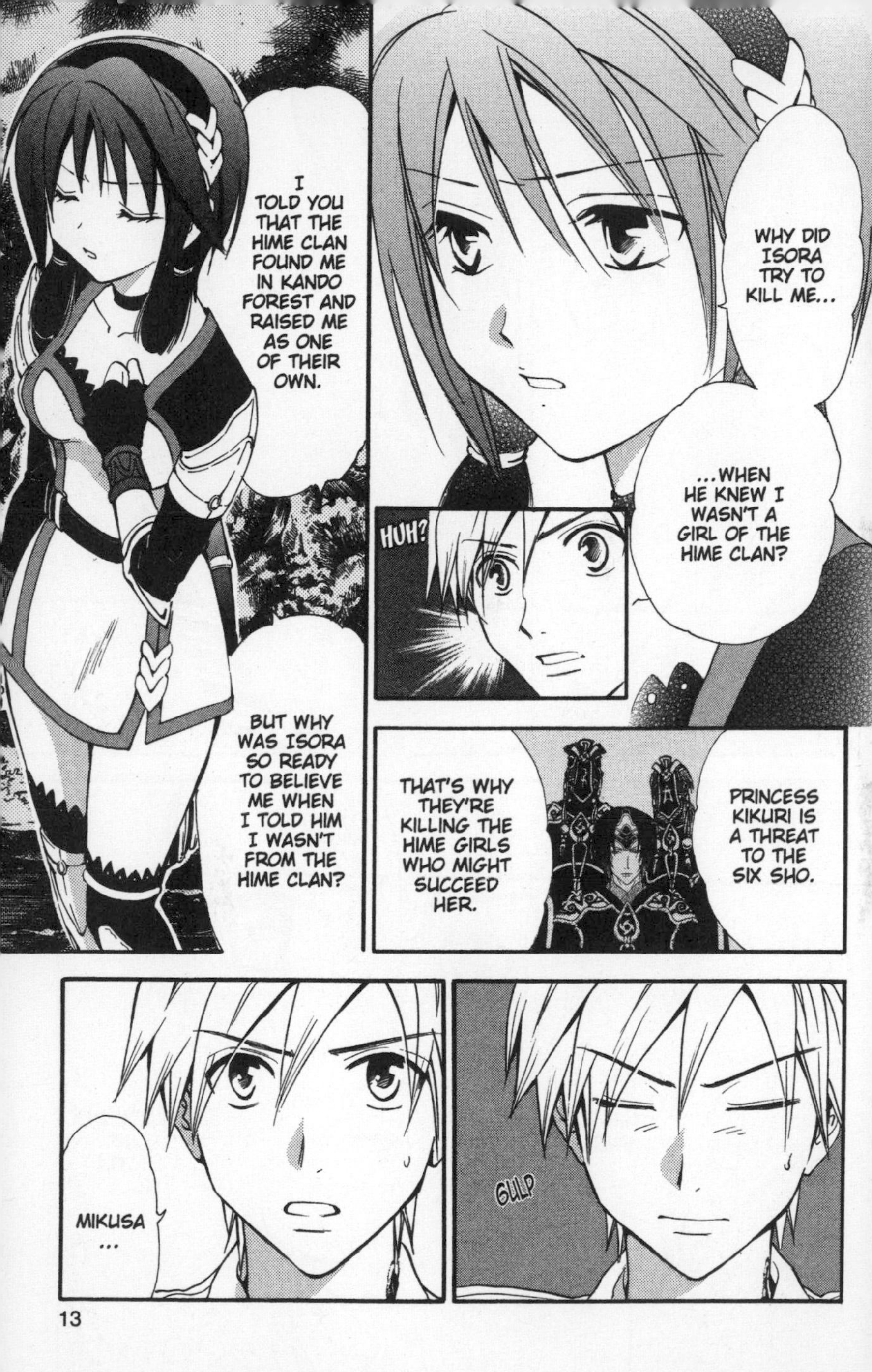
WHY DID ISORA TRY TO KILL ME...
...WHEN HE KNEW I WASN'T A GIRL OF THE HIME CLAN?
HUH?
PRINCESS KIKURI IS A THREAT TO THE SIX SHO.
THAT'S WHY THEY'RE KILLING THE HIME GIRLS WHO MIGHT SUCCEED HER.
I TOLD YOU THAT THE HIME CLAN FOUND ME IN KANDO FOREST AND RAISED ME AS ONE OF THEIR OWN.
BUT WHY WAS ISORA SO READY TO BELIEVE ME WHEN I TOLD HIM I WASN'T FROM THE HIME CLAN?
GULP
MIKUSA ...

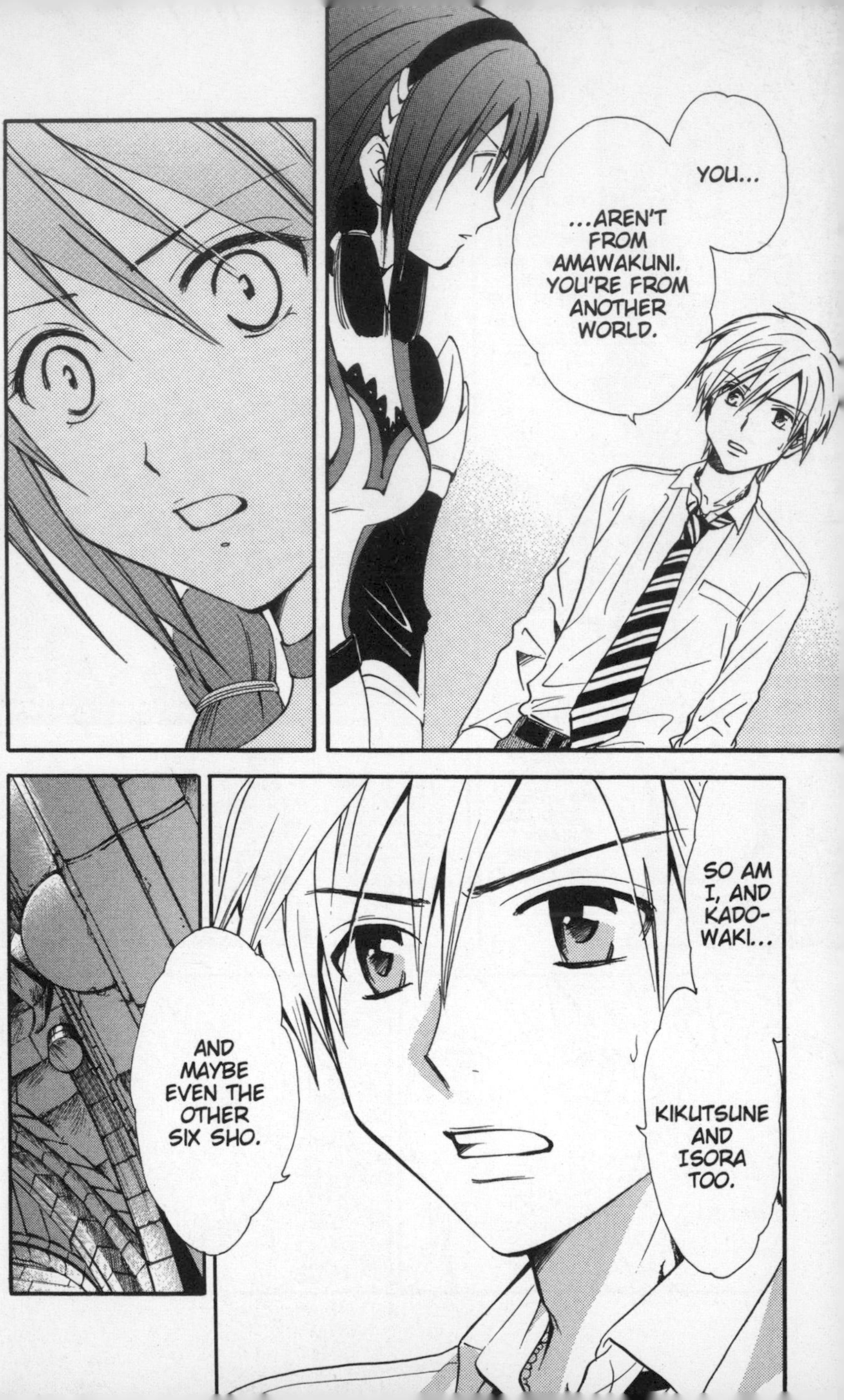
YOU...
...AREN'T FROM AMAWAKUNI. YOU'RE FROM ANOTHER WORLD.
SO AM I, AND KADO-WAKI...
KIKUTSUNE AND ISORA TOO.
AND MAYBE EVEN THE OTHER SIX SHO.

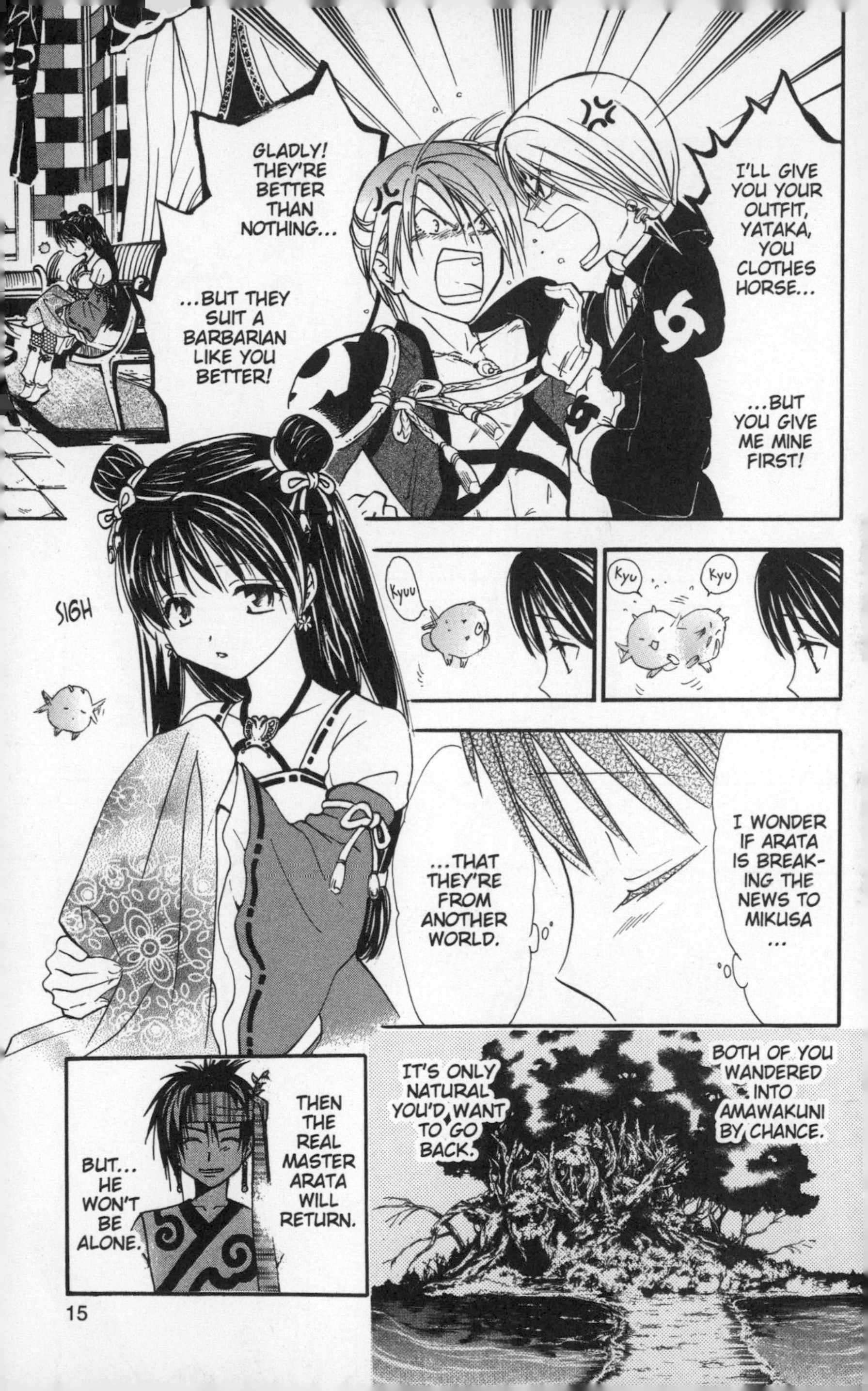
I'LL GIVE YOU YOUR OUTFIT, YATAKA, YOU CLOTHES HORSE...
...BUT YOU GIVE ME MINE FIRST!
GLADLY! THEY'RE BETTER THAN NOTHING...
...BUT THEY SUIT A BARBARIAN LIKE YOU BETTER!
Kyu
Kyu
Kyuu
I WONDER IF ARATA IS BREAKING THE NEWS TO MIKUSA...
...THAT THEY'RE FROM ANOTHER WORLD.
SIGH
BOTH OF YOU WANDERED INTO AMAWAKUNI BY CHANCE.
IT'S ONLY NATURAL YOU'D WANT TO GO BACK.
THEN THE REAL MASTER ARATA WILL RETURN.
BUT... HE WON'T BE ALONE.

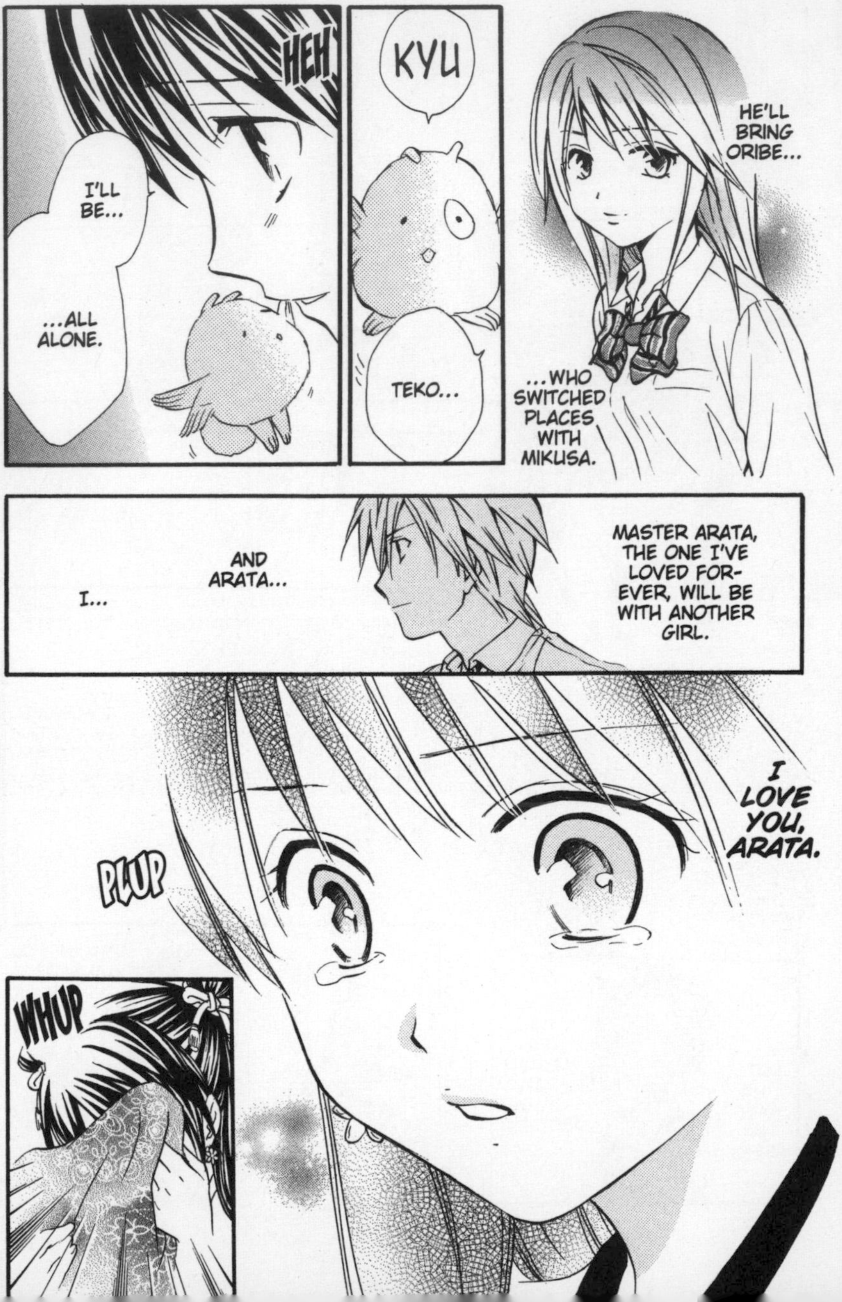
HE'LL BRING ORIBE...
...WHO SWITCHED PLACES WITH MIKUSA.
KYU
TEKO...
HEH
I'LL BE...
...ALL ALONE.
MASTER ARATA, THE ONE I'VE LOVED FOR-EVER, WILL BE WITH ANOTHER GIRL.
AND ARATA...
I...
I LOVE YOU, ARATA.
PLUP
WHUP

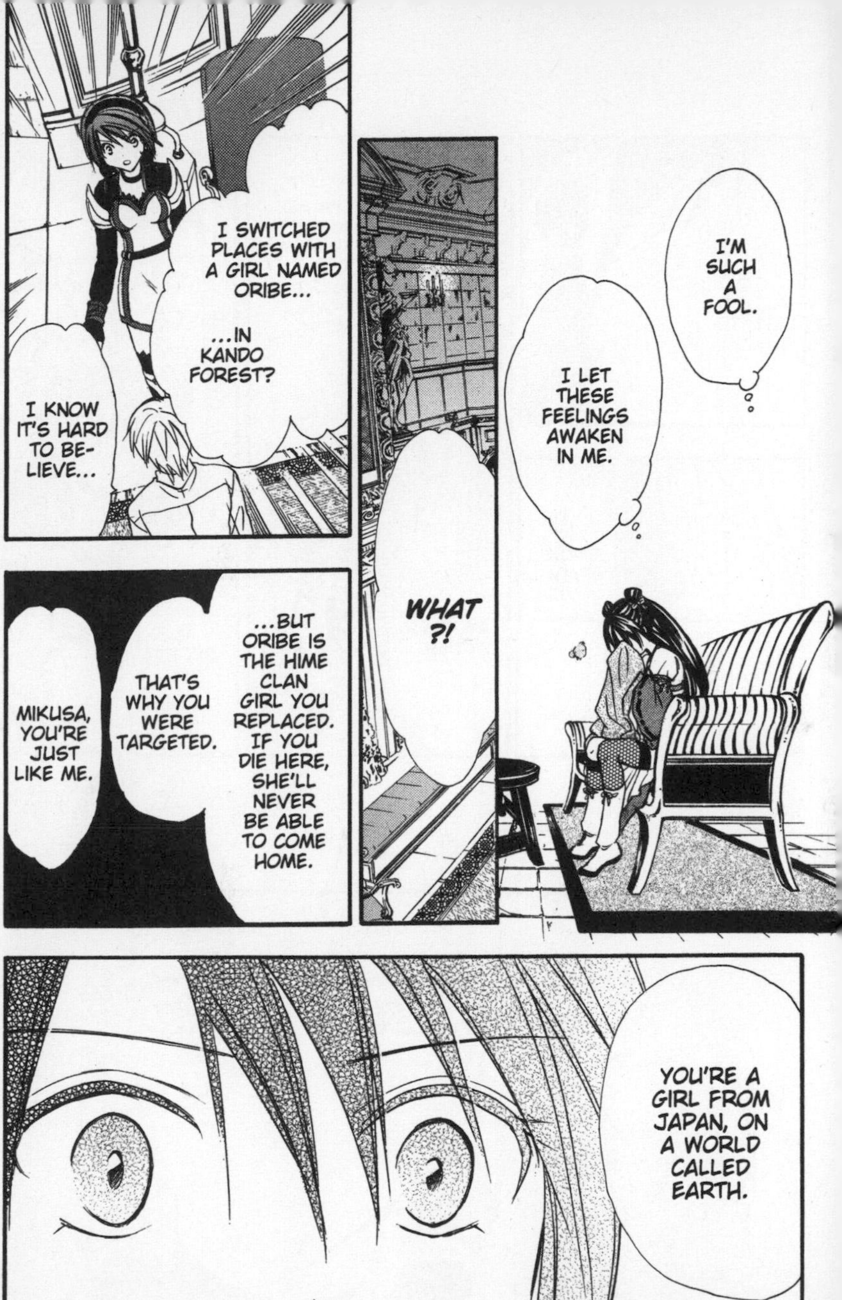
I'M SUCH A FOOL.
I LET THESE FEELINGS AWAKEN IN ME.
WHAT?!
I SWITCHED PLACES WITH A GIRL NAMED ORIBE...
...IN KANDO FOREST?
I KNOW IT'S HARD TO BE-LIEVE...
...BUT ORIBE IS THE HIME CLAN GIRL YOU REPLACED. IF YOU DIE HERE, SHE'LL NEVER BE ABLE TO COME HOME.
THAT'S WHY YOU WERE TARGETED.
MIKUSA, YOU'RE JUST LIKE ME.
YOU'RE A GIRL FROM JAPAN, ON A WORLD CALLED EARTH.

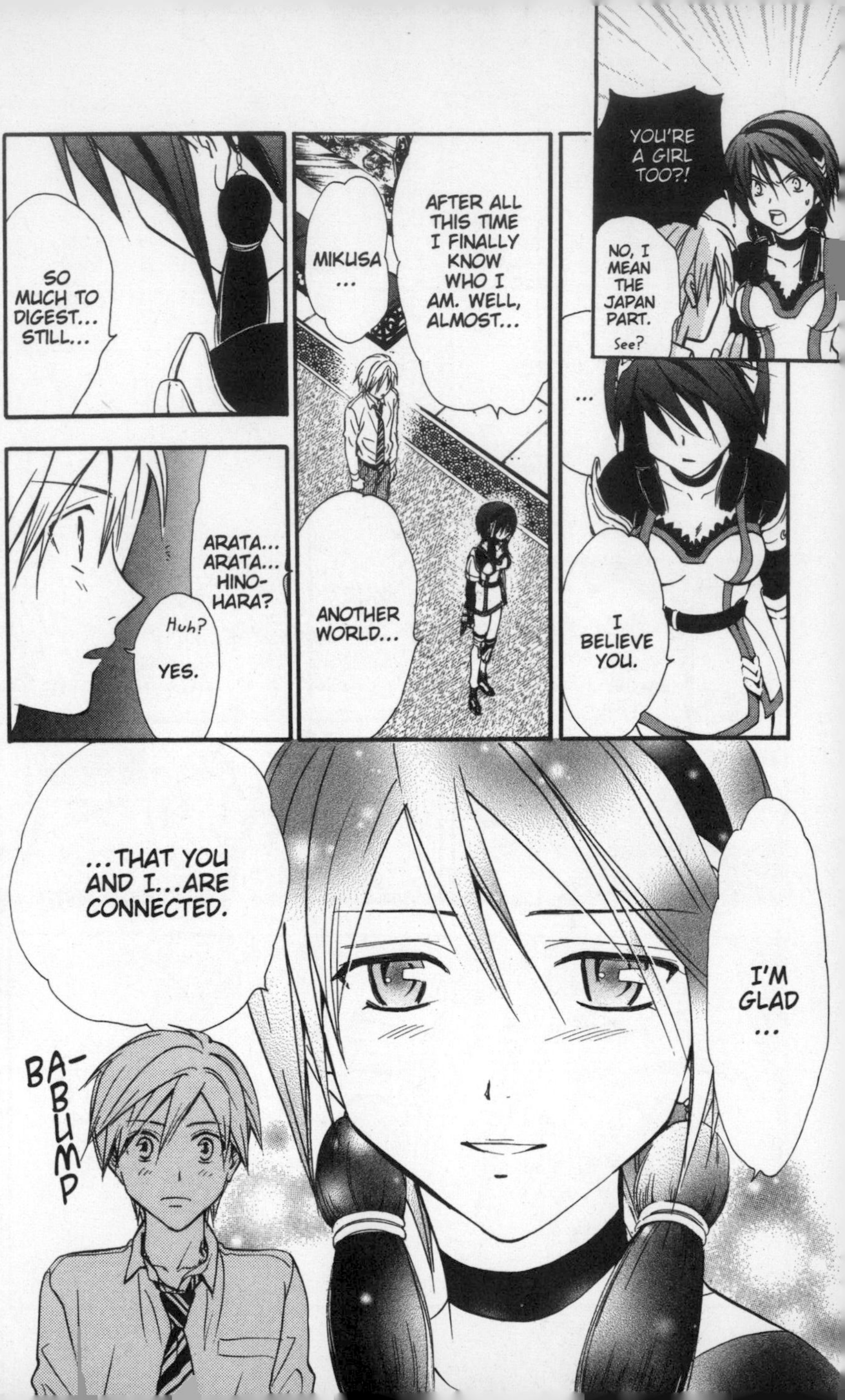
YOU'RE A GIRL TOO?!
NO, I MEAN THE JAPAN PART.
See?
...
I BELIEVE YOU.
AFTER ALL THIS TIME I FINALLY KNOW WHO I AM. WELL, ALMOST...
MIKUSA ...
ANOTHER WORLD...
SO MUCH TO DIGEST... STILL...
ARATA... ARATA... HINO-HARA?
Huh?
YES.
I'M GLAD ...
...THAT YOU AND I...ARE CONNECTED.
BA-BUMP

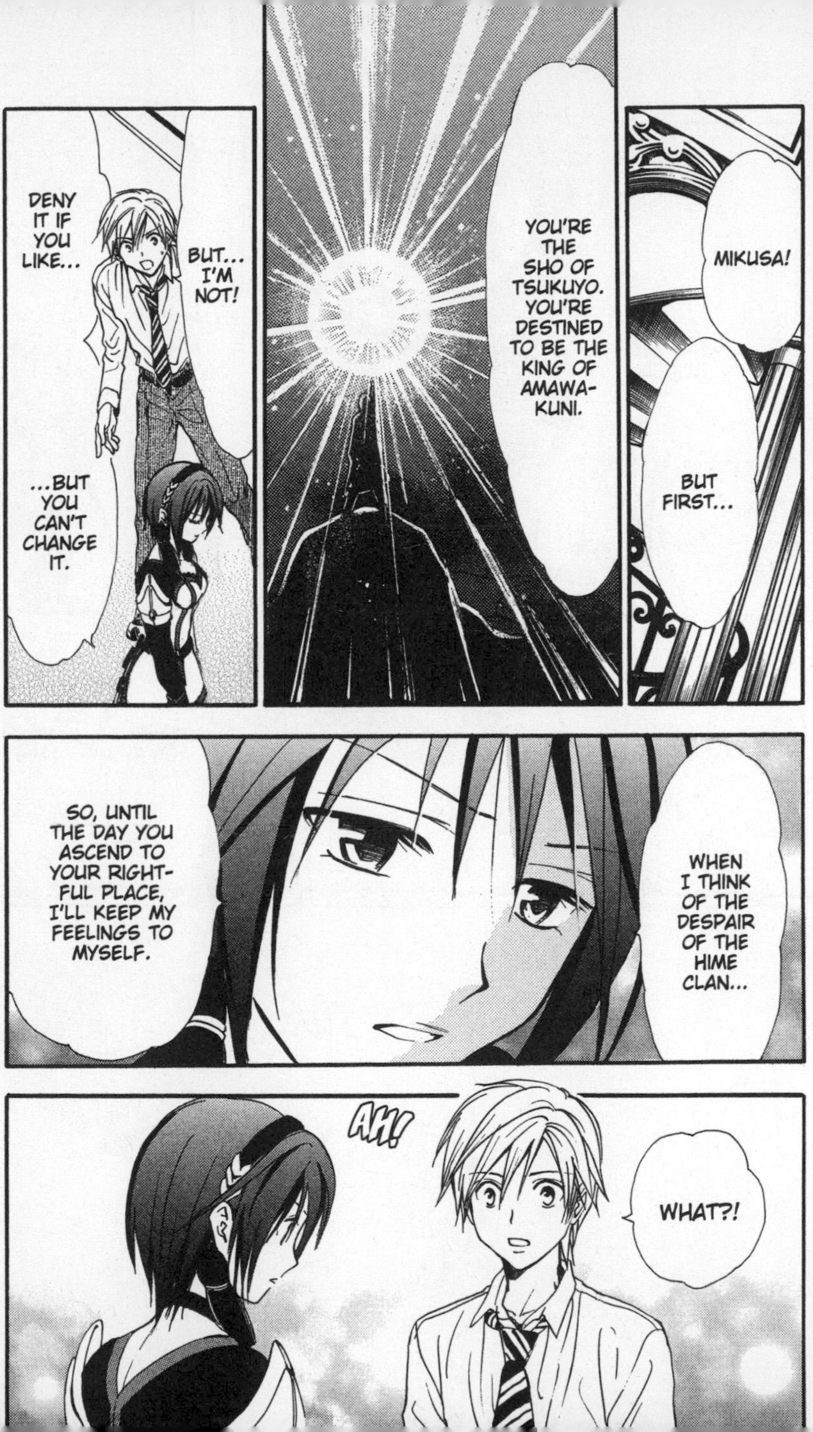
MIKUSA!
BUT FIRST...
YOU'RE THE SHO OF TSUKUYO. YOU'RE DESTINED TO BE THE KING OF AMAWA-KUNI.
BUT... I'M NOT!
DENY IT IF YOU LIKE...
...BUT YOU CAN'T CHANGE IT.
WHEN I THINK OF THE DESPAIR OF THE HIME CLAN...
SO, UNTIL THE DAY YOU ASCEND TO YOUR RIGHT-FUL PLACE, I'LL KEEP MY FEELINGS TO MYSELF.
WHAT?!
AH!

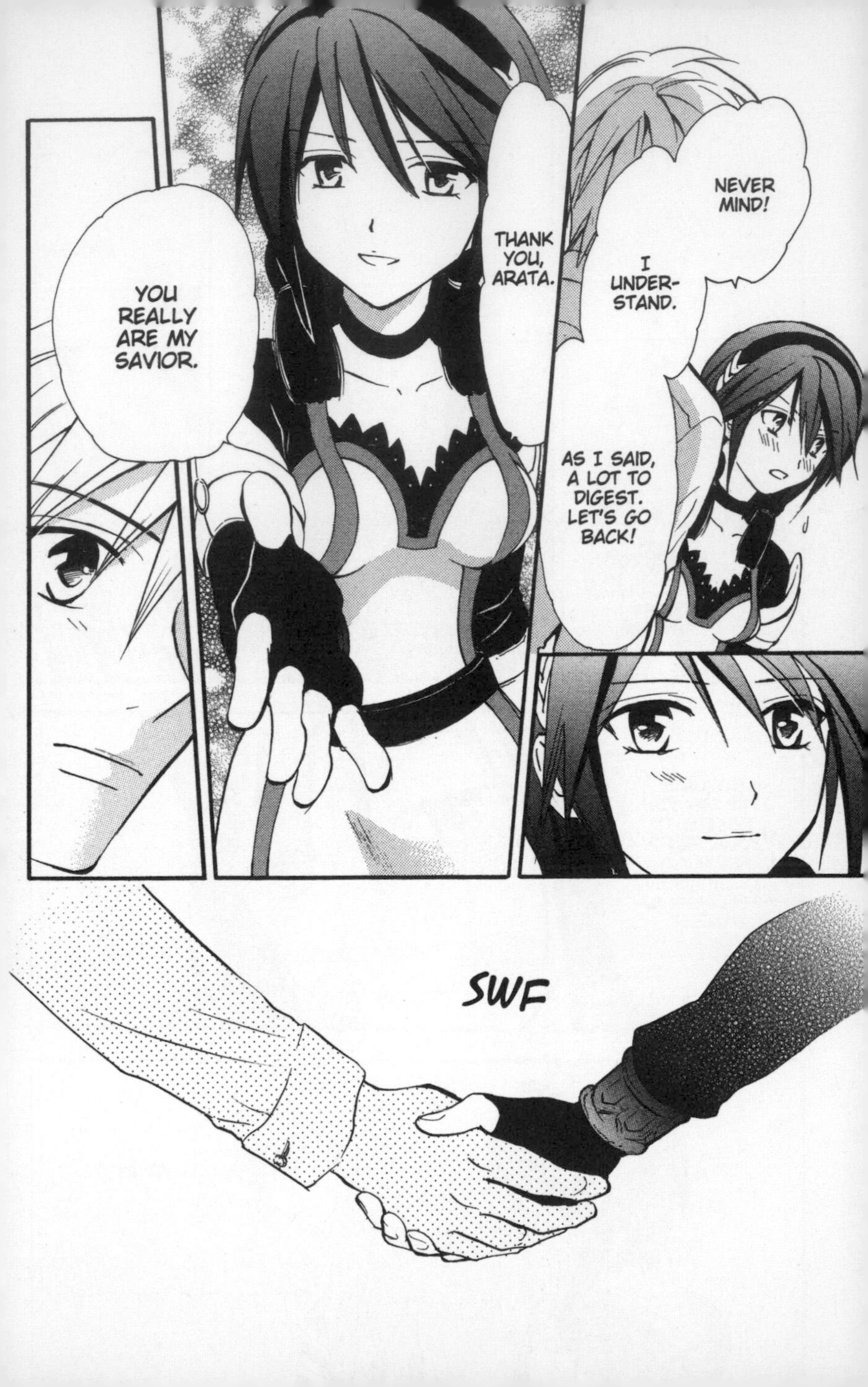
NEVER MIND!
I UNDER-STAND.
AS I SAID, A LOT TO DIGEST. LET'S GO BACK!
THANK YOU, ARATA.
YOU REALLY ARE MY SAVIOR.
SWF

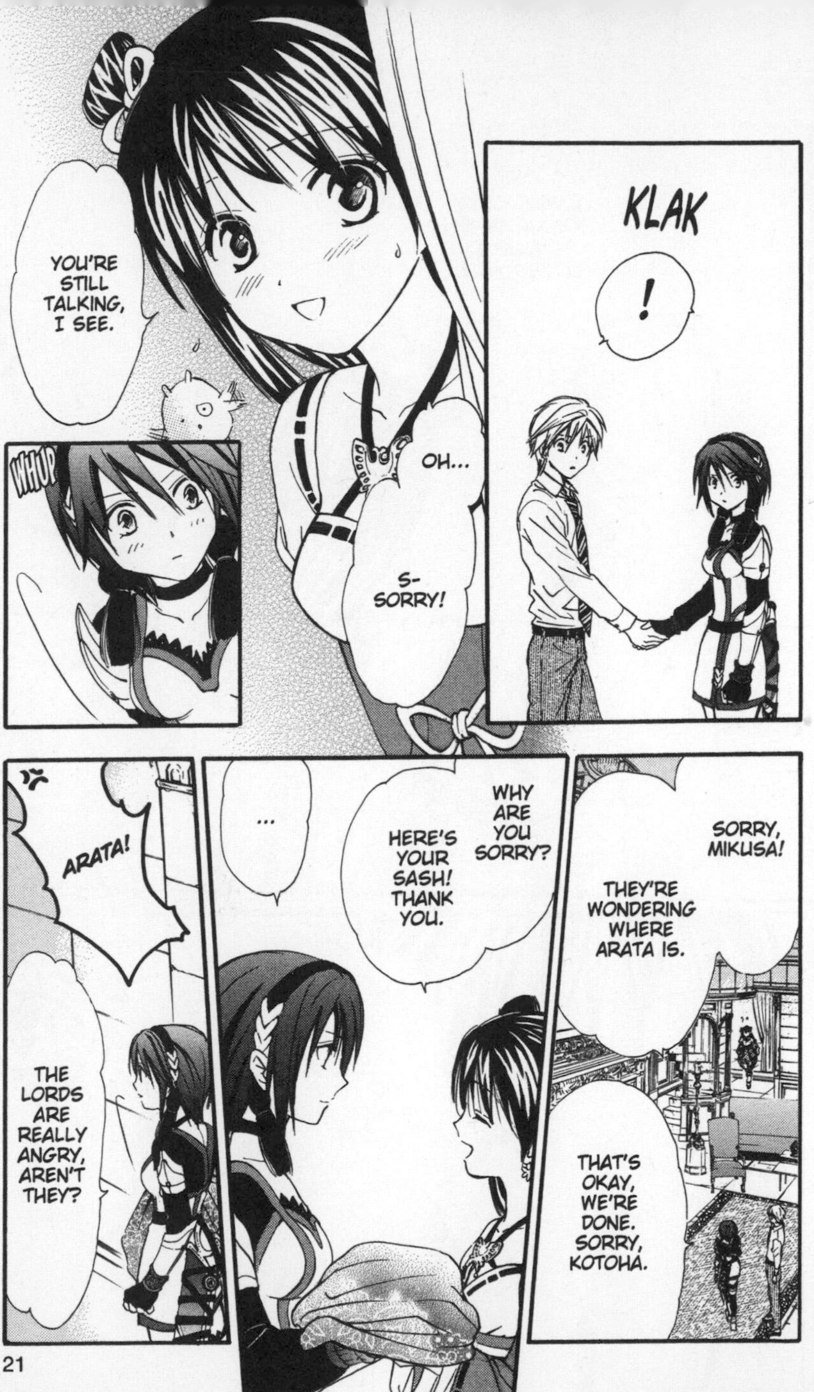
KLAK
!
YOU'RE STILL TALKING, I SEE.
OH...
S-SORRY!
WHOP
SORRY, MIKUSA!
THEY'RE WONDERING WHERE ARATA IS.
THAT'S OKAY, WE'RE DONE. SORRY, KOTOHA.
WHY ARE YOU SORRY?
HERE'S YOUR SASH! THANK YOU.
...
ARATA!
THE LORDS ARE REALLY ANGRY, AREN'T THEY?

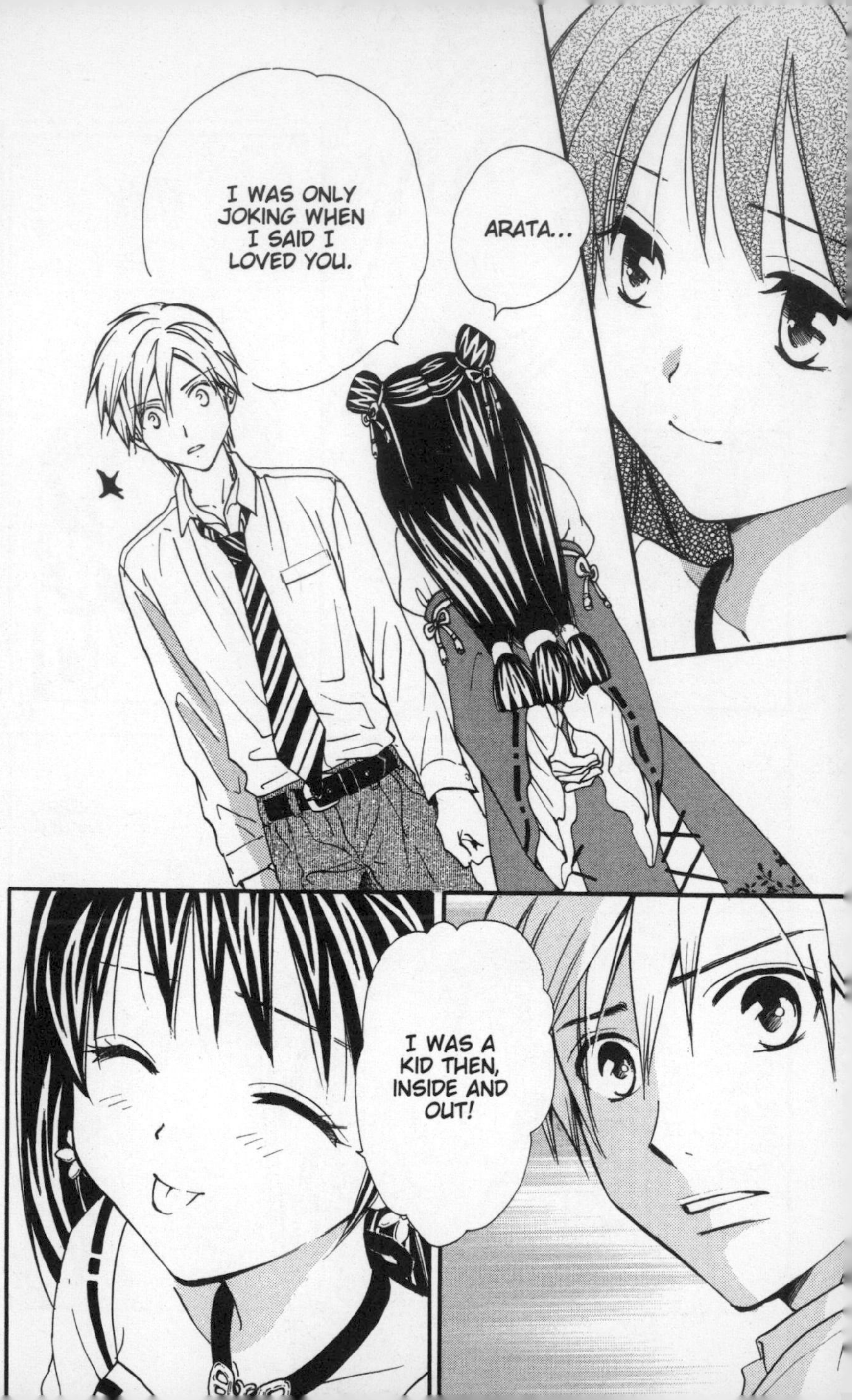
ARATA...
I WAS ONLY JOKING WHEN I SAID I LOVED YOU.
I WAS A KID THEN, INSIDE AND OUT!

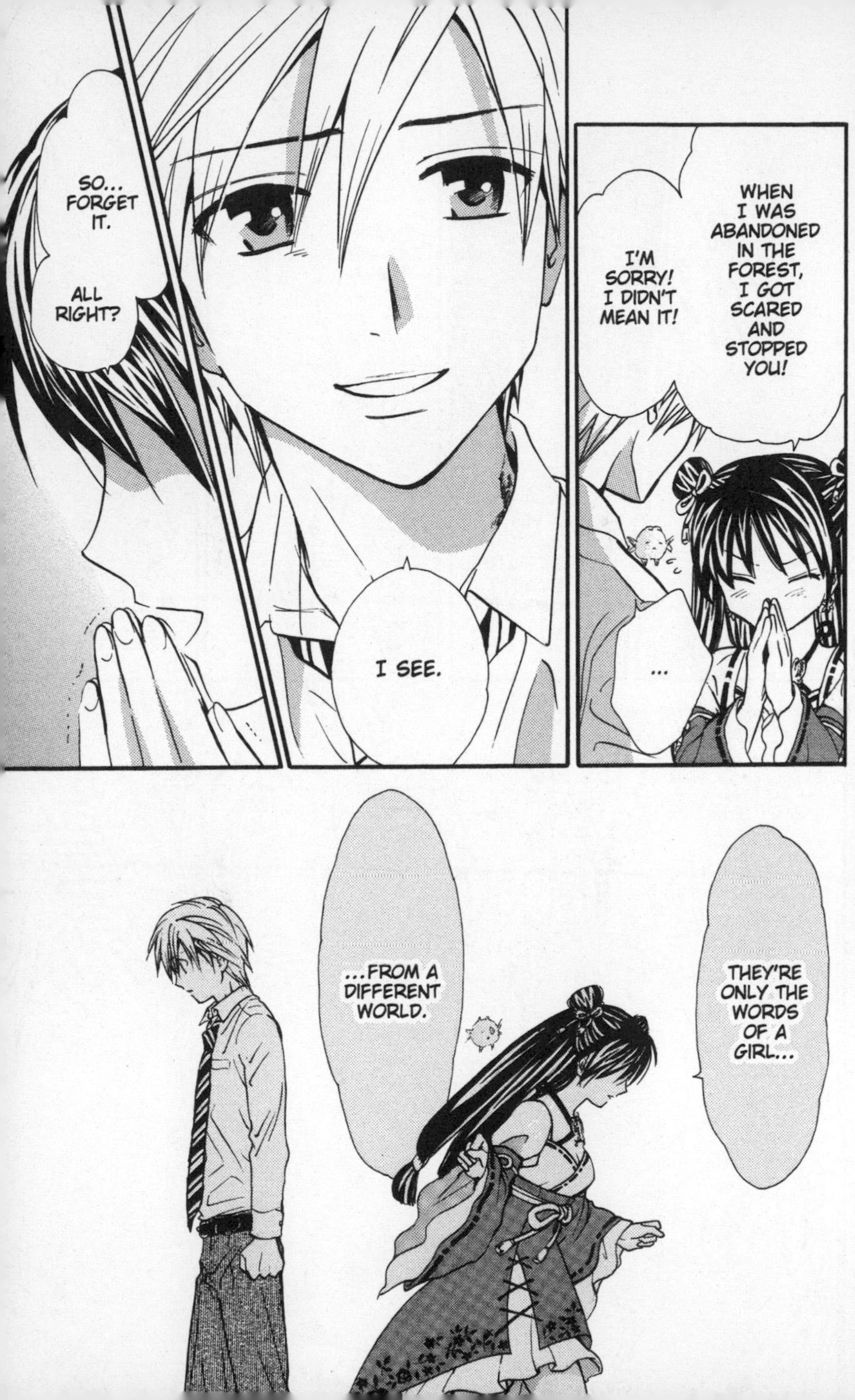
WHEN I WAS ABANDONED IN THE FOREST, I GOT SCARED AND STOPPED YOU!
I'M SORRY! I DIDN'T MEAN IT!
...
I SEE.
SO... FORGET IT.
ALL RIGHT?
THEY'RE ONLY THE WORDS OF A GIRL...
...FROM A DIFFERENT WORLD.

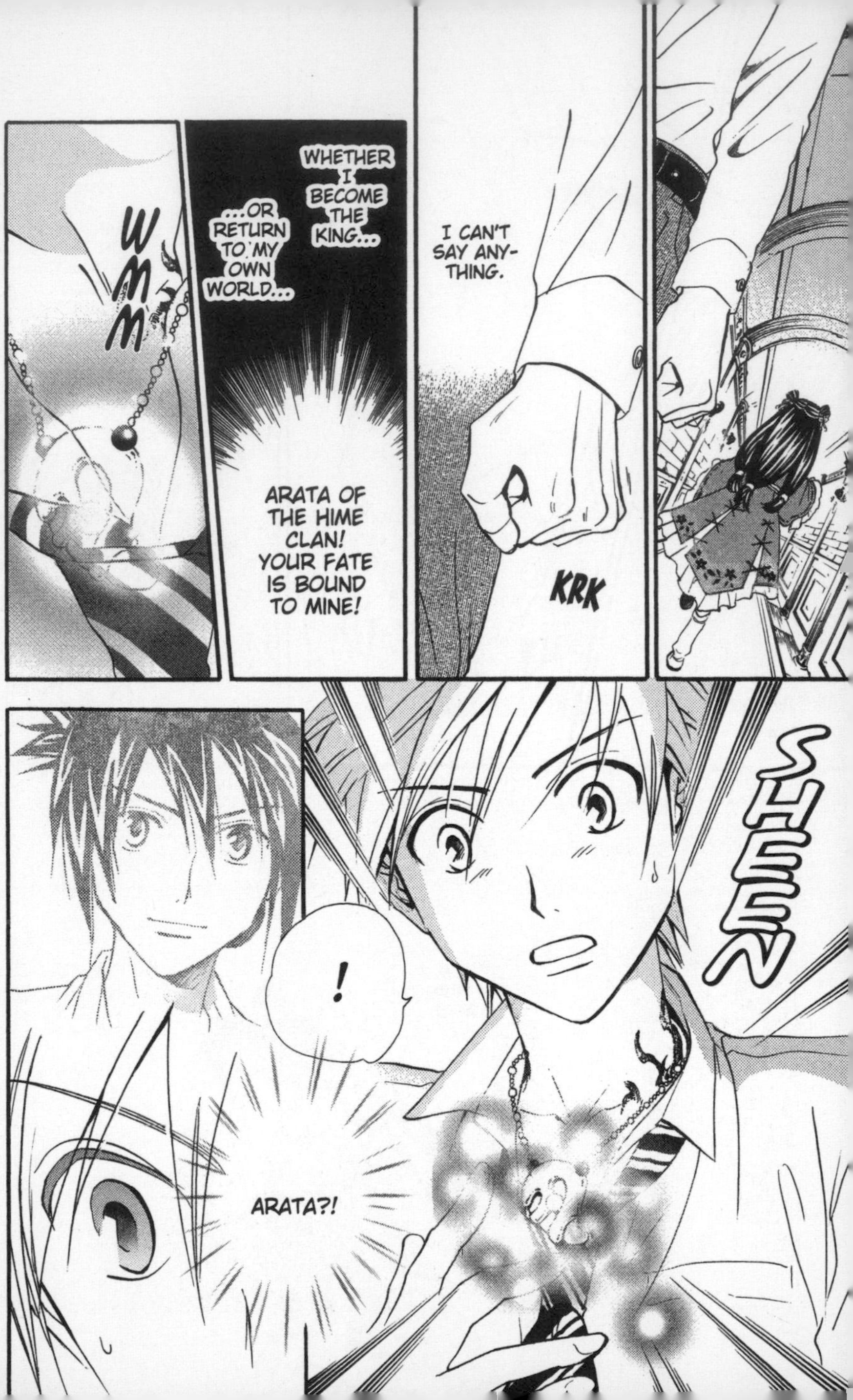
I CAN'T SAY ANY-THING.
KRK
WHETHER I BECOME THE KING...
...OR RETURN TO MY OWN WORLD...
ARATA OF THE HIME CLAN! YOUR FATE IS BOUND TO MINE!
WMM
SHEEN
!
ARATA?!

CHAPTER 189

THE SYMBOL

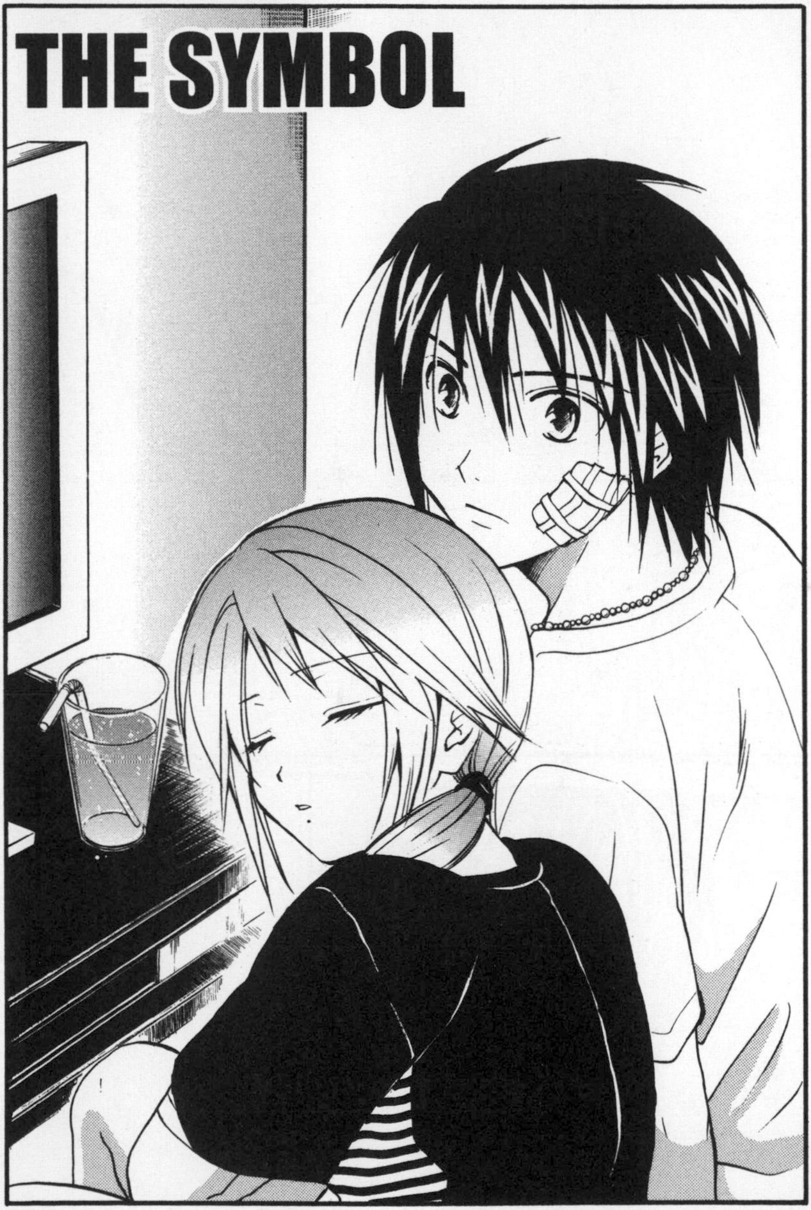

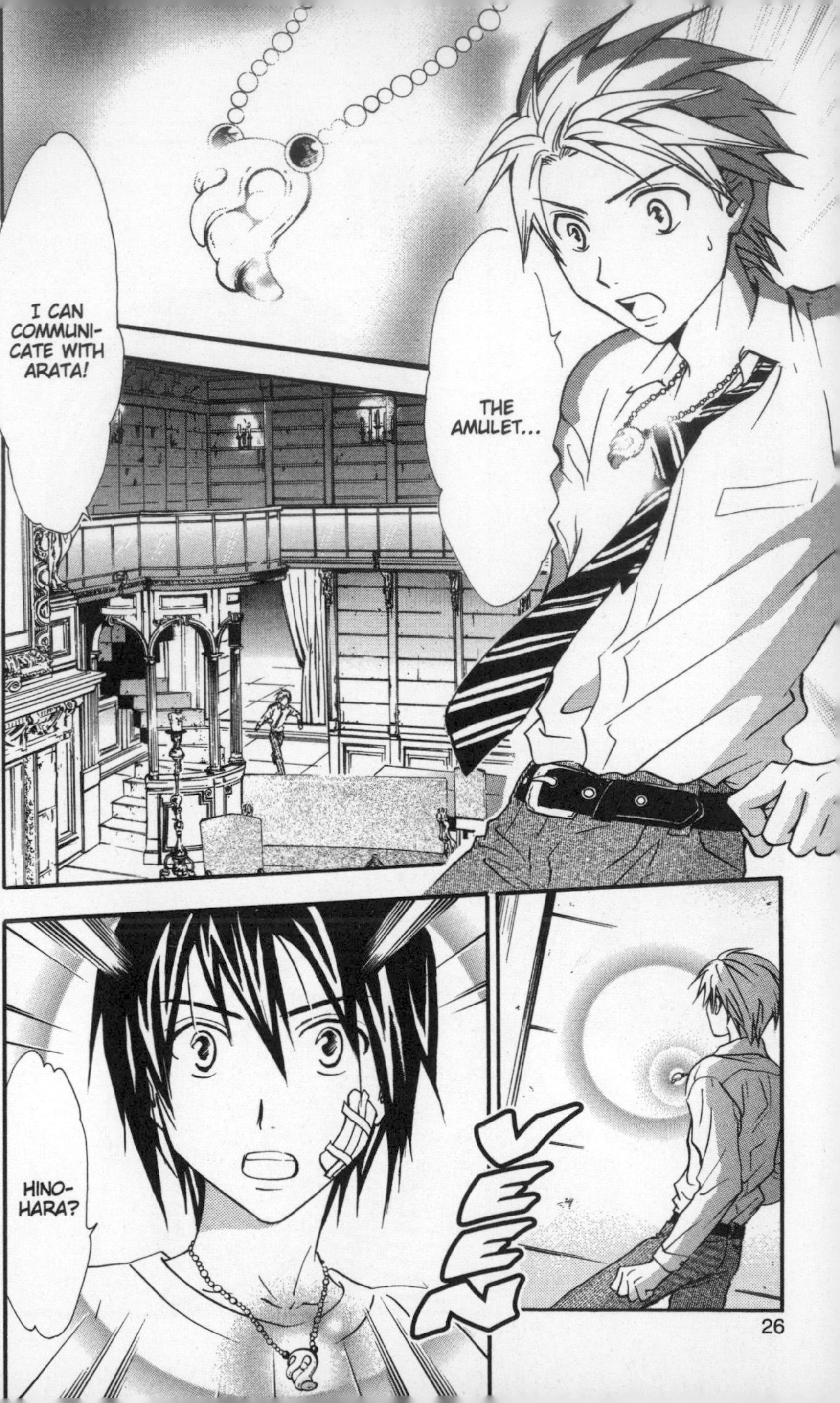
THE AMULET...
I CAN COMMUNI-CATE WITH ARATA!
HINO-HARA?

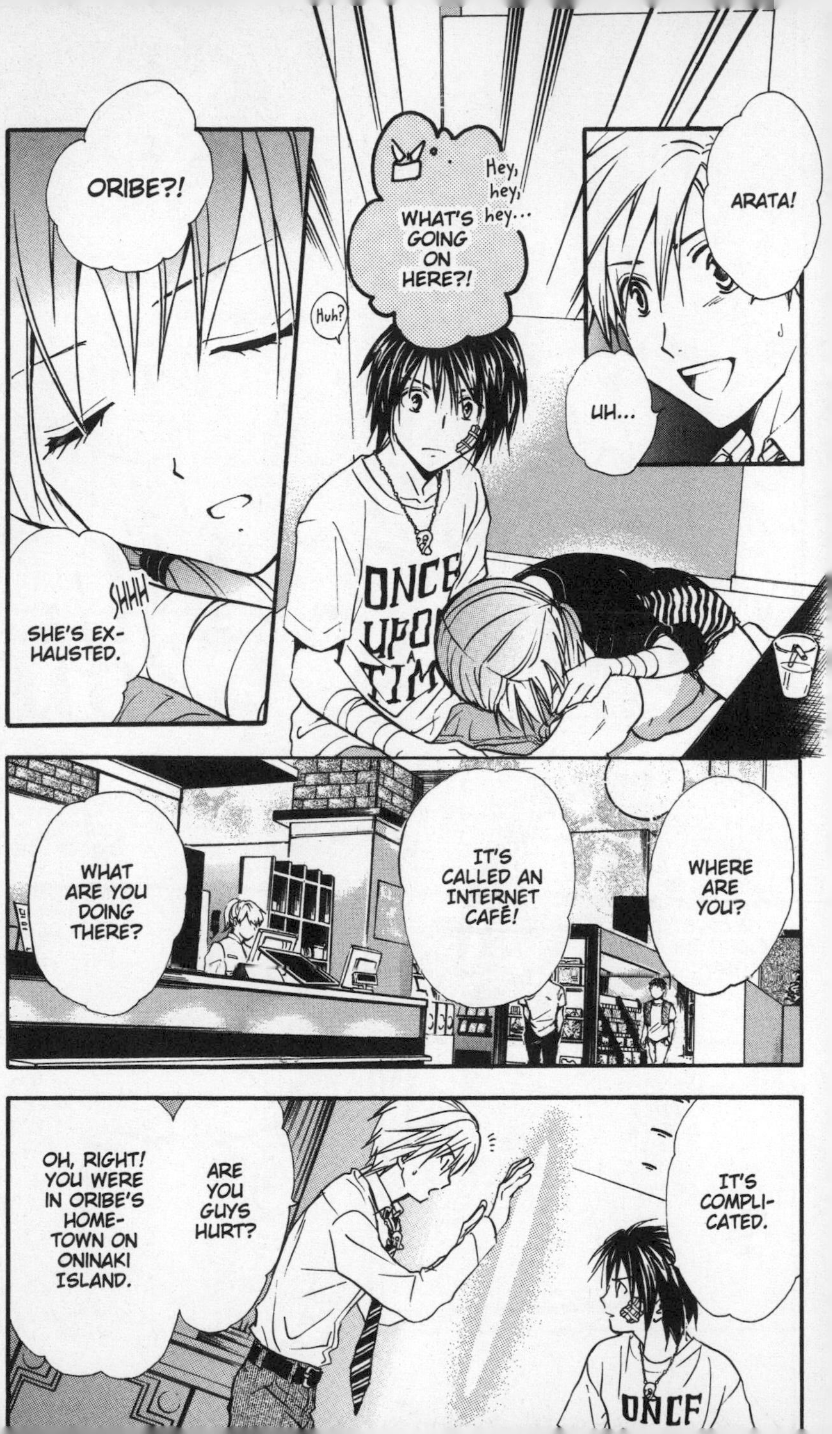
ARATA!
UH...
WHAT'S GOING ON HERE?!
Hey, hey, hey...
Huh?
ORIBE?!
SHHH
SHE'S EX-HAUSTED.
ONCE UPON A TIME
WHERE ARE YOU?
IT'S CALLED AN INTERNET CAFÉ!
WHAT ARE YOU DOING THERE?
IT'S COMPLI-CATED.
ARE YOU GUYS HURT?
OH, RIGHT! YOU WERE IN ORIBE'S HOME-TOWN ON ONINAKI ISLAND.

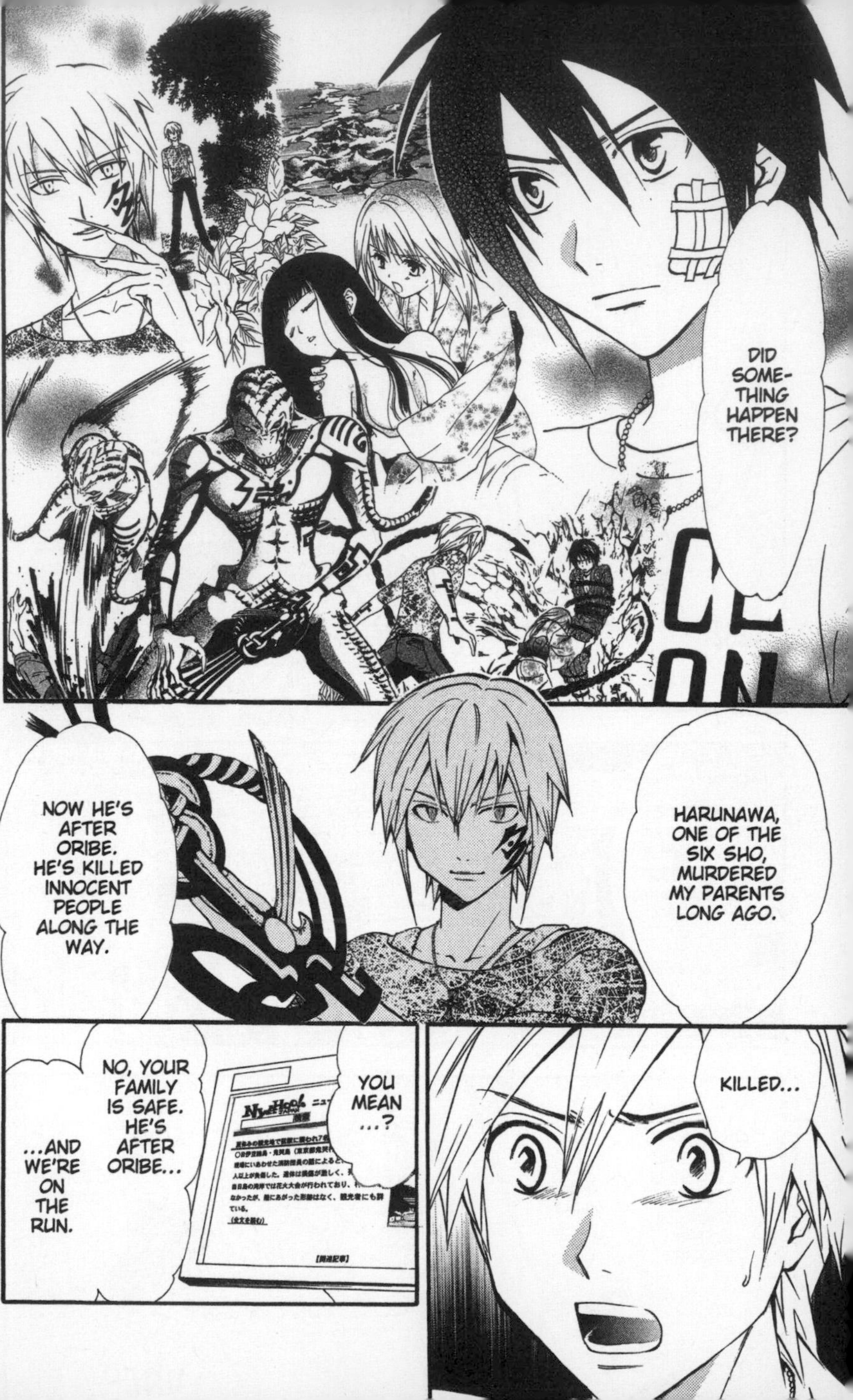
DID SOMETHING HAPPEN THERE?
HARUNAWA, ONE OF THE SIX SHO, MURDERED MY PARENTS LONG AGO.
NOW HE'S AFTER ORIBE. HE'S KILLED INNOCENT PEOPLE ALONG THE WAY.
KILLED...
YOU MEAN...?
NO, YOUR FAMILY IS SAFE. HE'S AFTER ORIBE...
...AND WE'RE ON THE RUN.

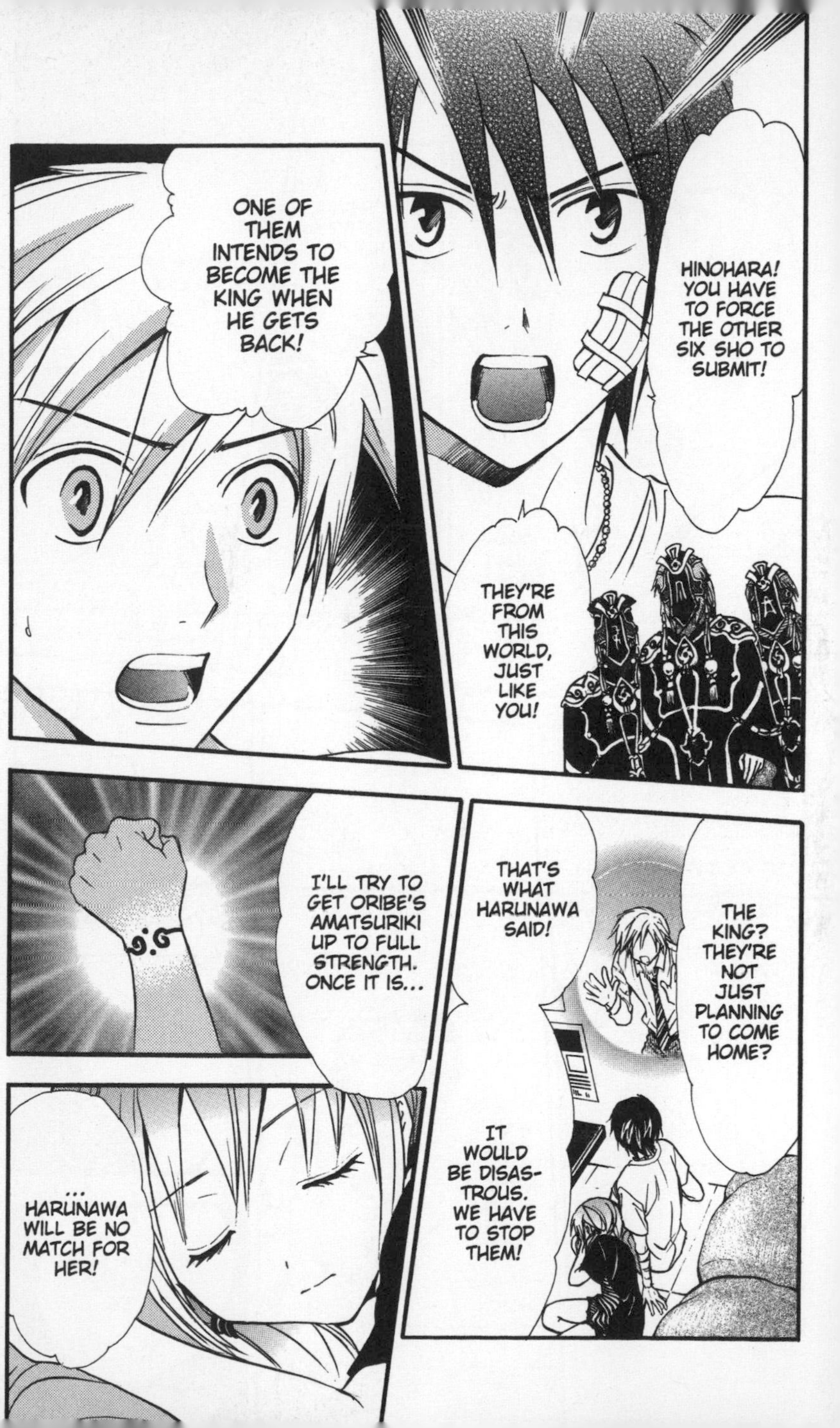
HINOHARA! YOU HAVE TO FORCE THE OTHER SIX SHO TO SUBMIT!
THEY'RE FROM THIS WORLD, JUST LIKE YOU!
ONE OF THEM INTENDS TO BECOME THE KING WHEN HE GETS BACK!
THE KING? THEY'RE NOT JUST PLANNING TO COME HOME?
THAT'S WHAT HARUNAWA SAID!
IT WOULD BE DISASTROUS. WE HAVE TO STOP THEM!
I'LL TRY TO GET ORIBE'S AMATSURIKI UP TO FULL STRENGTH. ONCE IT IS...
...HARUNAWA WILL BE NO MATCH FOR HER!

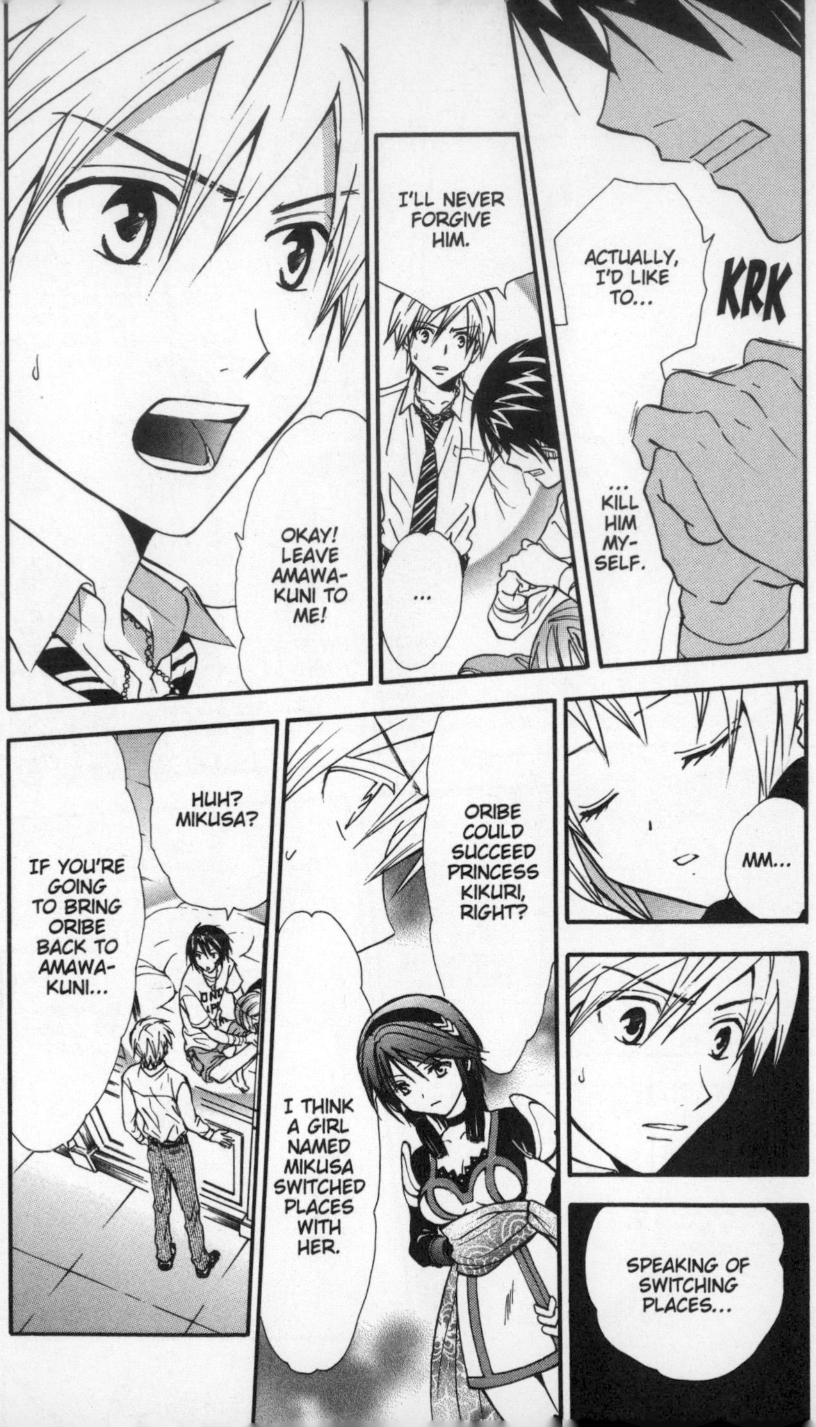
ACTUALLY, I'D LIKE TO...
KRK
...KILL HIM MY-SELF.
I'LL NEVER FORGIVE HIM.
...
OKAY! LEAVE AMAWA-KUNI TO ME!
MM...
SPEAKING OF SWITCHING PLACES...
ORIBE COULD SUCCEED PRINCESS KIKURI, RIGHT?
I THINK A GIRL NAMED MIKUSA SWITCHED PLACES WITH HER.
HUH? MIKUSA?
IF YOU'RE GOING TO BRING ORIBE BACK TO AMAWA-KUNI...

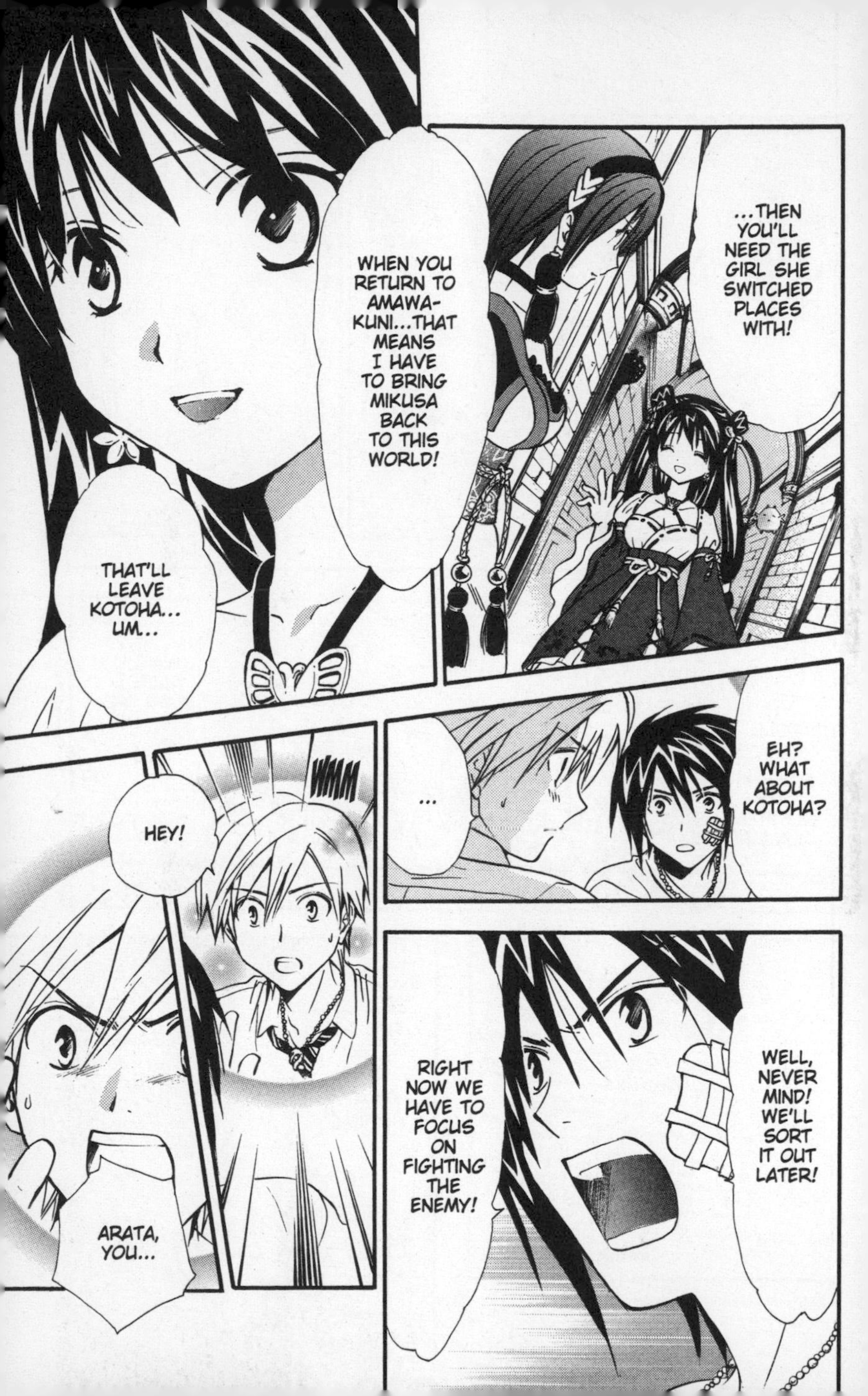
...THEN YOU'LL NEED THE GIRL SHE SWITCHED PLACES WITH!
WHEN YOU RETURN TO AMAWA-KUNI...THAT MEANS I HAVE TO BRING MIKUSA BACK TO THIS WORLD!
THAT'LL LEAVE KOTOHA... UM...
EH? WHAT ABOUT KOTOHA?
...
WELL, NEVER MIND! WE'LL SORT IT OUT LATER!
RIGHT NOW WE HAVE TO FOCUS ON FIGHTING THE ENEMY!
WMM
HEY!
ARATA, YOU...

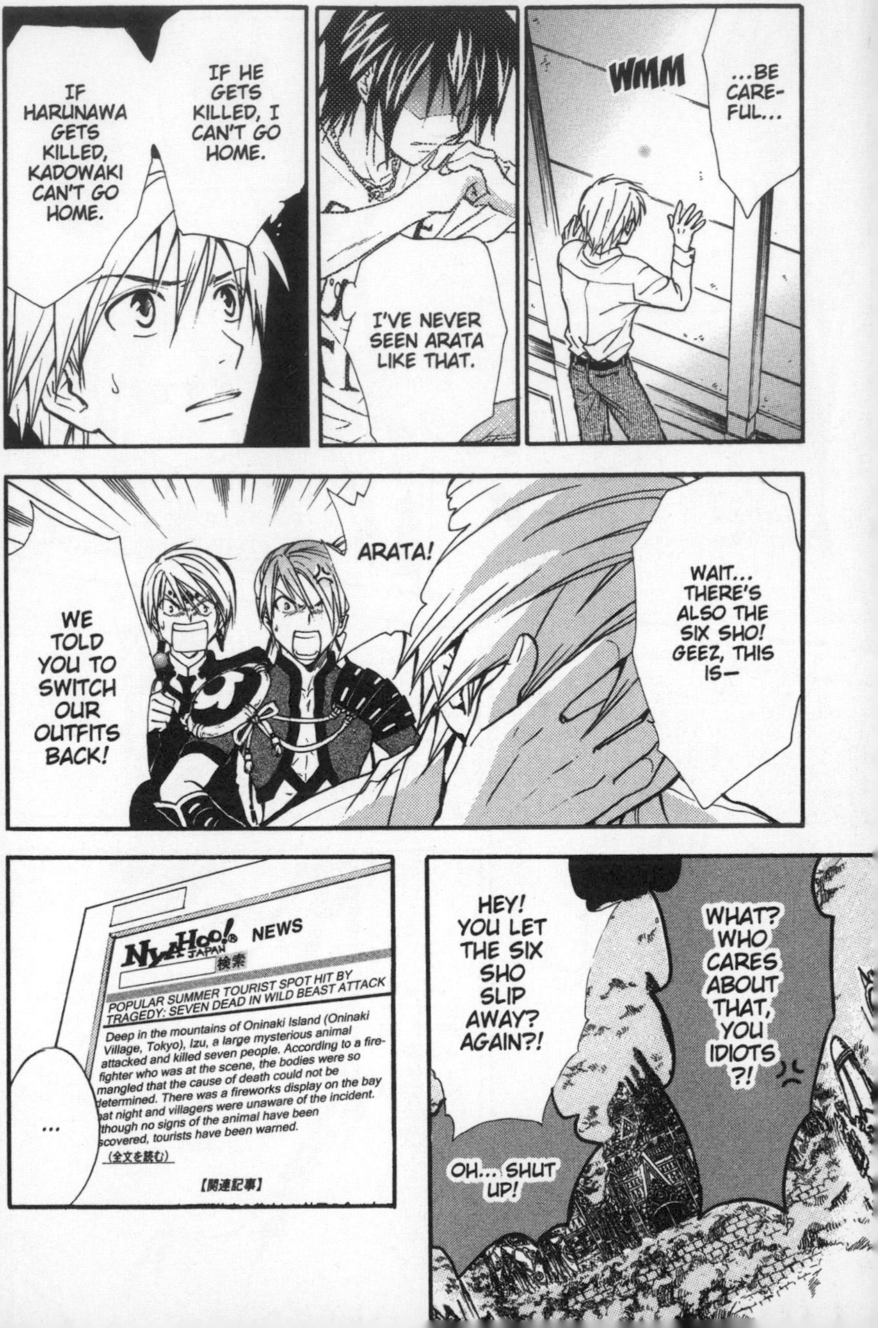
WMM
...BE CAREFUL...
I'VE NEVER SEEN ARATA LIKE THAT.
IF HE GETS KILLED, I CAN'T GO HOME.
IF HARUNAWA GETS KILLED, KADOWAKI CAN'T GO HOME.
WAIT... THERE'S ALSO THE SIX SHO! GEEZ, THIS IS—
ARATA!
WE TOLD YOU TO SWITCH OUR OUTFITS BACK!
WHAT? WHO CARES ABOUT THAT, YOU IDIOTS?!
HEY! YOU LET THE SIX SHO SLIP AWAY? AGAIN?!
OH... SHUT UP!
NYAHOO!® JAPAN
NEWS
検索
POPULAR SUMMER TOURIST SPOT HIT BY TRAGEDY: SEVEN DEAD IN WILD BEAST ATTACK
Deep in the mountains of Oninaki Island (Oninaki Village, Tokyo), Izu, a large mysterious animal attacked and killed seven people. According to a firefighter who was at the scene, the bodies were so mangled that the cause of death could not be determined. There was a fireworks display on the bay that night and villagers were unaware of the incident. Though no signs of the animal have been discovered, tourists have been warned.
(全文を読む)
【関連記事】
...

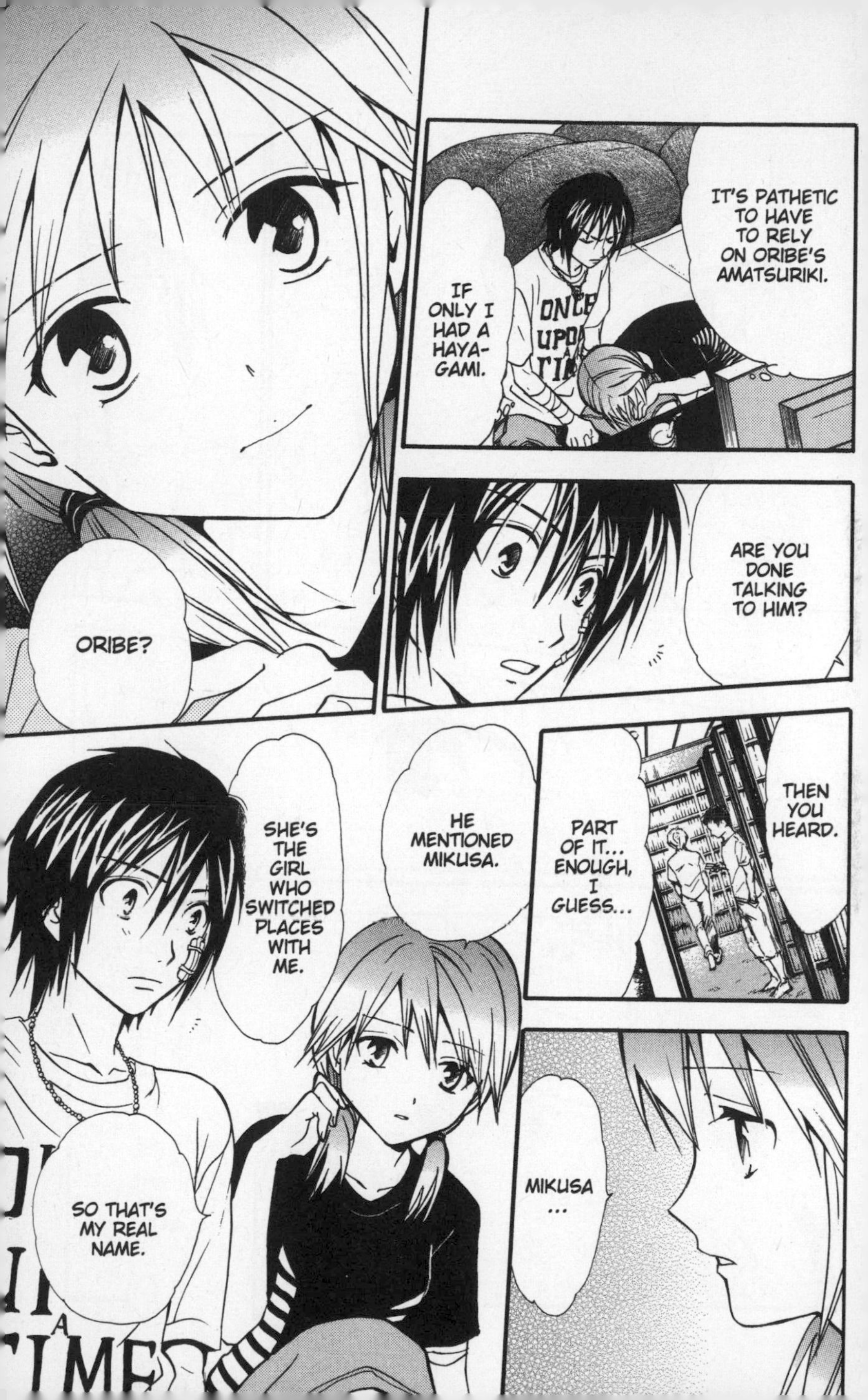
IT'S PATHETIC TO HAVE TO RELY ON ORIBE'S AMATSURIKI.
IF ONLY I HAD A HAYA-GAMI.
ARE YOU DONE TALKING TO HIM?
ORIBE?
THEN YOU HEARD.
PART OF IT... ENOUGH, I GUESS...
MIKUSA ...
HE MENTIONED MIKUSA.
SHE'S THE GIRL WHO SWITCHED PLACES WITH ME.
SO THAT'S MY REAL NAME.

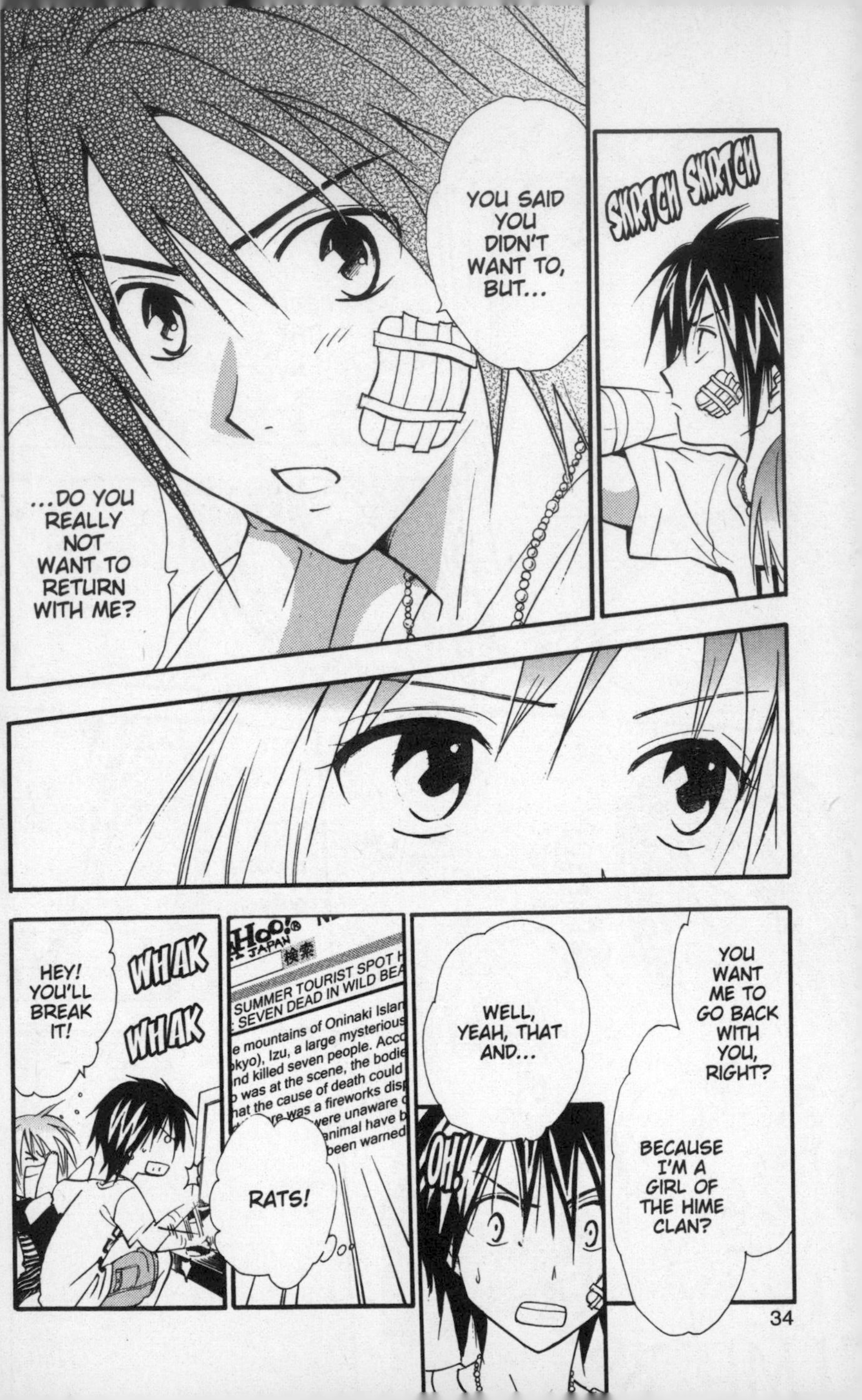
SKRTCH SKRTCH
YOU SAID YOU DIDN'T WANT TO, BUT...
...DO YOU REALLY NOT WANT TO RETURN WITH ME?
YOU WANT ME TO GO BACK WITH YOU, RIGHT?
BECAUSE I'M A GIRL OF THE HIME CLAN?
WELL, YEAH, THAT AND...
OH!
SUMMER TOURIST SPOT H
SEVEN DEAD IN WILD BEA
RATS!
WHAK
WHAK
HEY! YOU'LL BREAK IT!

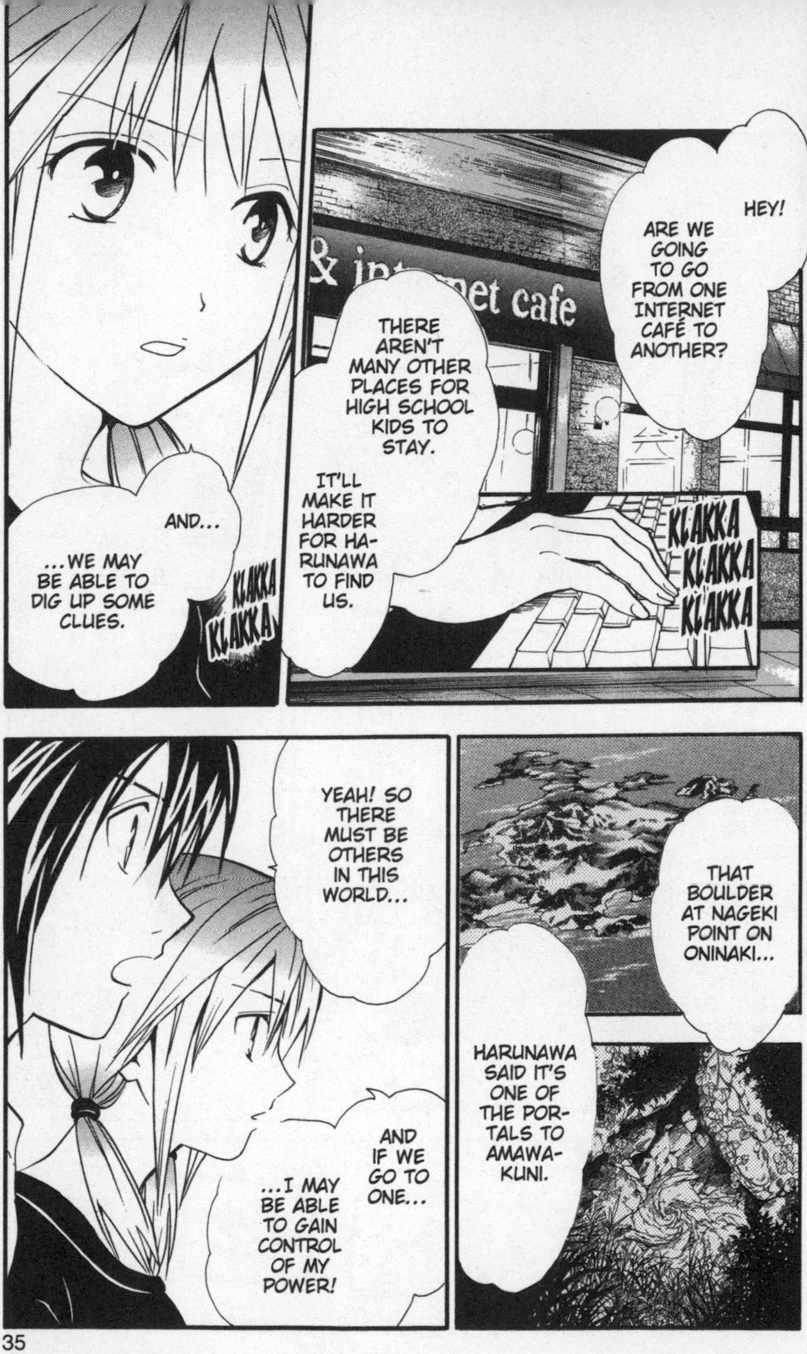
HEY! ARE WE GOING TO GO FROM ONE INTERNET CAFÉ TO ANOTHER?
& internet cafe
THERE AREN'T MANY OTHER PLACES FOR HIGH SCHOOL KIDS TO STAY.
IT'LL MAKE IT HARDER FOR HA-RUNAWA TO FIND US.
KLAKKA KLAKKA KLAKKA
AND...
...WE MAY BE ABLE TO DIG UP SOME CLUES.
KLAKKA KLAKKA
THAT BOULDER AT NAGEKI POINT ON ONINAKI...
HARUNAWA SAID IT'S ONE OF THE POR-TALS TO AMAWA-KUNI.
YEAH! SO THERE MUST BE OTHERS IN THIS WORLD...
AND IF WE GO TO ONE...
...I MAY BE ABLE TO GAIN CONTROL OF MY POWER!

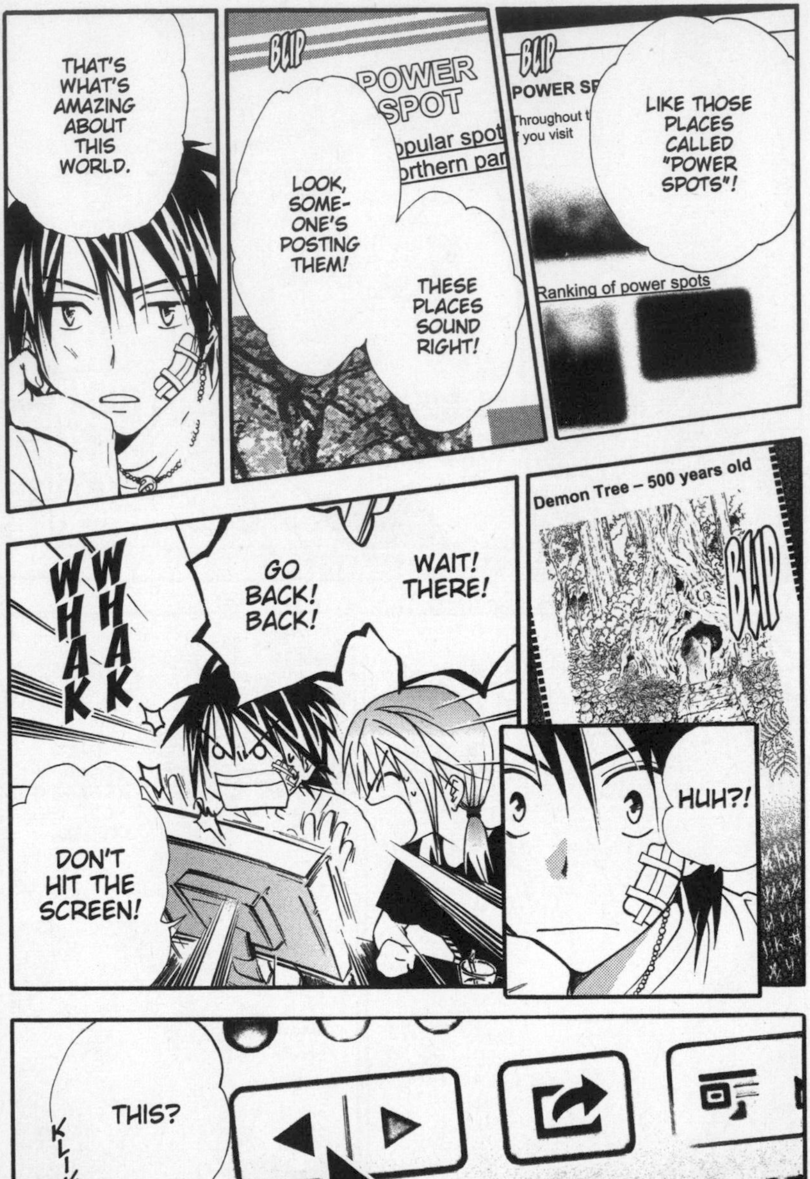
BLIP
POWER SP
Throughout t
f you visit
Ranking of power spots
LIKE THOSE PLACES CALLED "POWER SPOTS"!
BLIP
POWER SPOT
opular spot
orthern par
LOOK, SOME-ONE'S POSTING THEM!
THESE PLACES SOUND RIGHT!
THAT'S WHAT'S AMAZING ABOUT THIS WORLD.
Demon Tree – 500 years old
BLIP
HUH?!
WAIT! THERE!
GO BACK! BACK!
WHAK WHAK
DON'T HIT THE SCREEN!
THIS?
KLIK

...

IT'S A HUGE TREE...

YOU'RE TOO CLOSE!

I'll enlarge it.

THIS IS IT!

I KNEW IT!

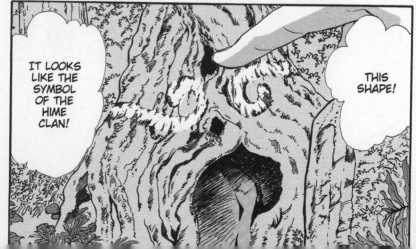

IT LOOKS LIKE THE SYMBOL OF THE HIME CLAN!

THIS SHAPE!

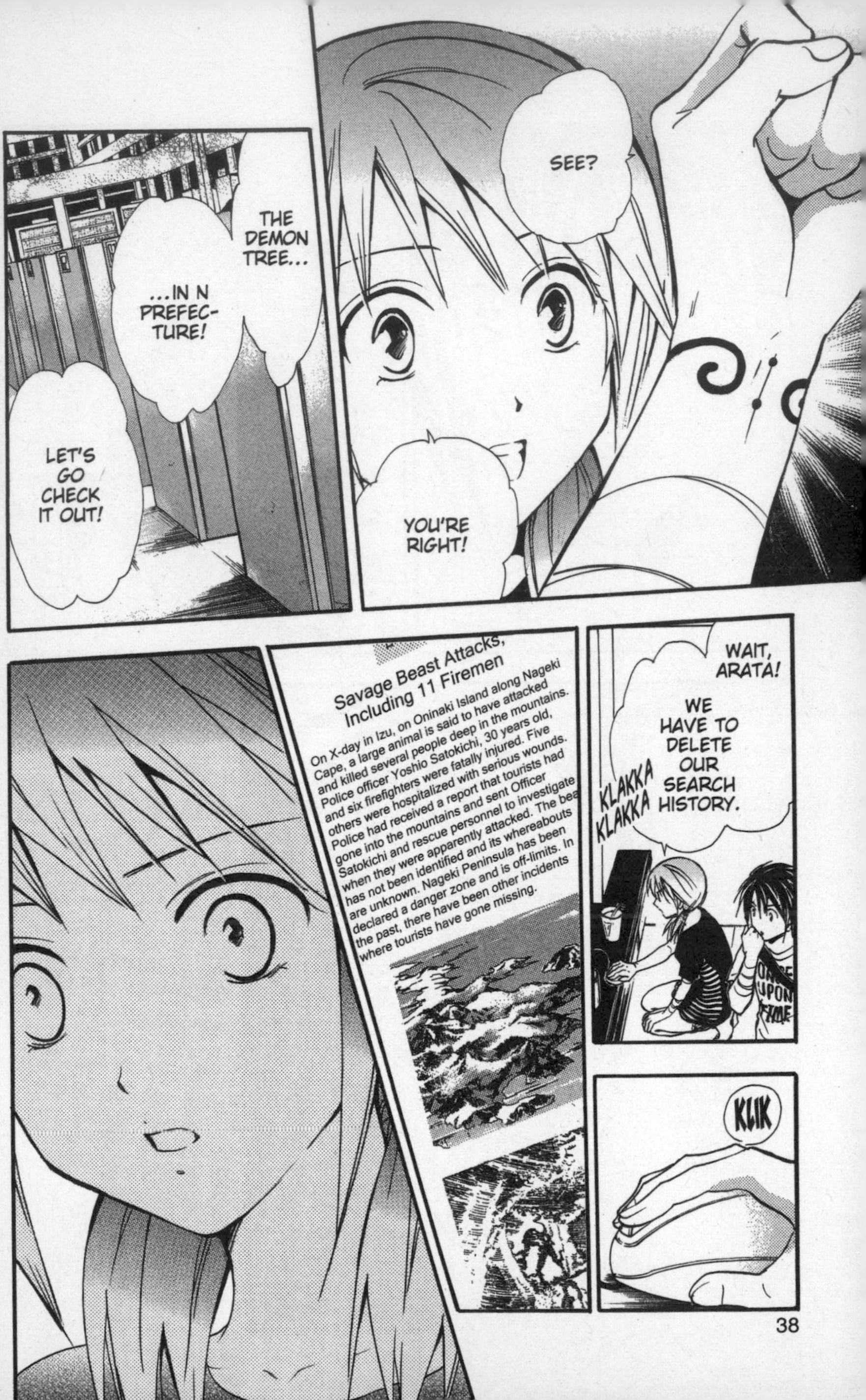
SEE?
YOU'RE RIGHT!
THE DEMON TREE...
...IN N PREFECTURE!
LET'S GO CHECK IT OUT!
WAIT, ARATA!
WE HAVE TO DELETE OUR SEARCH HISTORY.
KLAKKA KLAKKA
KLIK
Savage Beast Attacks, Including 11 Firemen
On X-day in Izu, on Oninaki Island along Nageki Cape, a large animal is said to have attacked and killed several people deep in the mountains. Police officer Yoshio Satokichi, 30 years old, and six firefighters were fatally injured. Five others were hospitalized with serious wounds. Police had received a report that tourists had gone into the mountains and sent Officer Satokichi and rescue personnel to investigate when they were apparently attacked. The bea has not been identified and its whereabouts are unknown. Nageki Peninsula has been declared a danger zone and is off-limits. In the past, there have been other incidents where tourists have gone missing.

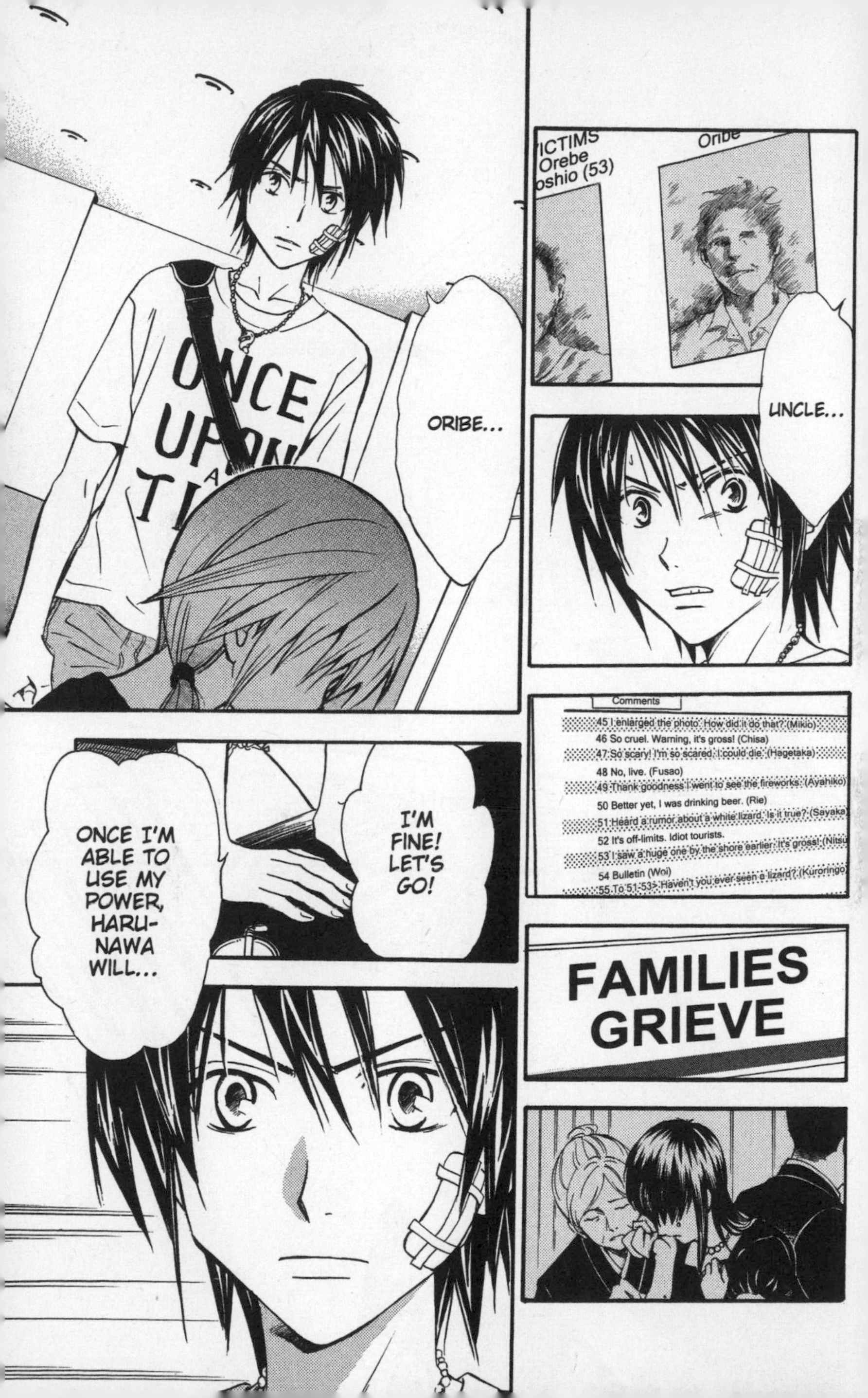
VICTIMS
Orebe
oshio (53)
Oribe
UNCLE...
Comments
45 I enlarged the photo. How did it do that? (Mikio)
46 So cruel. Warning, it's gross! (Chisa)
47 So scary! I'm so scared, I could die. (Hagetaka)
48 No, live. (Fusao)
49 Thank goodness I went to see the fireworks. (Ayahiko)
50 Better yet, I was drinking beer. (Rie)
51 Heard a rumor about a white lizard. Is it true? (Sayaka
52 It's off-limits. Idiot tourists.
53 I saw a huge one by the shore earlier. It's gross! (Nitsu
54 Bulletin (Woi)
55 To 51-53> Haven't you ever seen a lizard? (Kuroringo
FAMILIES GRIEVE
ORIBE...
I'M FINE! LET'S GO!
ONCE I'M ABLE TO USE MY POWER, HARUNAWA WILL...

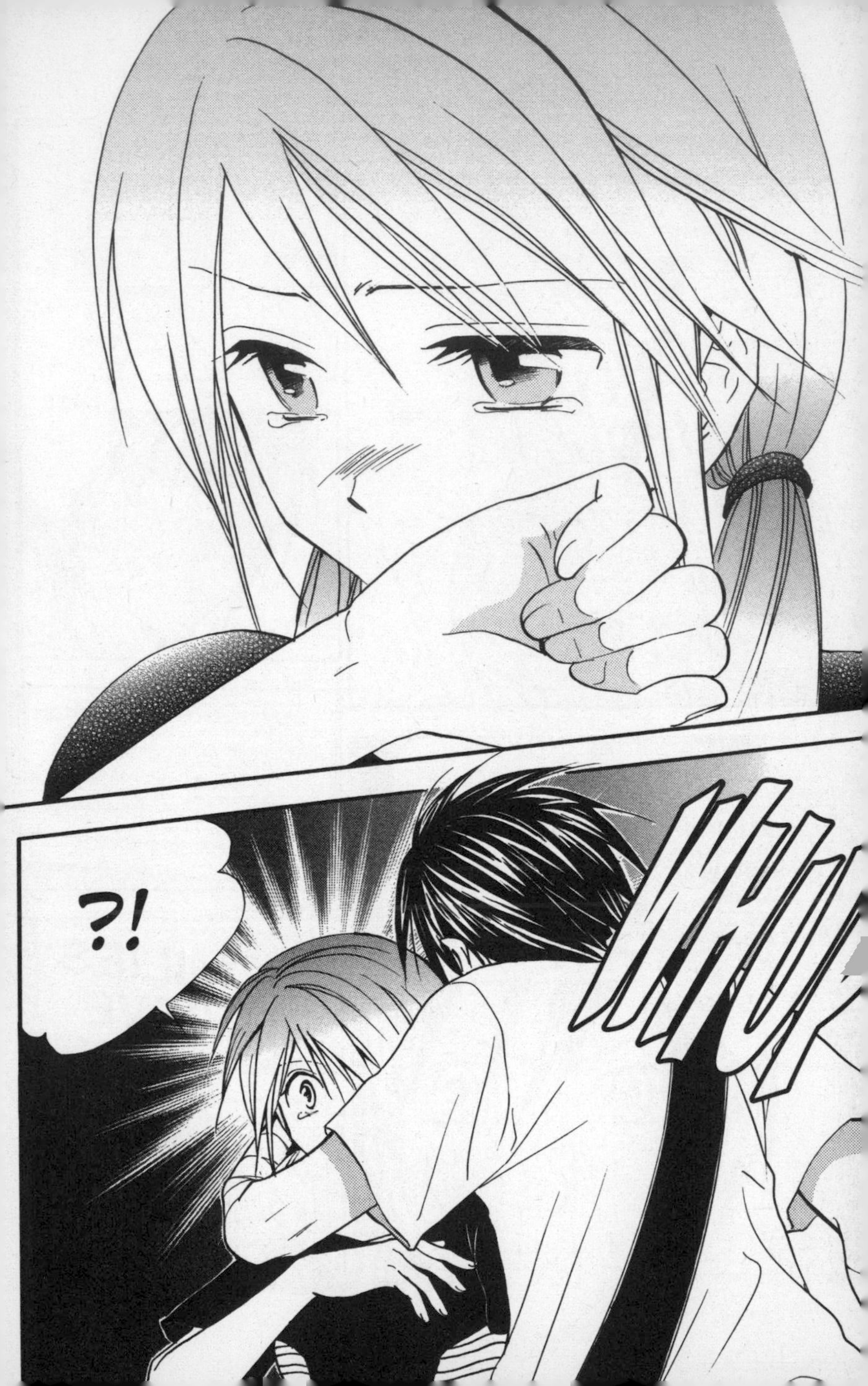
WHU
?!

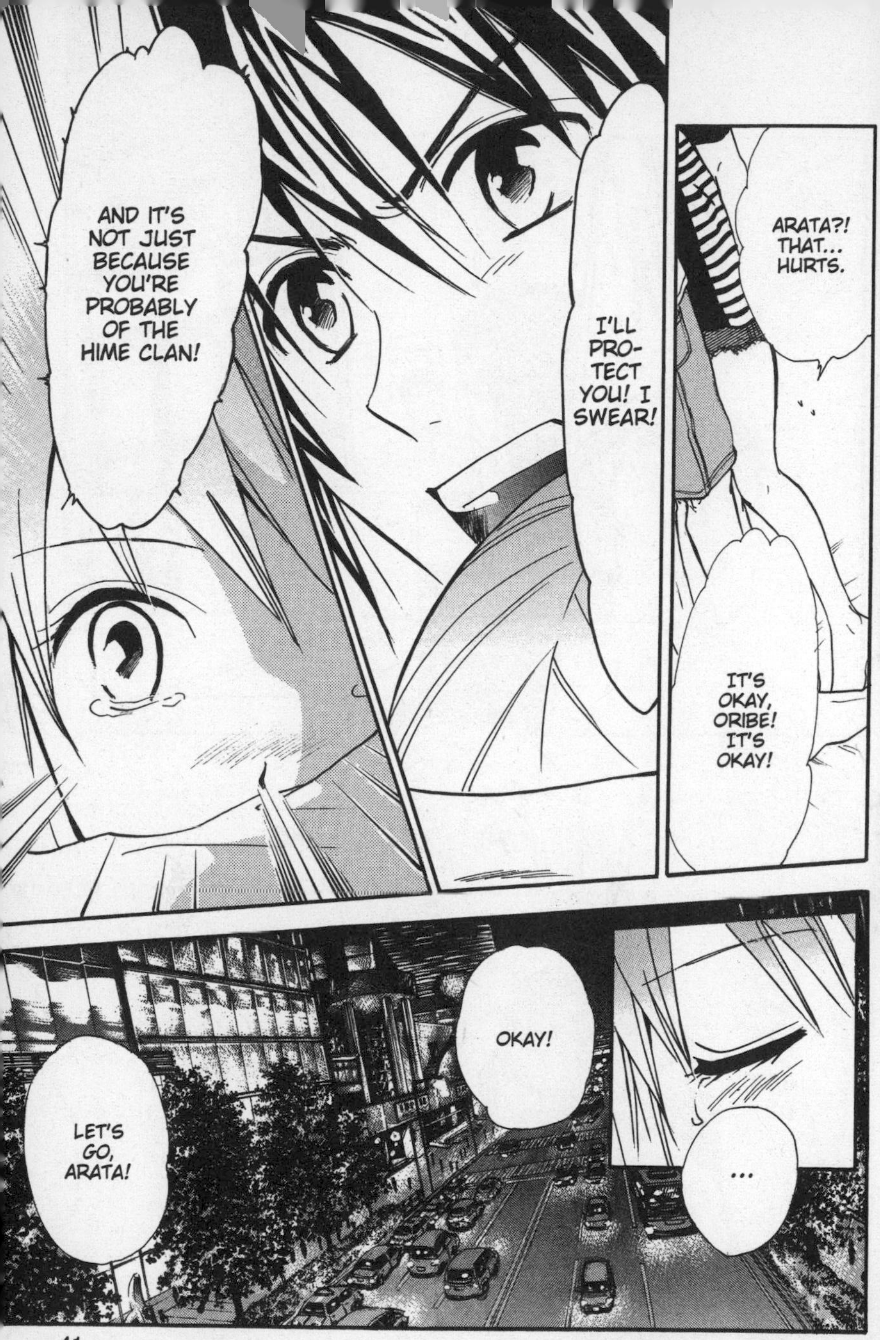
ARATA?! THAT... HURTS.
IT'S OKAY, ORIBE! IT'S OKAY!
I'LL PROTECT YOU! I SWEAR!
AND IT'S NOT JUST BECAUSE YOU'RE PROBABLY OF THE HIME CLAN!
...
OKAY!
LET'S GO, ARATA!

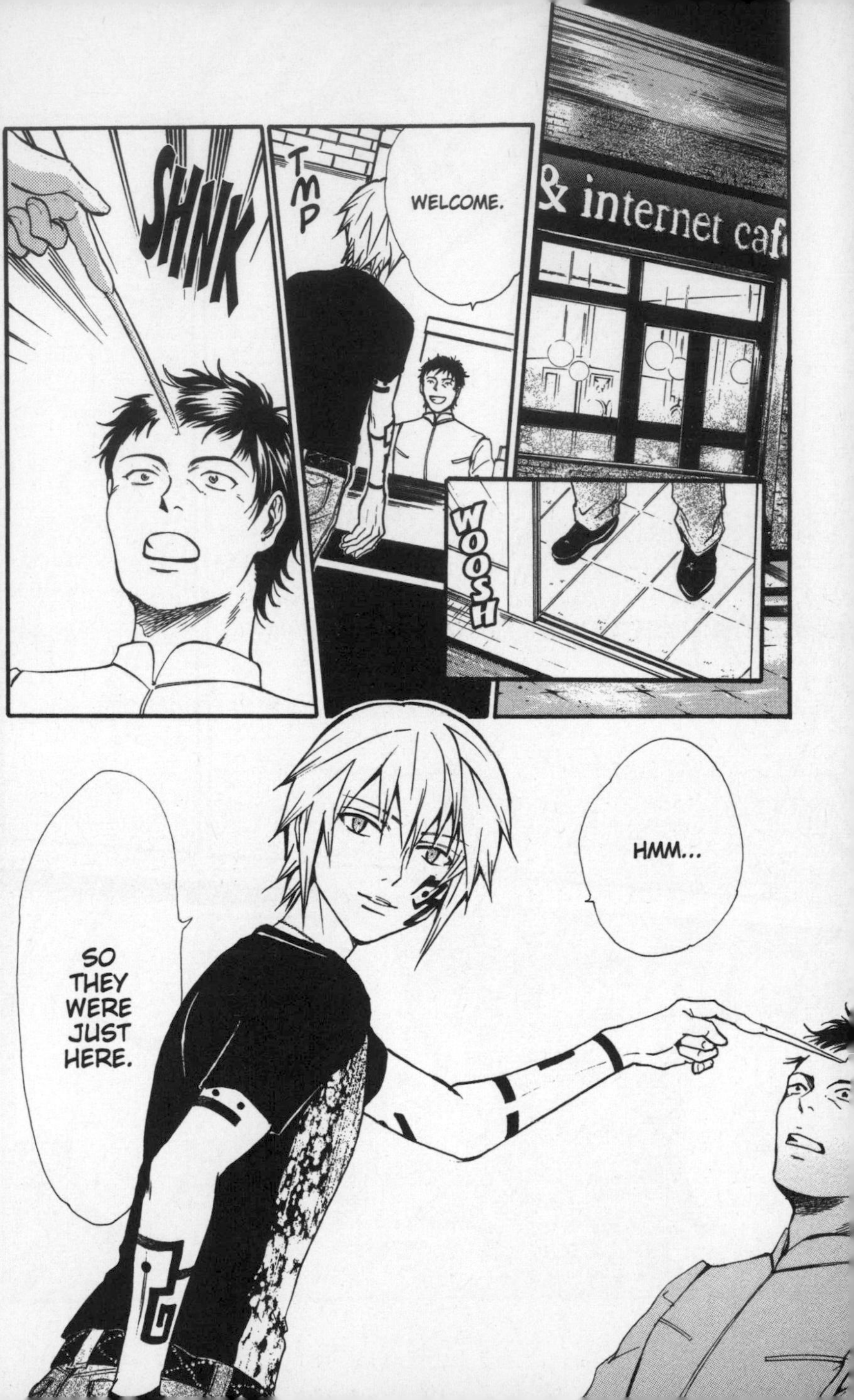
& internet caf
WOOSH
TMP
WELCOME.
SHNK
HMM...
SO THEY WERE JUST HERE.

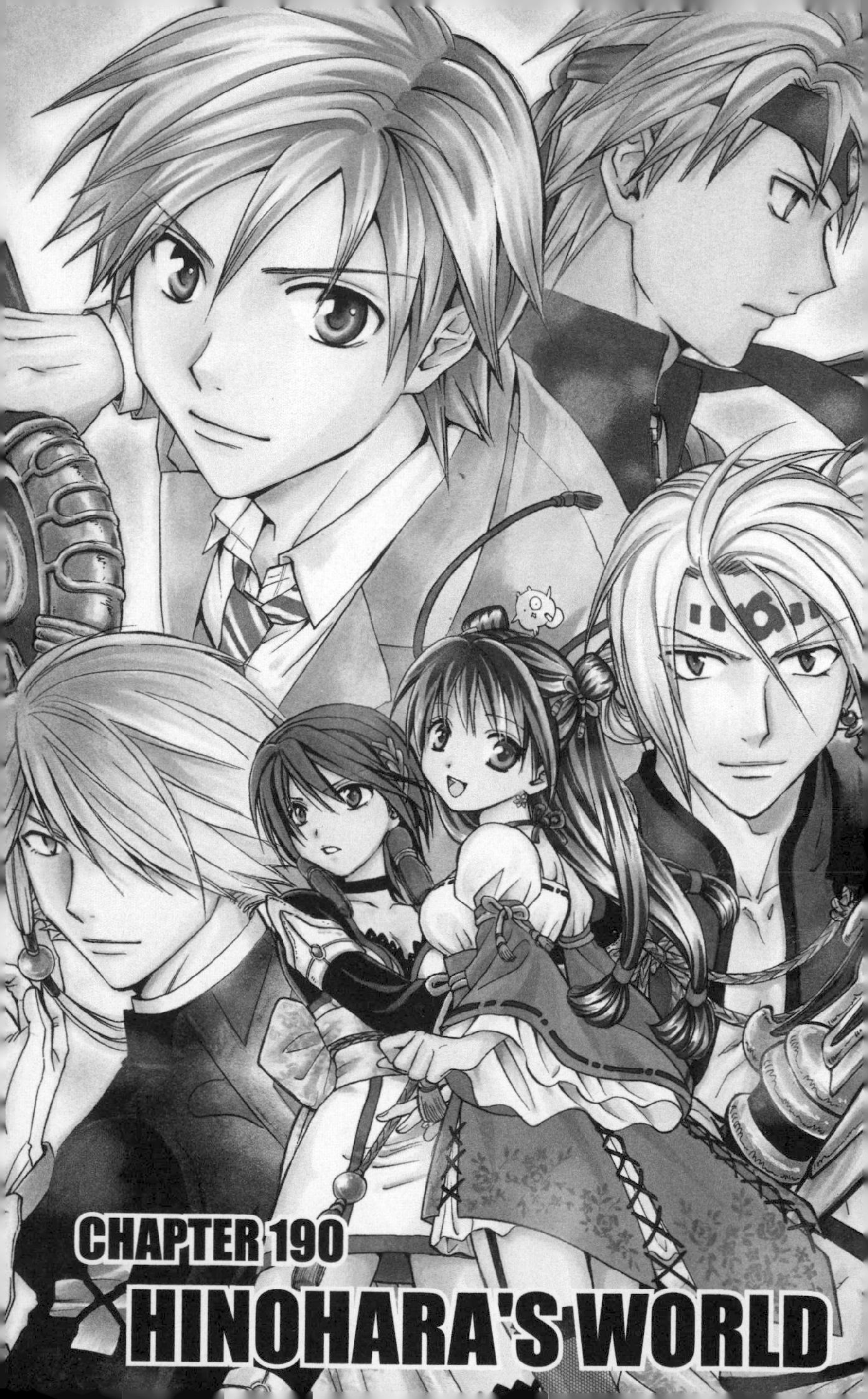
CHAPTER 190
HINOHARA'S WORLD

Arata
THE LEGEND

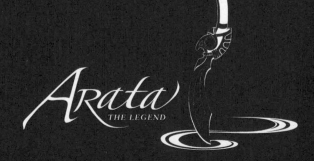

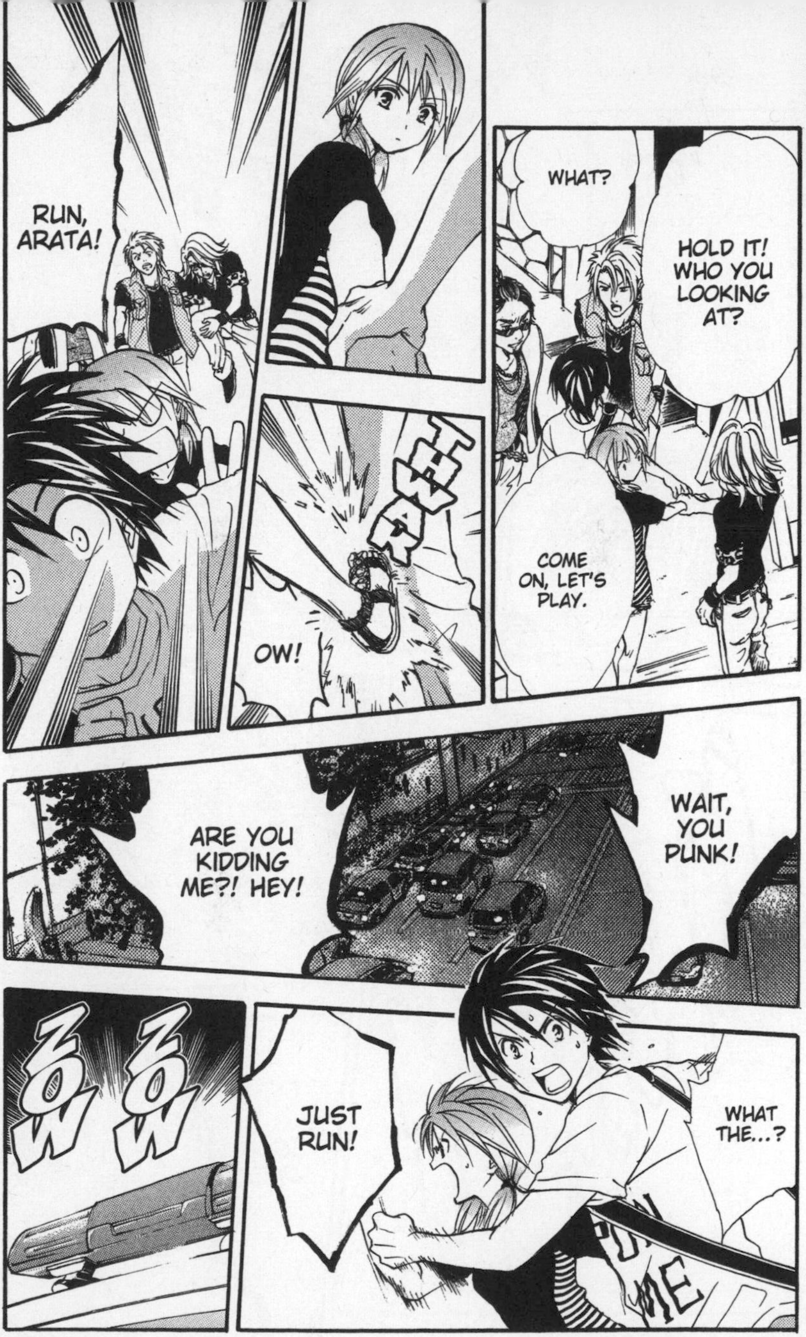
WHAT?
HOLD IT! WHO YOU LOOKING AT?
COME ON, LET'S PLAY.
THWAK
OW!
RUN, ARATA!
WAIT, YOU PUNK!
ARE YOU KIDDING ME?! HEY!
WHAT THE...?
JUST RUN!
ZOW
ZOW

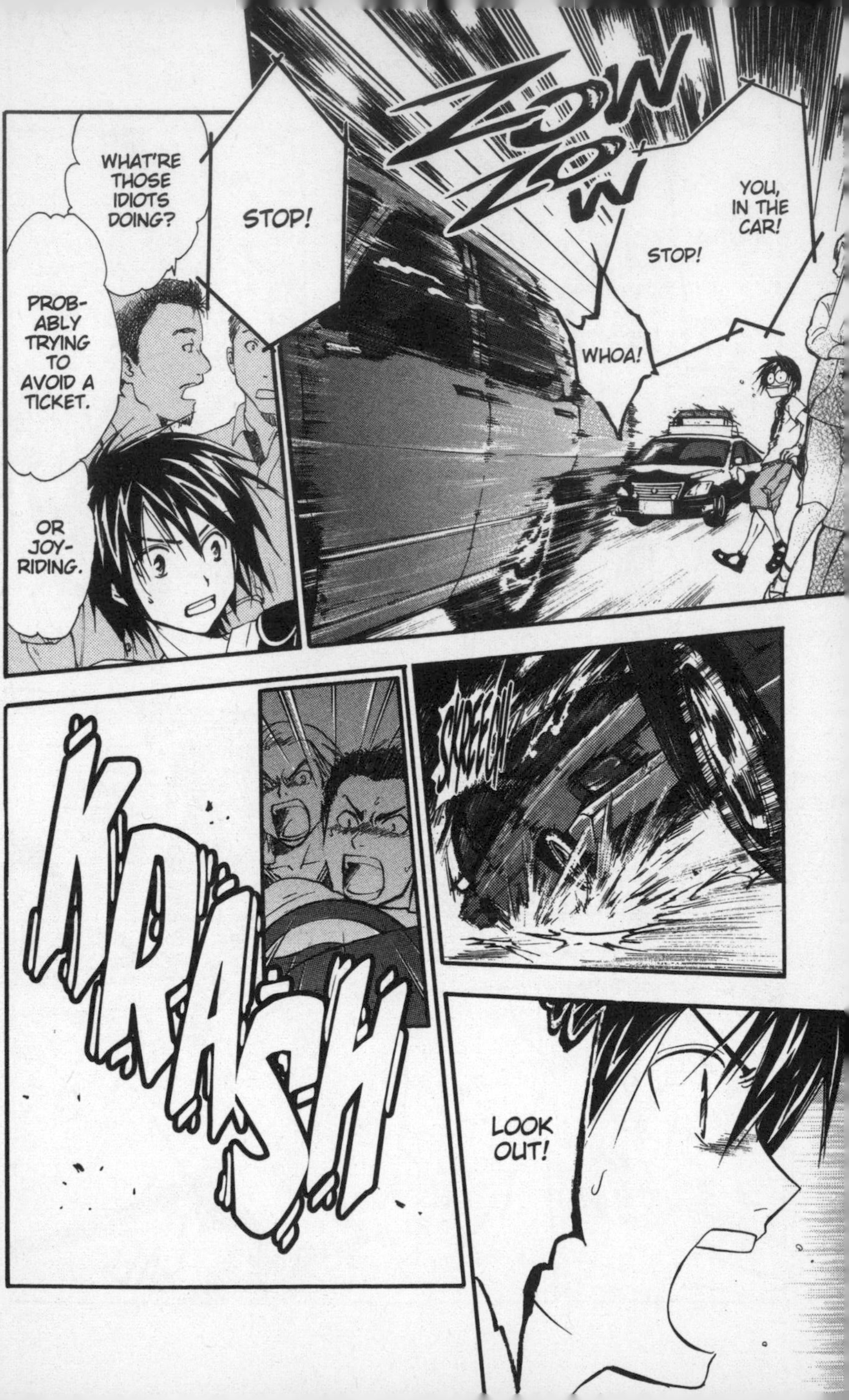
ZOOM ZOOM
YOU, IN THE CAR!
STOP!
STOP!
WHOA!
WHAT'RE THOSE IDIOTS DOING?
PROB-ABLY TRYING TO AVOID A TICKET.
OR JOY-RIDING.
SKREECH
LOOK OUT!
KRASH

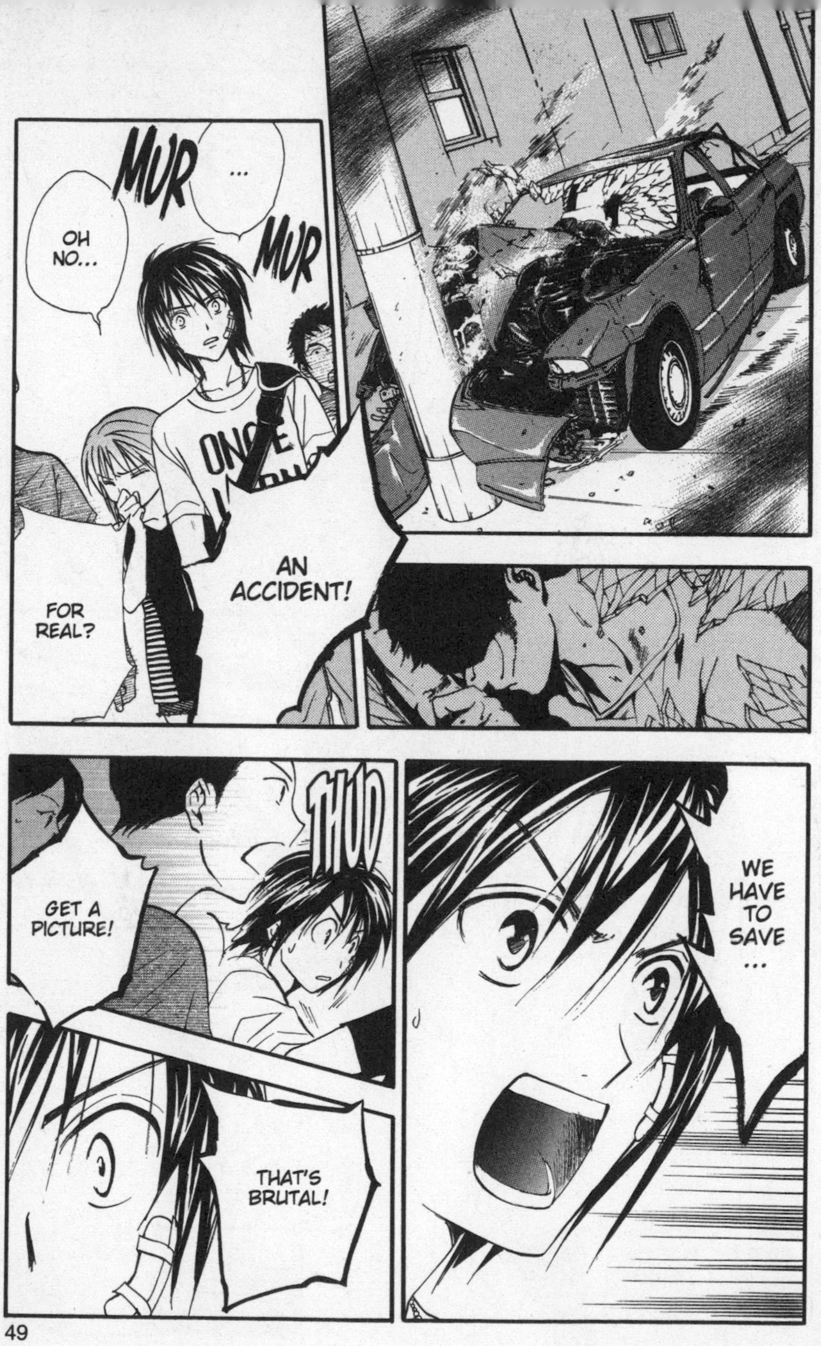
MUR MUR
...
OH NO...
AN ACCIDENT!
FOR REAL?
WE HAVE TO SAVE ...
THUD
GET A PICTURE!
THAT'S BRUTAL!

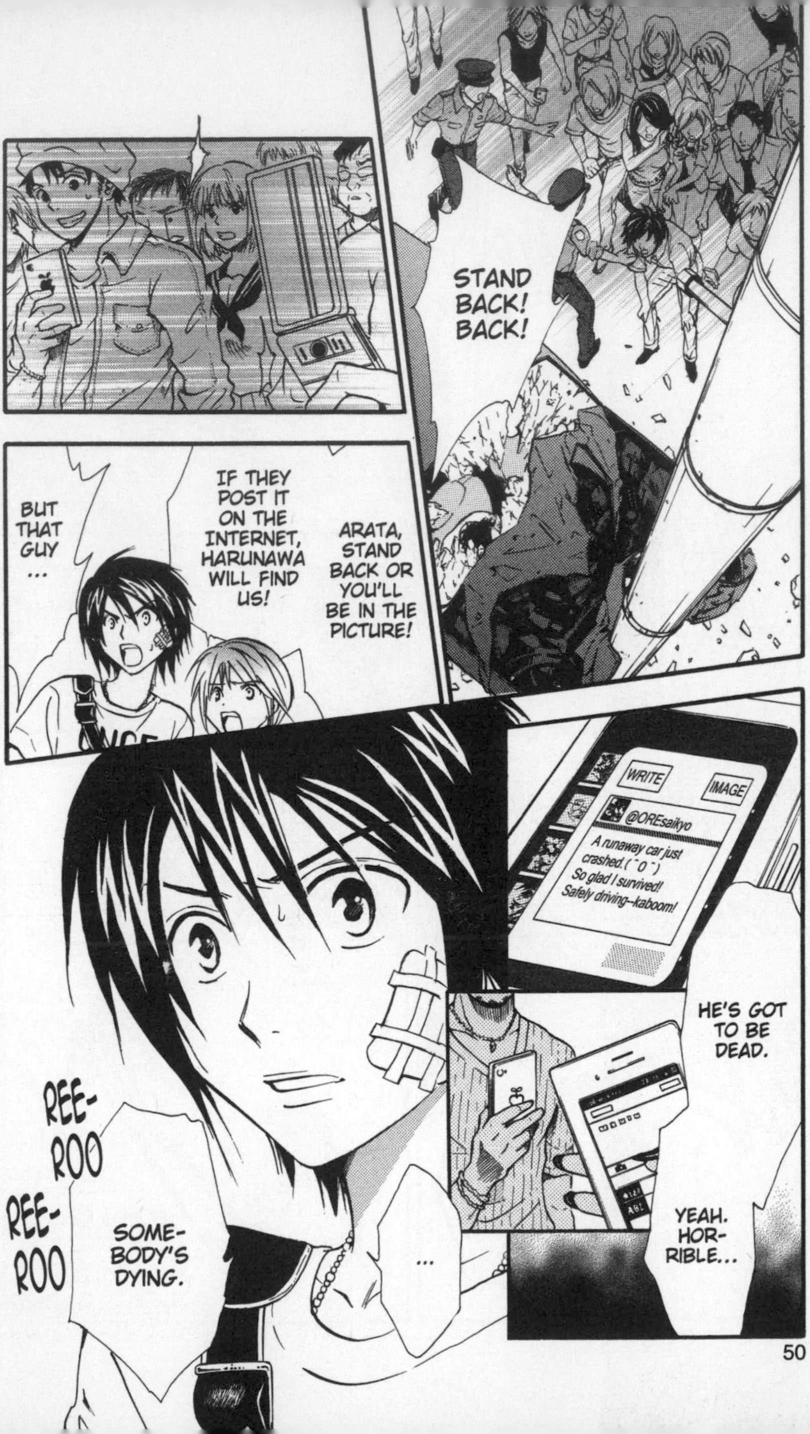
STAND BACK! BACK!
ARATA, STAND BACK OR YOU'LL BE IN THE PICTURE!
IF THEY POST IT ON THE INTERNET, HARUNAWA WILL FIND US!
BUT THAT GUY ...
WRITE
IMAGE
@OREsaikyo
A runaway car just crashed.(˘0˘) So glad I survived! Safely driving--kaboom!
HE'S GOT TO BE DEAD.
YEAH. HORRIBLE...
...
SOMEBODY'S DYING.
REE-ROO REE-ROO

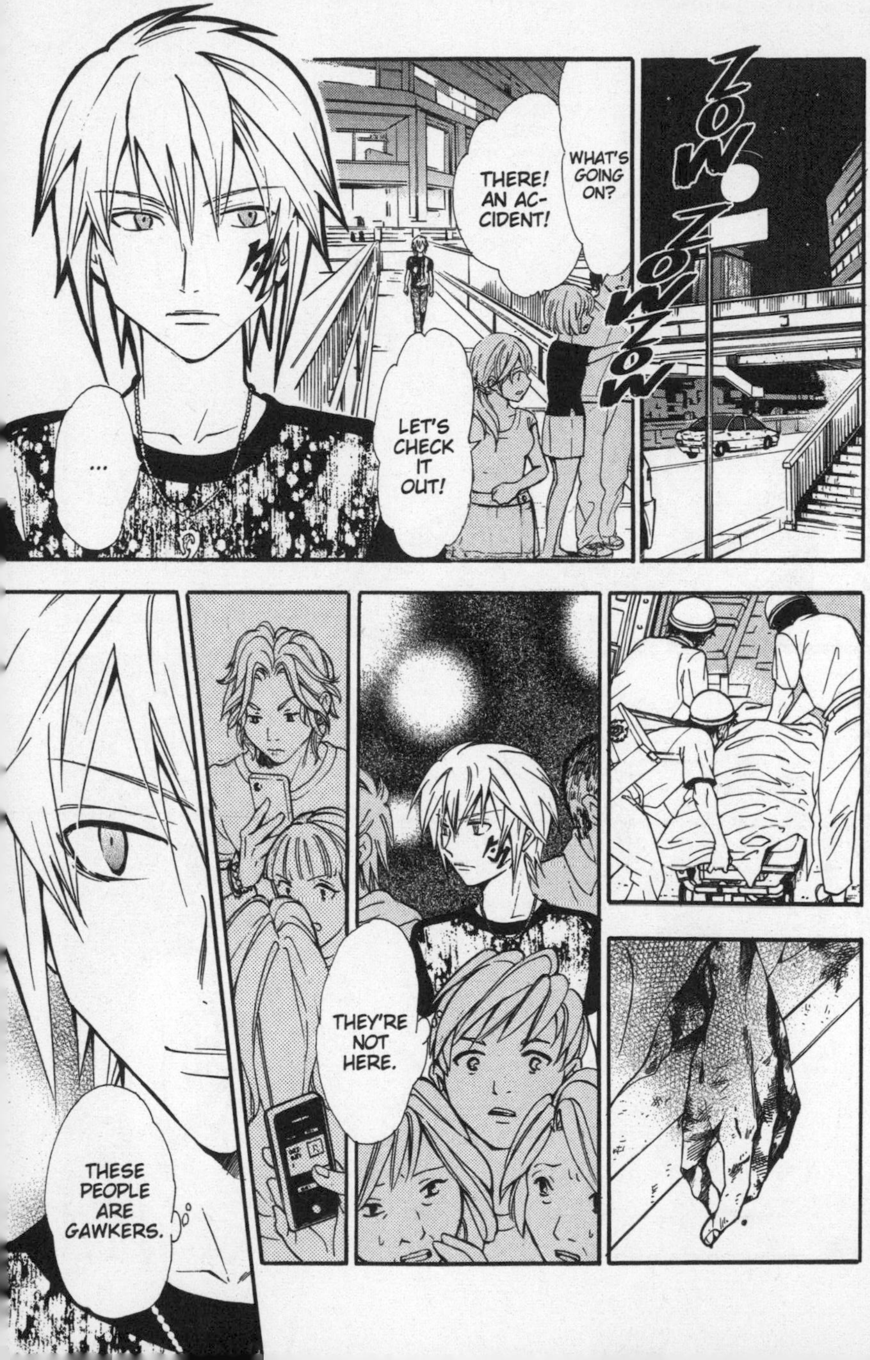
ZOW ZOWZOW
WHAT'S GOING ON?
THERE! AN ACCIDENT!
LET'S CHECK IT OUT!
...
THEY'RE NOT HERE.
THESE PEOPLE ARE GAWKERS.

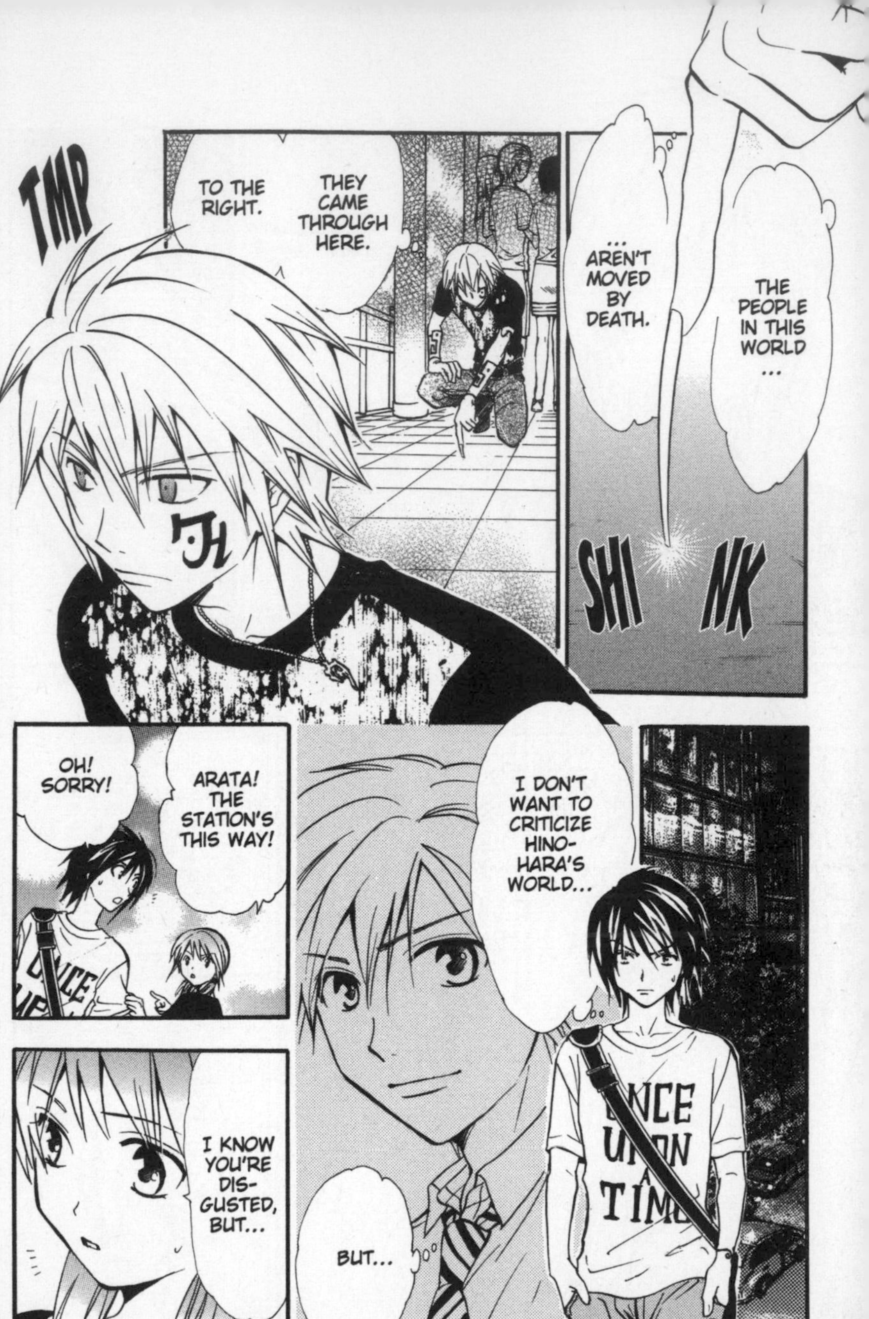
THE PEOPLE IN THIS WORLD...
...AREN'T MOVED BY DEATH.
SHINK
TMP
THEY CAME THROUGH HERE.
TO THE RIGHT.
I DON'T WANT TO CRITICIZE HINO-HARA'S WORLD...
BUT...
ARATA! THE STATION'S THIS WAY!
OH! SORRY!
I KNOW YOU'RE DIS-GUSTED, BUT...

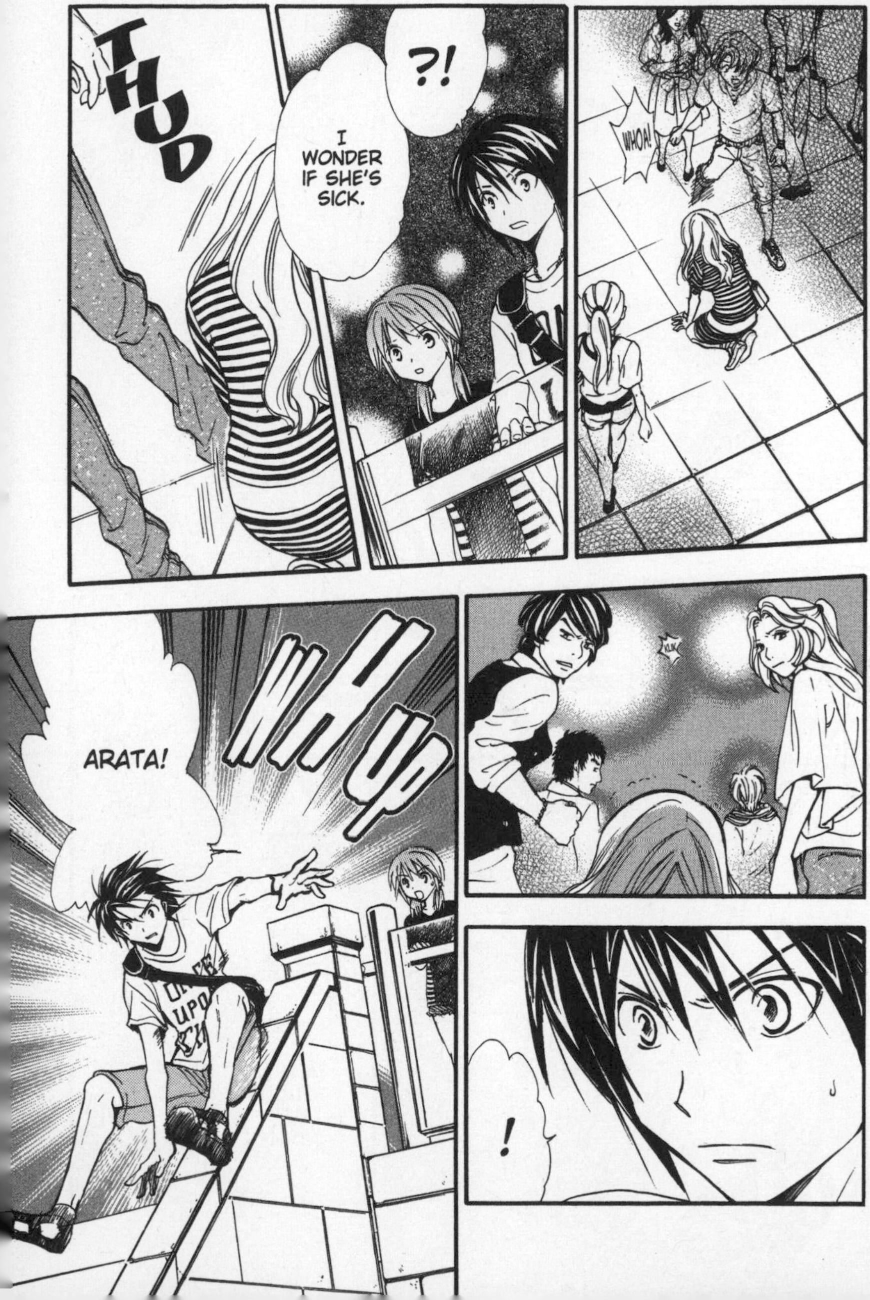
WHOA!
?!
I WONDER IF SHE'S SICK.
THUD
KLIK
!
WHUP
ARATA!

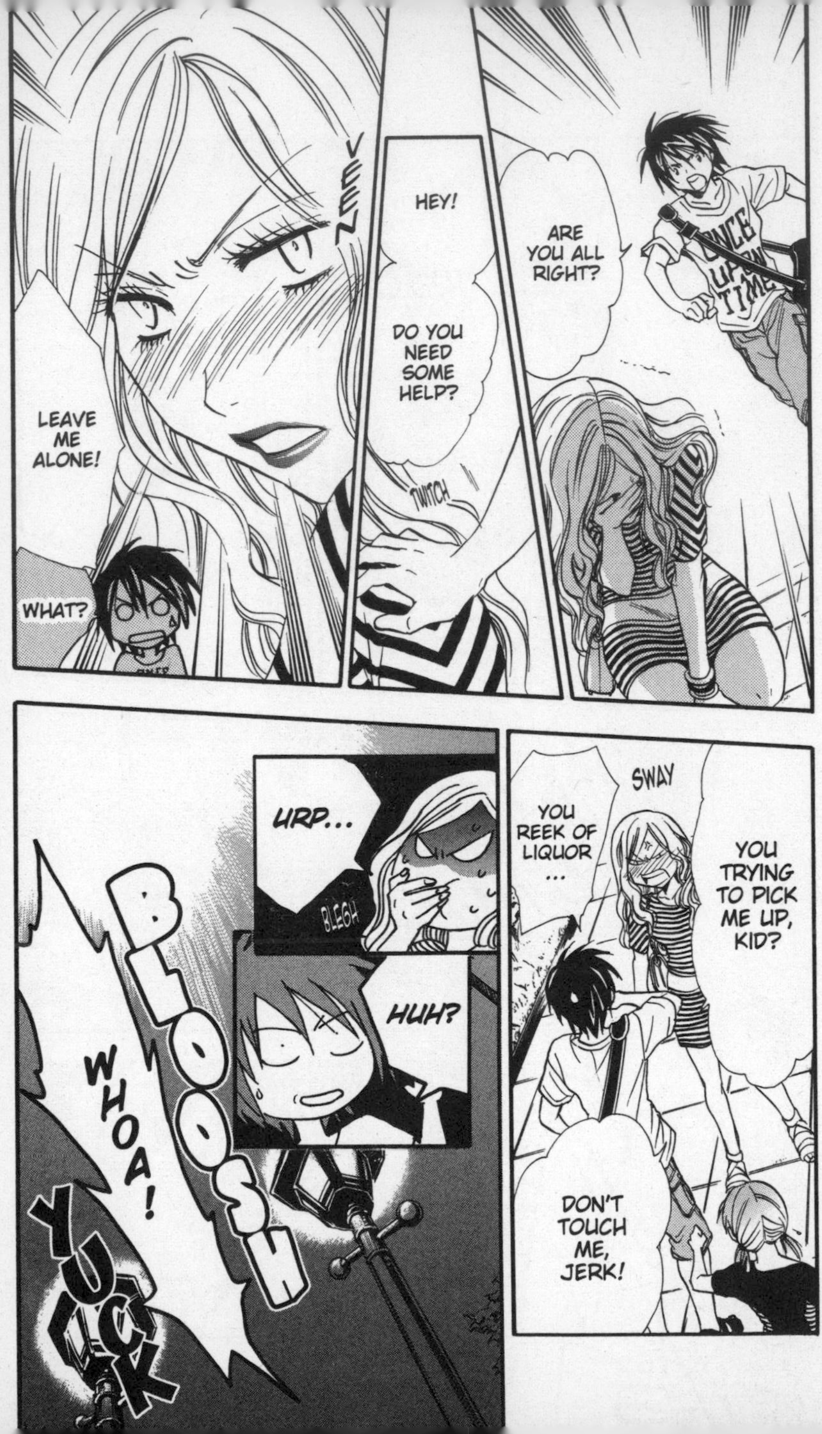
ARE YOU ALL RIGHT?
HEY!
DO YOU NEED SOME HELP?
TWITCH
VEEN
LEAVE ME ALONE!
WHAT?
YOU TRYING TO PICK ME UP, KID?
SWAY
YOU REEK OF LIQUOR ...
DON'T TOUCH ME, JERK!
URP...
BLEGH
HUH?
BLOOSH
WHOA!
YUCK

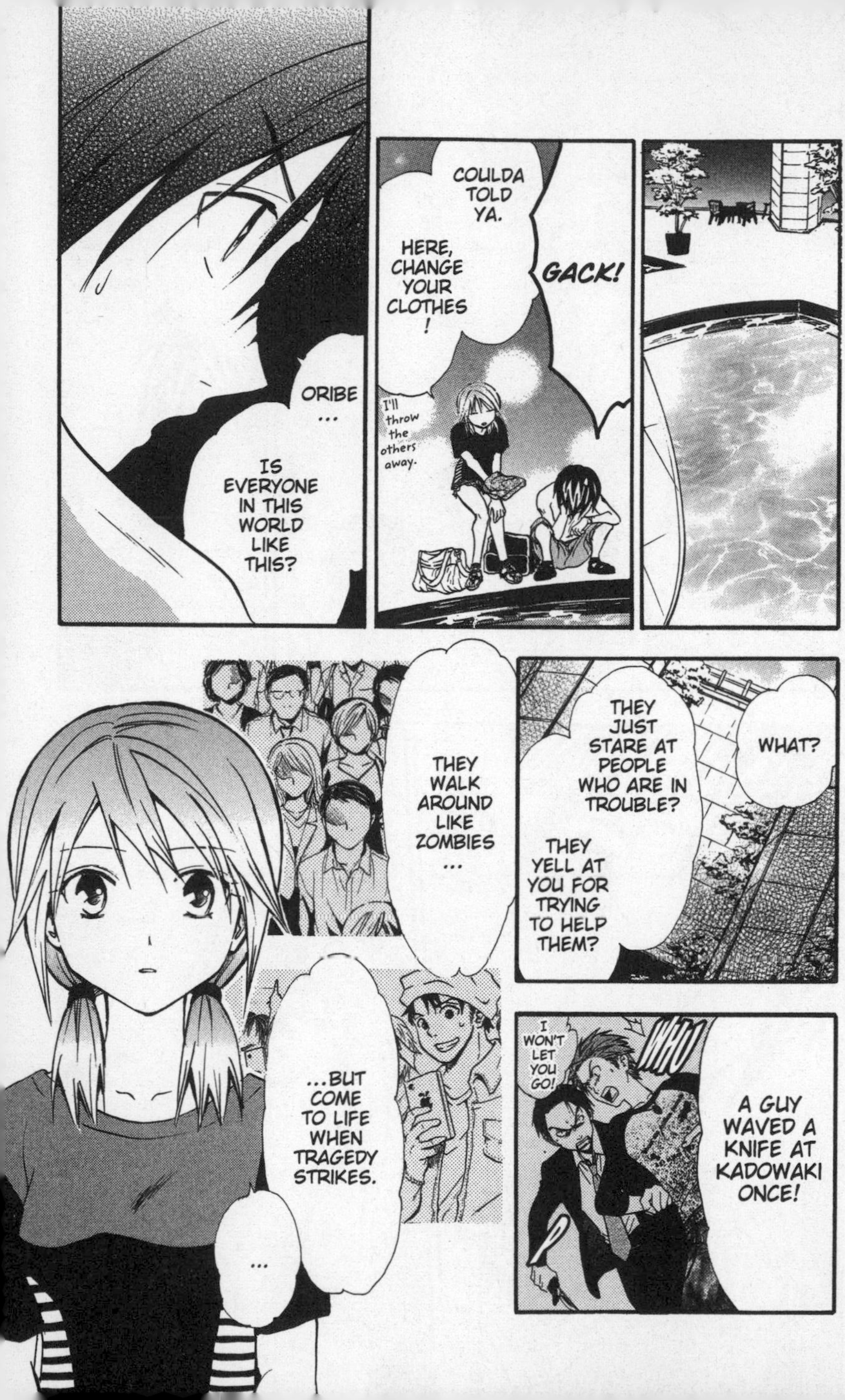
COULDA TOLD YA.
GACK!
HERE, CHANGE YOUR CLOTHES!
I'll throw the others away.
ORIBE...
IS EVERYONE IN THIS WORLD LIKE THIS?
WHAT?
THEY JUST STARE AT PEOPLE WHO ARE IN TROUBLE?
THEY YELL AT YOU FOR TRYING TO HELP THEM?
A GUY WAVED A KNIFE AT KADOWAKI ONCE!
I WON'T LET YOU GO!
THEY WALK AROUND LIKE ZOMBIES...
...BUT COME TO LIFE WHEN TRAGEDY STRIKES.
...

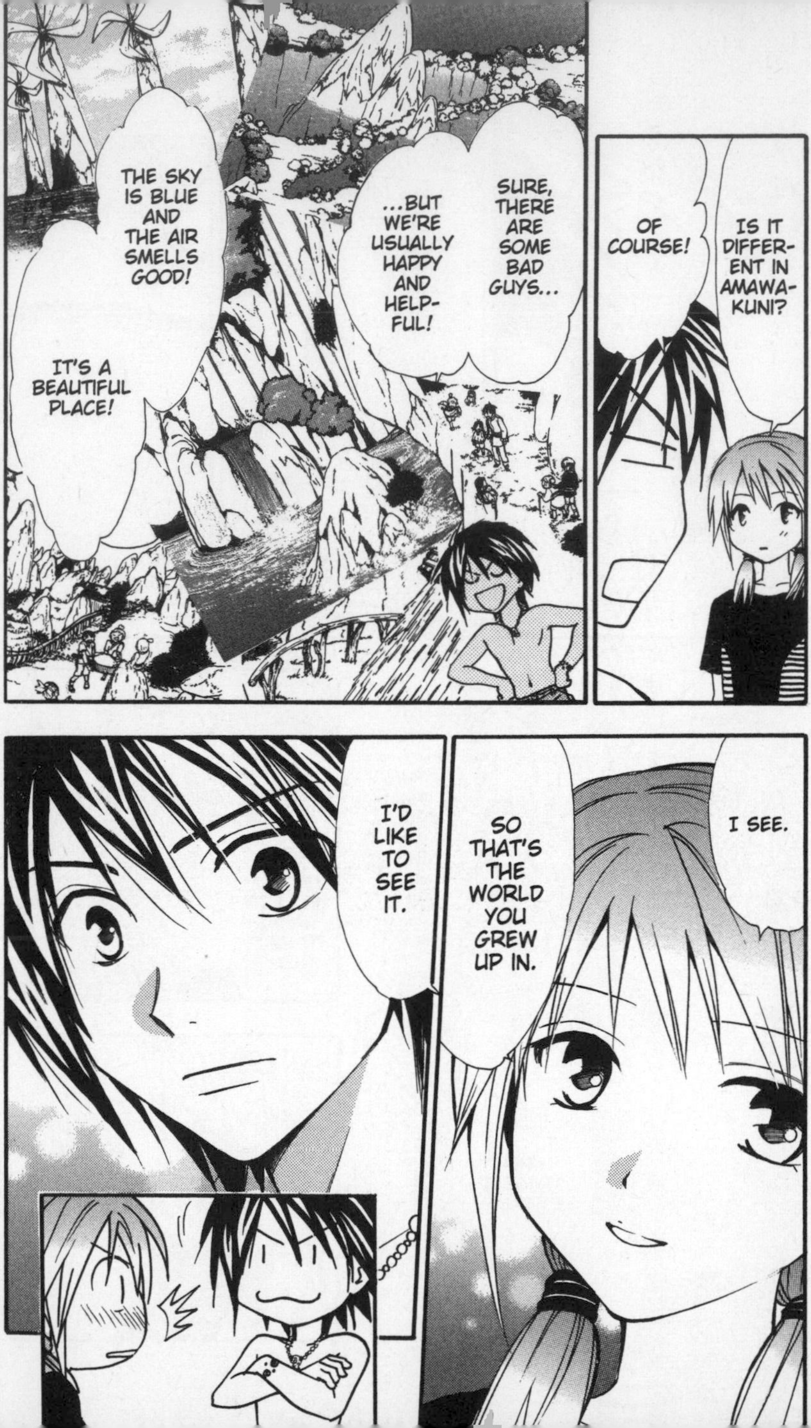
IS IT DIFFER-ENT IN AMAWA-KUNI?
OF COURSE!
SURE, THERE ARE SOME BAD GUYS...
...BUT WE'RE USUALLY HAPPY AND HELP-FUL!
THE SKY IS BLUE AND THE AIR SMELLS GOOD!
IT'S A BEAUTIFUL PLACE!
I SEE.
SO THAT'S THE WORLD YOU GREW UP IN.
I'D LIKE TO SEE IT.

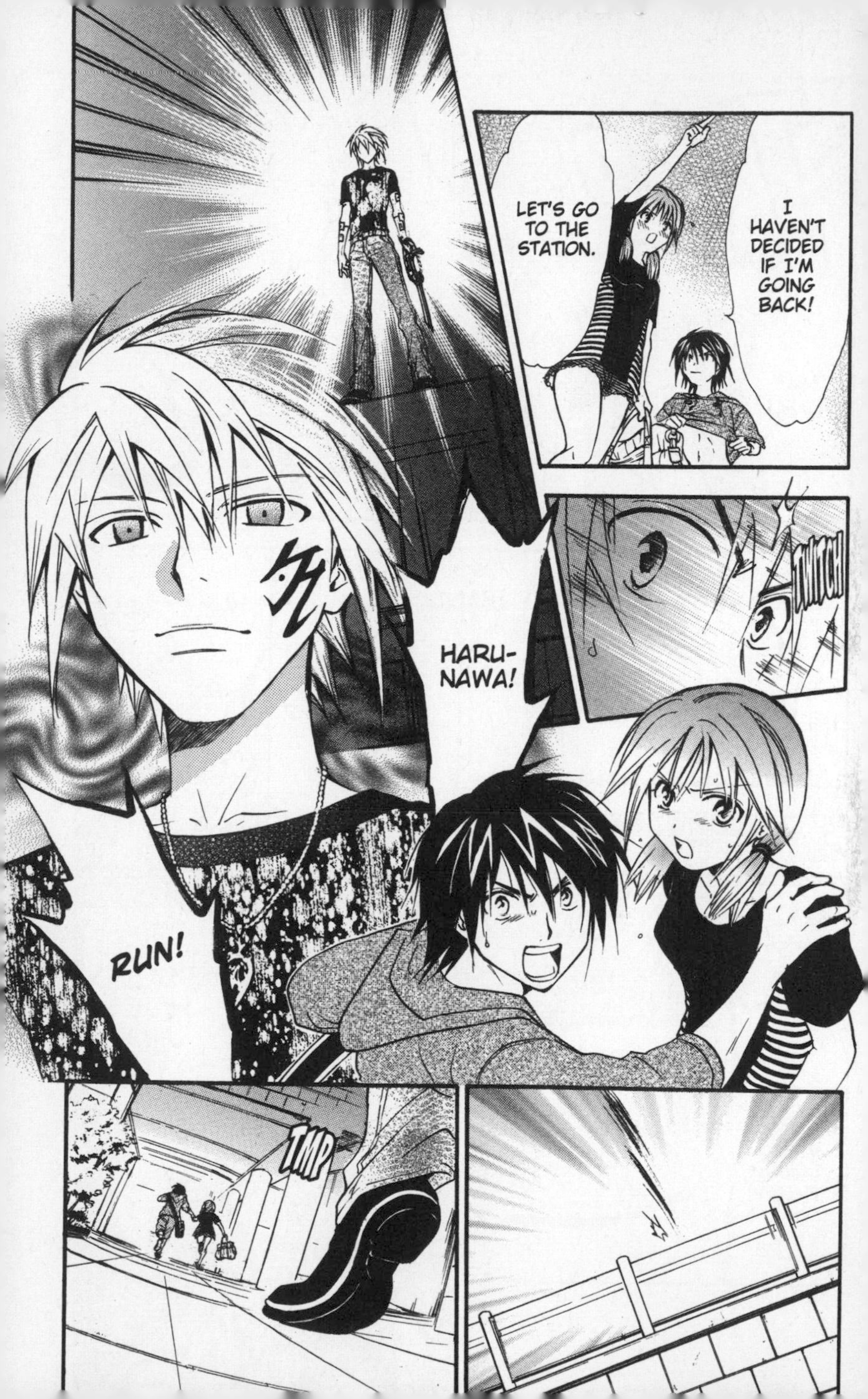
I HAVEN'T DECIDED IF I'M GOING BACK!
LET'S GO TO THE STATION.
TWITCH
HARU-NAWA!
RUN!
TMP

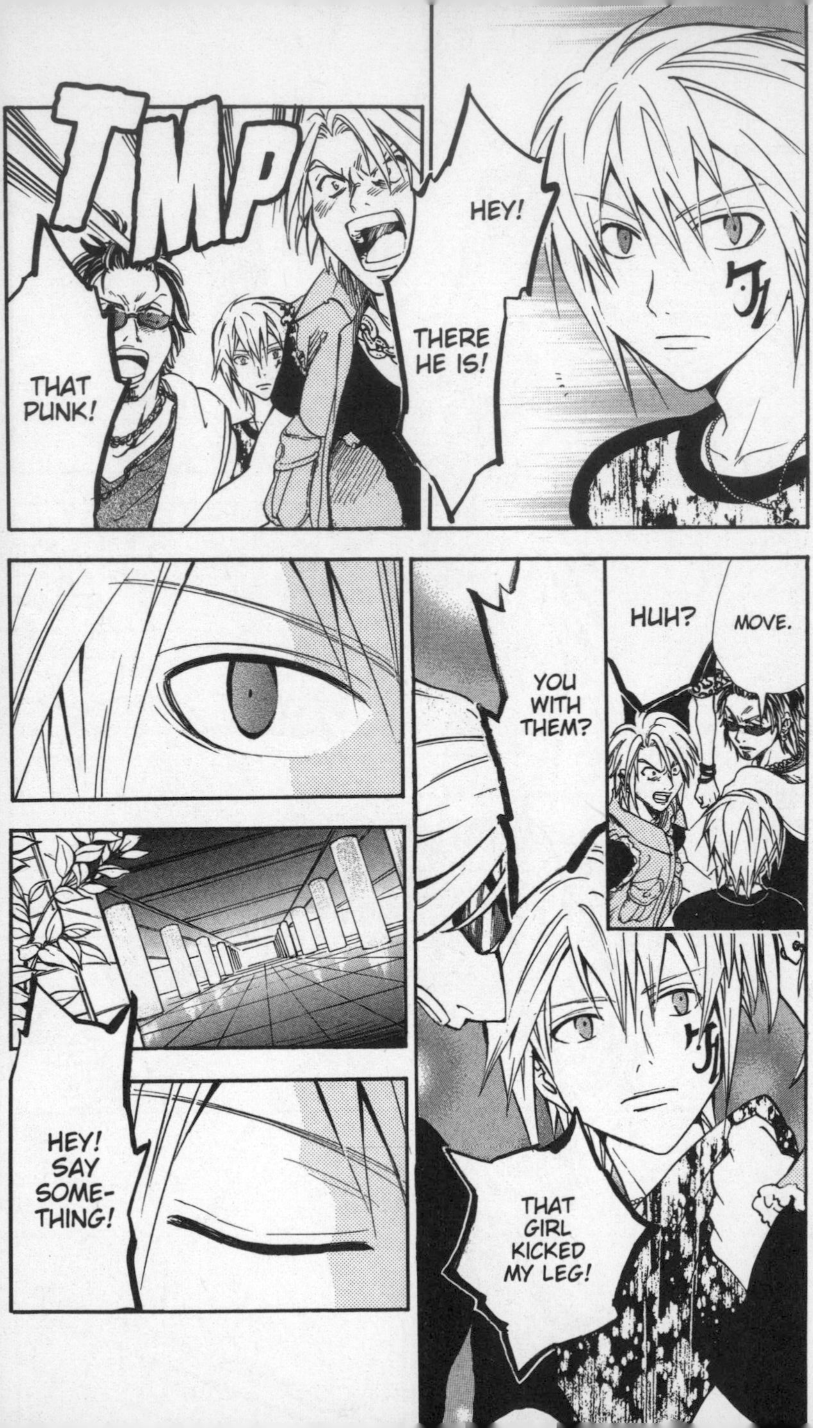
HEY!
THERE HE IS!
TIMP
THAT PUNK!
MOVE.
HUH?
YOU WITH THEM?
THAT GIRL KICKED MY LEG!
HEY! SAY SOMETHING!

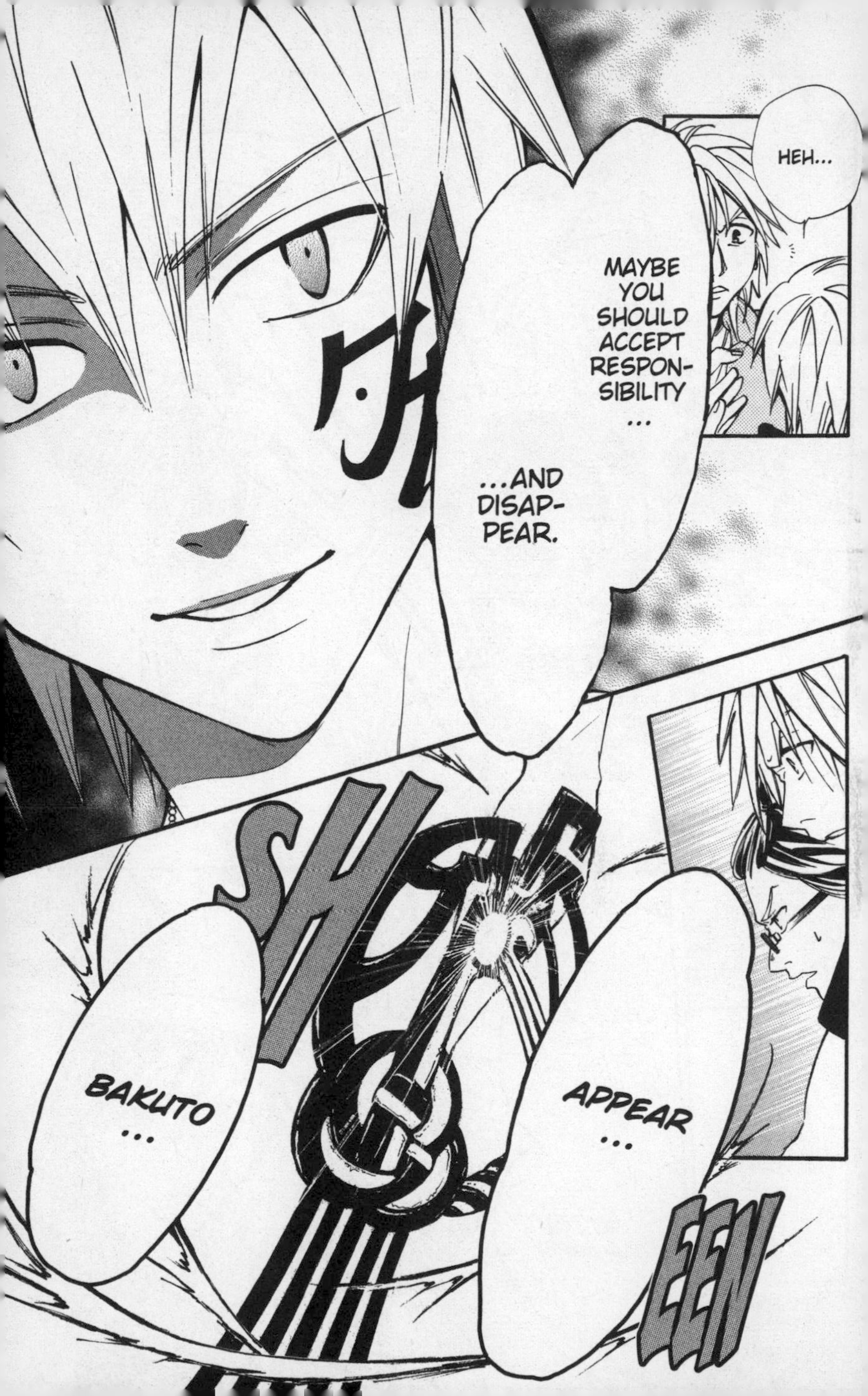

HEH...
MAYBE YOU SHOULD ACCEPT RESPON-SIBILITY ...
...AND DISAP-PEAR.
APPEAR ...
BAKUTO ...
SH
EEN

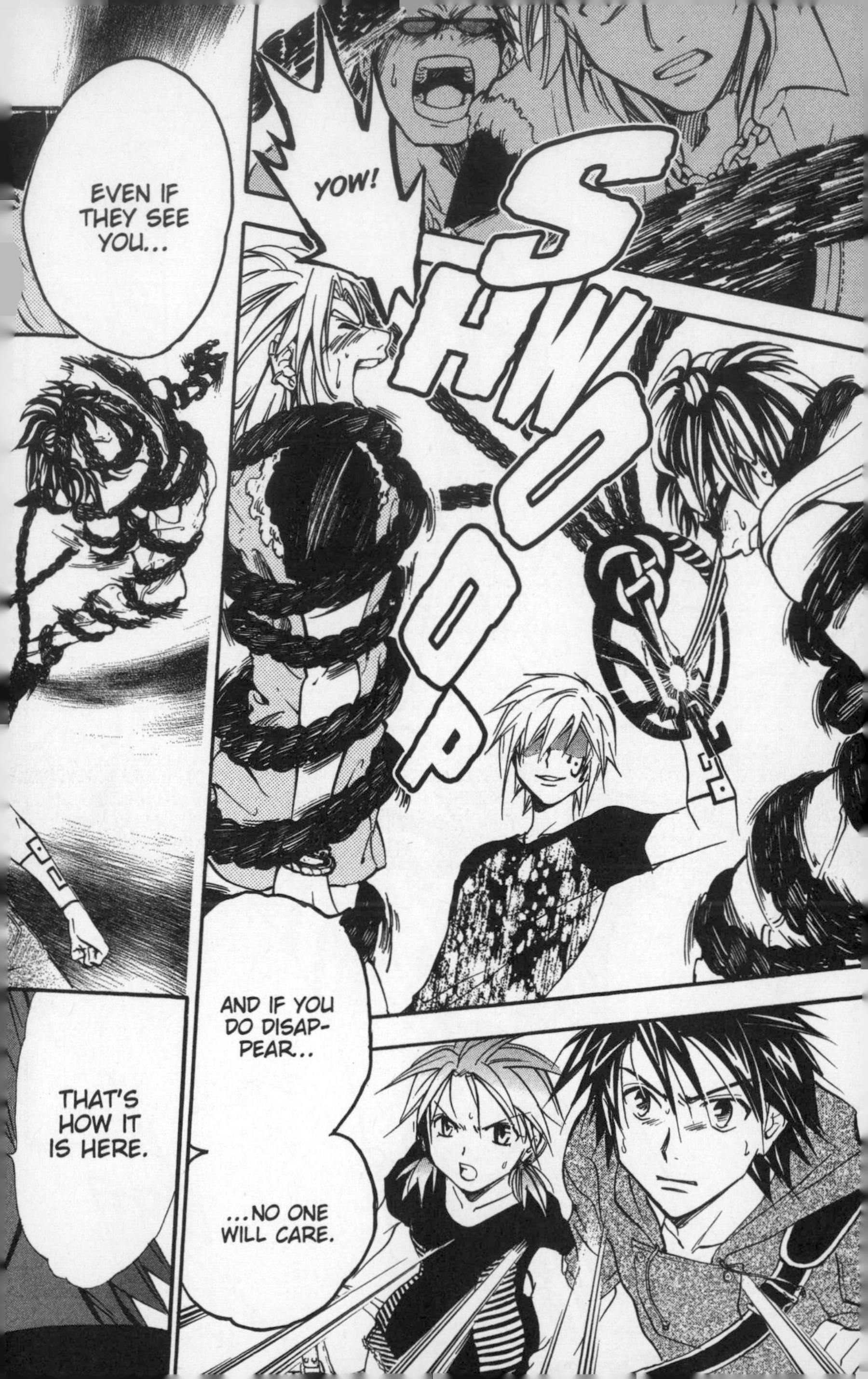
YOW!
SHWOOP
EVEN IF THEY SEE YOU...
AND IF YOU DO DISAPPEAR...
...NO ONE WILL CARE.
THAT'S HOW IT IS HERE.

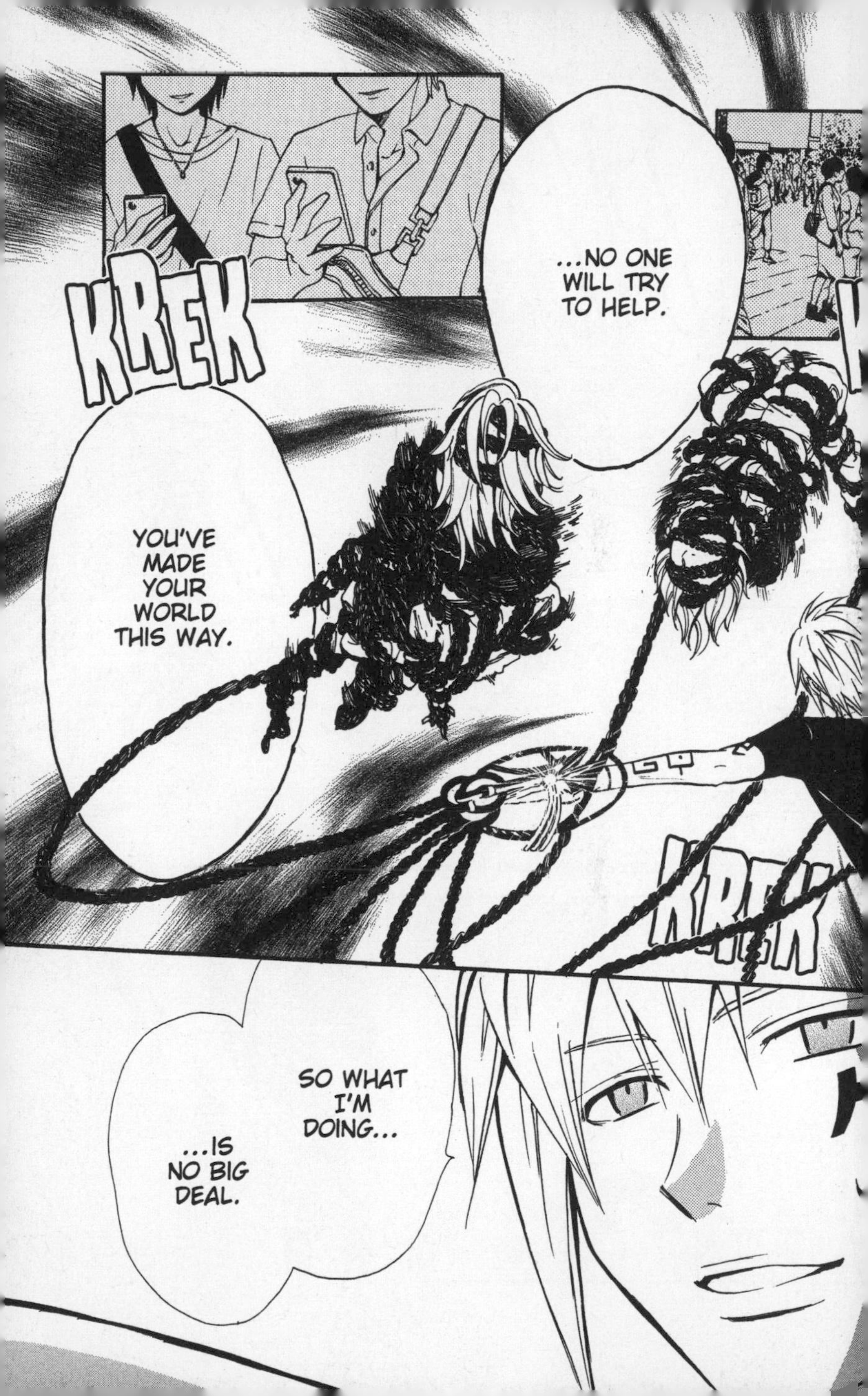
...NO ONE WILL TRY TO HELP.
KREK
YOU'VE MADE YOUR WORLD THIS WAY.
KREK
SO WHAT I'M DOING...
...IS NO BIG DEAL.

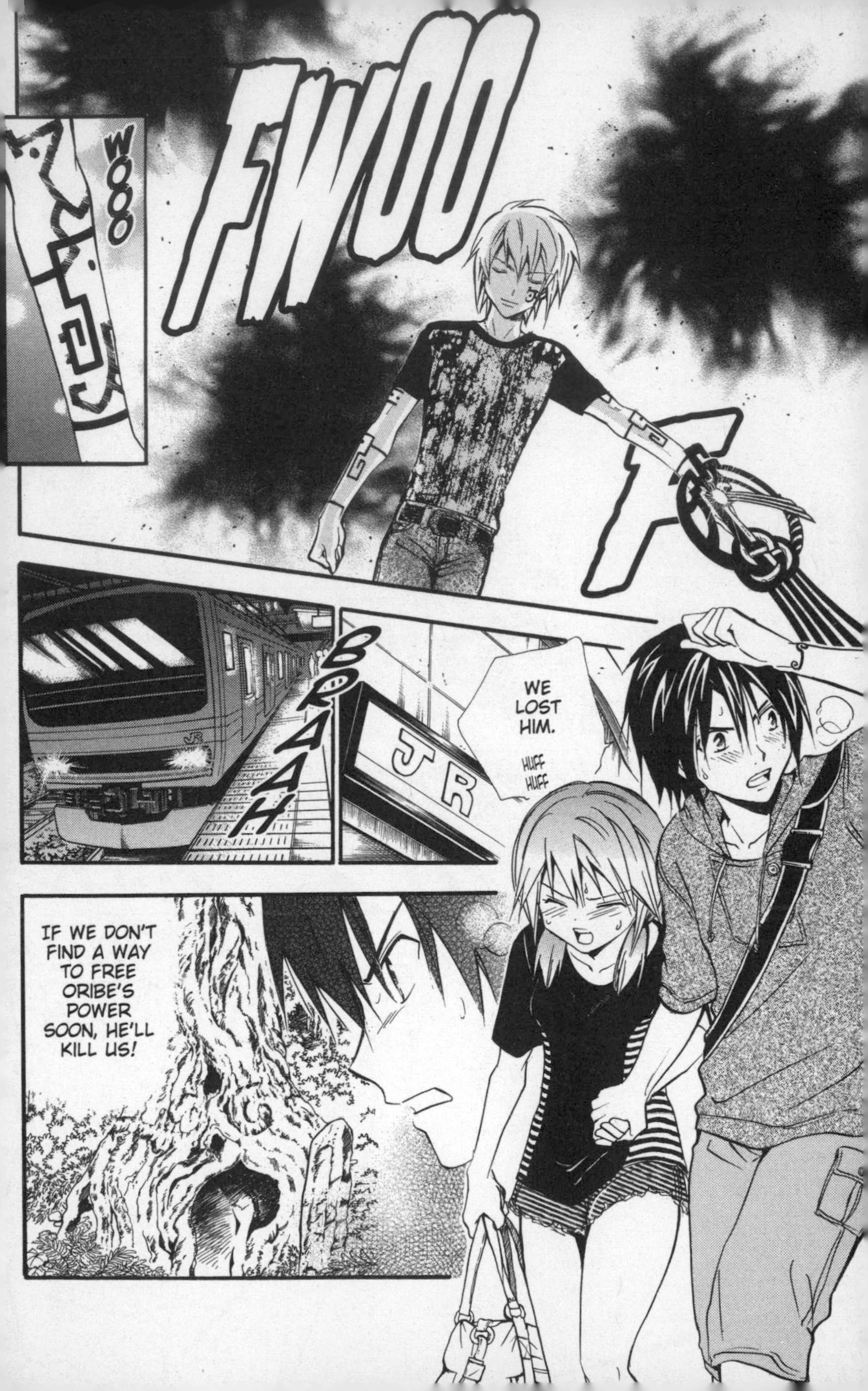
FWOO
WOOO
WE LOST HIM.
HUFF HUFF
BRAAAH
JR
IF WE DON'T FIND A WAY TO FREE ORIBE'S POWER SOON, HE'LL KILL US!

CHAPTER 191
PORTAL

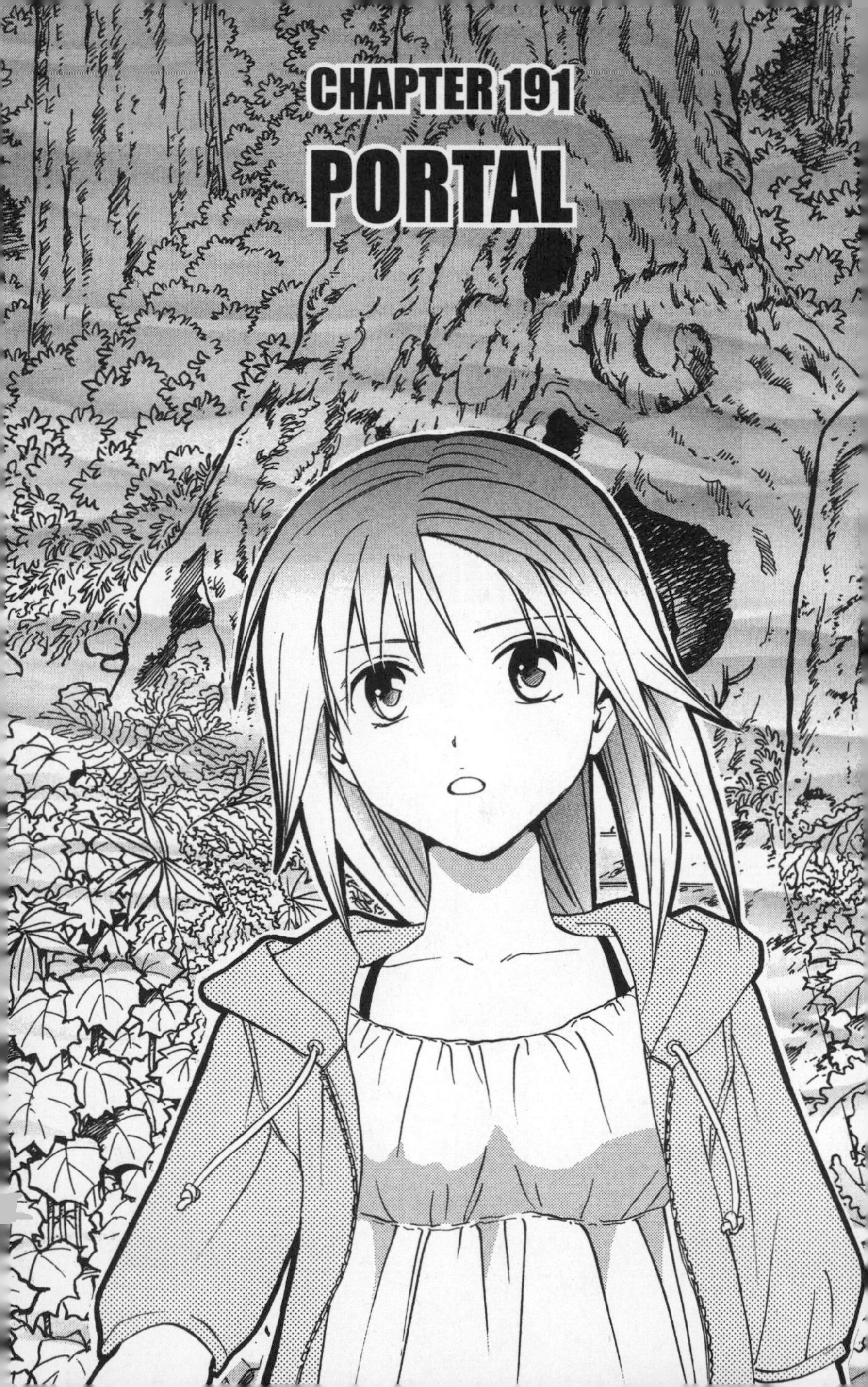

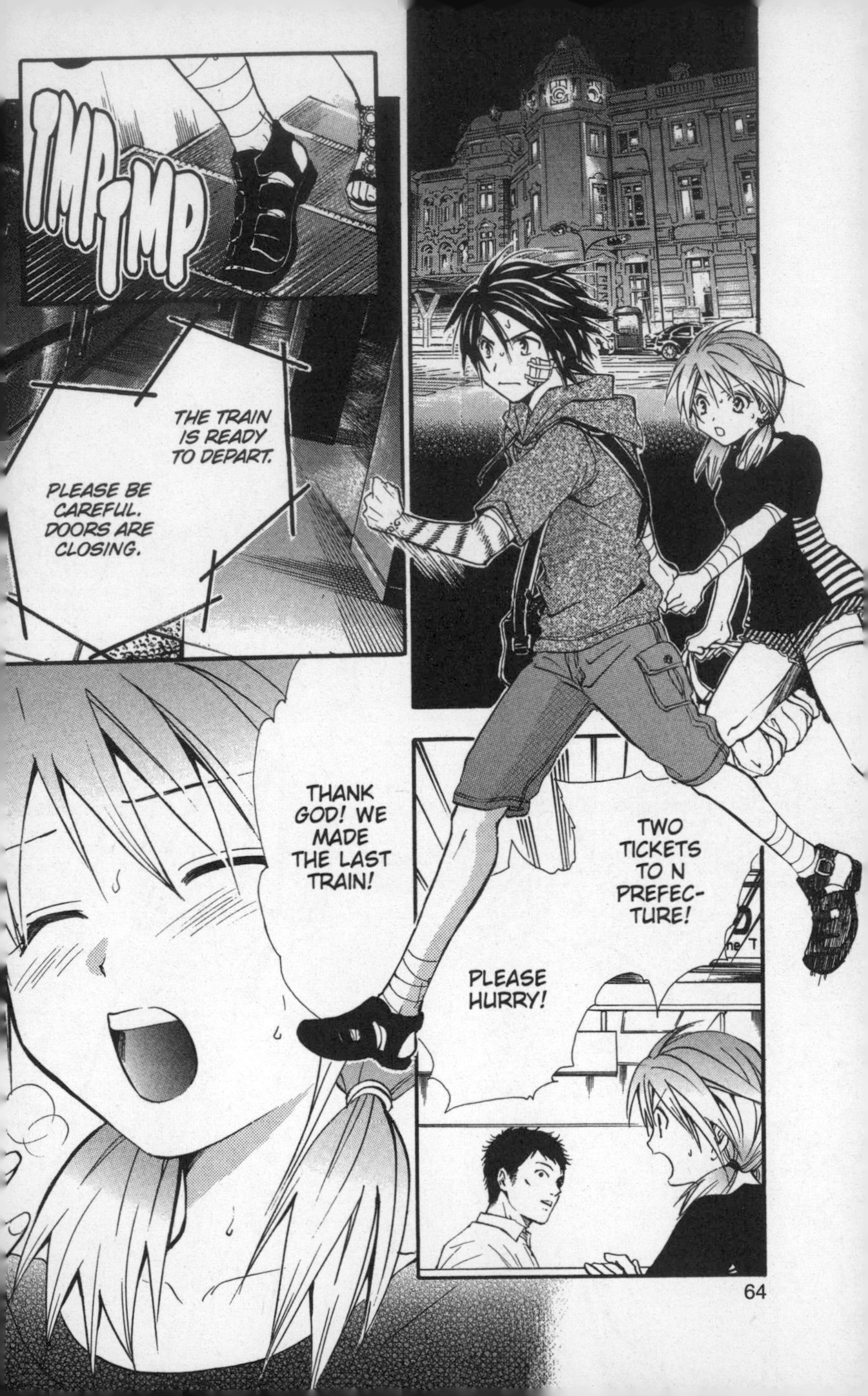
TMP TMP
THE TRAIN IS READY TO DEPART.
PLEASE BE CAREFUL. DOORS ARE CLOSING.
TWO TICKETS TO N PREFECTURE!
PLEASE HURRY!
THANK GOD! WE MADE THE LAST TRAIN!

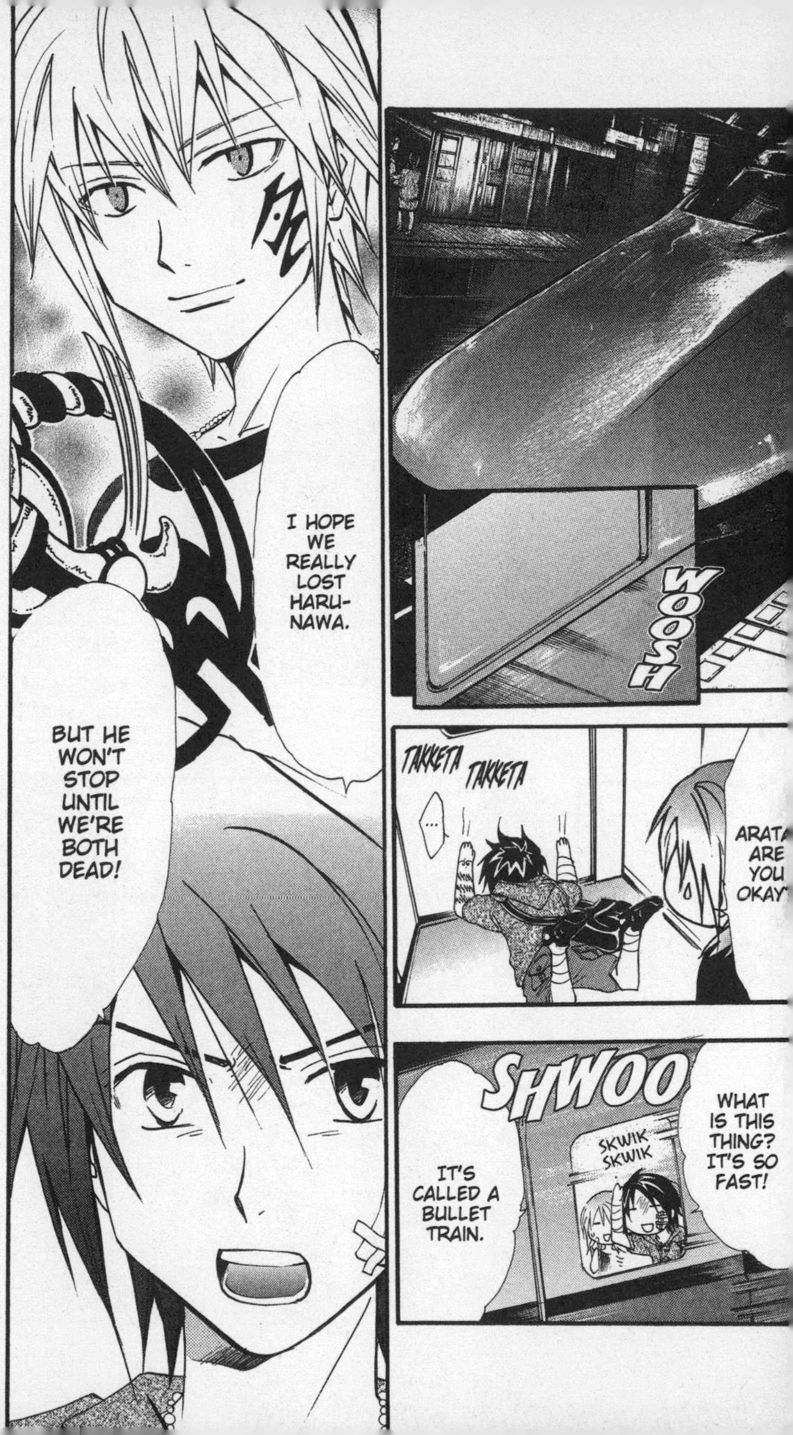
WOOSH
TAKKETA TAKKETA
...
ARATA ARE YOU OKAY
SHWOO
WHAT IS THIS THING? IT'S SO FAST!
SKWIK SKWIK
IT'S CALLED A BULLET TRAIN.
I HOPE WE REALLY LOST HARUNAWA.
BUT HE WON'T STOP UNTIL WE'RE BOTH DEAD!

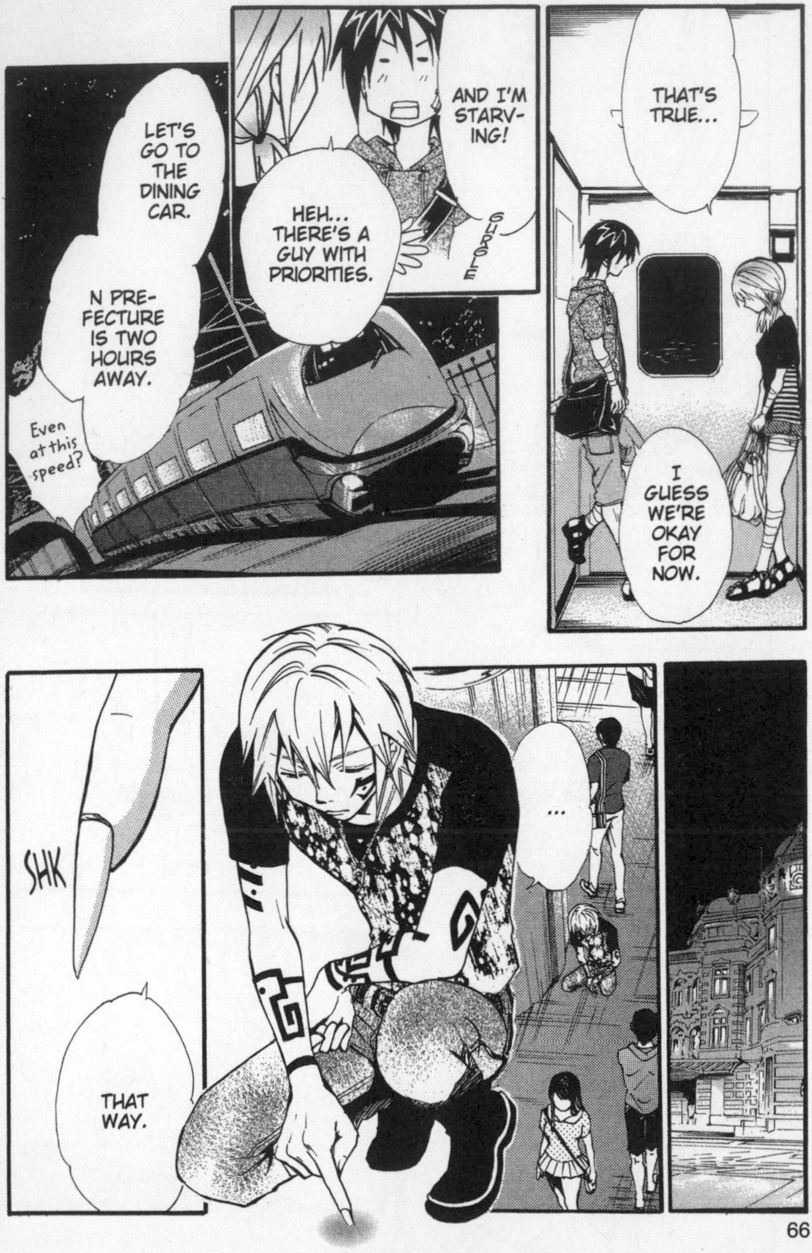
THAT'S TRUE...
I GUESS WE'RE OKAY FOR NOW.
AND I'M STARVING!
GURGLE
HEH... THERE'S A GUY WITH PRIORITIES.
LET'S GO TO THE DINING CAR.
N PREFECTURE IS TWO HOURS AWAY.
Even at this speed?
...
SHK
THAT WAY.

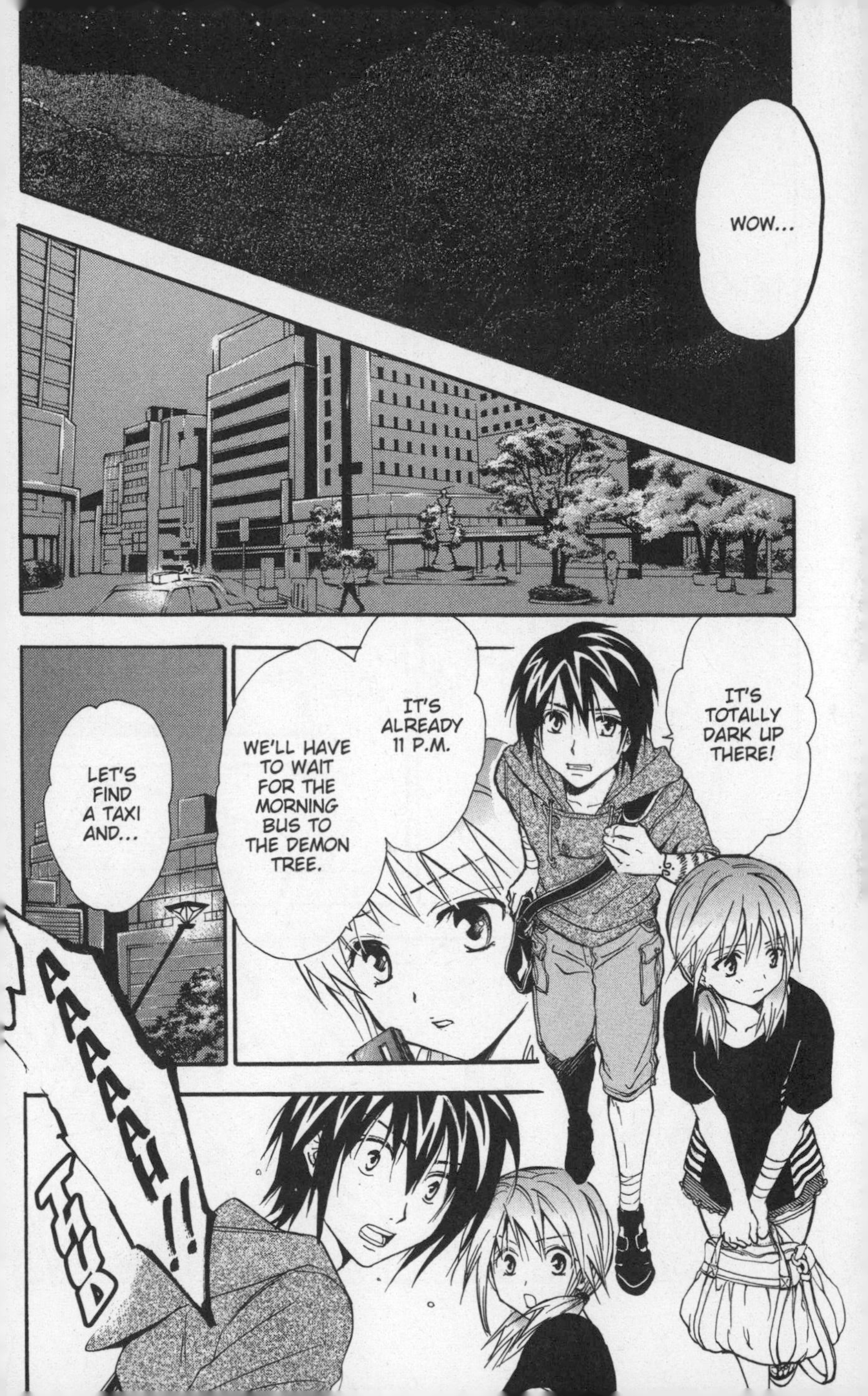
WOW...
IT'S TOTALLY DARK UP THERE!
IT'S ALREADY 11 P.M.
WE'LL HAVE TO WAIT FOR THE MORNING BUS TO THE DEMON TREE.
LET'S FIND A TAXI AND...
AAAAAH!!
THUD

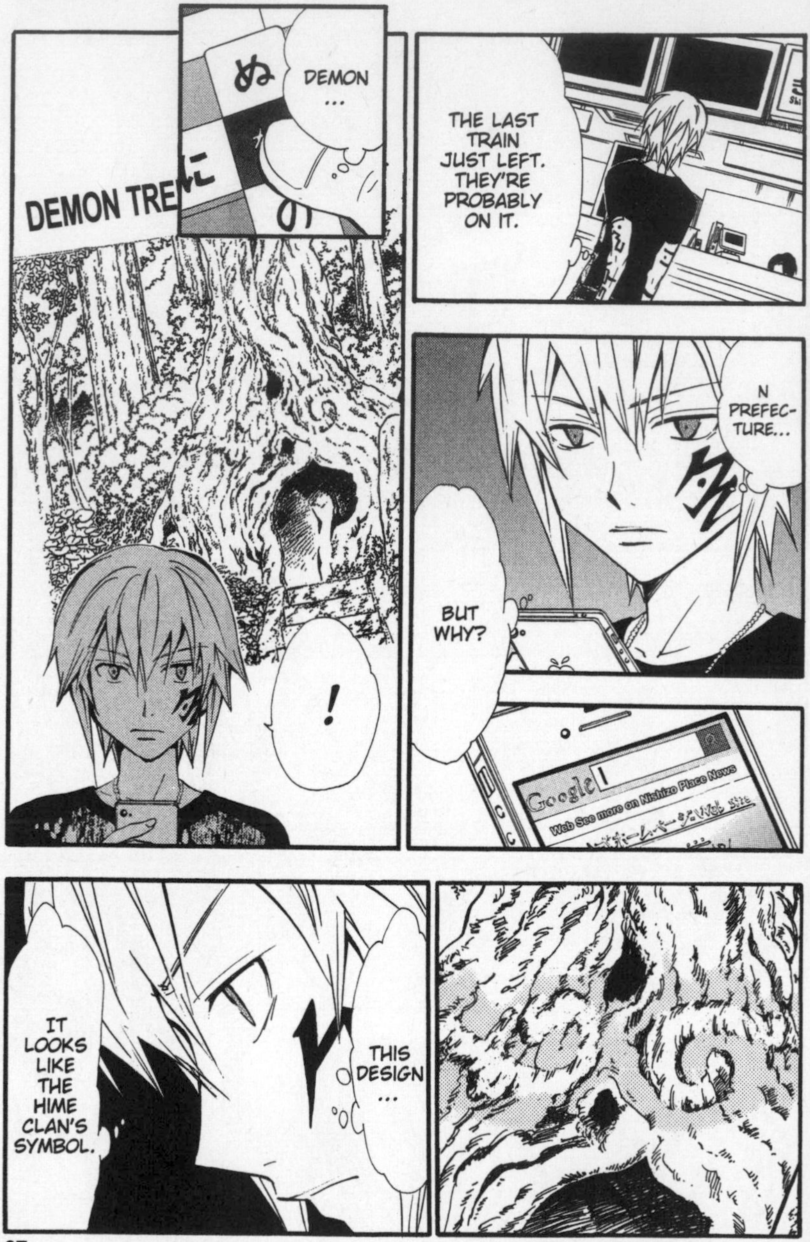
THE LAST TRAIN JUST LEFT. THEY'RE PROBABLY ON IT.
N PREFECTURE...
BUT WHY?
Google
Web See more on Nishizo Place News
DEMON...
DEMON TRE
!
THIS DESIGN...
IT LOOKS LIKE THE HIME CLAN'S SYMBOL.

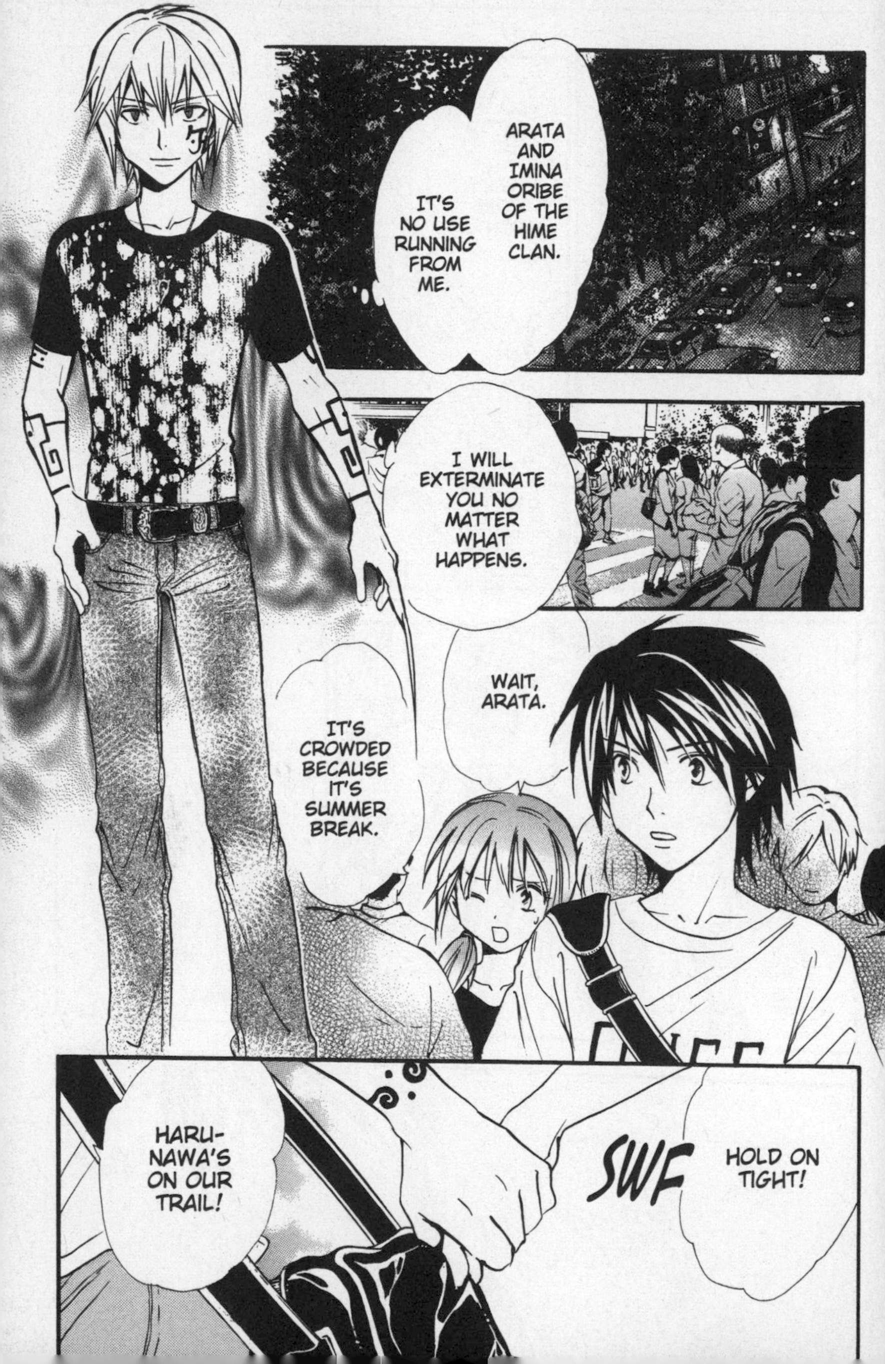
ARATA AND IMINA ORIBE OF THE HIME CLAN.
IT'S NO USE RUNNING FROM ME.
I WILL EXTERMINATE YOU NO MATTER WHAT HAPPENS.
WAIT, ARATA.
IT'S CROWDED BECAUSE IT'S SUMMER BREAK.
HOLD ON TIGHT!
SWF
HARU-NAWA'S ON OUR TRAIL!

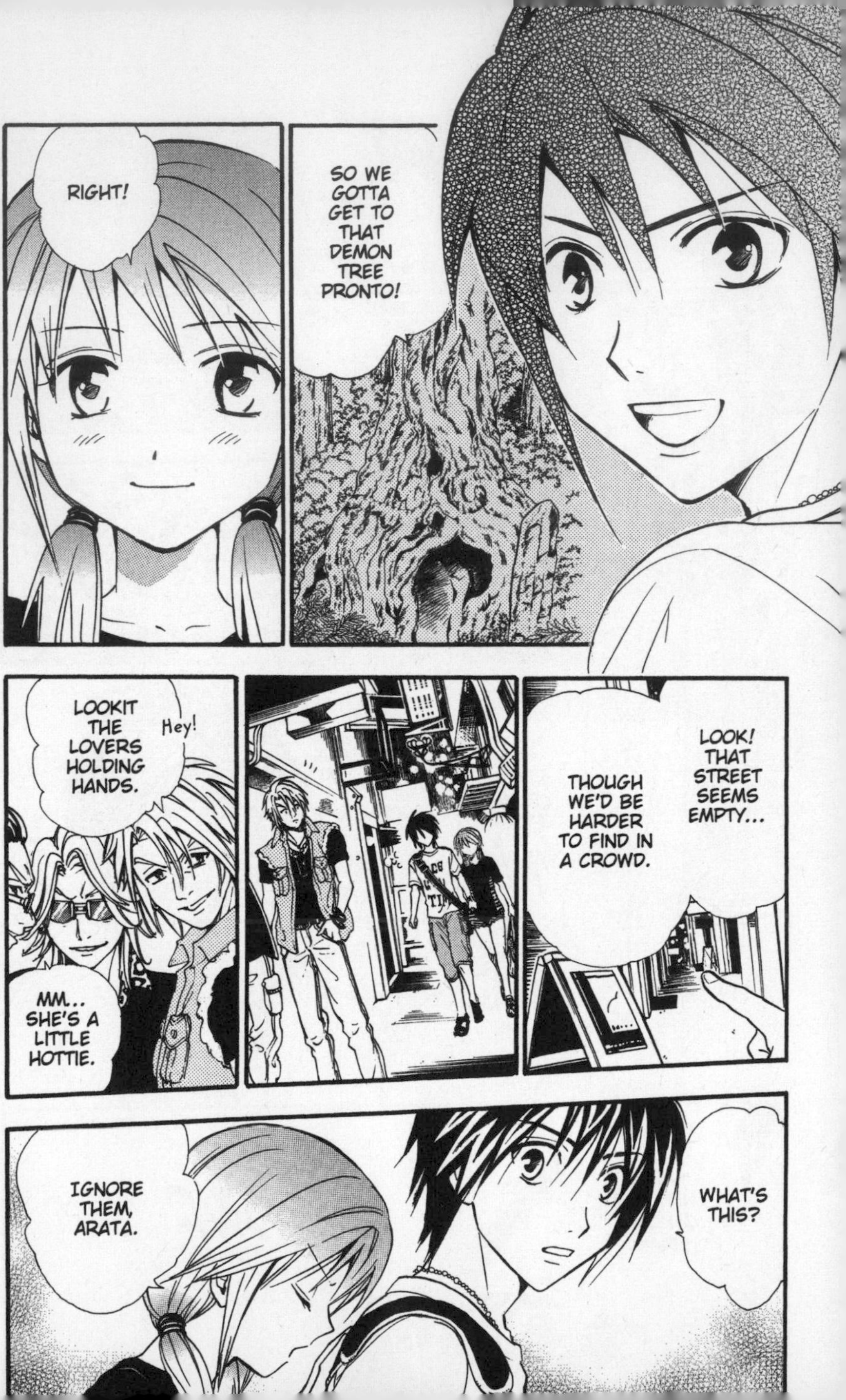
SO WE GOTTA GET TO THAT DEMON TREE PRONTO!
RIGHT!
LOOK! THAT STREET SEEMS EMPTY...
THOUGH WE'D BE HARDER TO FIND IN A CROWD.
LOOKIT THE LOVERS HOLDING HANDS.
Hey!
MM... SHE'S A LITTLE HOTTIE.
WHAT'S THIS?
IGNORE THEM, ARATA.

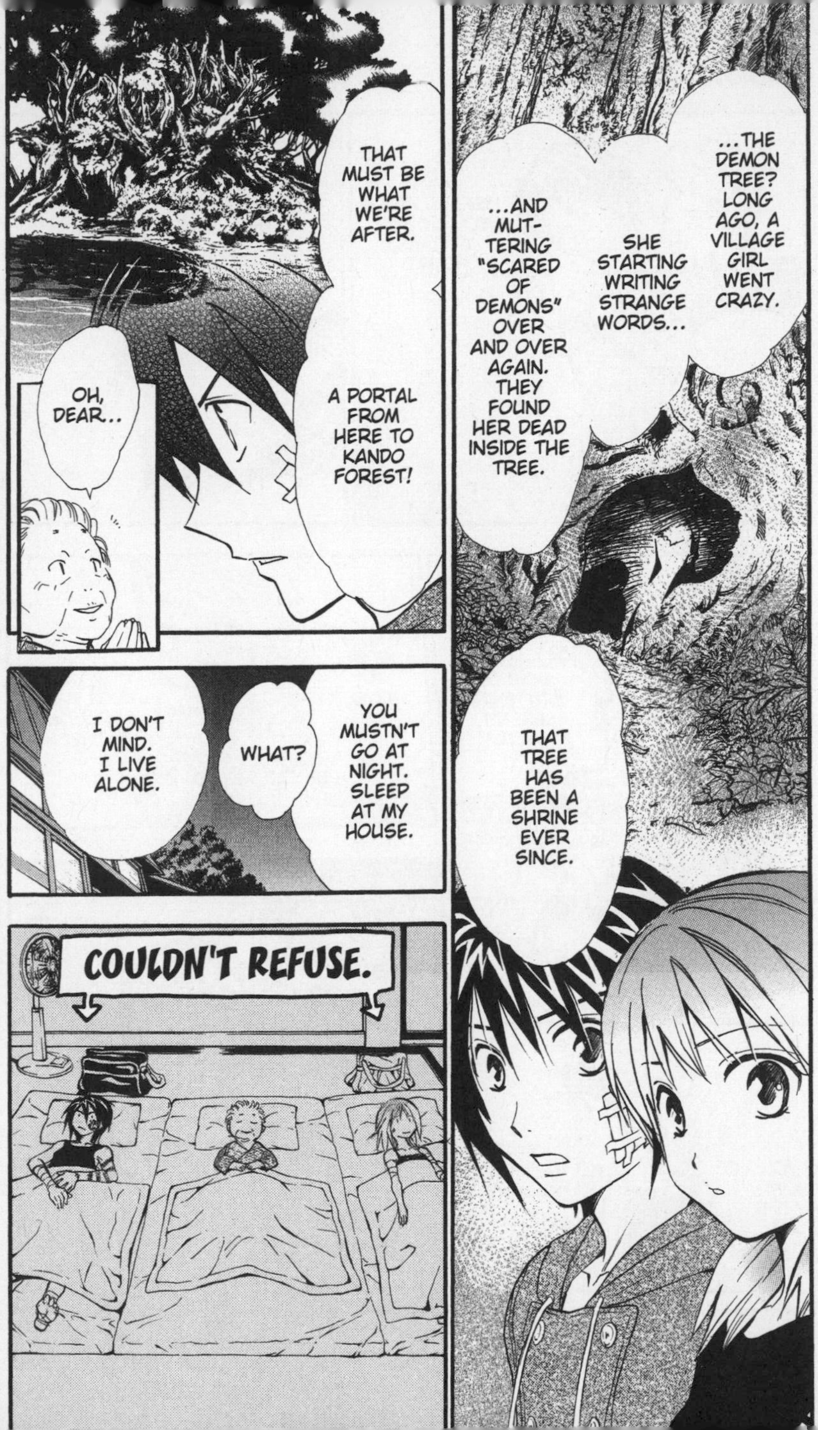
...THE DEMON TREE? LONG AGO, A VILLAGE GIRL WENT CRAZY.
SHE STARTING WRITING STRANGE WORDS...
...AND MUT-TERING "SCARED OF DEMONS" OVER AND OVER AGAIN. THEY FOUND HER DEAD INSIDE THE TREE.
THAT TREE HAS BEEN A SHRINE EVER SINCE.
THAT MUST BE WHAT WE'RE AFTER.
A PORTAL FROM HERE TO KANDO FOREST!
OH, DEAR...
YOU MUSTN'T GO AT NIGHT. SLEEP AT MY HOUSE.
WHAT?
I DON'T MIND. I LIVE ALONE.
COULDN'T REFUSE.

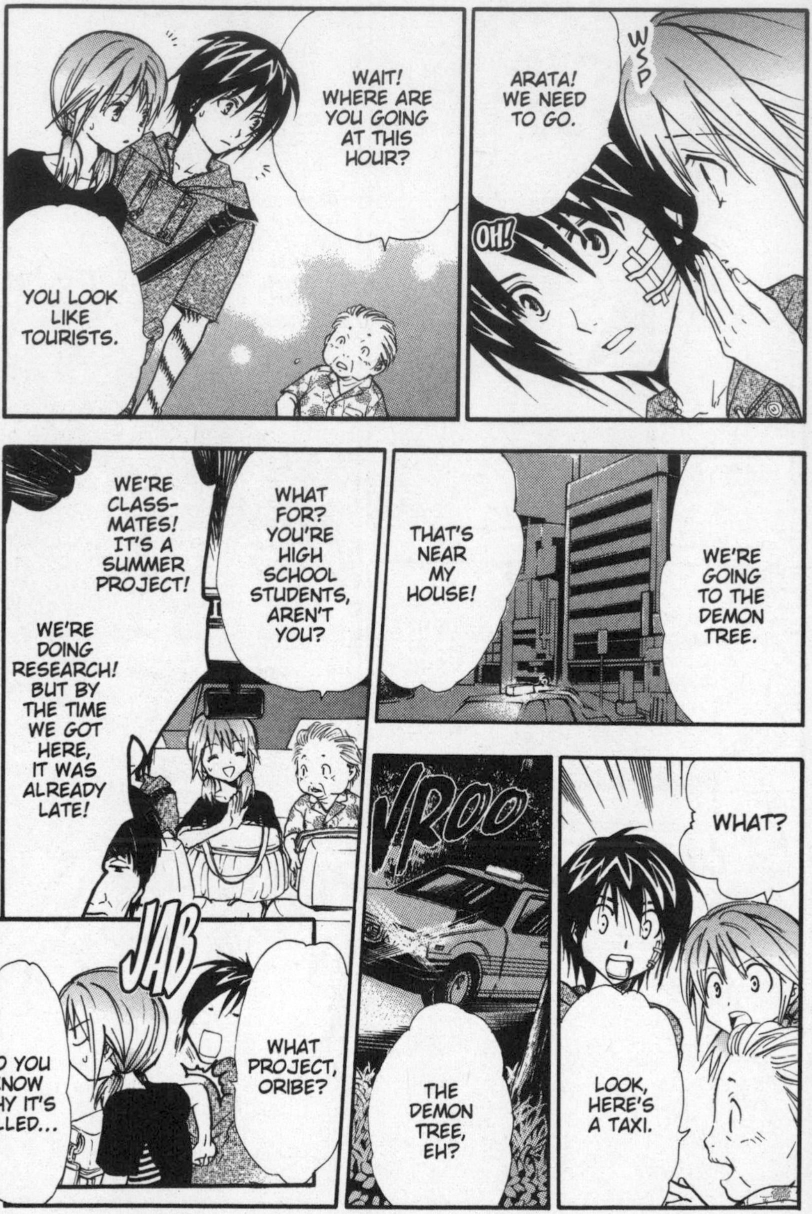
WSP
ARATA! WE NEED TO GO.
OH!
WAIT! WHERE ARE YOU GOING AT THIS HOUR?
YOU LOOK LIKE TOURISTS.
WE'RE GOING TO THE DEMON TREE.
THAT'S NEAR MY HOUSE!
WHAT?
LOOK, HERE'S A TAXI.
VROO
THE DEMON TREE, EH?
WHAT FOR? YOU'RE HIGH SCHOOL STUDENTS, AREN'T YOU?
WE'RE CLASSMATES! IT'S A SUMMER PROJECT!
WE'RE DOING RESEARCH! BUT BY THE TIME WE GOT HERE, IT WAS ALREADY LATE!
JAB
WHAT PROJECT, ORIBE?
DO YOU KNOW WHY IT'S CALLED...

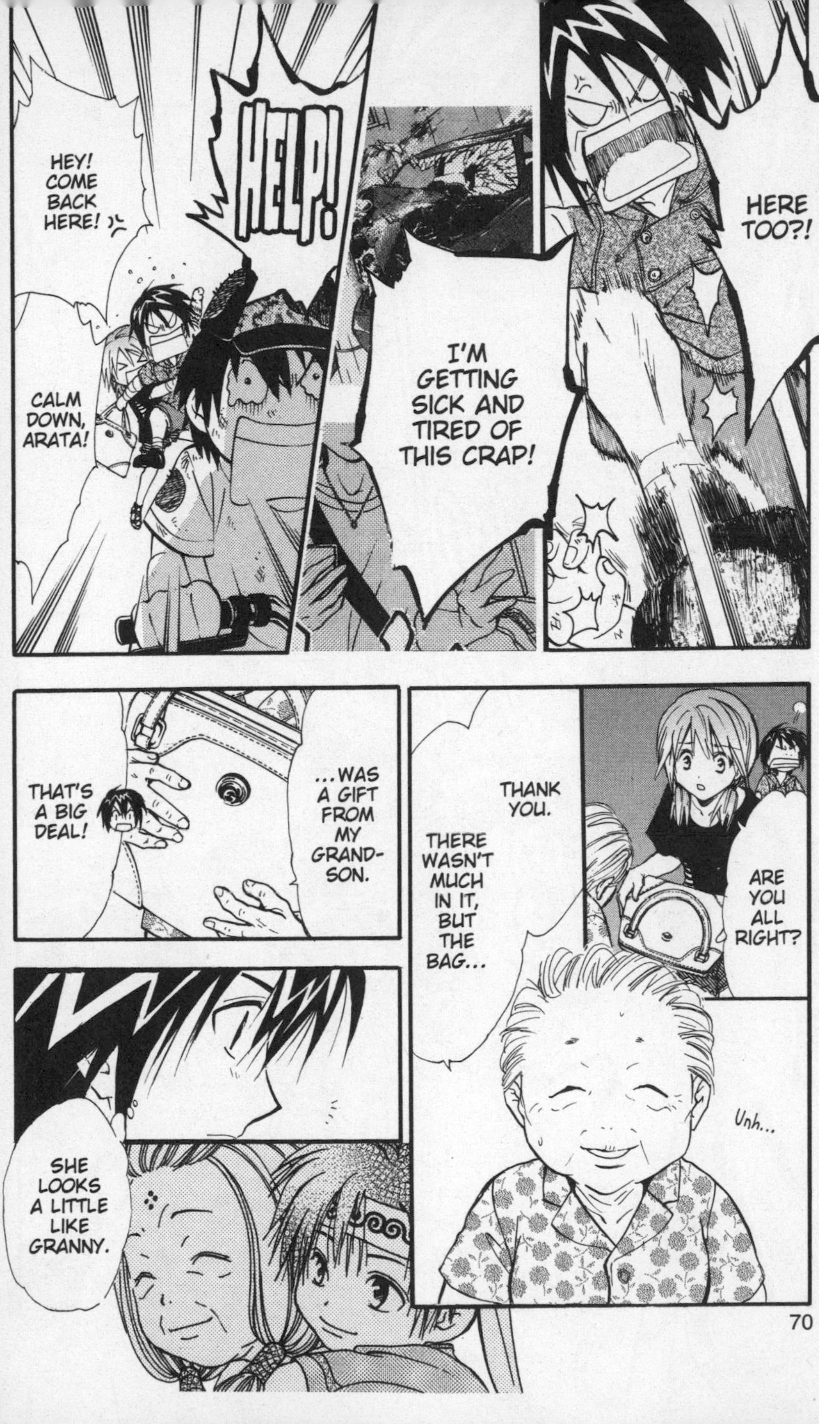
HERE TOO?!
I'M GETTING SICK AND TIRED OF THIS CRAP!
HELP!
HEY! COME BACK HERE!
CALM DOWN, ARATA!
ARE YOU ALL RIGHT?
THANK YOU.
THERE WASN'T MUCH IN IT, BUT THE BAG...
...WAS A GIFT FROM MY GRANDSON.
THAT'S A BIG DEAL!
Unh...
SHE LOOKS A LITTLE LIKE GRANNY.

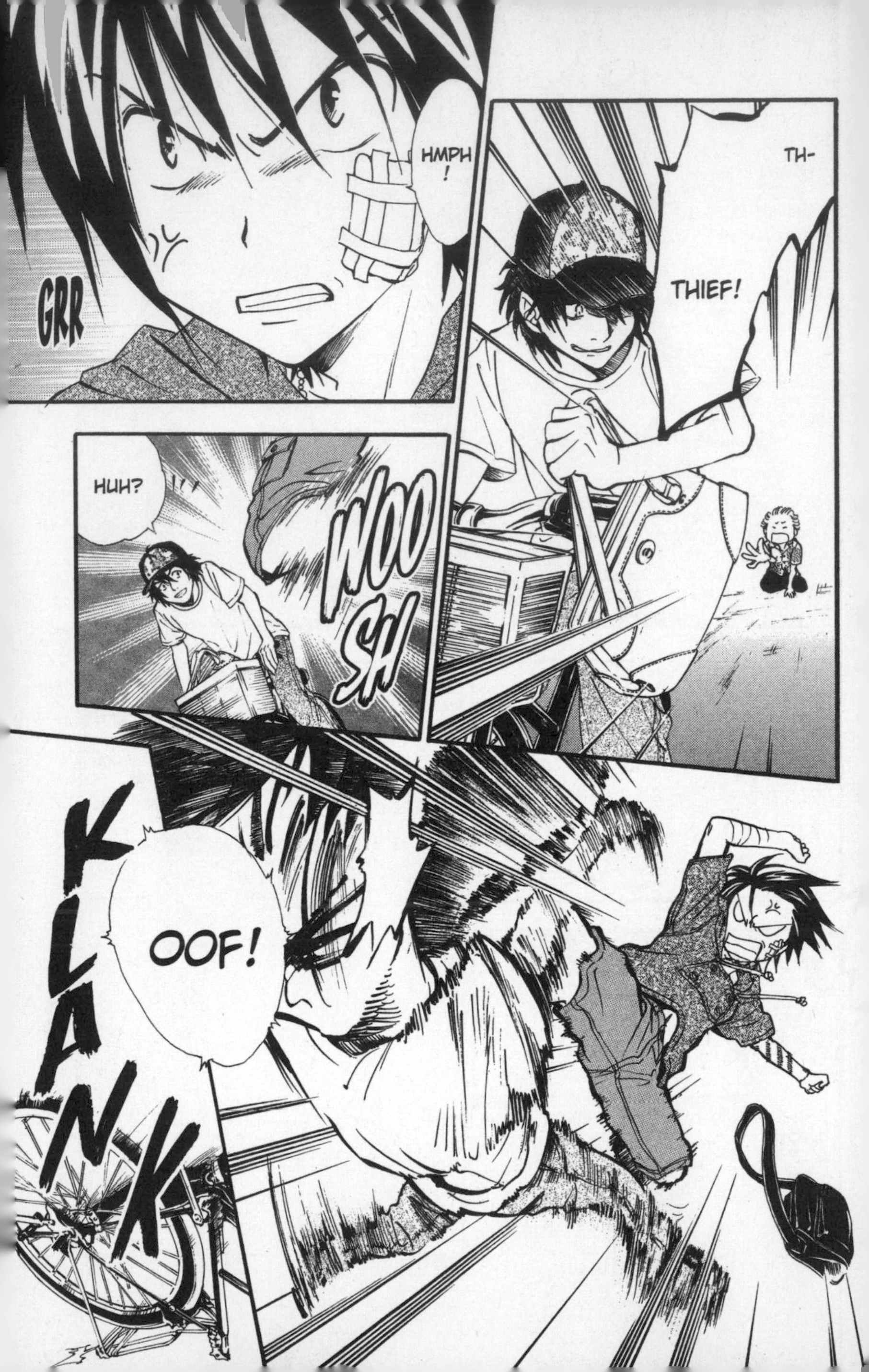
TH-
THIEF!
HMPH!
GRR
HUH?
WOOSH
OOF!
KLANK

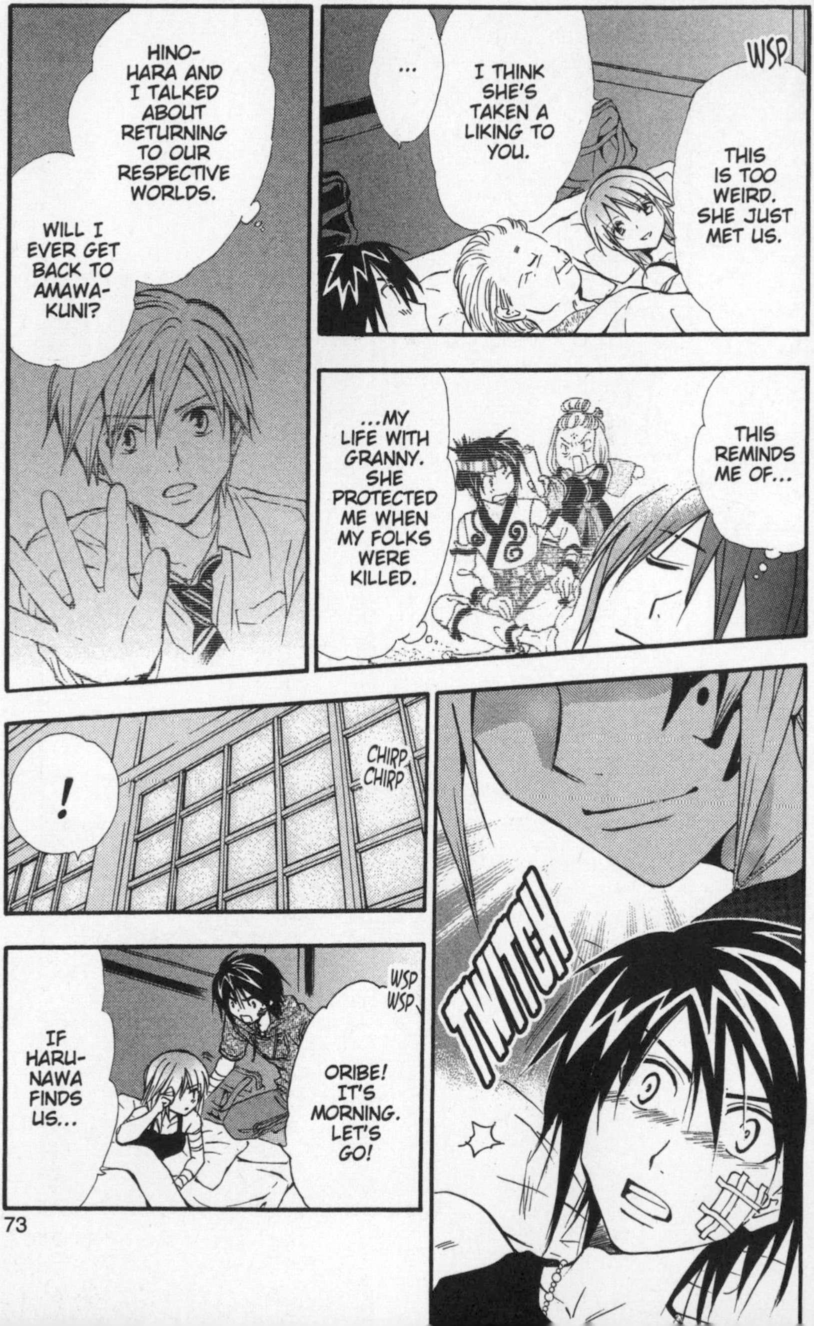
WSP
THIS IS TOO WEIRD. SHE JUST MET US.
I THINK SHE'S TAKEN A LIKING TO YOU.
...
THIS REMINDS ME OF...
...MY LIFE WITH GRANNY. SHE PROTECTED ME WHEN MY FOLKS WERE KILLED.
HINO-HARA AND I TALKED ABOUT RETURNING TO OUR RESPECTIVE WORLDS.
WILL I EVER GET BACK TO AMAWA-KUNI?
TWITCH
CHIRP CHIRP
!
WSP WSP
ORIBE! IT'S MORNING. LET'S GO!
IF HARU-NAWA FINDS US...

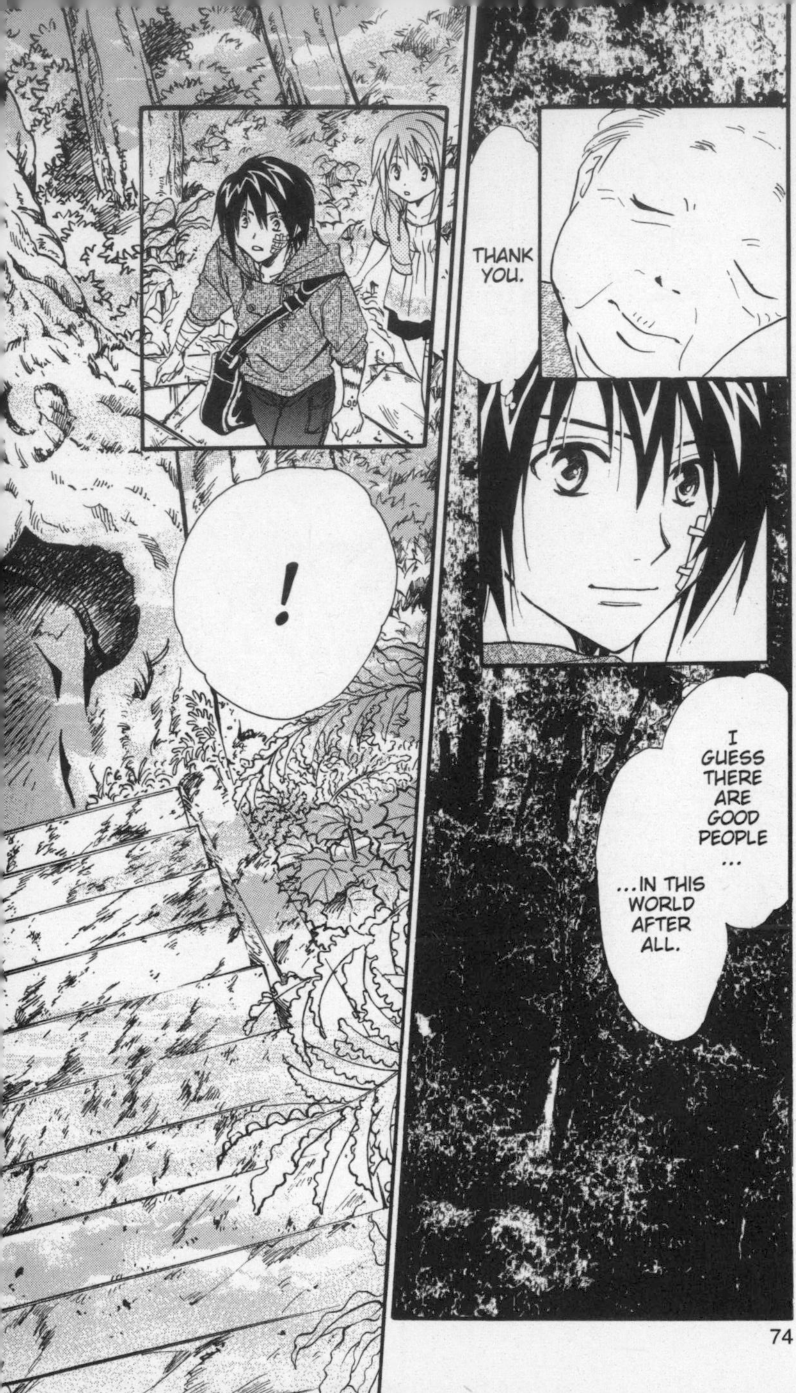
THANK YOU.
I GUESS THERE ARE GOOD PEOPLE ...
...IN THIS WORLD AFTER ALL.
!

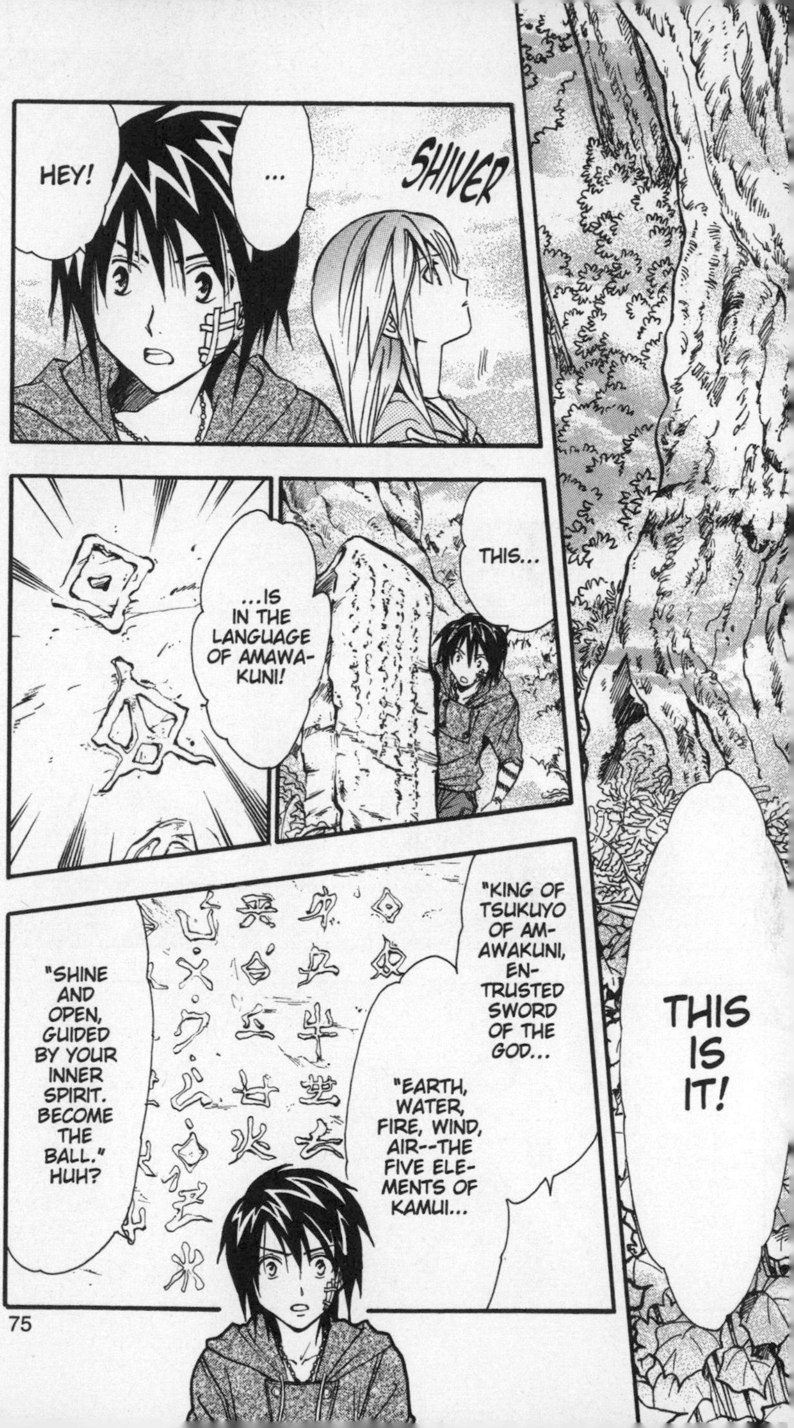
THIS IS IT!
SHIVER
...
HEY!
THIS...
...IS IN THE LANGUAGE OF AMAWA-KUNI!
"KING OF TSUKUYO OF AM-AWAKUNI, EN-TRUSTED SWORD OF THE GOD...
"EARTH, WATER, FIRE, WIND, AIR--THE FIVE ELE-MENTS OF KAMUI...
"SHINE AND OPEN, GUIDED BY YOUR INNER SPIRIT. BECOME THE BALL." HUH?

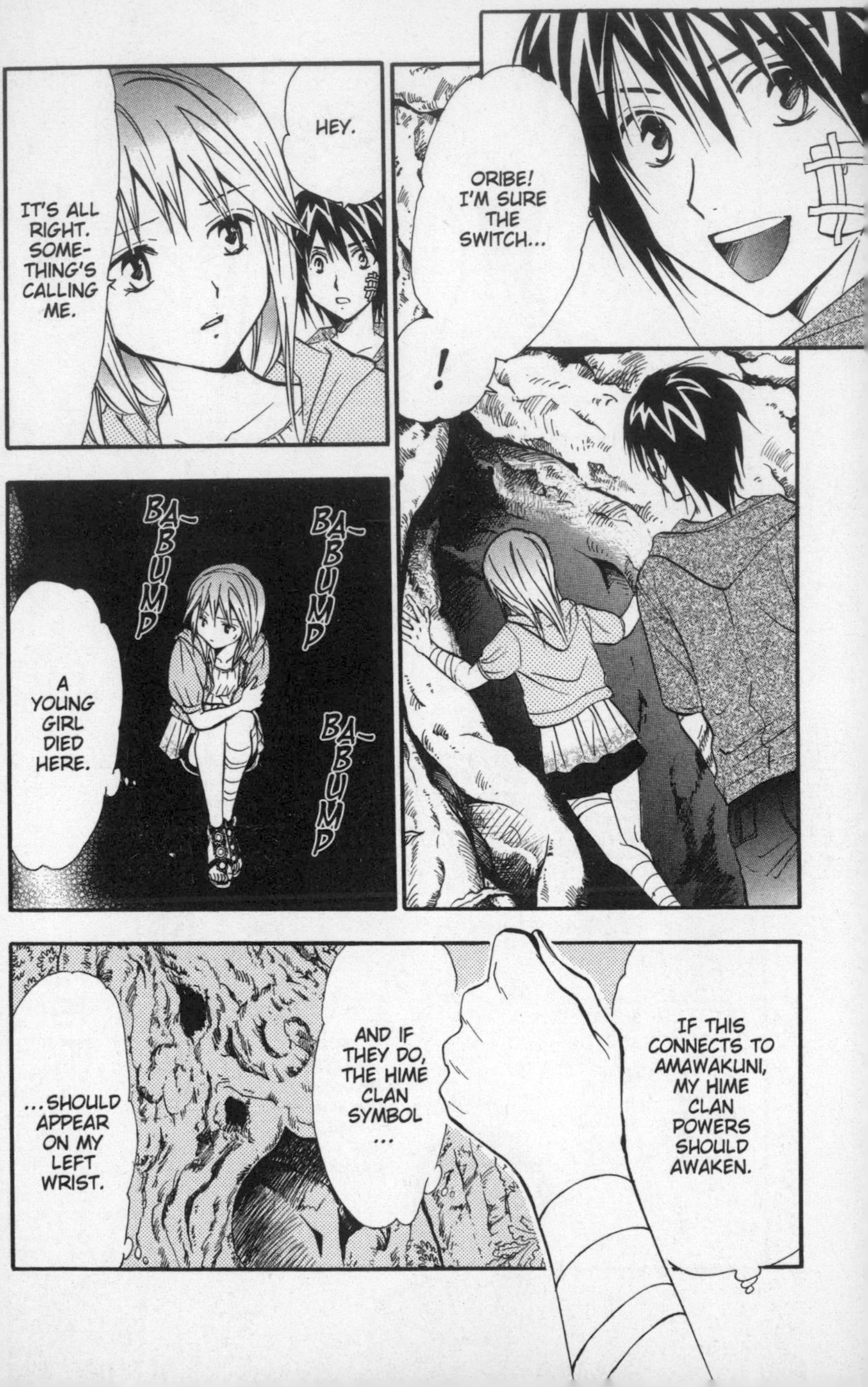
ORIBE! I'M SURE THE SWITCH...
!
HEY.
IT'S ALL RIGHT. SOMETHING'S CALLING ME.
BA-BUMP
BA-BUMP
BA-BUMP
A YOUNG GIRL DIED HERE.
IF THIS CONNECTS TO AMAWAKUNI, MY HIME CLAN POWERS SHOULD AWAKEN.
AND IF THEY DO, THE HIME CLAN SYMBOL...
...SHOULD APPEAR ON MY LEFT WRIST.

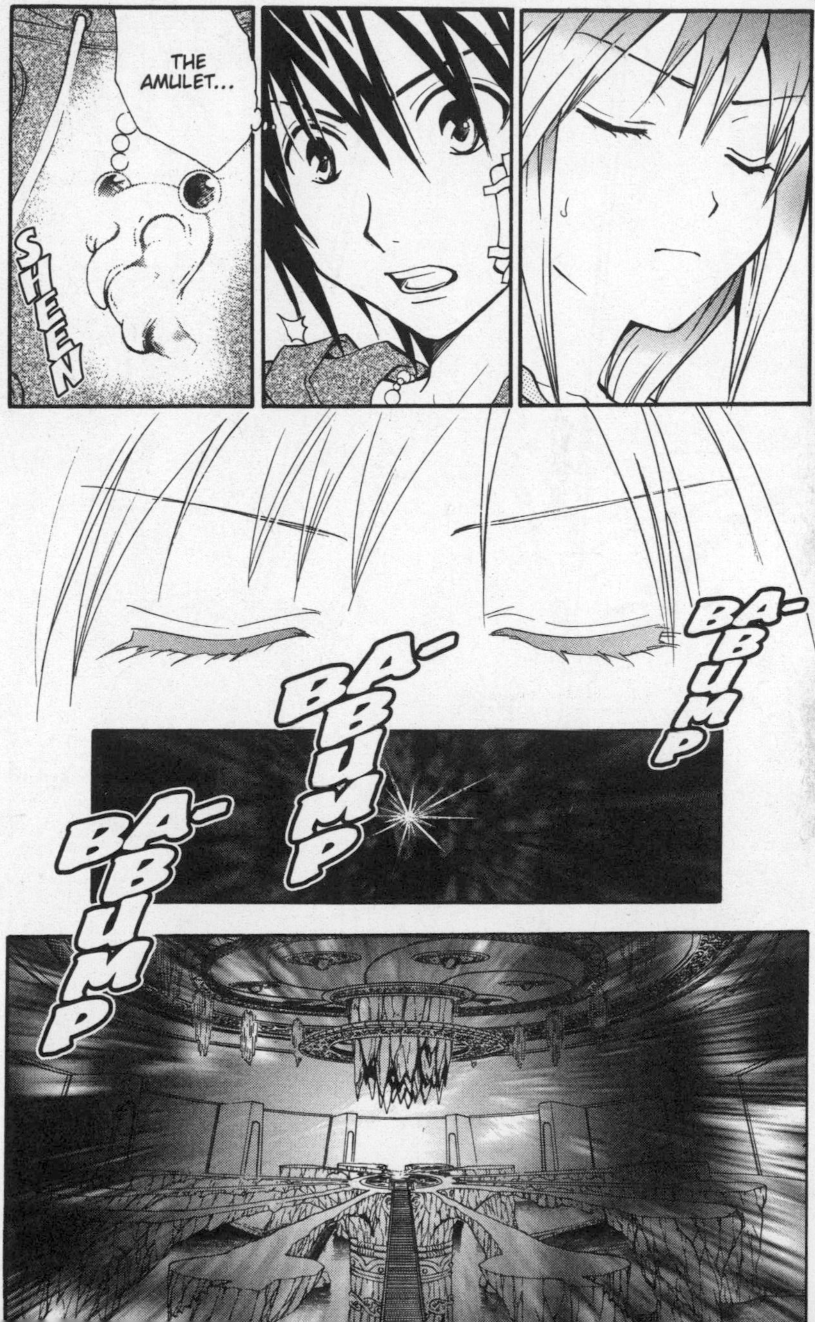
THE AMULET...
SHEEN
BA-BUMP
BA-BUMP
BA-BUMP

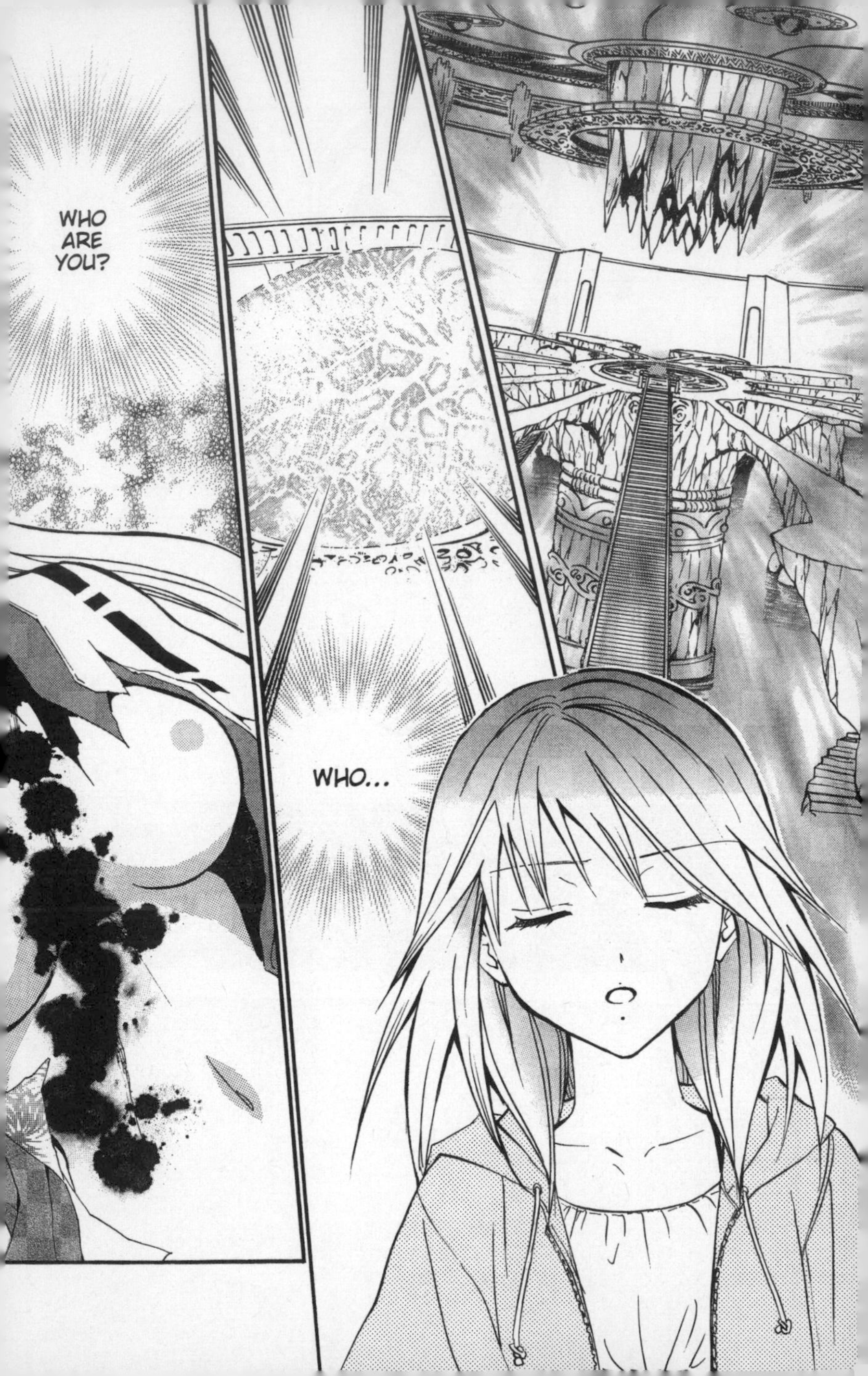
WHO...
WHO ARE YOU?

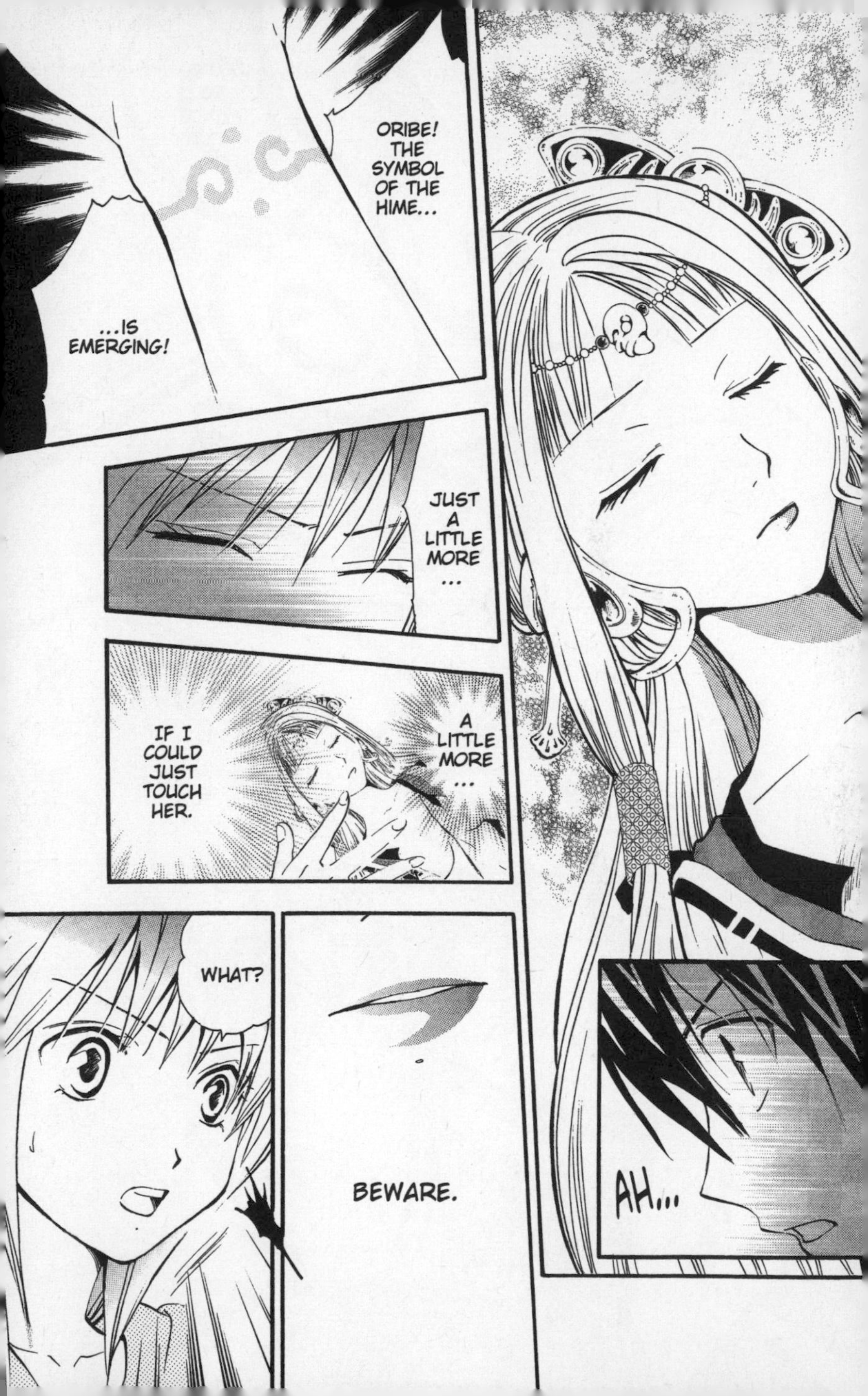
ORIBE! THE SYMBOL OF THE HIME...
...IS EMERGING!
JUST A LITTLE MORE...
A LITTLE MORE...
IF I COULD JUST TOUCH HER.
AH...
BEWARE.
WHAT?

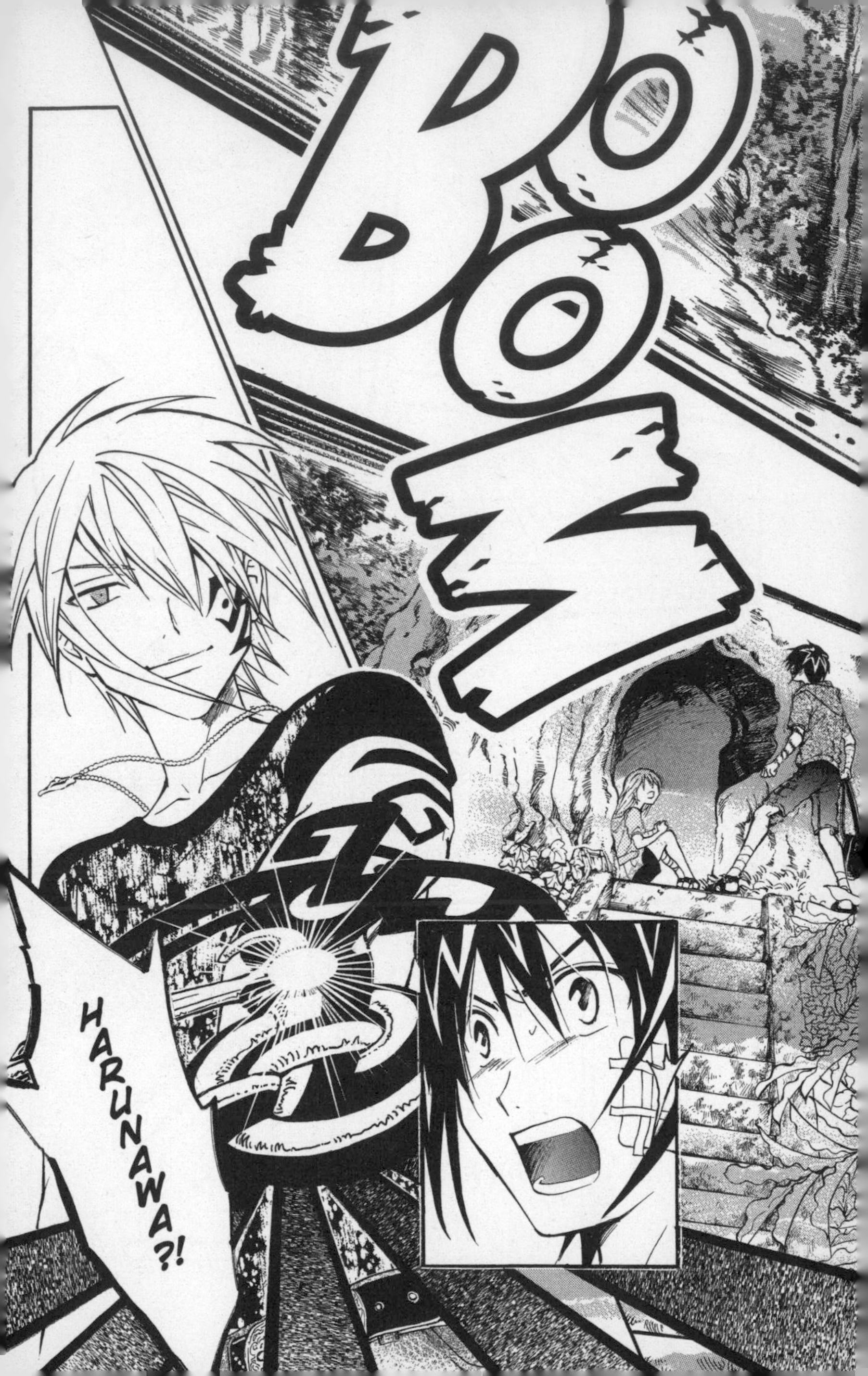
DOOM
HARUNAWA?!

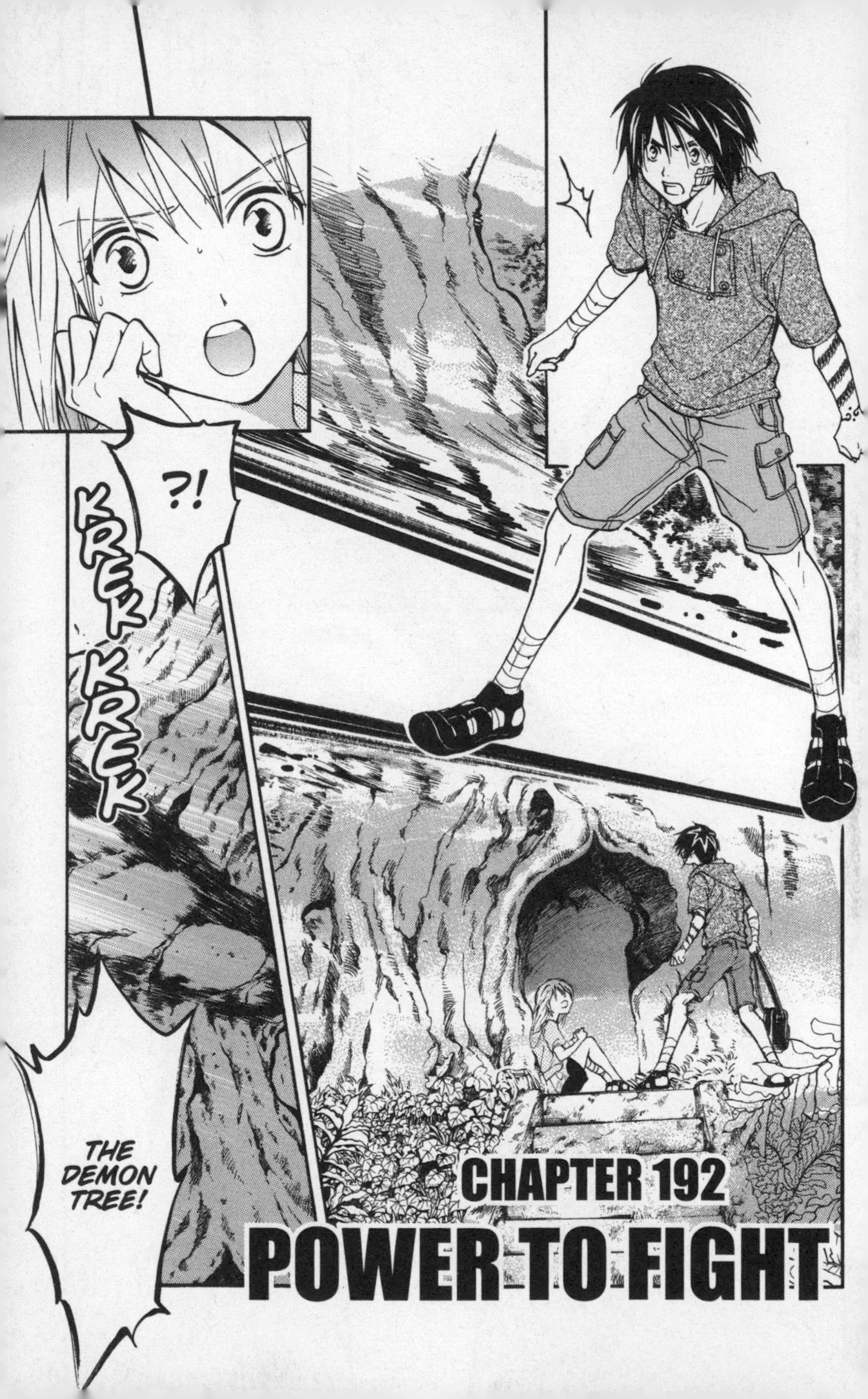
?!
KREK KREK
THE DEMON TREE!
CHAPTER 192
POWER TO FIGHT

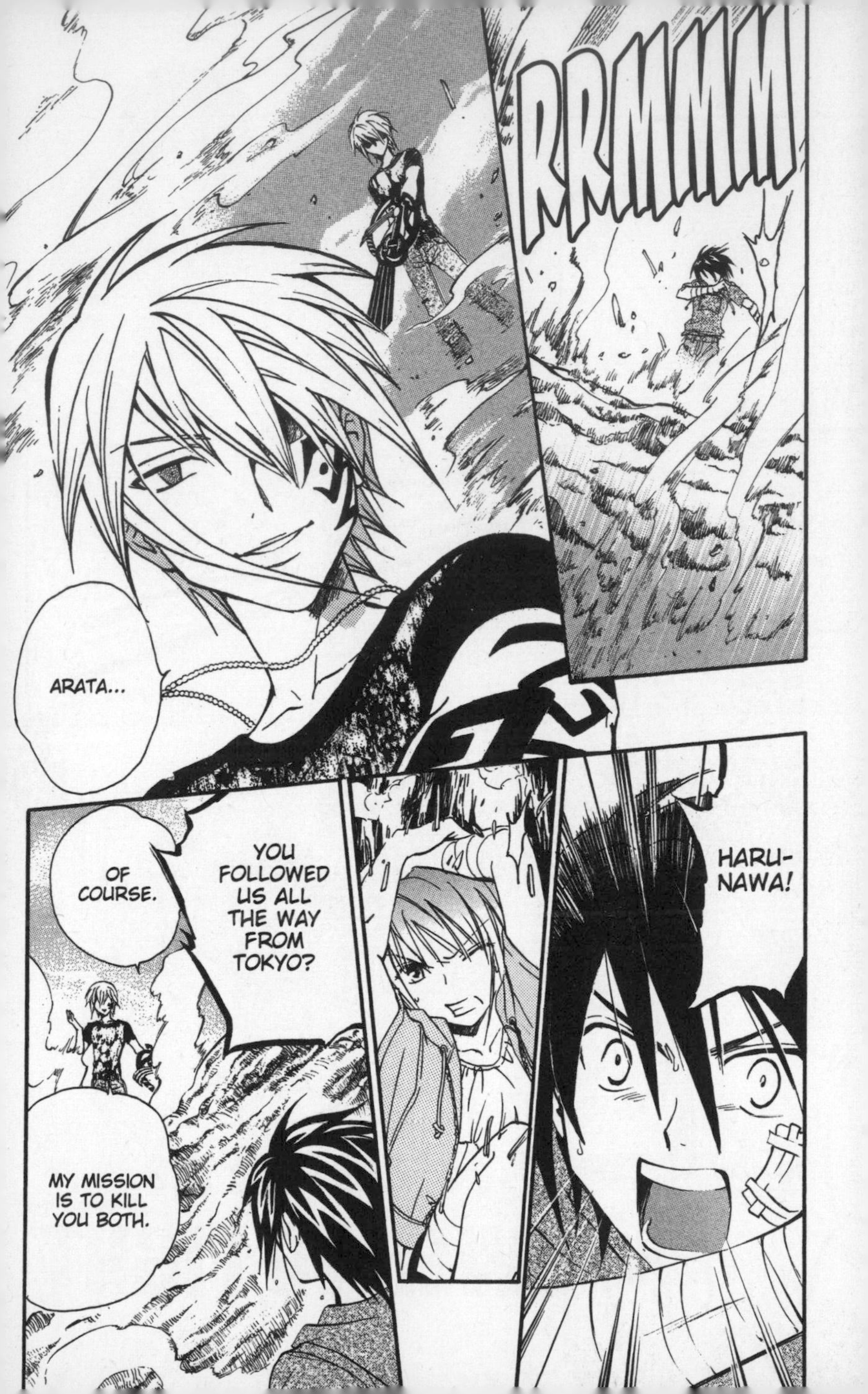
RRMMMM
ARATA...
HARU-NAWA!
YOU FOLLOWED US ALL THE WAY FROM TOKYO?
OF COURSE.
MY MISSION IS TO KILL YOU BOTH.

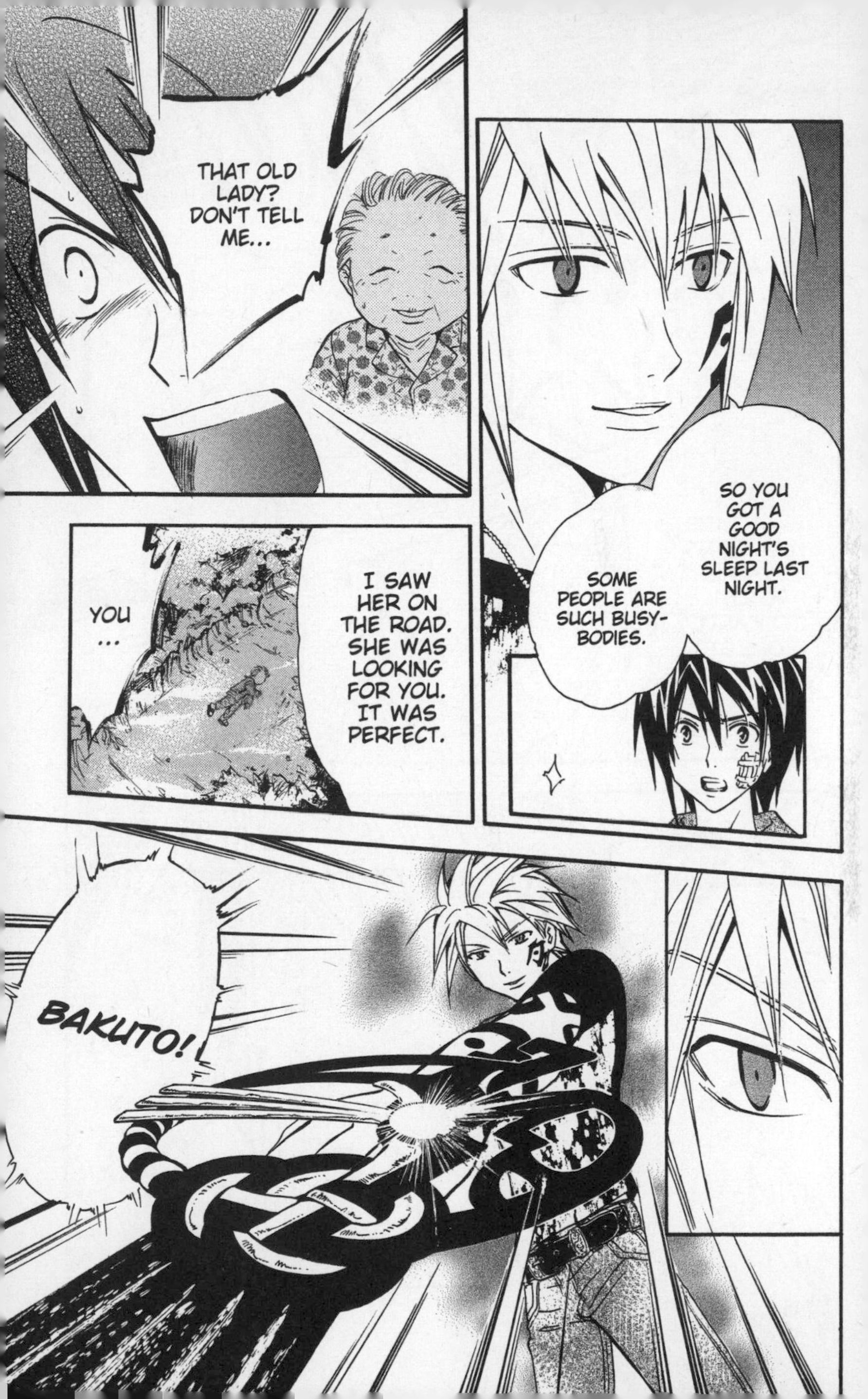
SO YOU GOT A GOOD NIGHT'S SLEEP LAST NIGHT.
SOME PEOPLE ARE SUCH BUSY-BODIES.
THAT OLD LADY? DON'T TELL ME...
I SAW HER ON THE ROAD. SHE WAS LOOKING FOR YOU. IT WAS PERFECT.
YOU...
BAKUTO!

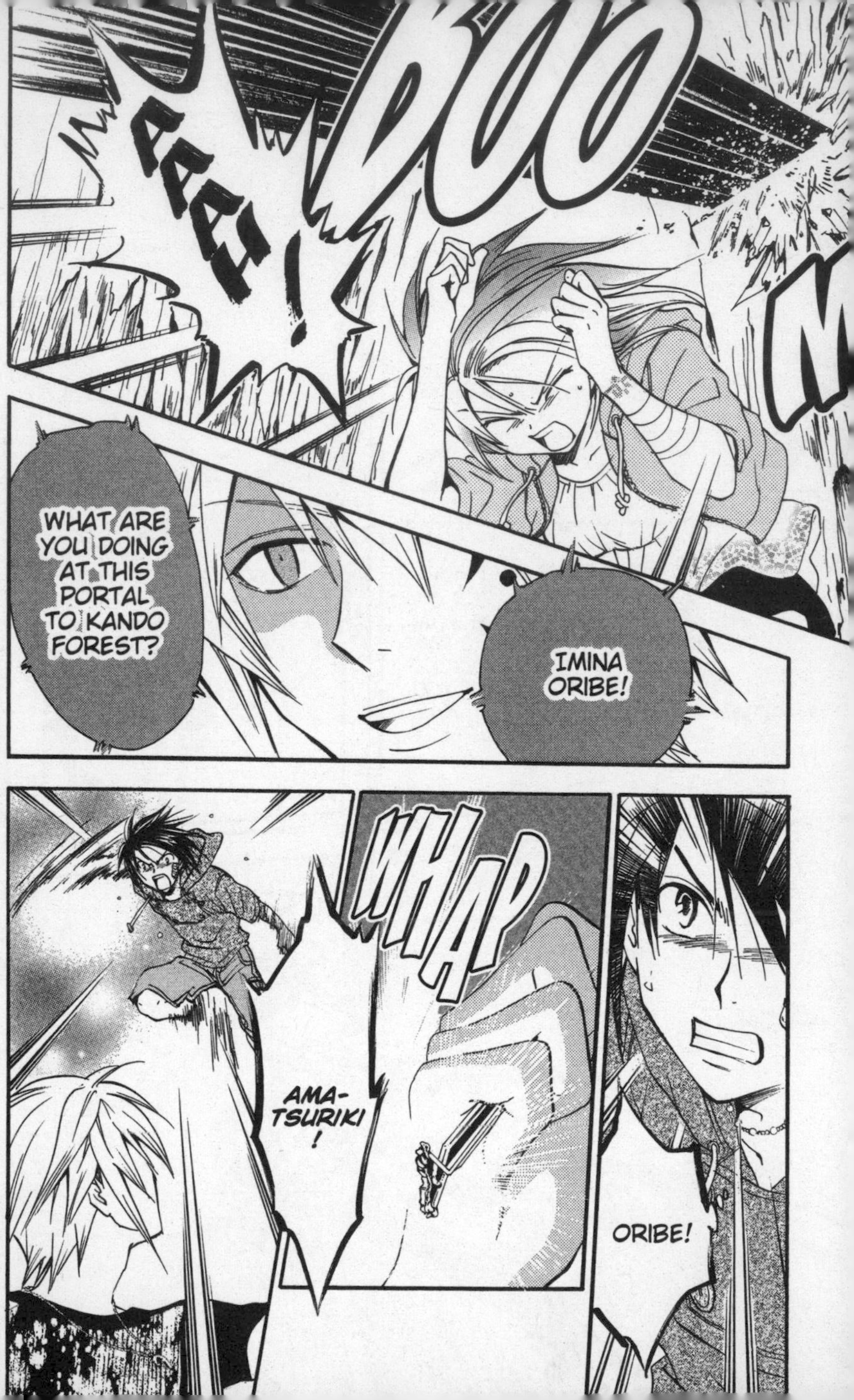
WHAT ARE YOU DOING AT THIS PORTAL TO KANDO FOREST?
IMINA ORIBE!
ORIBE!
WHAP
AMA-TSURIKI!

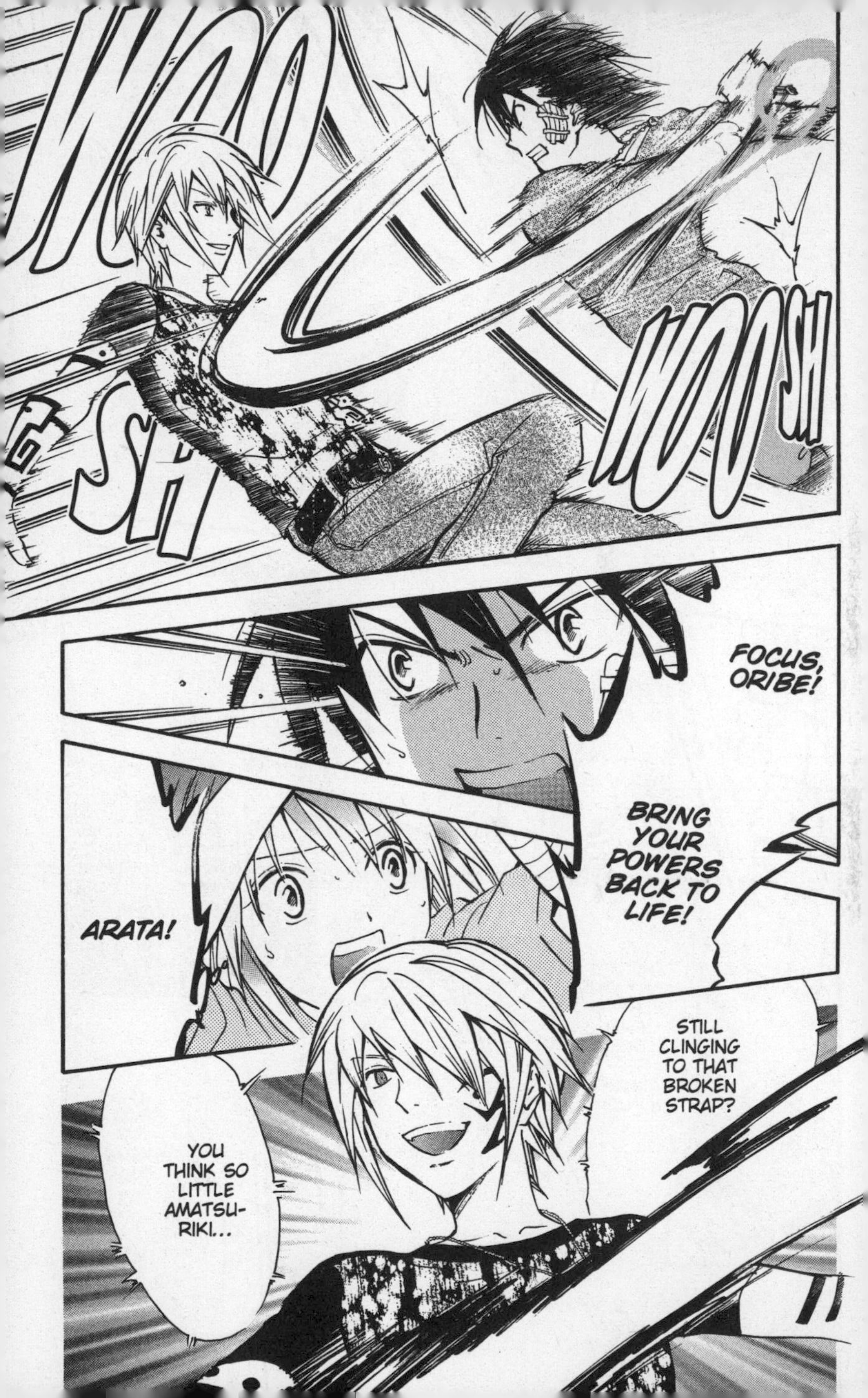
WHOOSH
WHOOSH
FOCUS, ORIBE!
BRING YOUR POWERS BACK TO LIFE!
ARATA!
STILL CLINGING TO THAT BROKEN STRAP?
YOU THINK SO LITTLE AMATSU-RIKI...

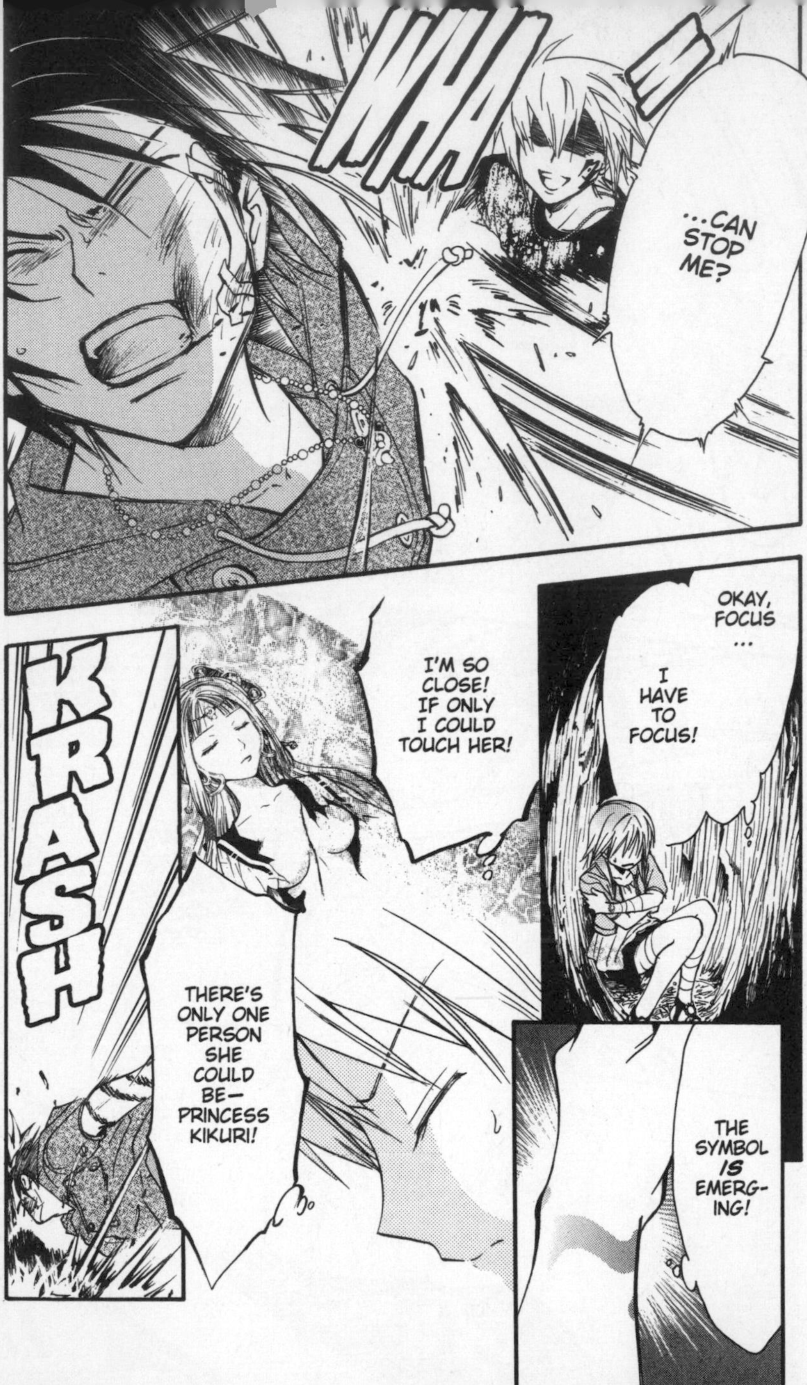
WHA
...CAN STOP ME?
OKAY, FOCUS ...
I HAVE TO FOCUS!
THE SYMBOL *IS* EMERGING!
I'M SO CLOSE! IF ONLY I COULD TOUCH HER!
THERE'S ONLY ONE PERSON SHE COULD BE—PRINCESS KIKURI!
KRASH

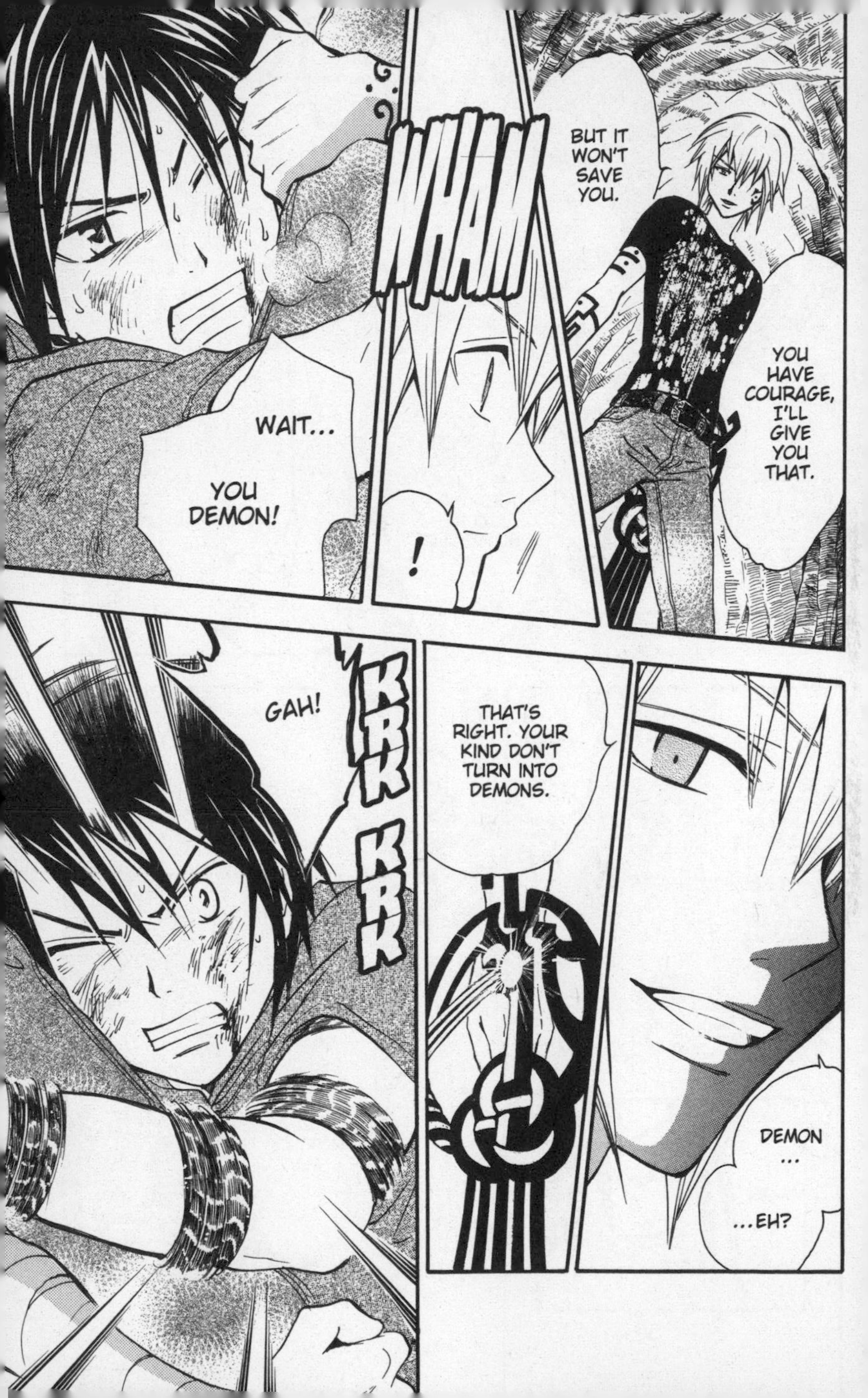
YOU HAVE COURAGE, I'LL GIVE YOU THAT.
BUT IT WON'T SAVE YOU.
WHAM
!
WAIT...
YOU DEMON!
DEMON ...
...EH?
THAT'S RIGHT. YOUR KIND DON'T TURN INTO DEMONS.
KRK KRK
GAH!

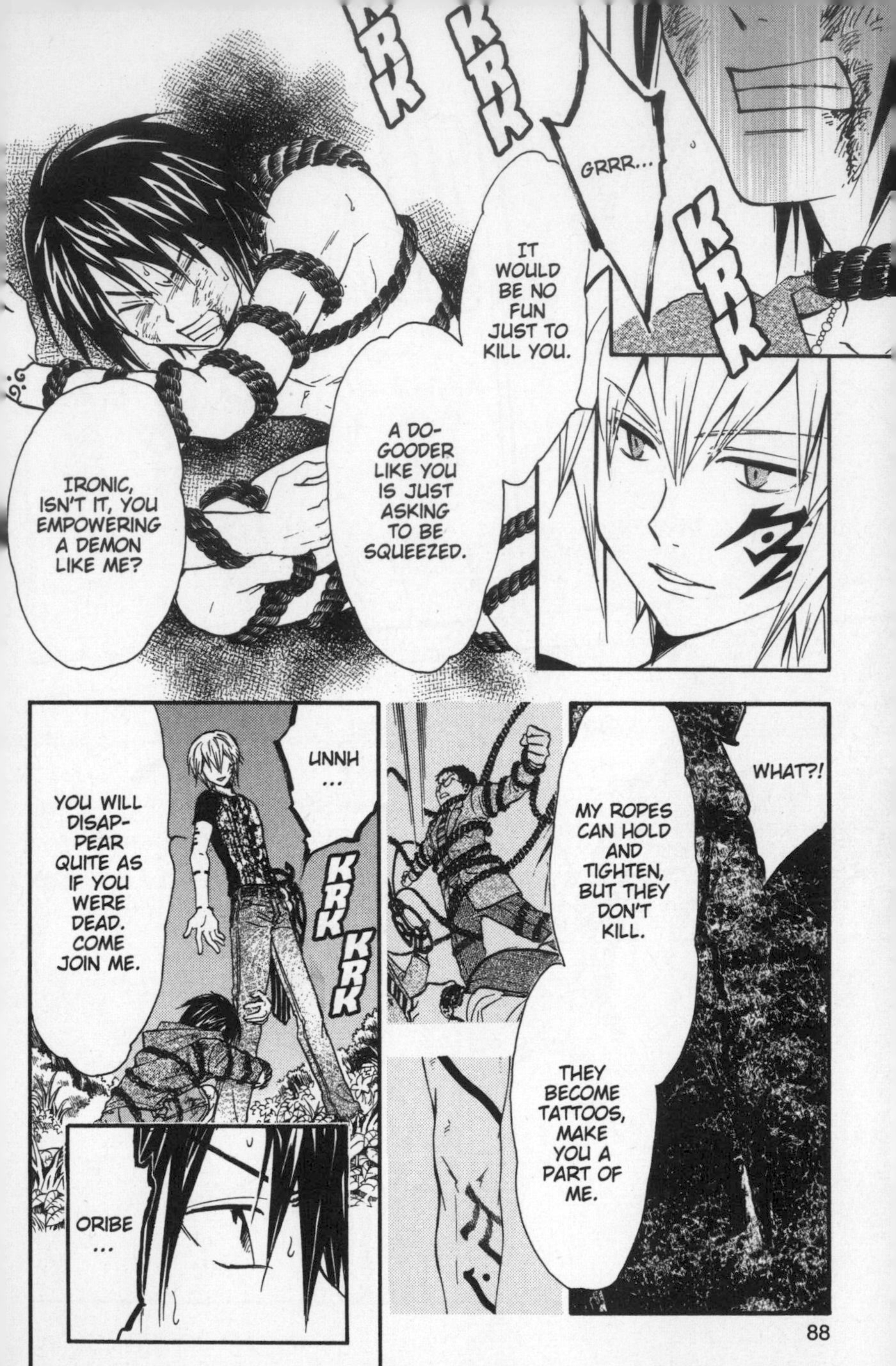
GRRR...
KRK
KRK
KRK
IT WOULD BE NO FUN JUST TO KILL YOU.
A DO-GOODER LIKE YOU IS JUST ASKING TO BE SQUEEZED.
IRONIC, ISN'T IT, YOU EMPOWERING A DEMON LIKE ME?
WHAT?!
MY ROPES CAN HOLD AND TIGHTEN, BUT THEY DON'T KILL.
THEY BECOME TATTOOS, MAKE YOU A PART OF ME.
UNNH ...
KRK KRK
YOU WILL DISAP-PEAR QUITE AS IF YOU WERE DEAD. COME JOIN ME.
ORIBE ...

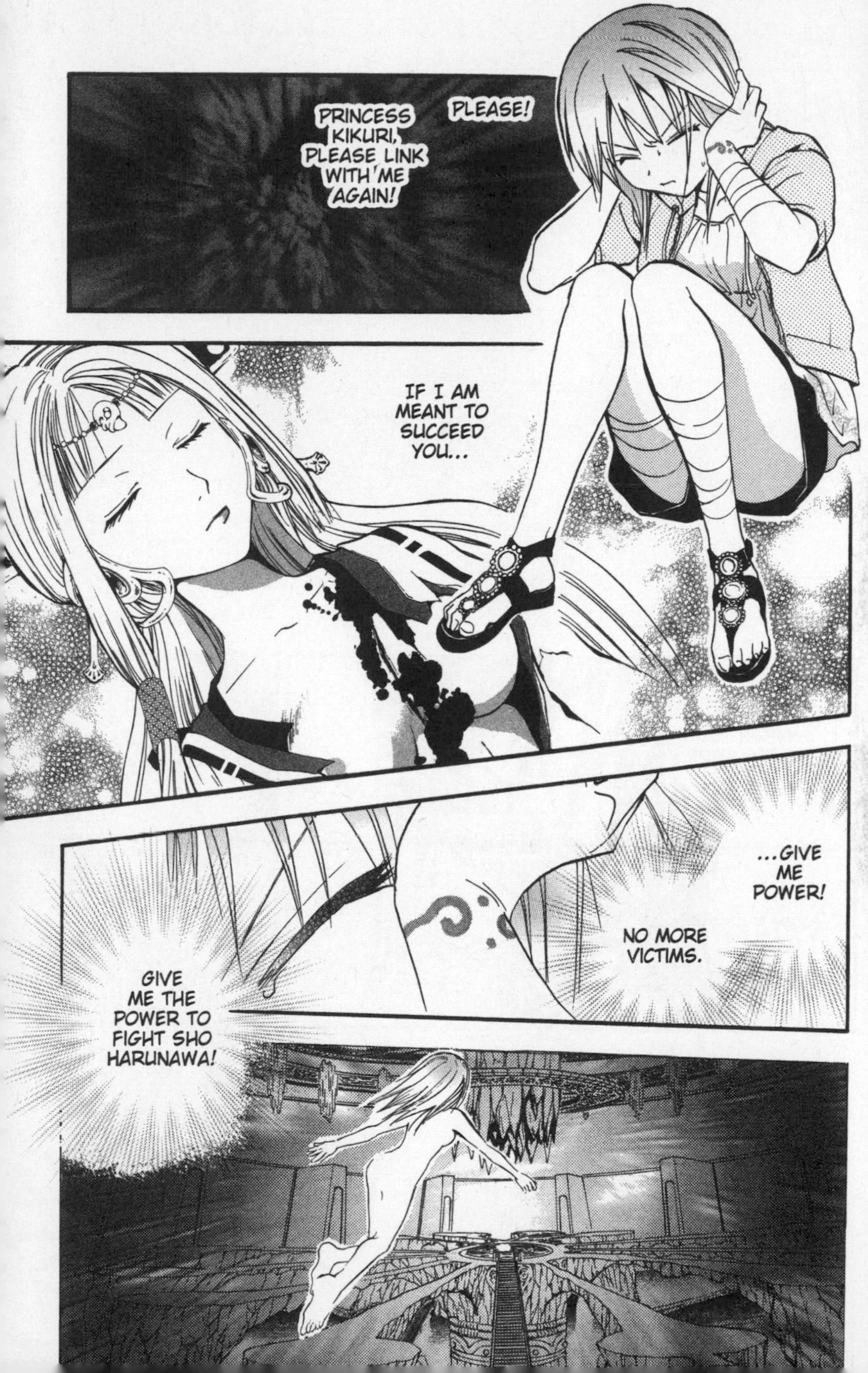
PLEASE!
PRINCESS KIKURI, PLEASE LINK WITH ME AGAIN!
IF I AM MEANT TO SUCCEED YOU...
...GIVE ME POWER!
NO MORE VICTIMS.
GIVE ME THE POWER TO FIGHT SHO HARUNAWA!

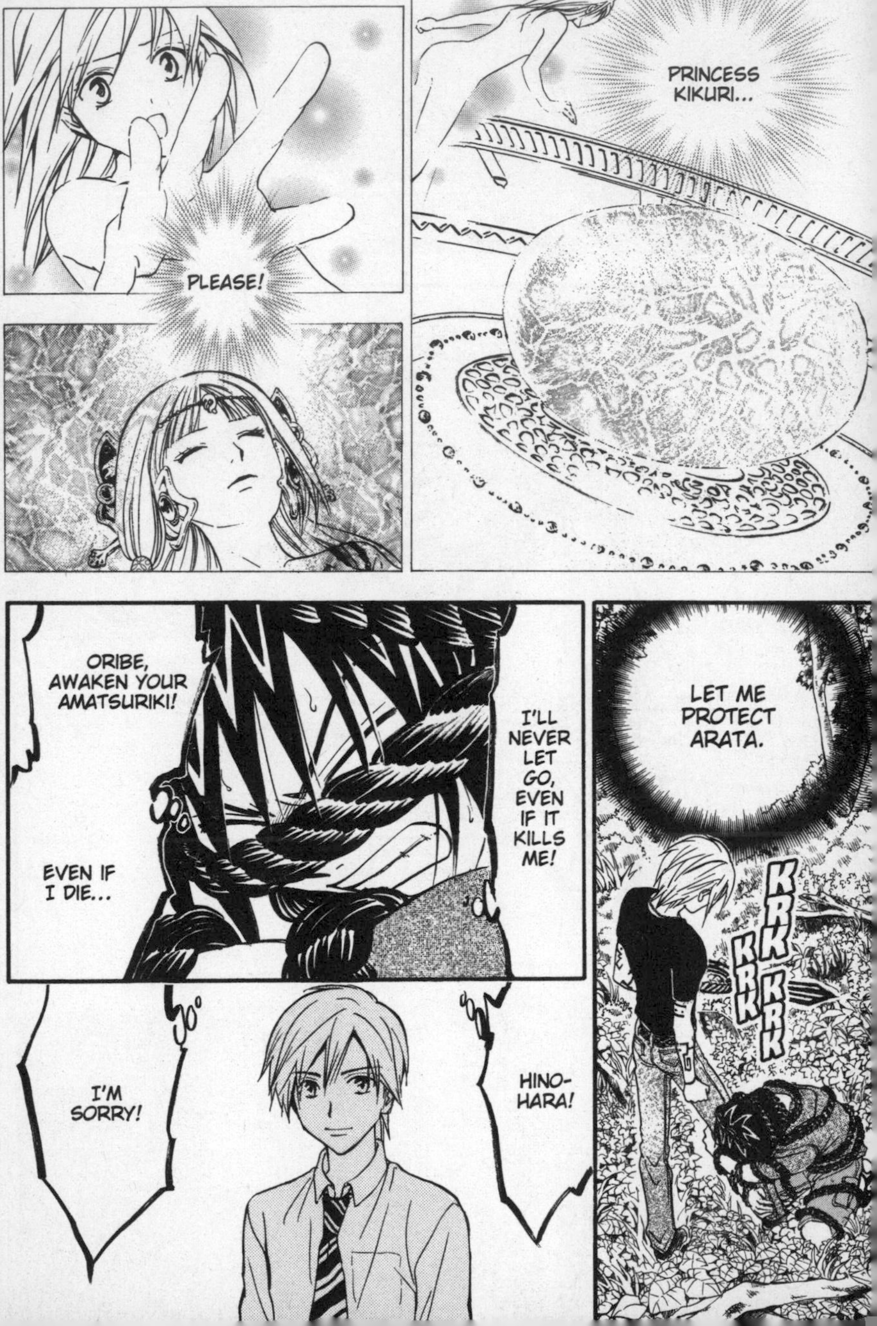
PRINCESS KIKURI...
PLEASE!
LET ME PROTECT ARATA.
KRK KRK
KRK KRK
I'LL NEVER LET GO, EVEN IF IT KILLS ME!
ORIBE, AWAKEN YOUR AMATSURIKI!
EVEN IF I DIE...
HINO-HARA!
I'M SORRY!

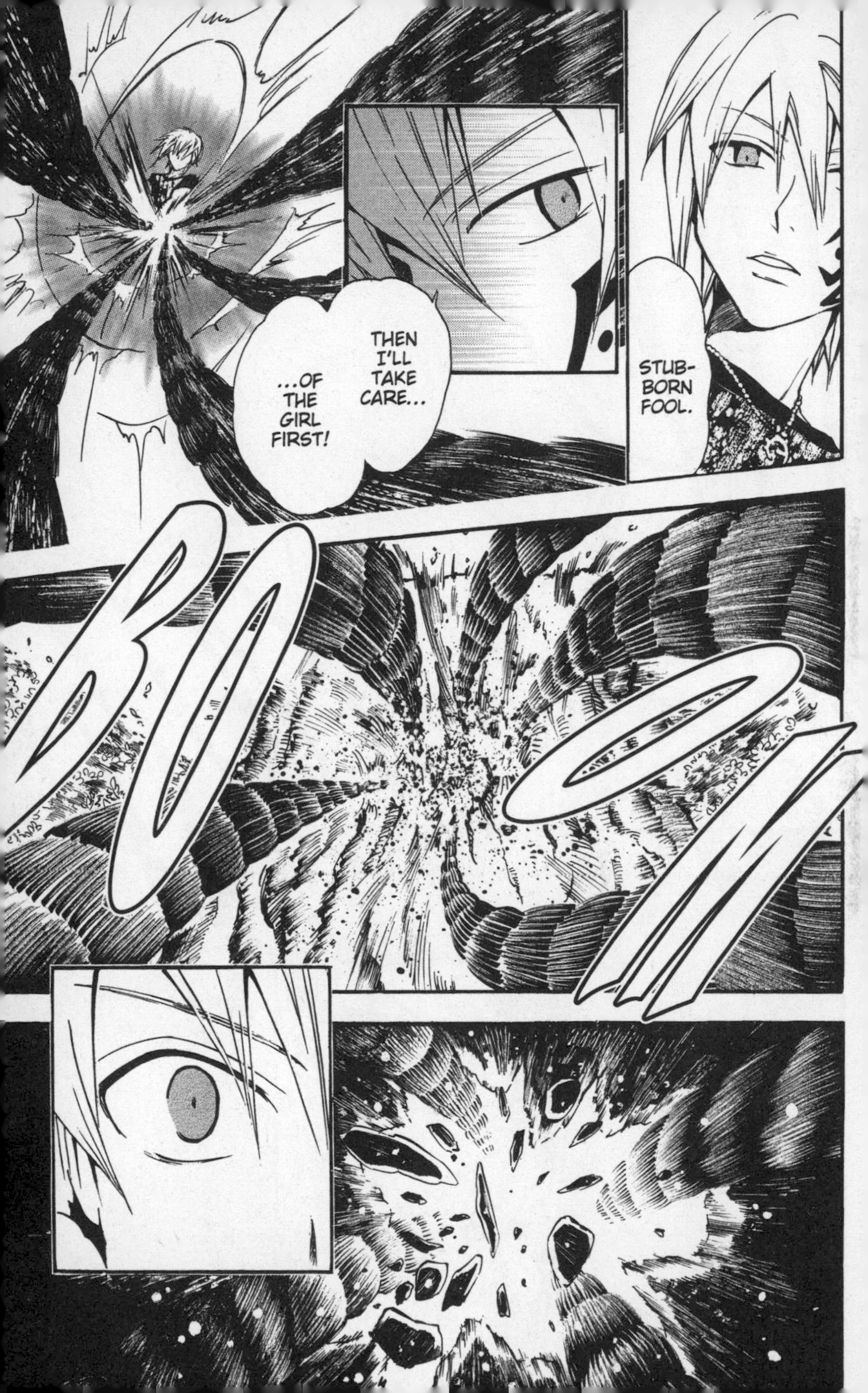
STUB-BORN FOOL.
THEN I'LL TAKE CARE...
...OF THE GIRL FIRST!
BOOM

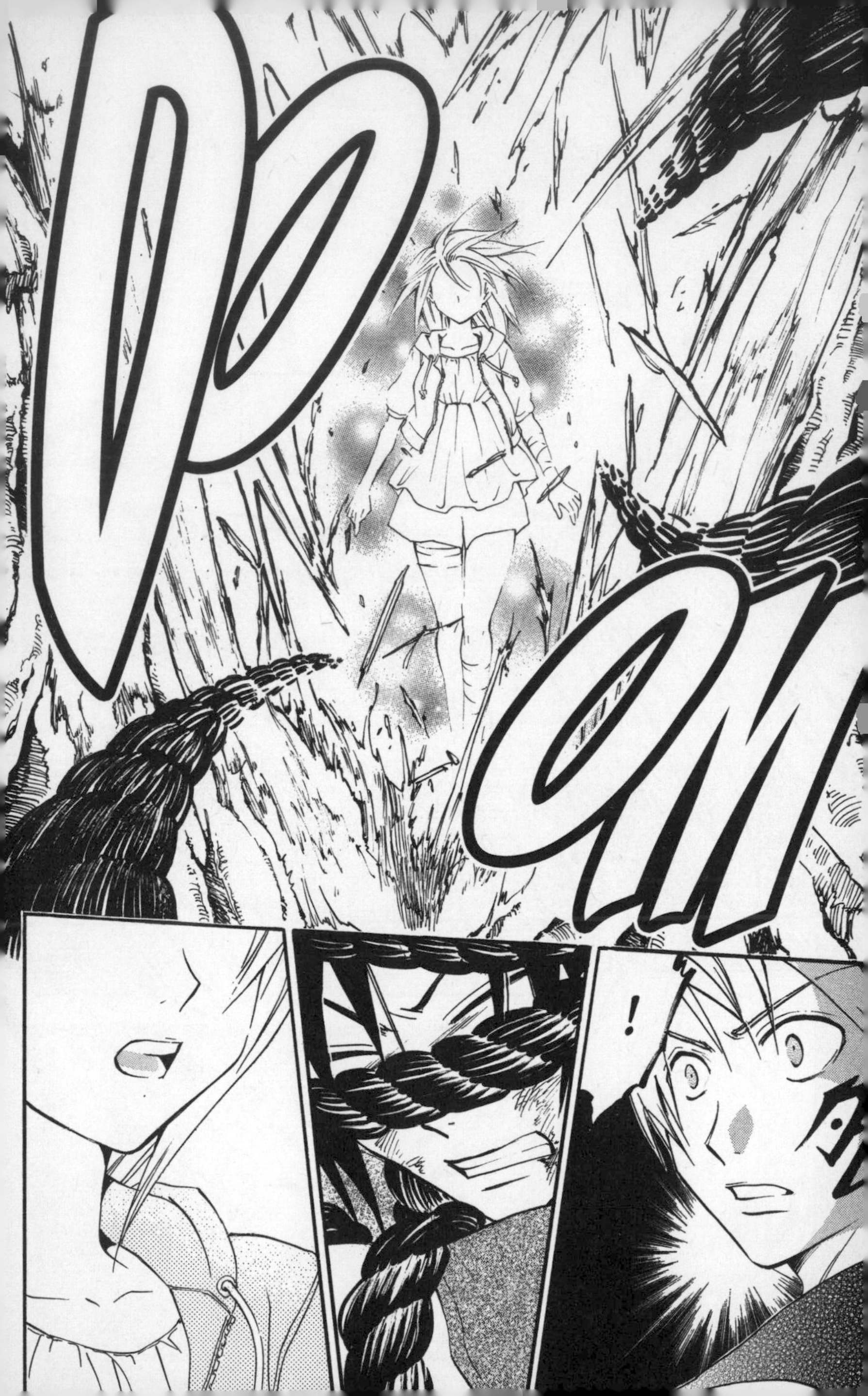
Doom
!

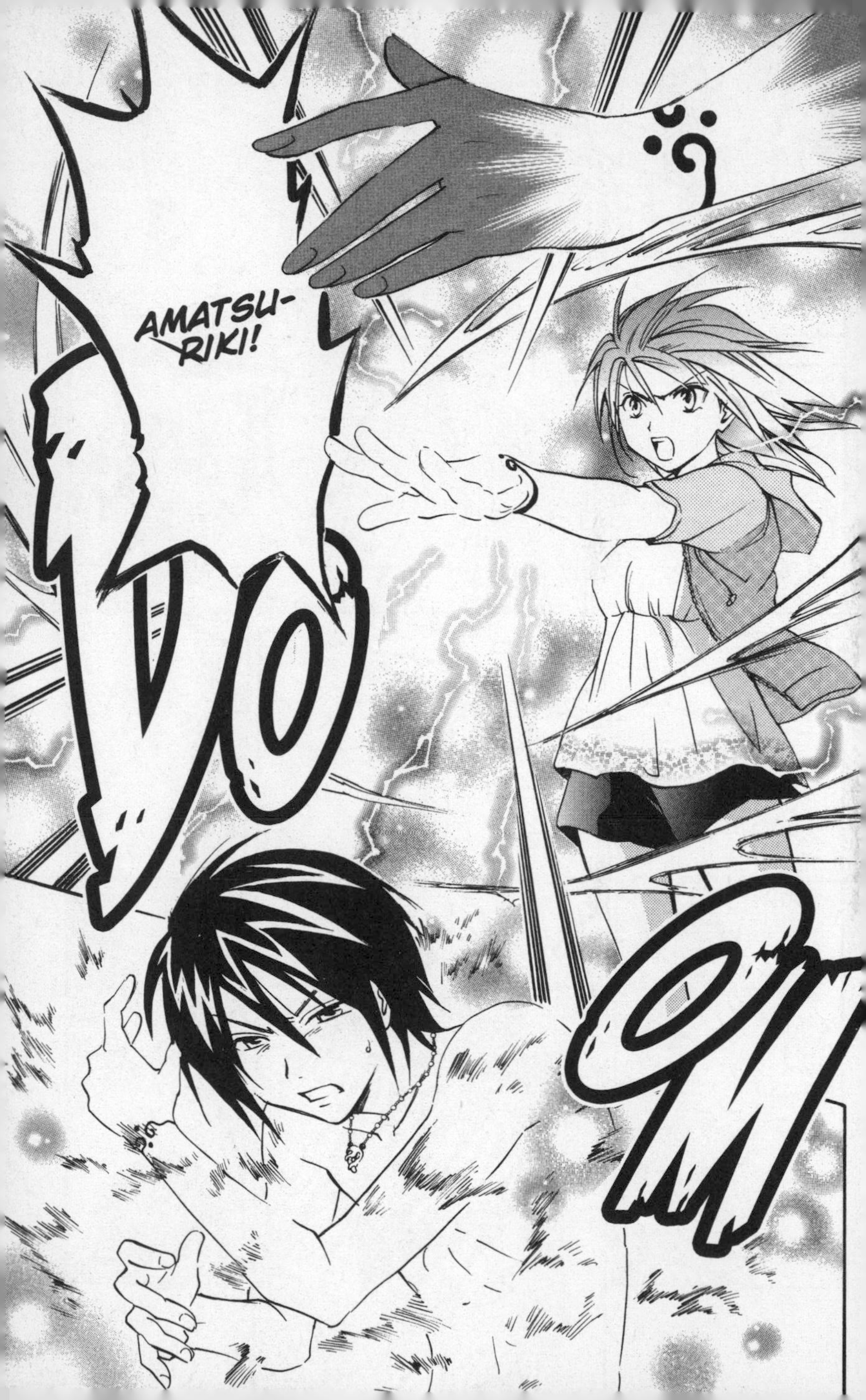
AMATSU-RIKI!
DOOM

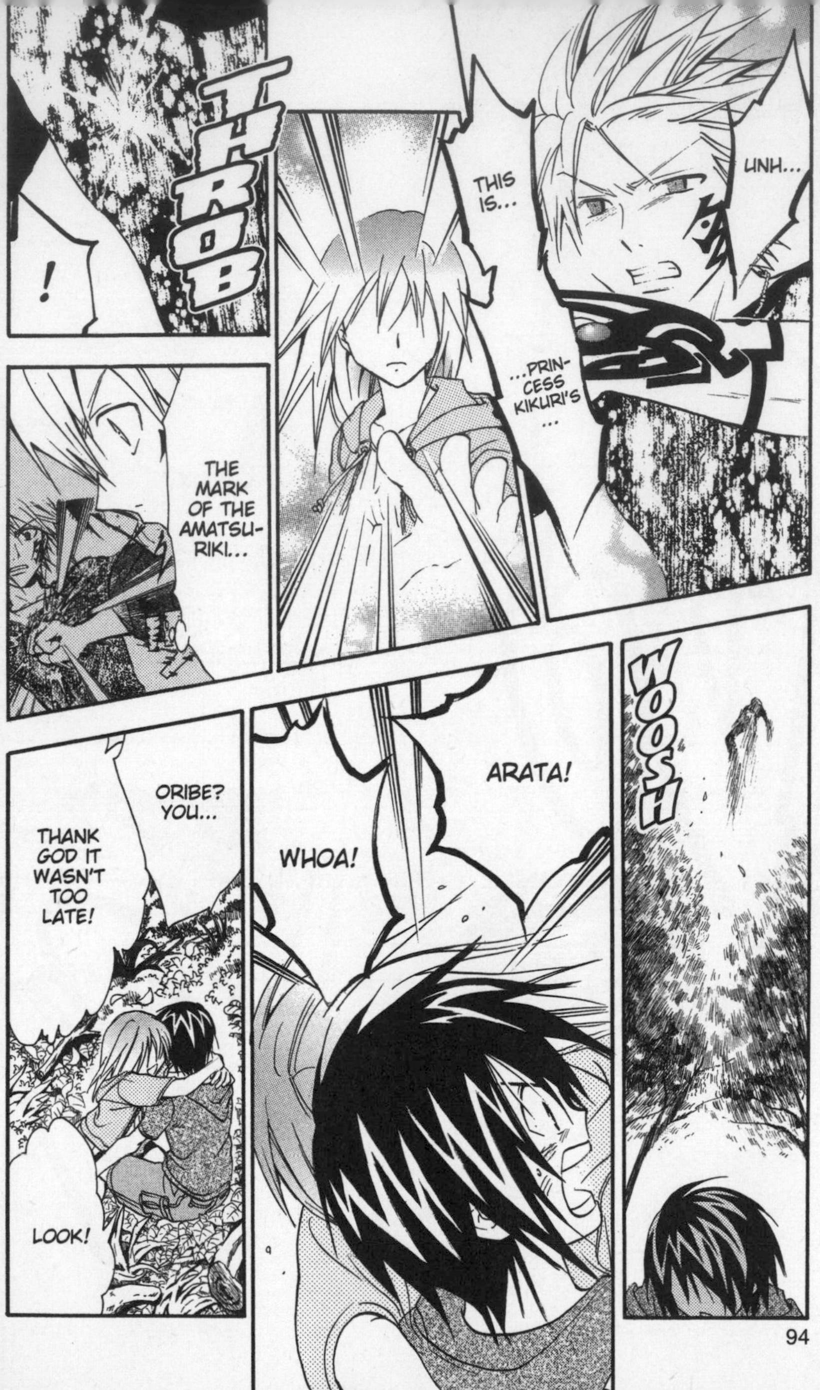
UNH...
THIS IS...
...PRINCESS KIKURI'S...
THROB
!
THE MARK OF THE AMATSURIKI...
WOOSH
ARATA!
WHOA!
ORIBE? YOU...
THANK GOD IT WASN'T TOO LATE!
LOOK!

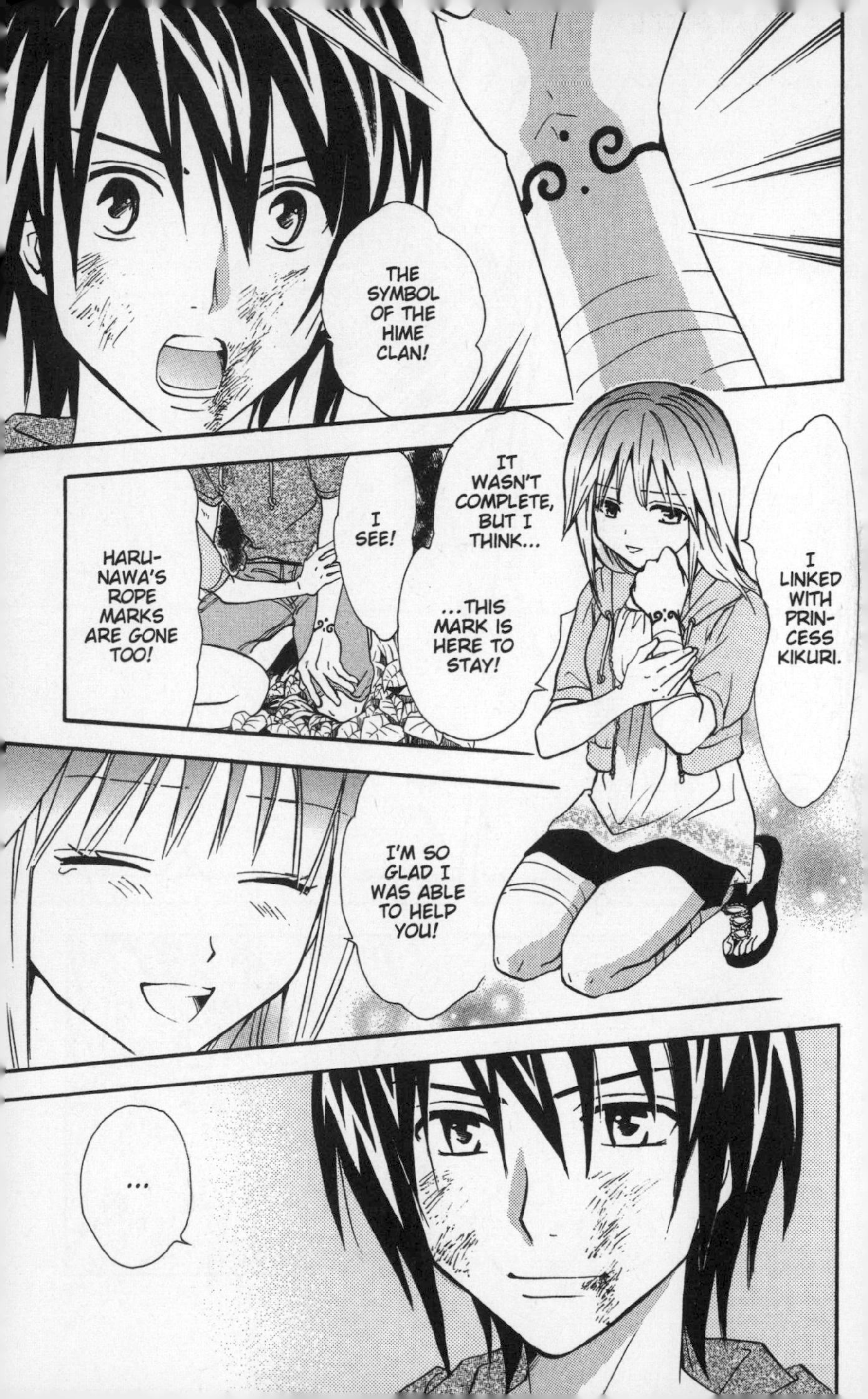
THE SYMBOL OF THE HIME CLAN!
I LINKED WITH PRIN-CESS KIKURI.
IT WASN'T COMPLETE, BUT I THINK...
...THIS MARK IS HERE TO STAY!
I SEE!
HARU-NAWA'S ROPE MARKS ARE GONE TOO!
I'M SO GLAD I WAS ABLE TO HELP YOU!
...

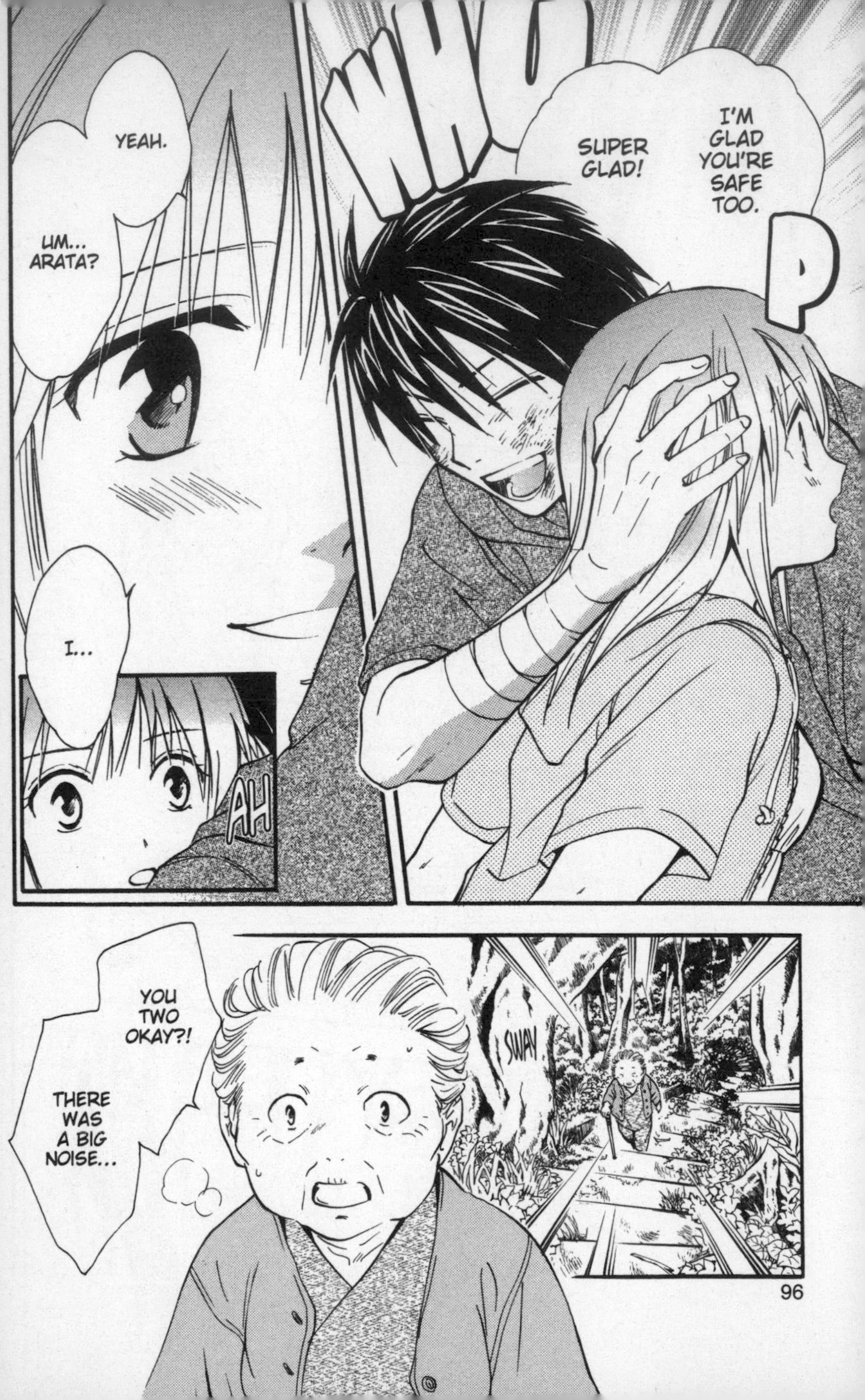
I'M GLAD YOU'RE SAFE TOO.
SUPER GLAD!
YEAH.
UM... ARATA?
I...
AH
SWAY
YOU TWO OKAY?!
THERE WAS A BIG NOISE...

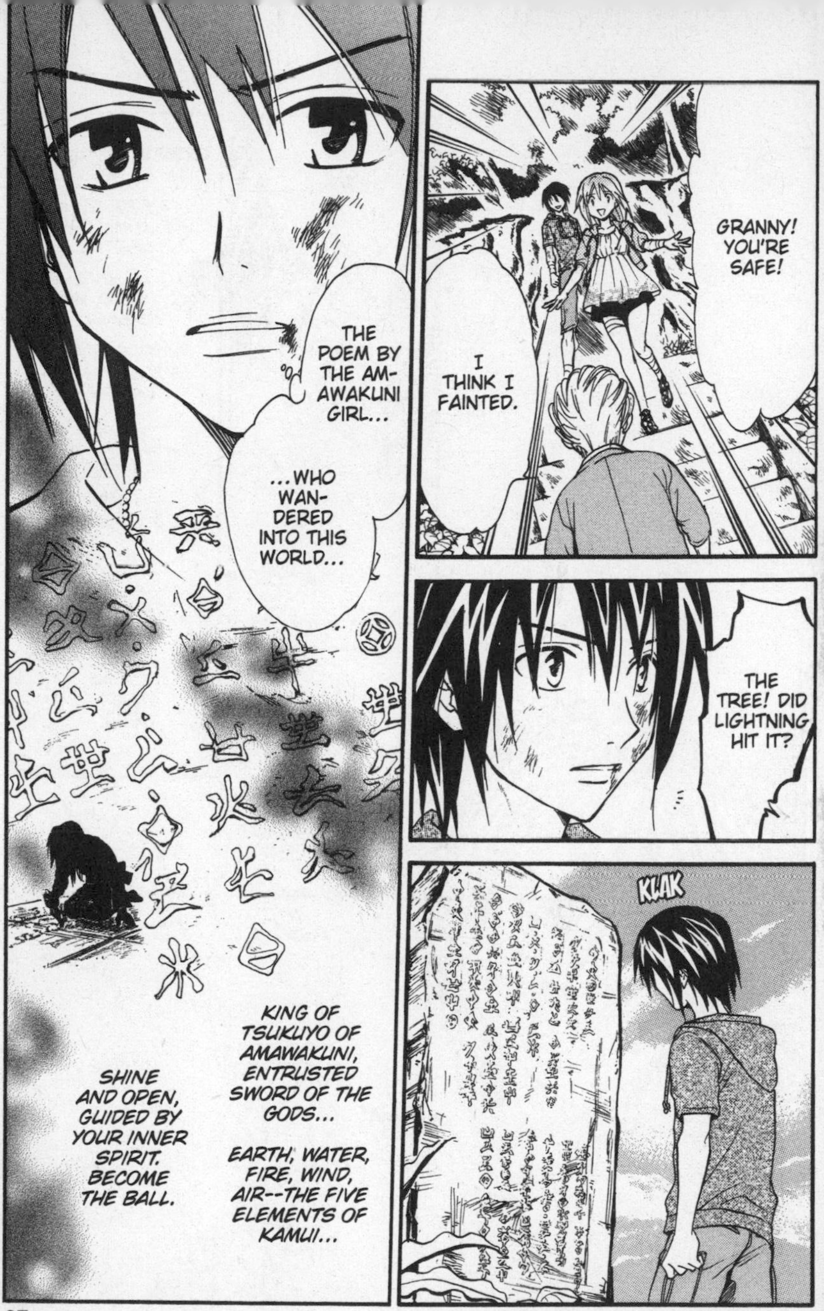
GRANNY! YOU'RE SAFE!
I THINK I FAINTED.
THE TREE! DID LIGHTNING HIT IT?
KLAK
THE POEM BY THE AM-AWAKUNI GIRL...
...WHO WAN-DERED INTO THIS WORLD...
KING OF TSUKUYO OF AMAWAKUNI, ENTRUSTED SWORD OF THE GODS...
EARTH, WATER, FIRE, WIND, AIR--THE FIVE ELEMENTS OF KAMUI...
SHINE AND OPEN, GUIDED BY YOUR INNER SPIRIT. BECOME THE BALL.

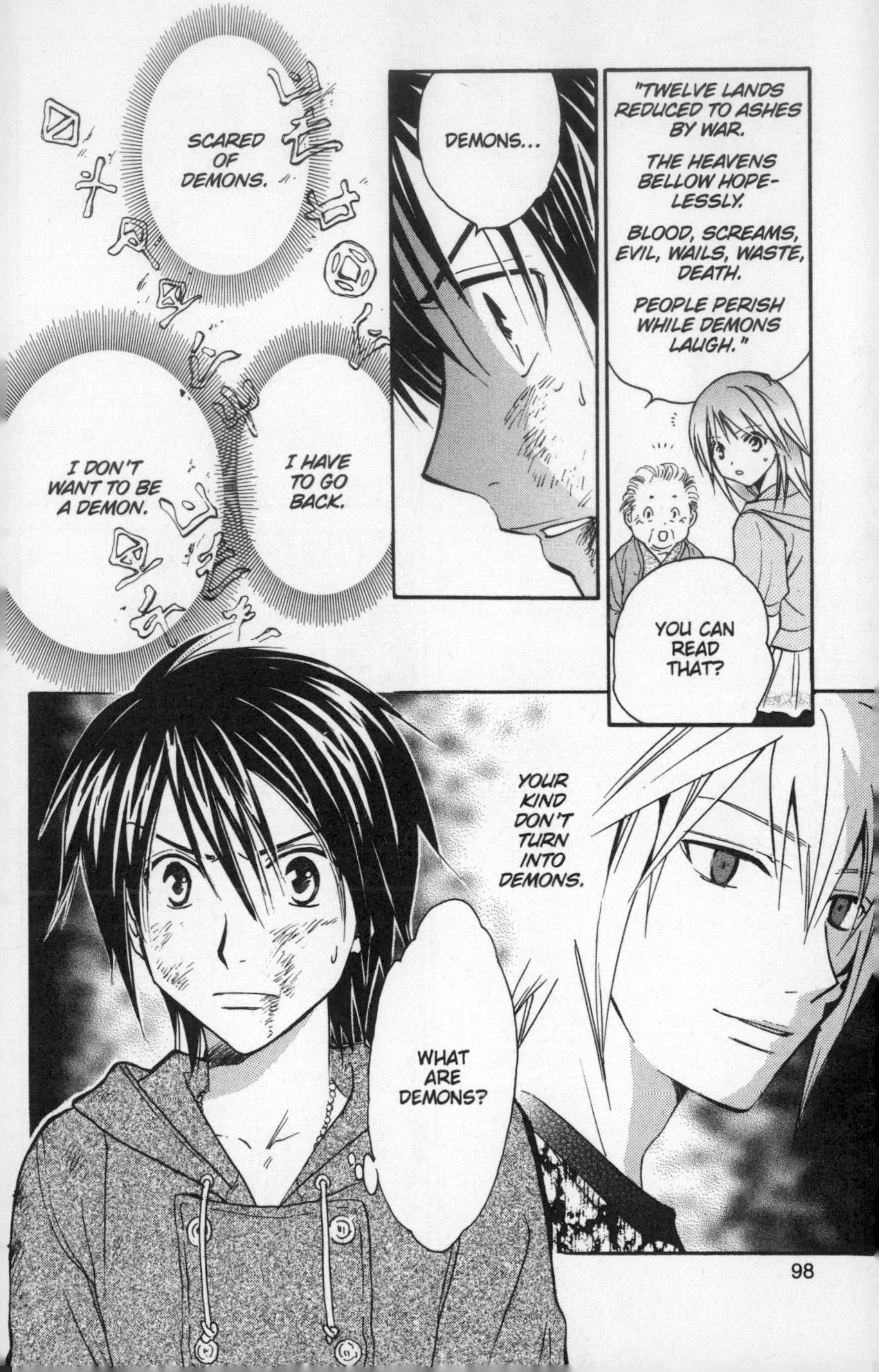
"TWELVE LANDS REDUCED TO ASHES BY WAR.
THE HEAVENS BELLOW HOPE-LESSLY.
BLOOD, SCREAMS, EVIL, WAILS, WASTE, DEATH.
PEOPLE PERISH WHILE DEMONS LAUGH."
YOU CAN READ THAT?
DEMONS...
SCARED OF DEMONS.
I HAVE TO GO BACK.
I DON'T WANT TO BE A DEMON.
YOUR KIND DON'T TURN INTO DEMONS.
WHAT ARE DEMONS?

CHAPTER 193
MOVING FORWARD

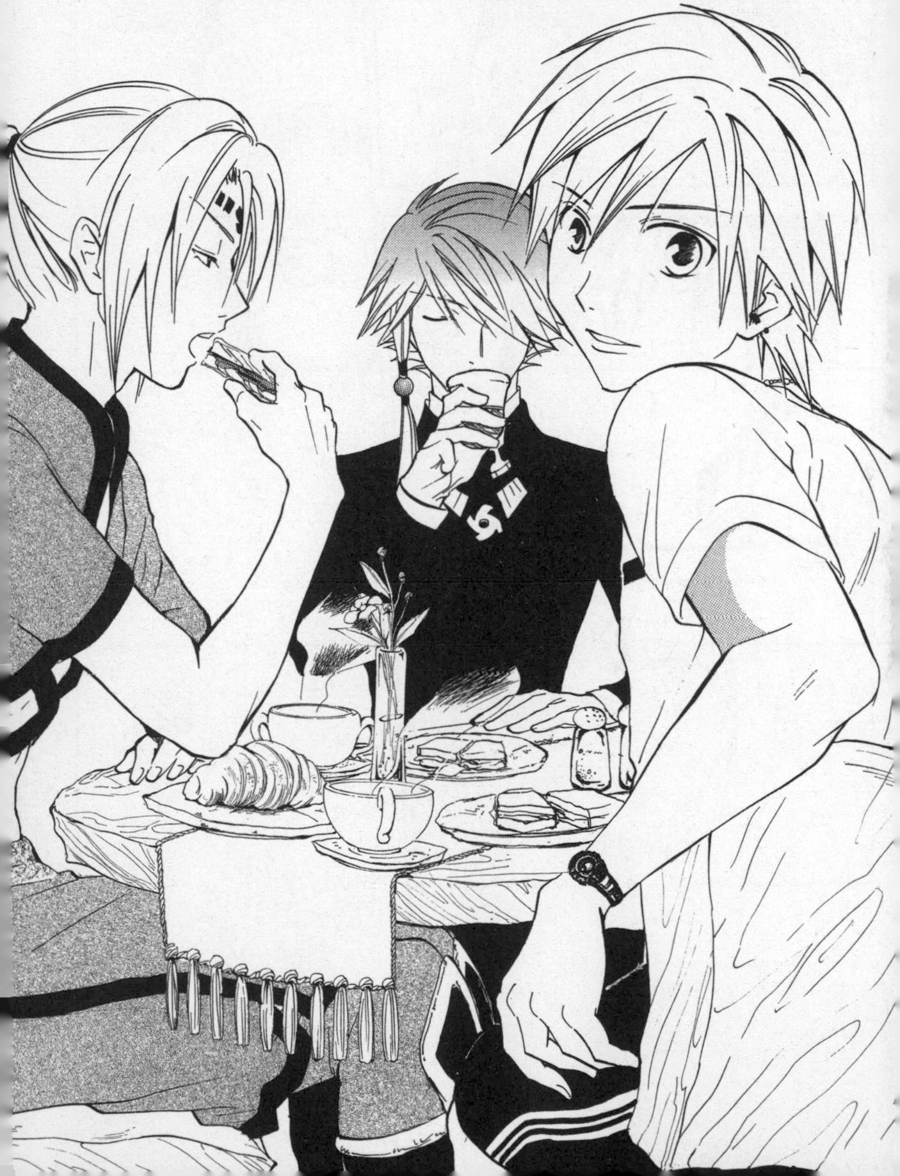

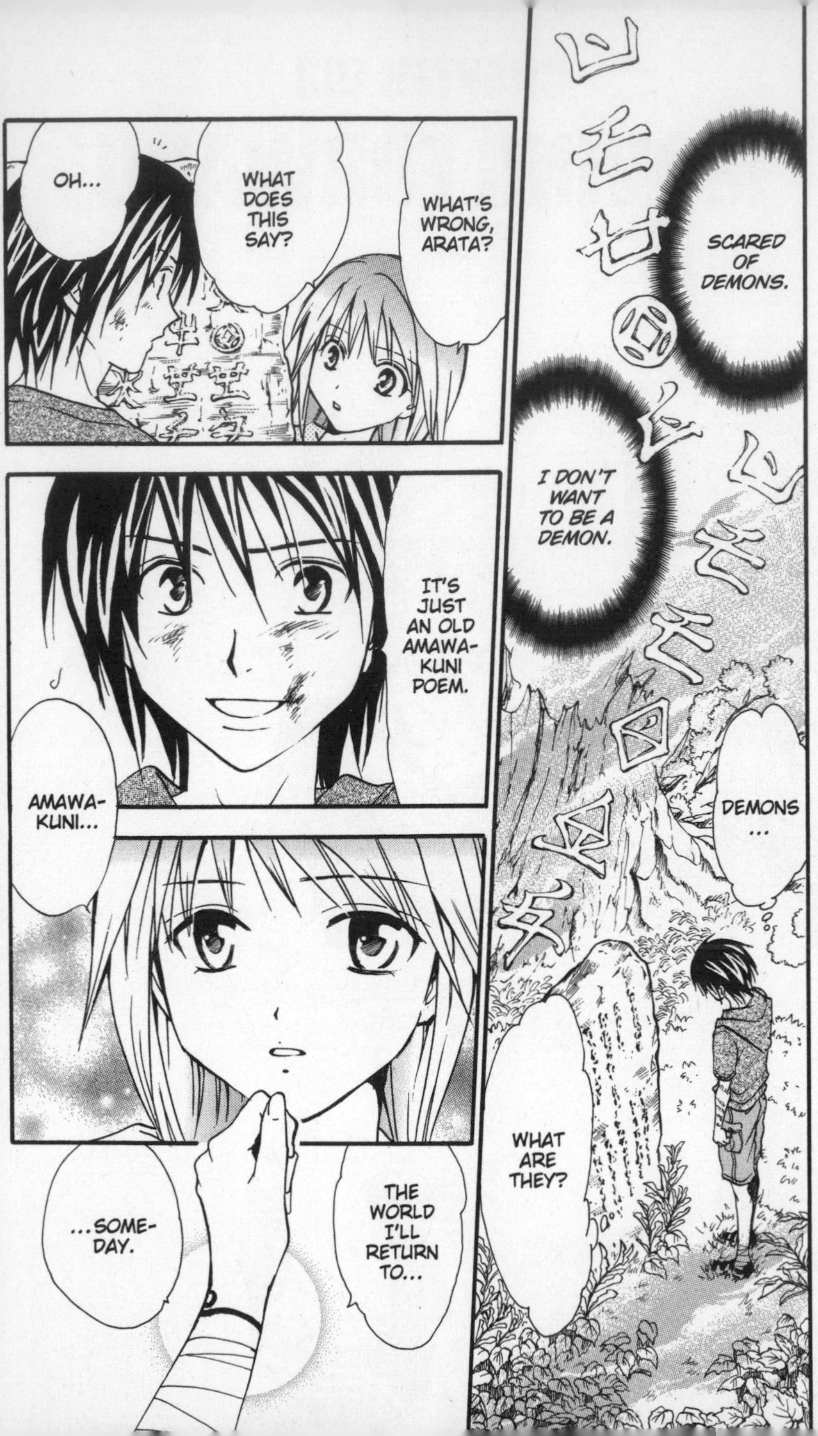
SCARED OF DEMONS.
I DON'T WANT TO BE A DEMON.
DEMONS...
WHAT ARE THEY?
WHAT'S WRONG, ARATA?
WHAT DOES THIS SAY?
OH...
IT'S JUST AN OLD AMAWA-KUNI POEM.
AMAWA-KUNI...
THE WORLD I'LL RETURN TO...
...SOME-DAY.

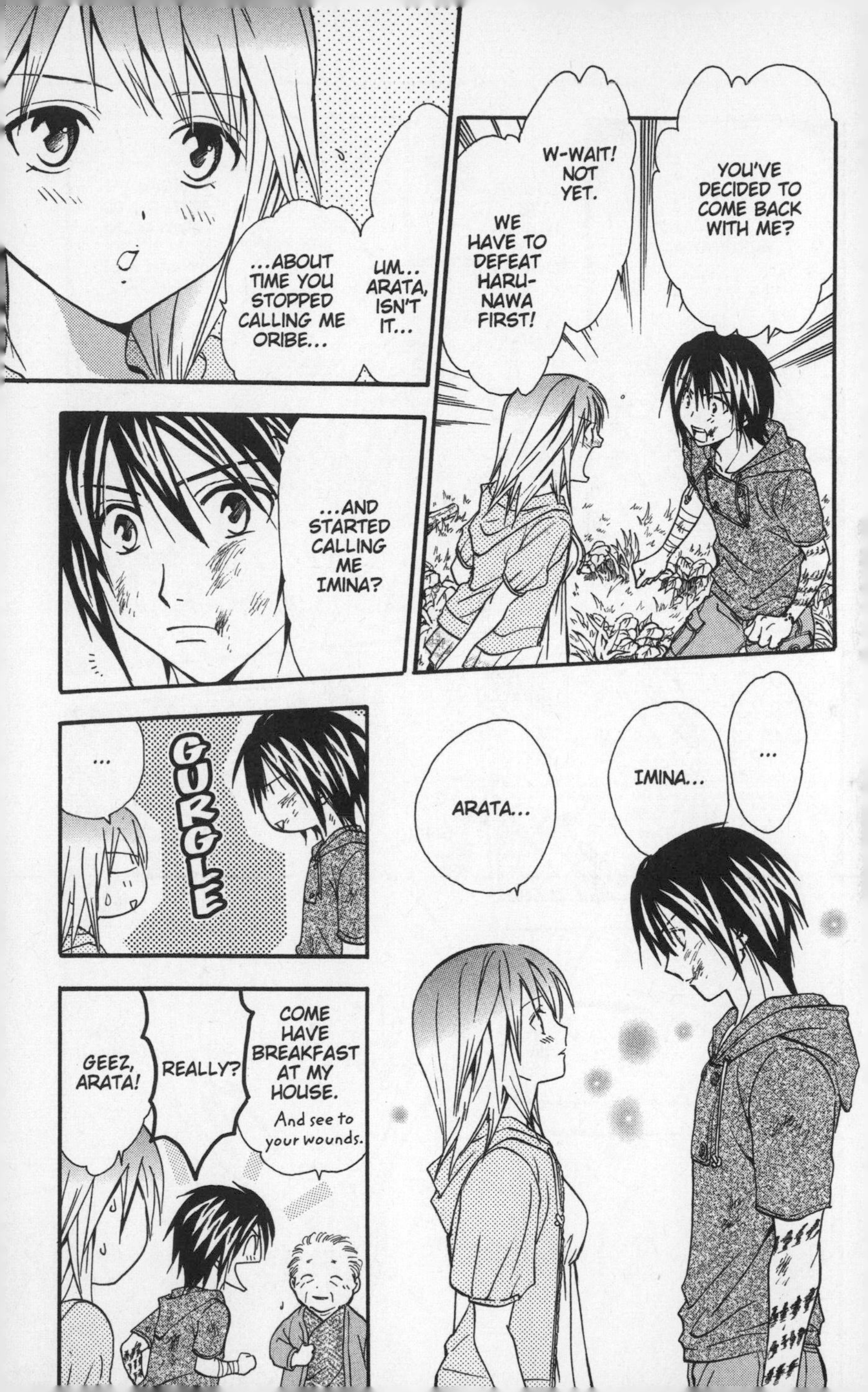
YOU'VE DECIDED TO COME BACK WITH ME?
W-WAIT! NOT YET.
WE HAVE TO DEFEAT HARU-NAWA FIRST!
UM... ARATA, ISN'T IT...
...ABOUT TIME YOU STOPPED CALLING ME ORIBE...
...AND STARTED CALLING ME IMINA?
...
IMINA...
ARATA...
...
GURGLE
COME HAVE BREAKFAST AT MY HOUSE.
And see to your wounds.
REALLY?
GEEZ, ARATA!

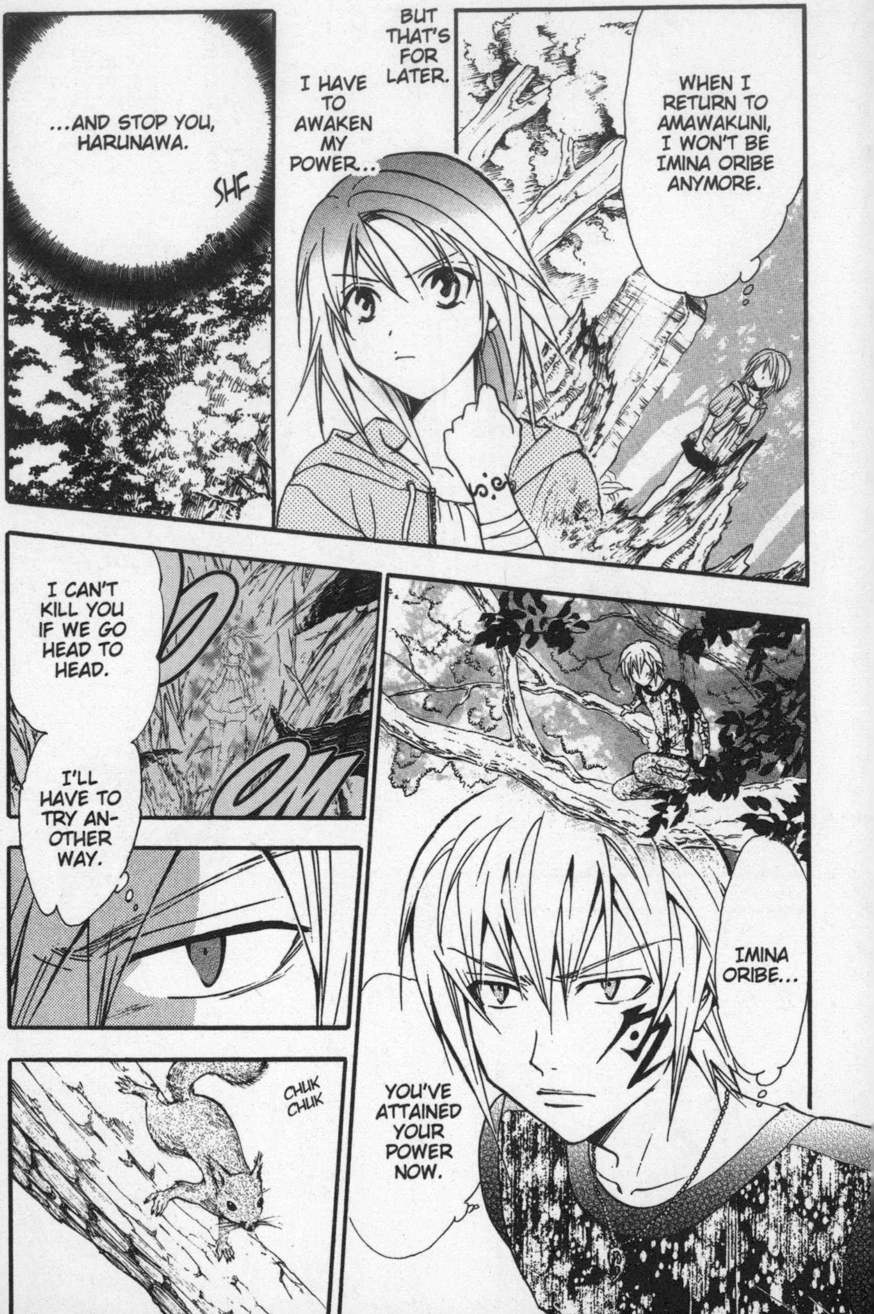
WHEN I RETURN TO AMAWAKUNI, I WON'T BE IMINA ORIBE ANYMORE.
BUT THAT'S FOR LATER.
I HAVE TO AWAKEN MY POWER...
...AND STOP YOU, HARUNAWA.
SHF
IMINA ORIBE...
YOU'VE ATTAINED YOUR POWER NOW.
I CAN'T KILL YOU IF WE GO HEAD TO HEAD.
I'LL HAVE TO TRY AN-OTHER WAY.
CHUK CHUK

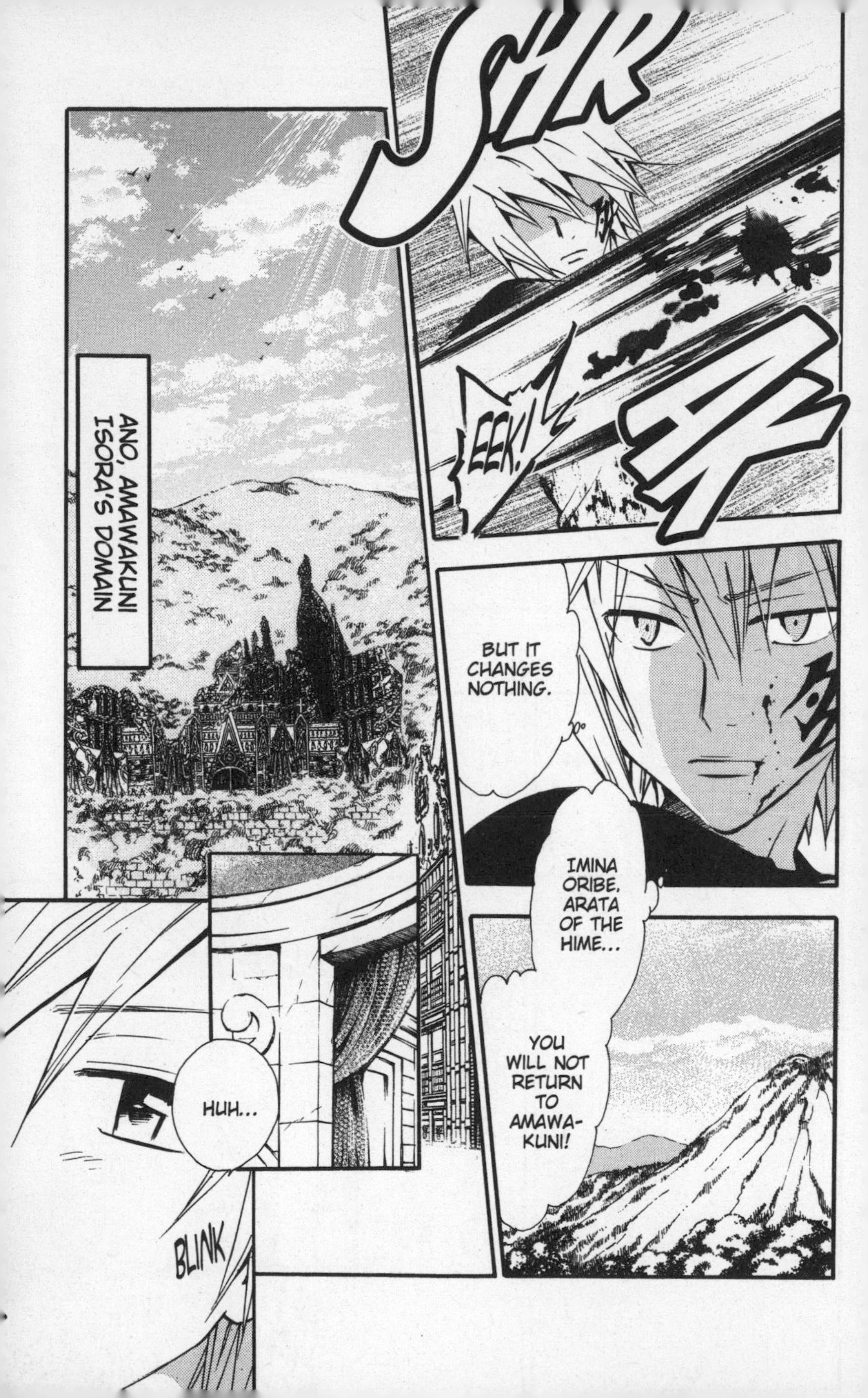
SHK
EEK!
AK
BUT IT CHANGES NOTHING.
IMINA ORIBE, ARATA OF THE HIME...
YOU WILL NOT RETURN TO AMAWA-KUNI!
ANO, AMAWAKUNI ISORA'S DOMAIN
HUH...
BLINK

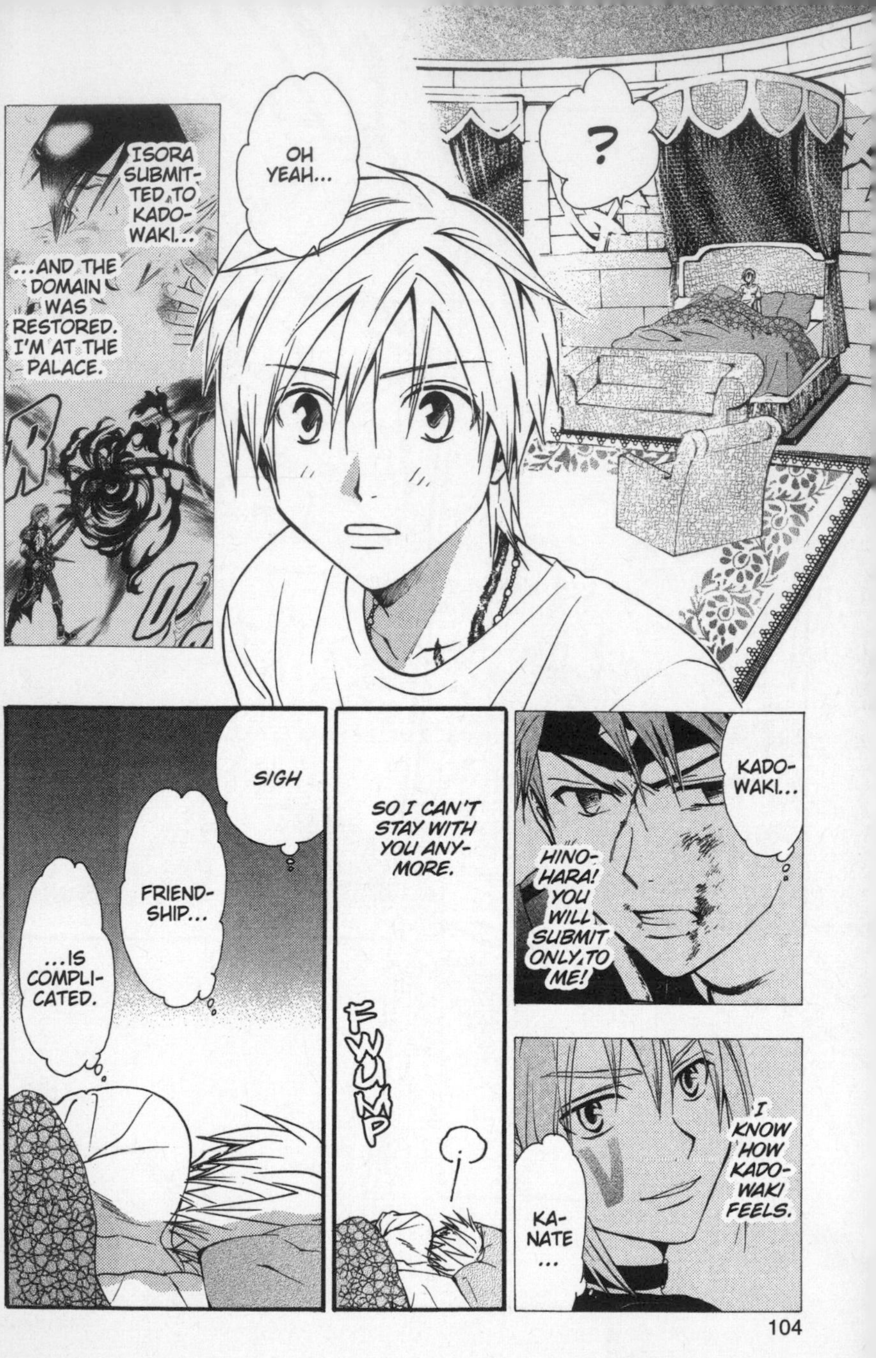
?
OH YEAH...
ISORA SUBMIT-TED TO KADO-WAKI...
...AND THE DOMAIN WAS RESTORED. I'M AT THE PALACE.
KADO-WAKI...
HINO-HARA! YOU WILL SUBMIT ONLY TO ME!
I KNOW HOW KADO-WAKI FEELS.
KA-NATE ...
SO I CAN'T STAY WITH YOU ANY-MORE.
FWUMP
SIGH
FRIEND-SHIP...
...IS COMPLI-CATED.

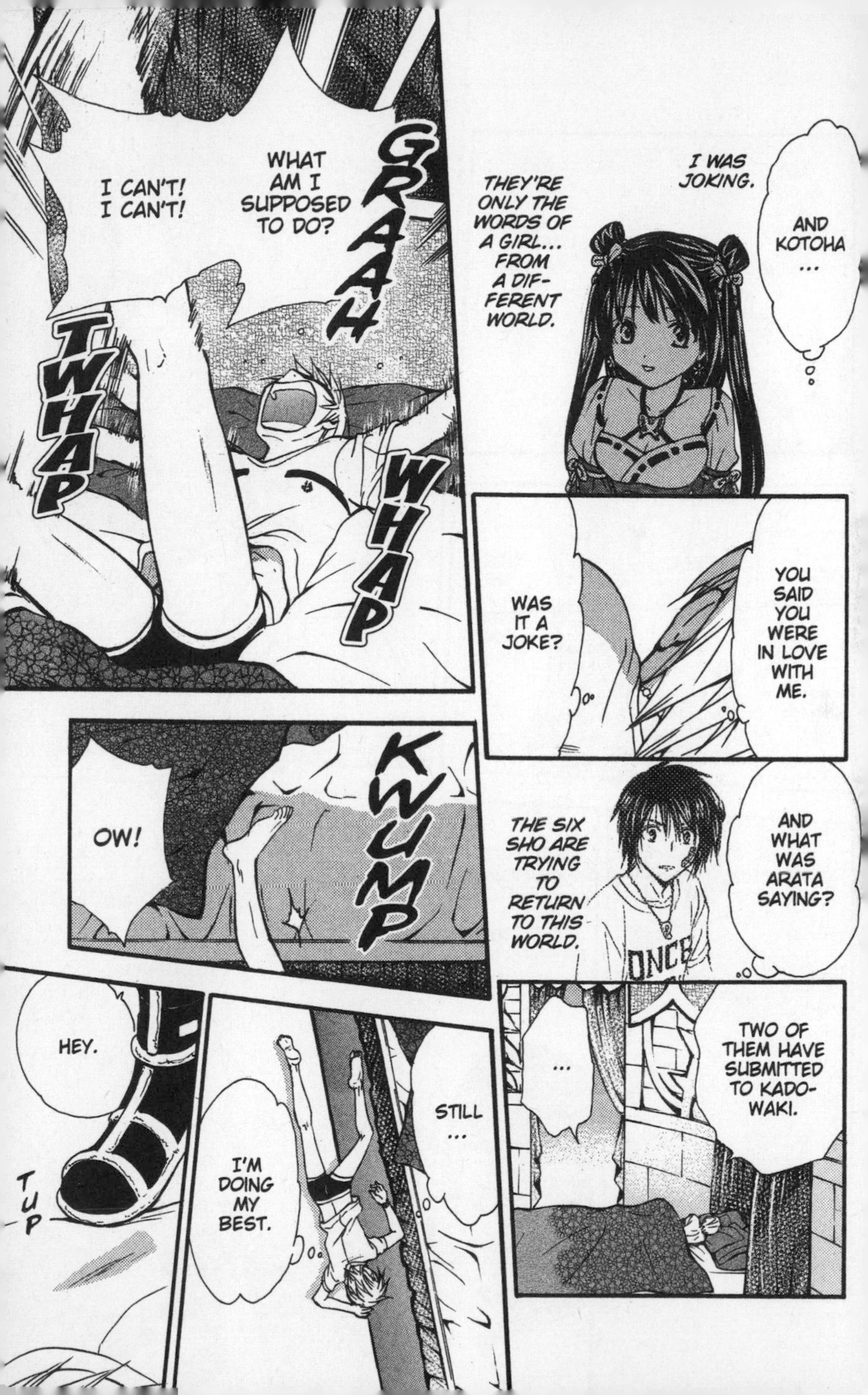
AND KOTOHA ...
I WAS JOKING.
THEY'RE ONLY THE WORDS OF A GIRL... FROM A DIF-FERENT WORLD.
YOU SAID YOU WERE IN LOVE WITH ME.
WAS IT A JOKE?
AND WHAT WAS ARATA SAYING?
THE SIX SHO ARE TRYING TO RETURN TO THIS WORLD.
GRAAH
WHAT AM I SUPPOSED TO DO?
I CAN'T! I CAN'T!
WHAP
TWHAP
KWUMP
OW!
TWO OF THEM HAVE SUBMITTED TO KADO-WAKI.
...
STILL ...
I'M DOING MY BEST.
HEY.
TUP

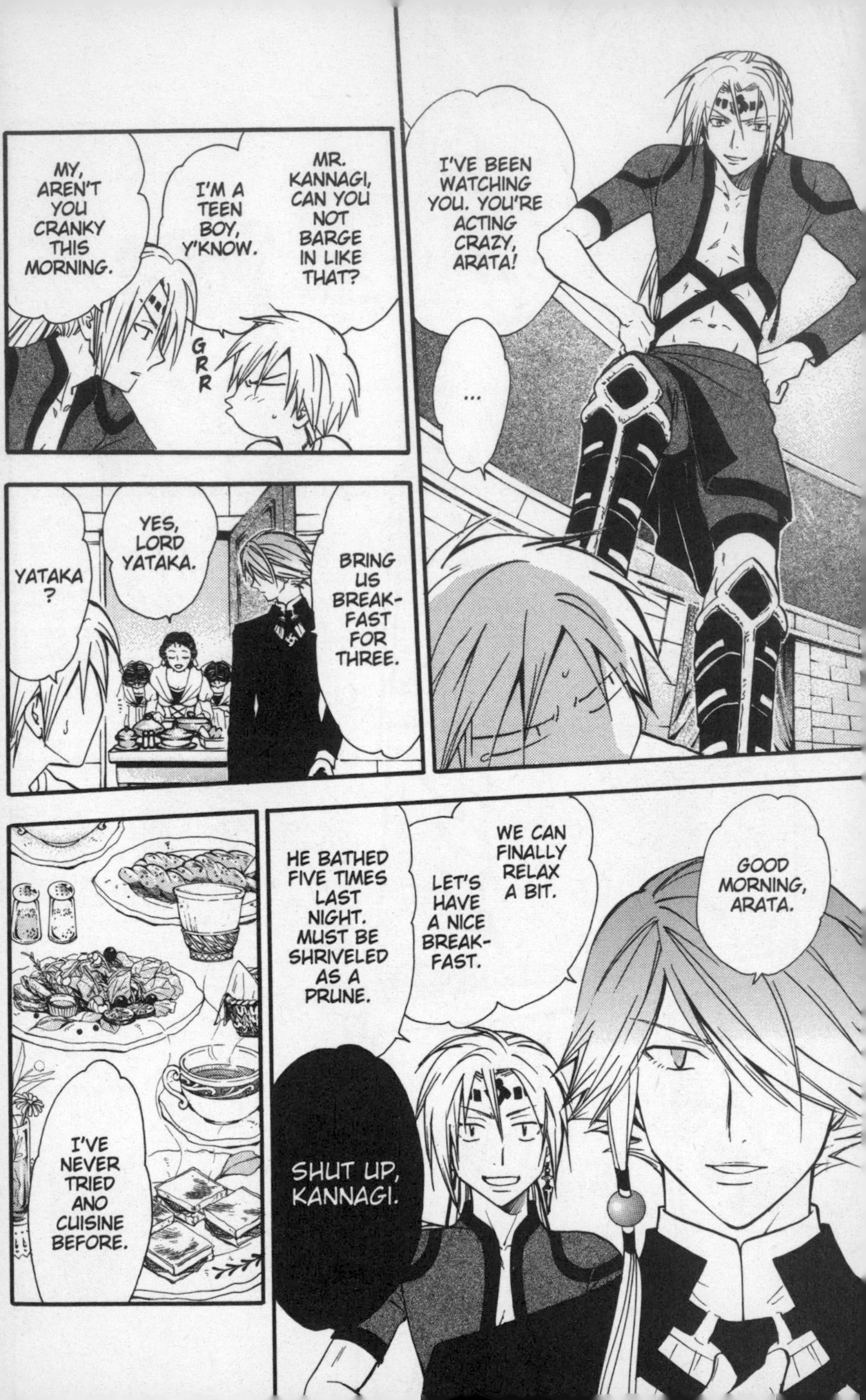
I'VE BEEN WATCHING YOU. YOU'RE ACTING CRAZY, ARATA!
...
MR. KANNAGI, CAN YOU NOT BARGE IN LIKE THAT?
I'M A TEEN BOY, Y'KNOW.
MY, AREN'T YOU CRANKY THIS MORNING.
GRR
BRING US BREAK-FAST FOR THREE.
YES, LORD YATAKA.
YATAKA?
GOOD MORNING, ARATA.
WE CAN FINALLY RELAX A BIT.
LET'S HAVE A NICE BREAK-FAST.
HE BATHED FIVE TIMES LAST NIGHT. MUST BE SHRIVELED AS A PRUNE.
SHUT UP, KANNAGI.
I'VE NEVER TRIED ANO CUISINE BEFORE.

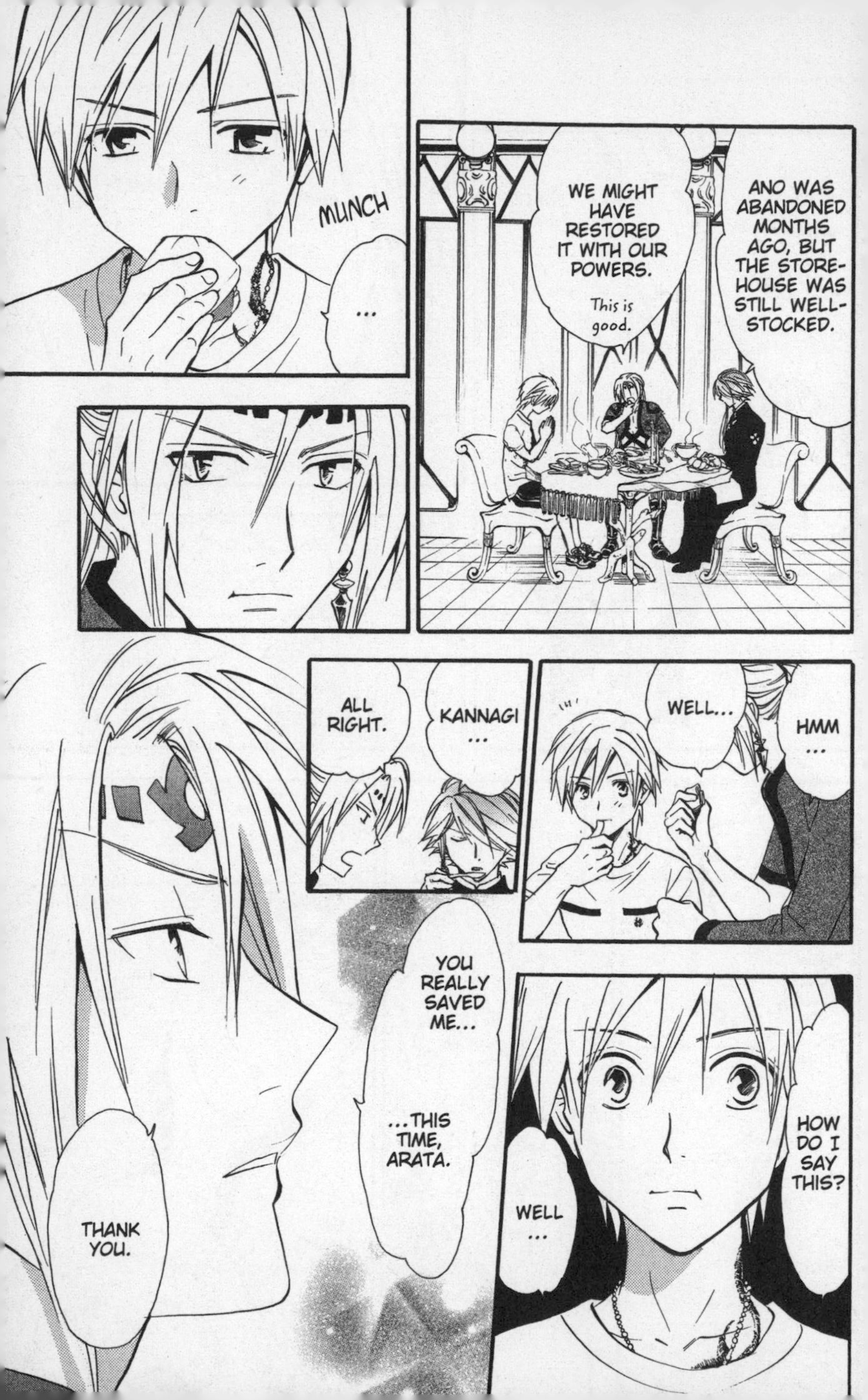
ANO WAS ABANDONED MONTHS AGO, BUT THE STOREHOUSE WAS STILL WELL-STOCKED.
WE MIGHT HAVE RESTORED IT WITH OUR POWERS.
This is good.
MUNCH
...
HMM...
WELL...
KANNAGI...
ALL RIGHT.
HOW DO I SAY THIS?
WELL...
YOU REALLY SAVED ME...
...THIS TIME, ARATA.
THANK YOU.

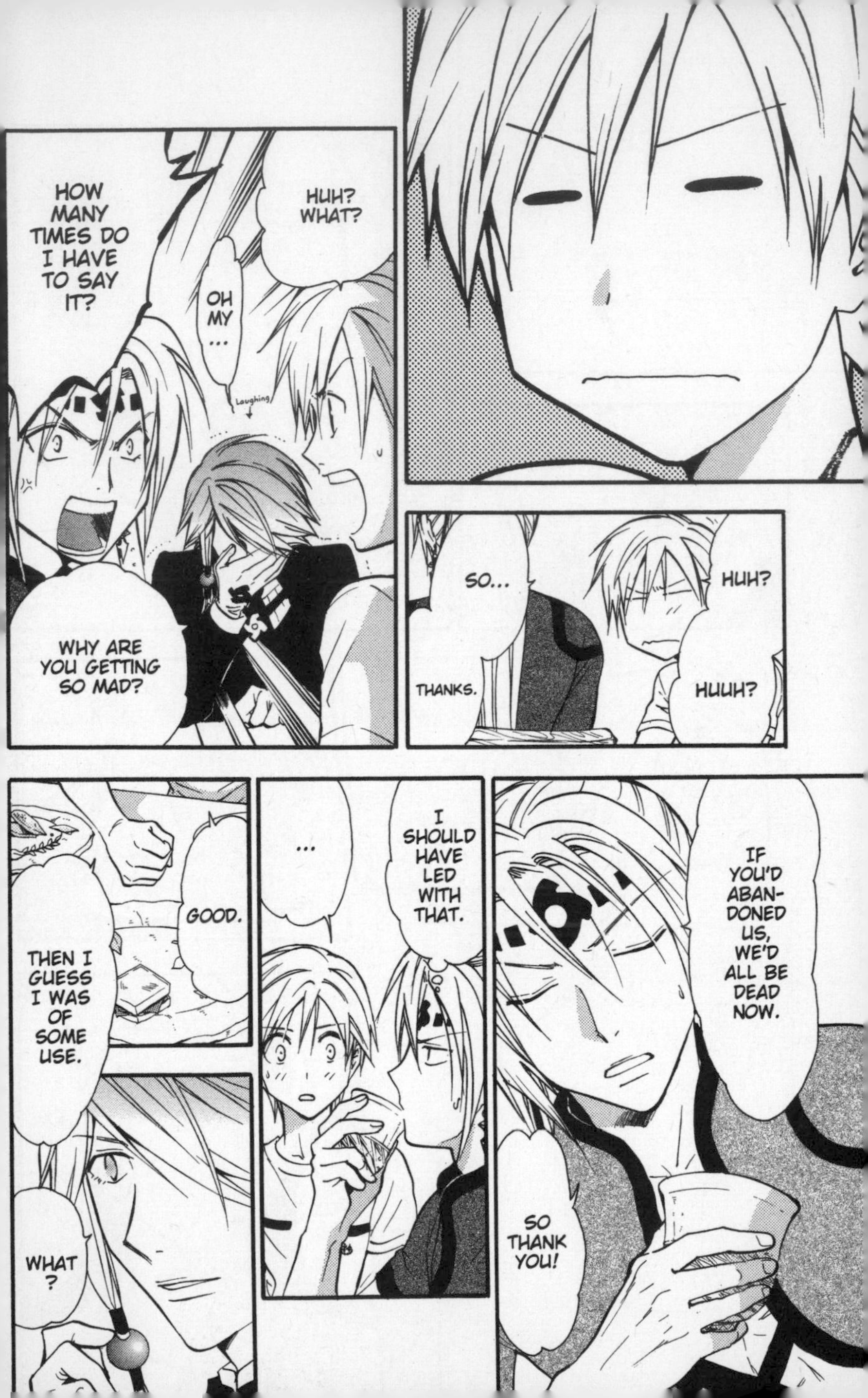
HUH?
SO...
HUUH?
THANKS.
HUH? WHAT?
HOW MANY TIMES DO I HAVE TO SAY IT?
OH MY ...
Laughing
WHY ARE YOU GETTING SO MAD?
IF YOU'D ABANDONED US, WE'D ALL BE DEAD NOW.
SO THANK YOU!
I SHOULD HAVE LED WITH THAT.
...
GOOD.
THEN I GUESS I WAS OF SOME USE.
WHAT ?

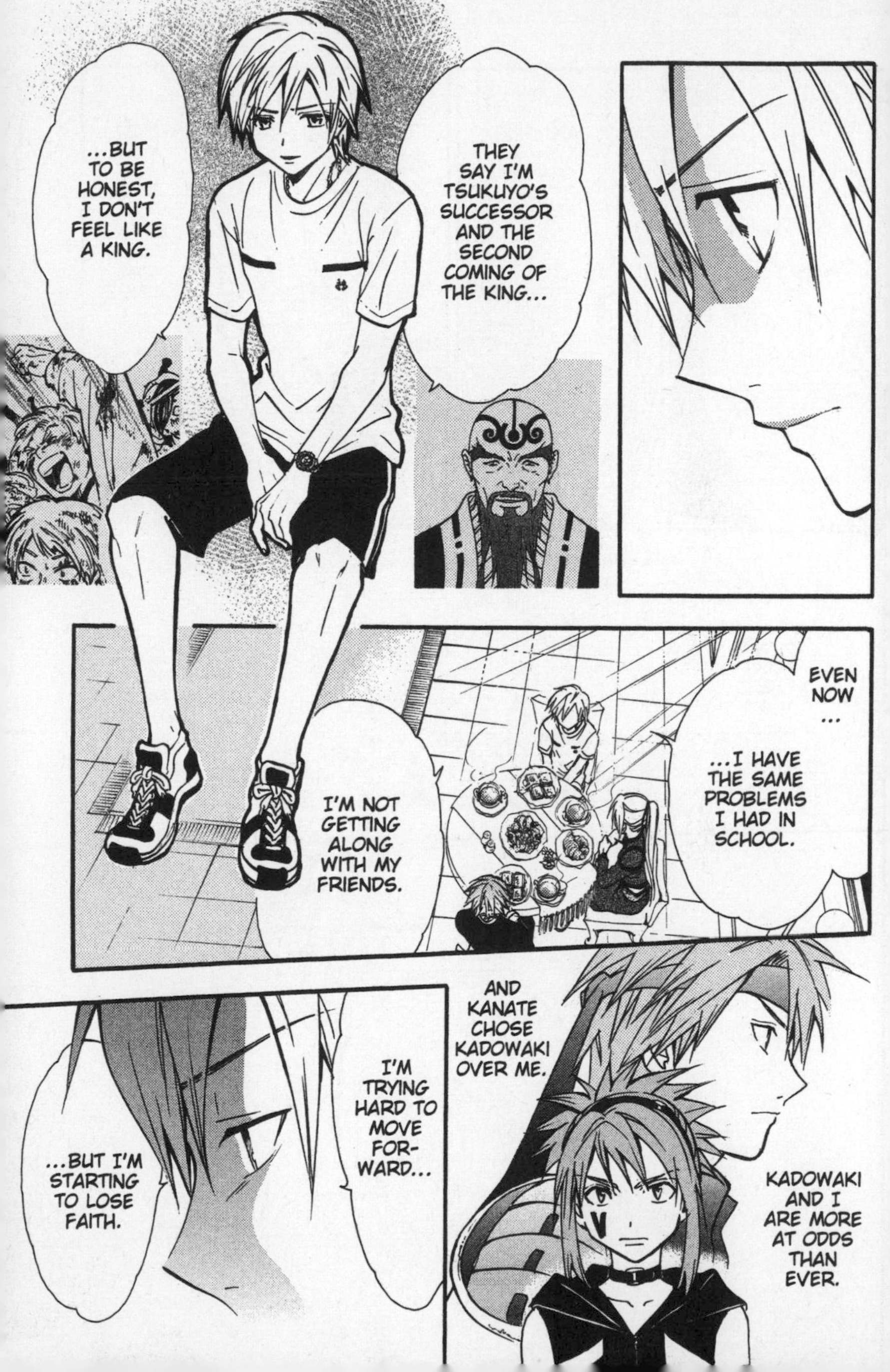
THEY SAY I'M TSUKUYO'S SUCCESSOR AND THE SECOND COMING OF THE KING...
...BUT TO BE HONEST, I DON'T FEEL LIKE A KING.
EVEN NOW...
...I HAVE THE SAME PROBLEMS I HAD IN SCHOOL.
I'M NOT GETTING ALONG WITH MY FRIENDS.
AND KANATE CHOSE KADOWAKI OVER ME.
KADOWAKI AND I ARE MORE AT ODDS THAN EVER.
I'M TRYING HARD TO MOVE FOR-WARD...
...BUT I'M STARTING TO LOSE FAITH.

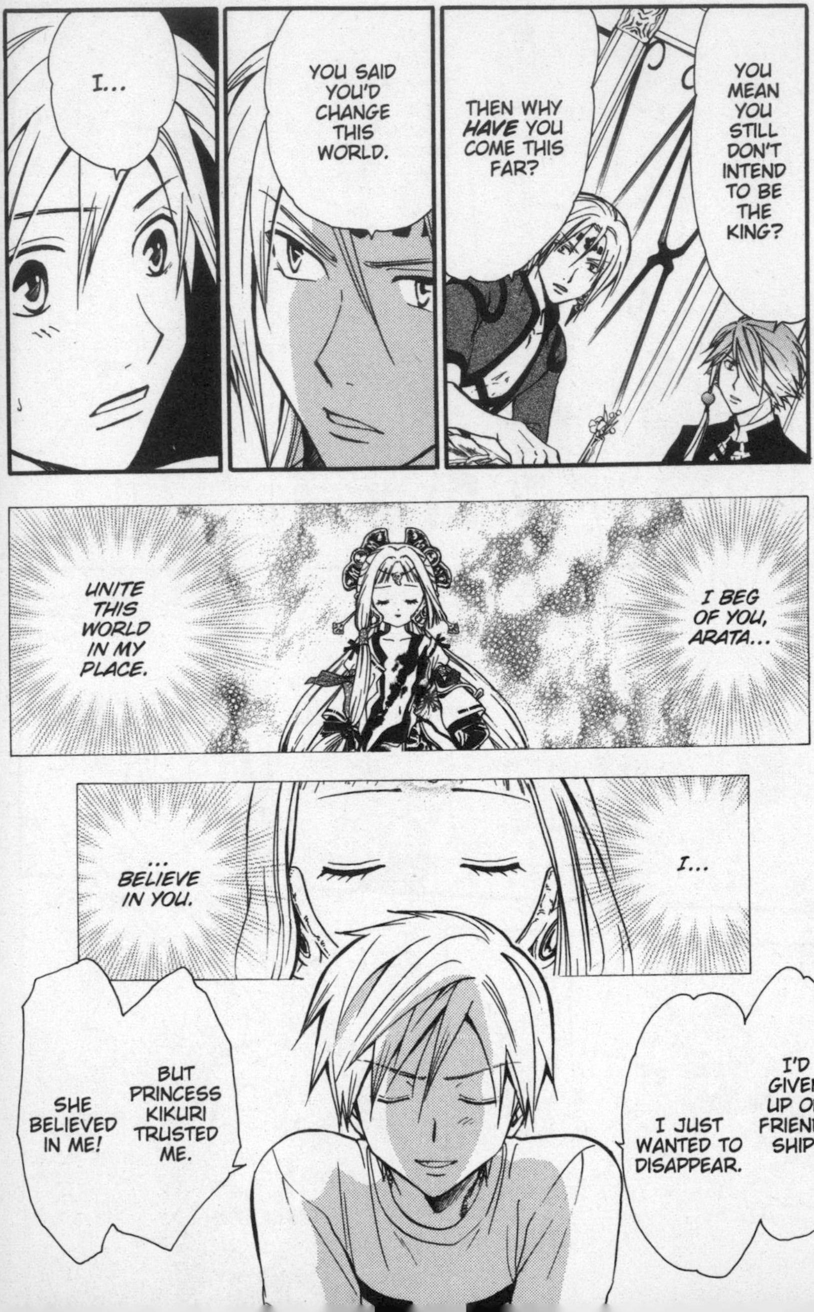
YOU MEAN YOU STILL DON'T INTEND TO BE THE KING?
THEN WHY HAVE YOU COME THIS FAR?
YOU SAID YOU'D CHANGE THIS WORLD.
I...
I BEG OF YOU, ARATA...
UNITE THIS WORLD IN MY PLACE.
I...
...BELIEVE IN YOU.
I'D GIVEN UP ON FRIEND-SHIP.
I JUST WANTED TO DISAPPEAR.
BUT PRINCESS KIKURI TRUSTED ME.
SHE BELIEVED IN ME!

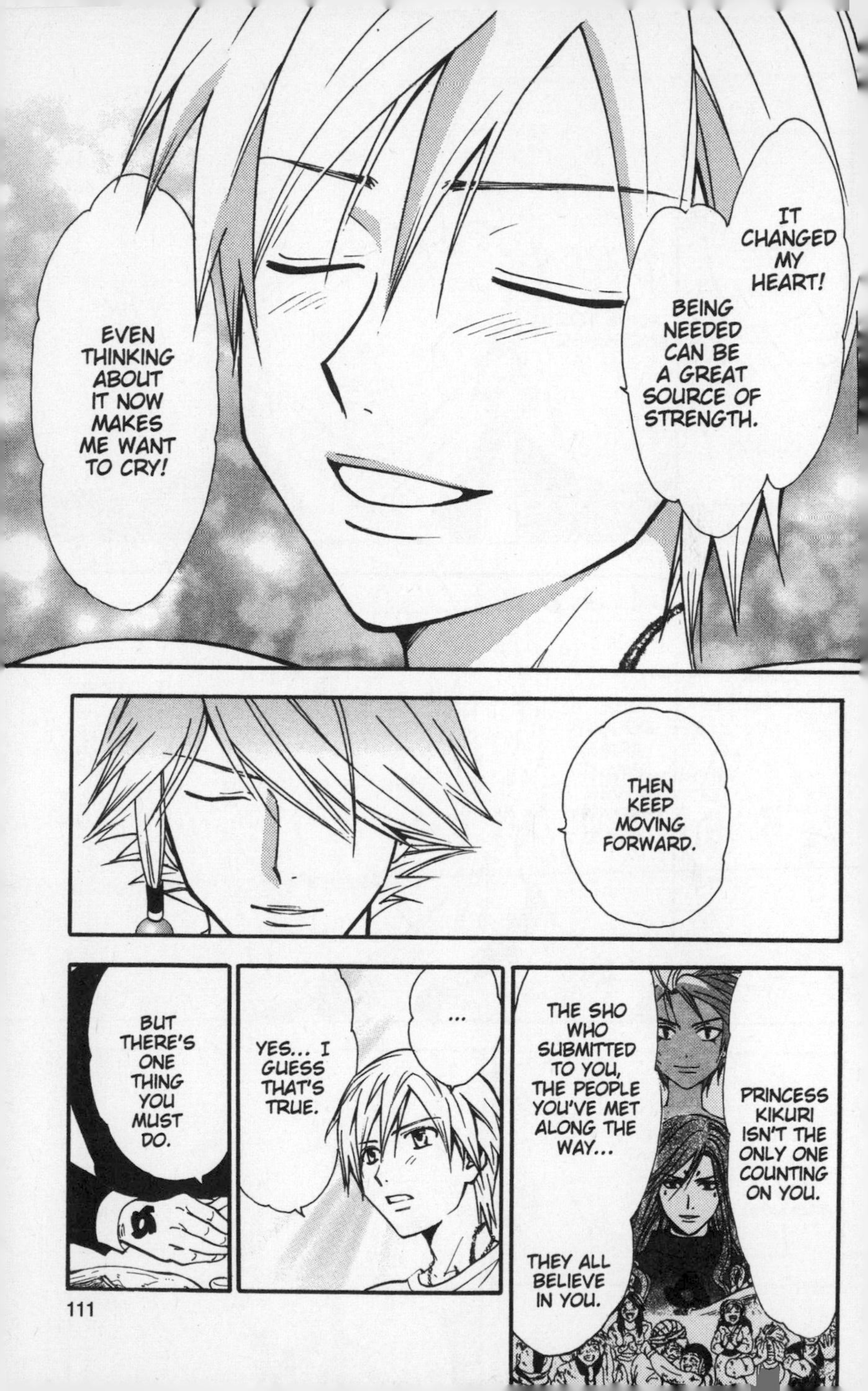
IT CHANGED MY HEART!
BEING NEEDED CAN BE A GREAT SOURCE OF STRENGTH.
EVEN THINKING ABOUT IT NOW MAKES ME WANT TO CRY!
THEN KEEP MOVING FORWARD.
PRINCESS KIKURI ISN'T THE ONLY ONE COUNTING ON YOU.
THE SHO WHO SUBMITTED TO YOU, THE PEOPLE YOU'VE MET ALONG THE WAY...
THEY ALL BELIEVE IN YOU.
...
YES... I GUESS THAT'S TRUE.
BUT THERE'S ONE THING YOU MUST DO.

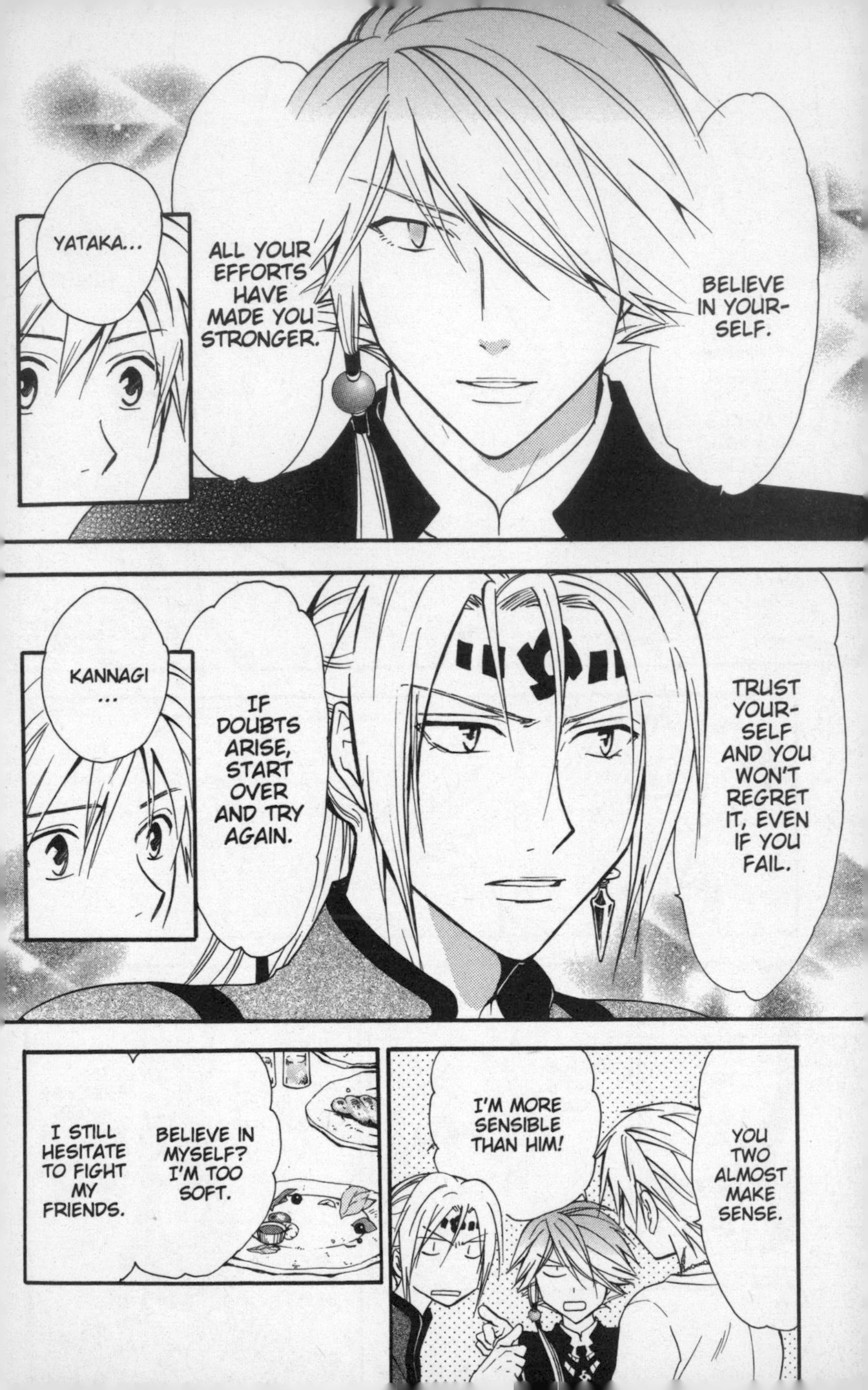
BELIEVE IN YOURSELF.
ALL YOUR EFFORTS HAVE MADE YOU STRONGER.
YATAKA...
TRUST YOURSELF AND YOU WON'T REGRET IT, EVEN IF YOU FAIL.
IF DOUBTS ARISE, START OVER AND TRY AGAIN.
KANNAGI...
YOU TWO ALMOST MAKE SENSE.
I'M MORE SENSIBLE THAN HIM!
BELIEVE IN MYSELF? I'M TOO SOFT.
I STILL HESITATE TO FIGHT MY FRIENDS.

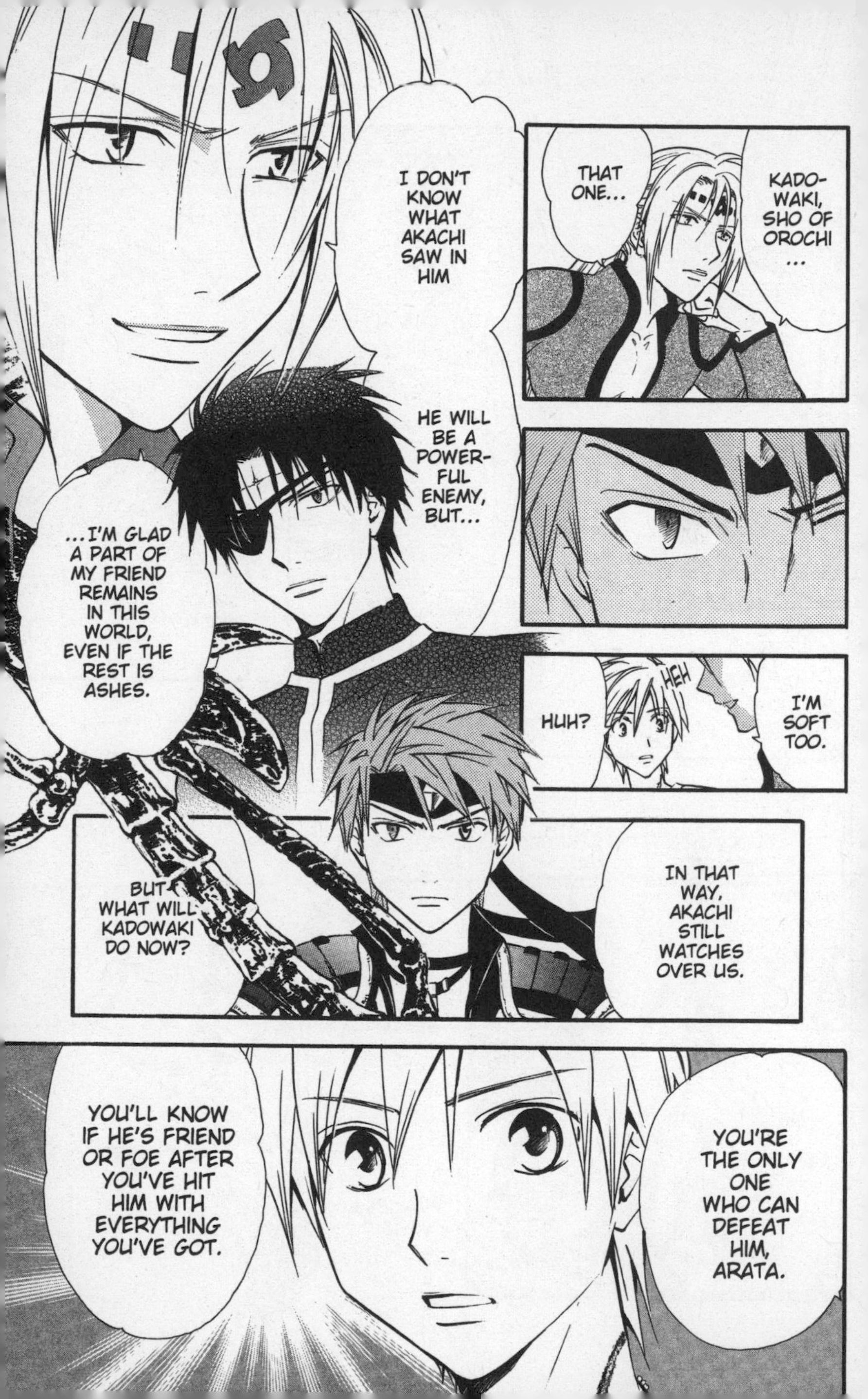
KADO-WAKI, SHO OF OROCHI ...
THAT ONE...
I'M SOFT TOO.
HEH
HUH?
I DON'T KNOW WHAT AKACHI SAW IN HIM
HE WILL BE A POWER-FUL ENEMY, BUT...
...I'M GLAD A PART OF MY FRIEND REMAINS IN THIS WORLD, EVEN IF THE REST IS ASHES.
IN THAT WAY, AKACHI STILL WATCHES OVER US.
BUT WHAT WILL KADOWAKI DO NOW?
YOU'RE THE ONLY ONE WHO CAN DEFEAT HIM, ARATA.
YOU'LL KNOW IF HE'S FRIEND OR FOE AFTER YOU'VE HIT HIM WITH EVERYTHING YOU'VE GOT.

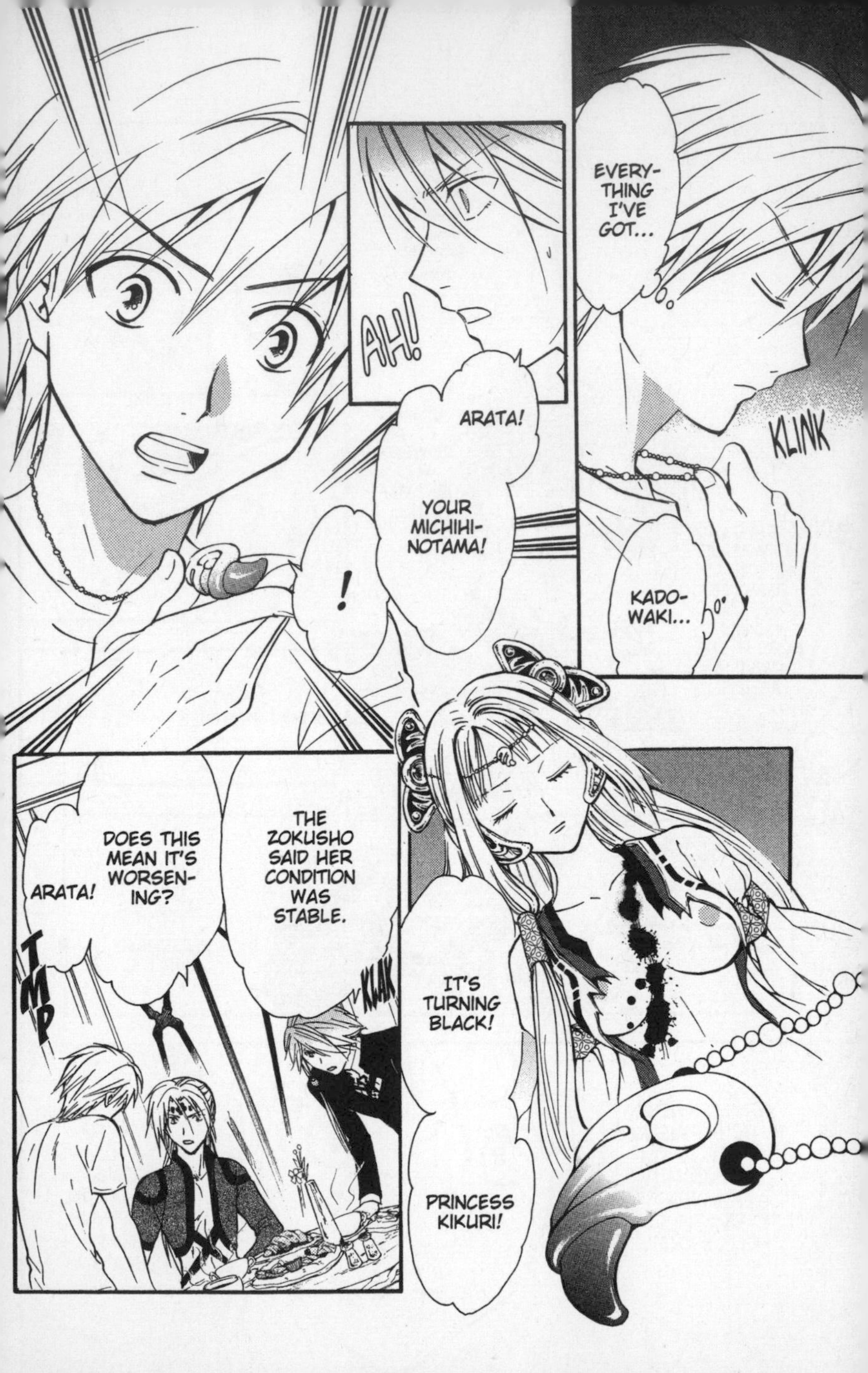
EVERY-THING I'VE GOT...
KLINK
KADO-WAKI...
AH!
ARATA!
YOUR MICHIHI-NOTAMA!
!
IT'S TURNING BLACK!
PRINCESS KIKURI!
THE ZOKUSHO SAID HER CONDITION WAS STABLE.
DOES THIS MEAN IT'S WORSEN-ING?
ARATA!
KLAK
TMP

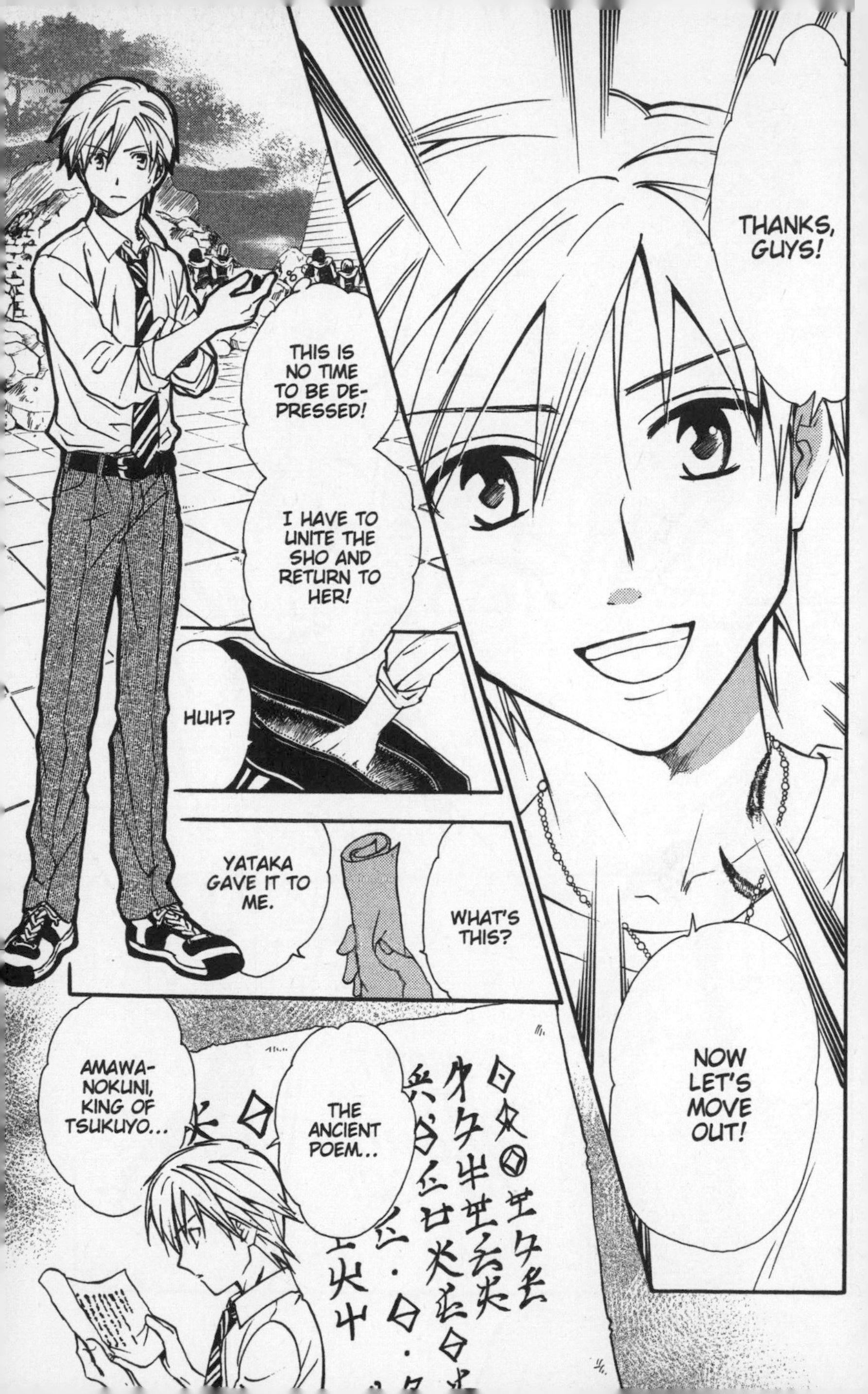
THANKS, GUYS!
NOW LET'S MOVE OUT!
THIS IS NO TIME TO BE DE-PRESSED!
I HAVE TO UNITE THE SHO AND RETURN TO HER!
HUH?
WHAT'S THIS?
YATAKA GAVE IT TO ME.
THE ANCIENT POEM...
AMAWA-NOKUNI, KING OF TSUKUYO...

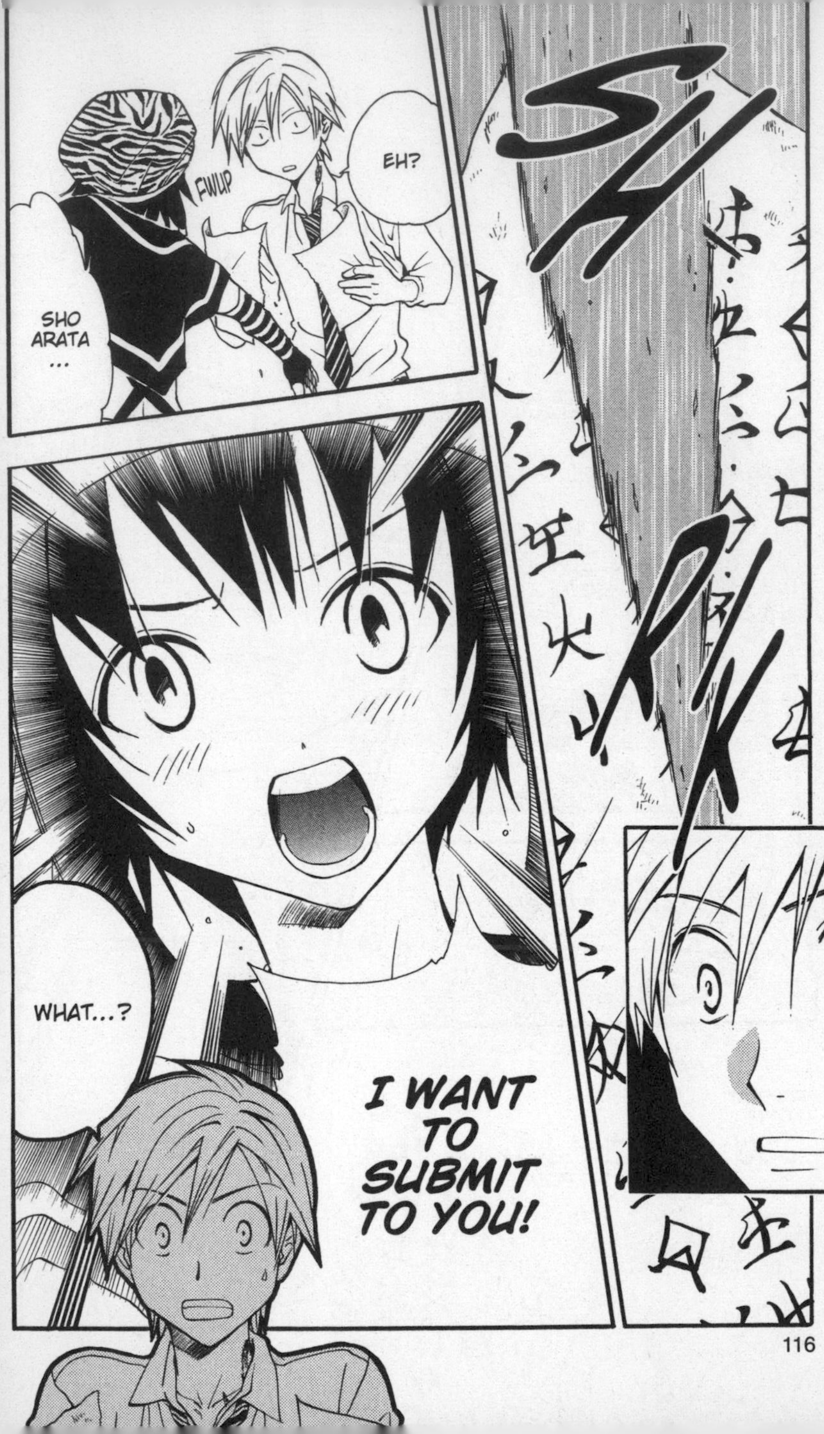
EH?
FWUP
SHO ARATA ...
I WANT TO SUBMIT TO YOU!
WHAT...?

CHAPTER 194

PLEASE

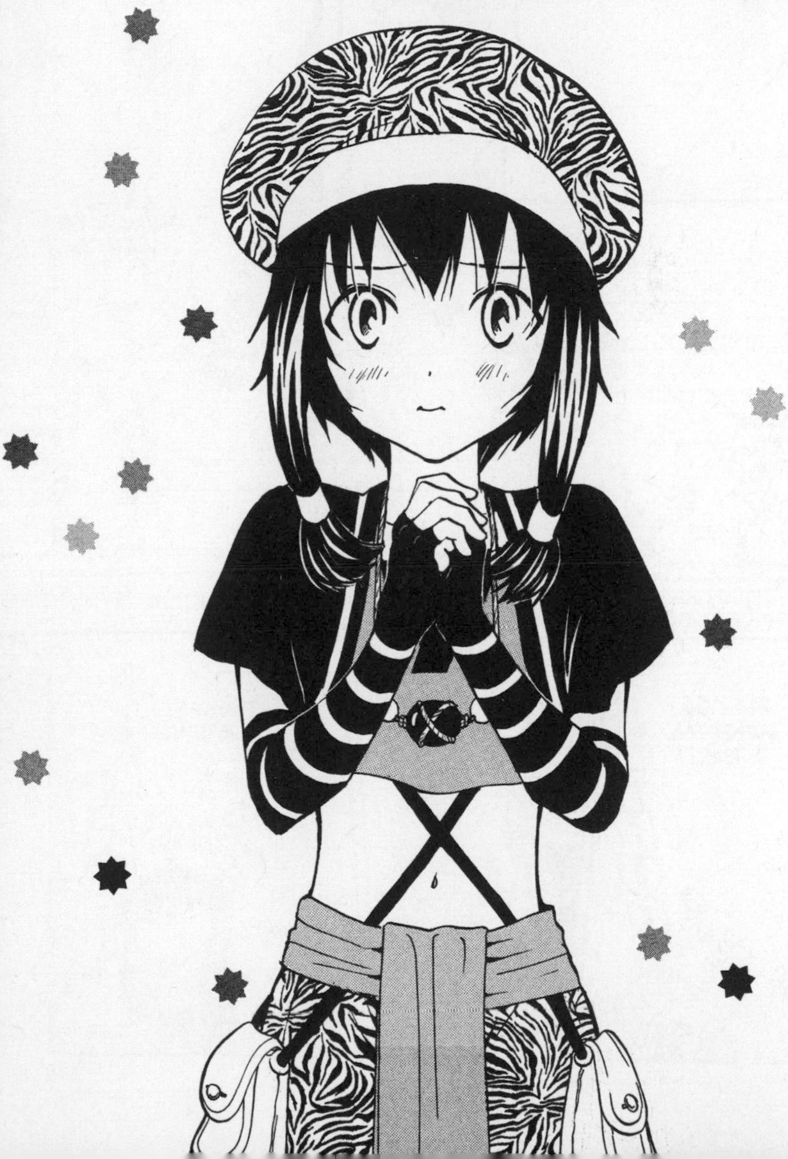

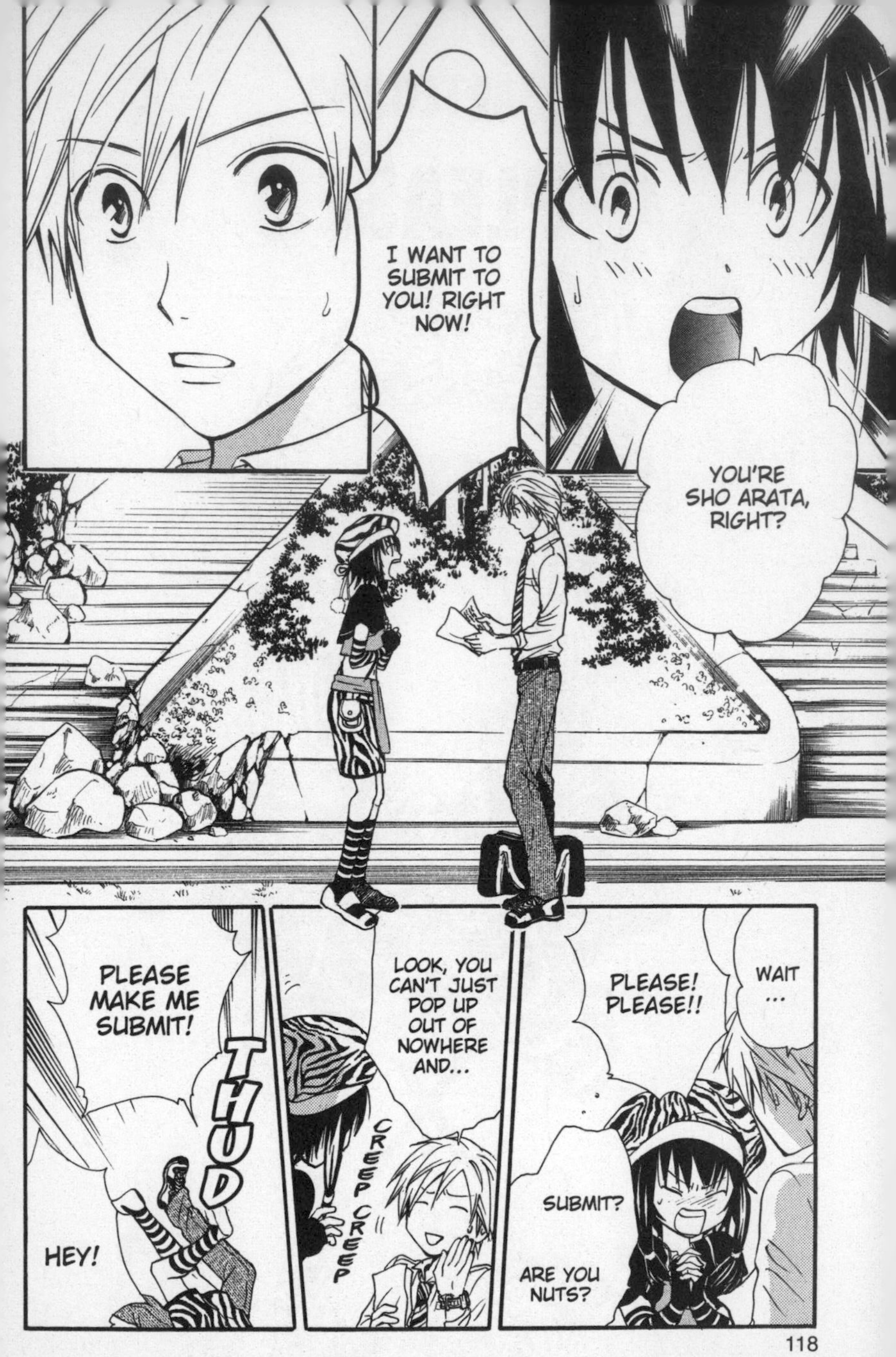
YOU'RE SHO ARATA, RIGHT?
I WANT TO SUBMIT TO YOU! RIGHT NOW!
WAIT ...
PLEASE! PLEASE!!
SUBMIT?
ARE YOU NUTS?
LOOK, YOU CAN'T JUST POP UP OUT OF NOWHERE AND...
CREEP CREEP
PLEASE MAKE ME SUBMIT!
THUD
HEY!

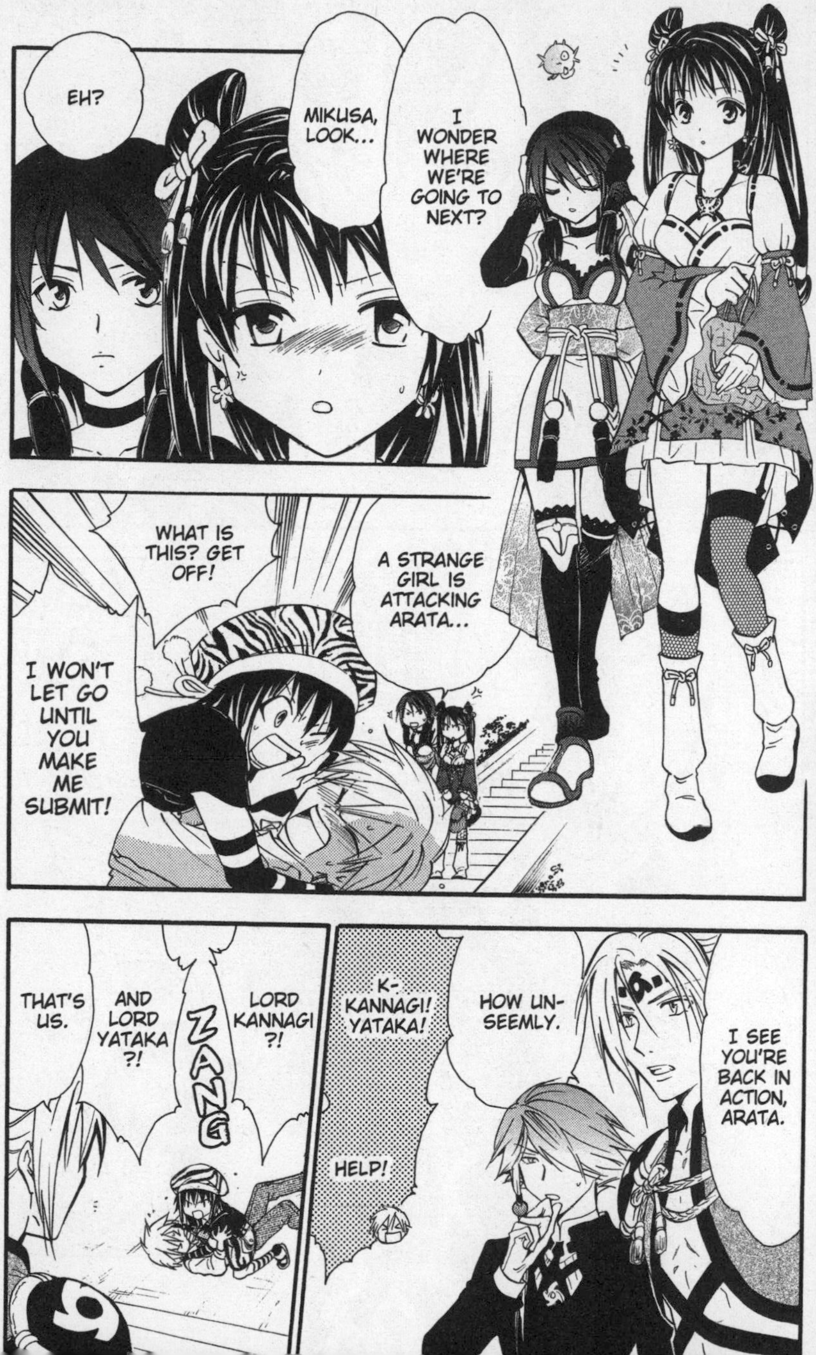
I WONDER WHERE WE'RE GOING TO NEXT?
MIKUSA, LOOK...
EH?
A STRANGE GIRL IS ATTACKING ARATA...
WHAT IS THIS? GET OFF!
I WON'T LET GO UNTIL YOU MAKE ME SUBMIT!
I SEE YOU'RE BACK IN ACTION, ARATA.
HOW UN-SEEMLY.
K-KANNAGI! YATAKA!
HELP!
LORD KANNAGI?!
ZANG
AND LORD YATAKA?!
THAT'S US.

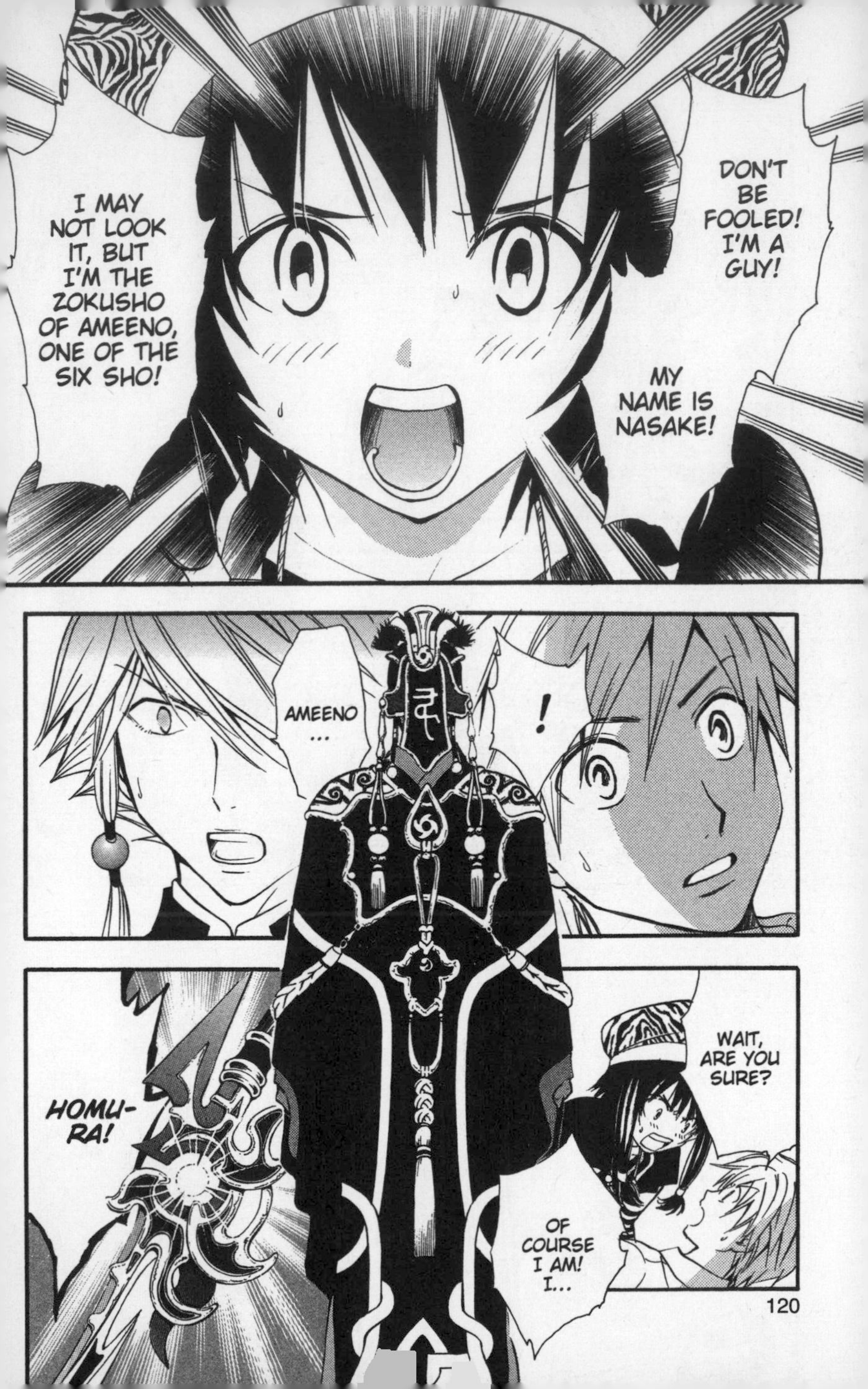
DON'T BE FOOLED! I'M A GUY!
MY NAME IS NASAKE!
I MAY NOT LOOK IT, BUT I'M THE ZOKUSHO OF AMEENO, ONE OF THE SIX SHO!
!
AMEENO ...
WAIT, ARE YOU SURE?
OF COURSE I AM! I...
HOMU-RA!

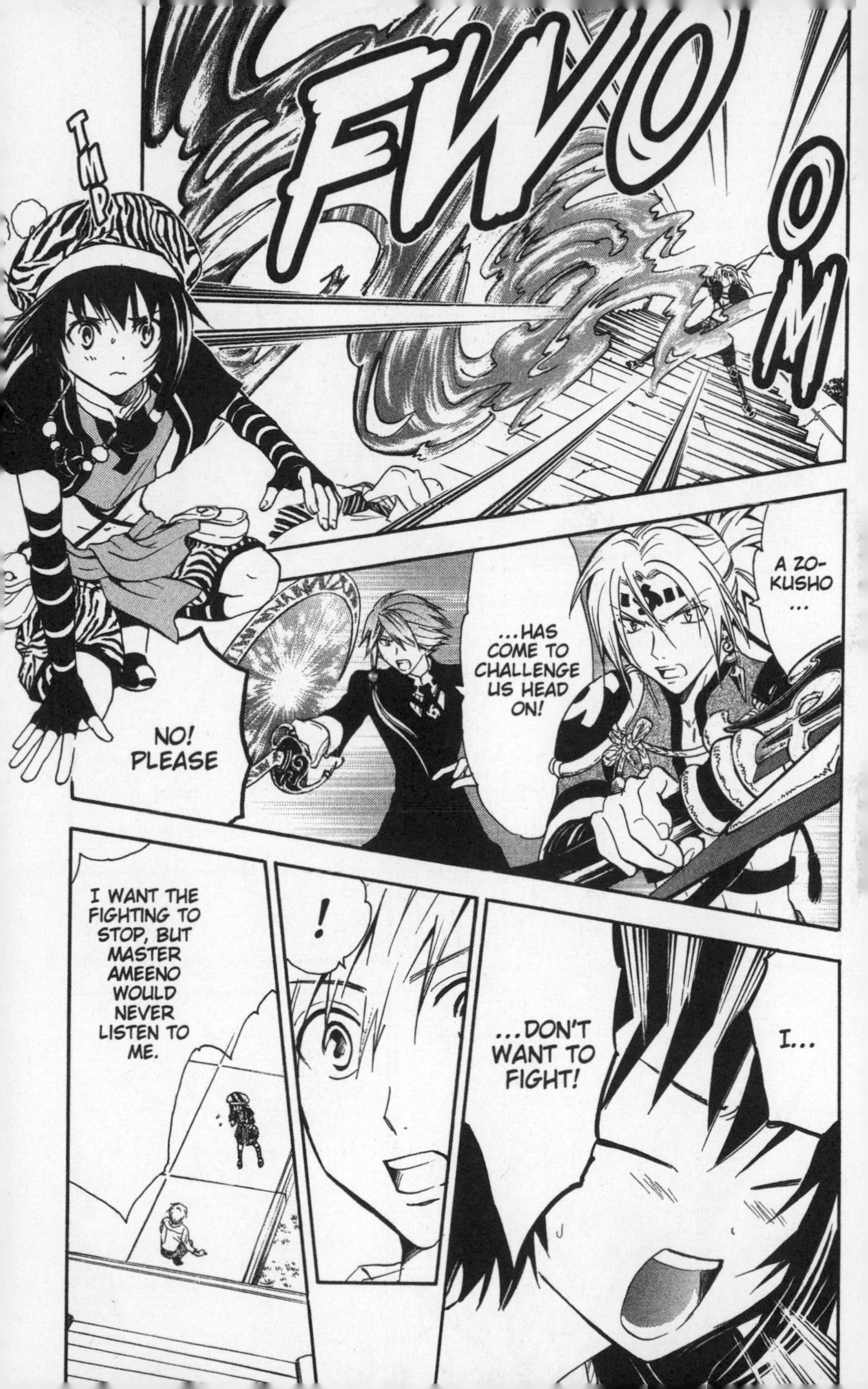
FWOOOM
TMP
A ZO-KUSHO...
...HAS COME TO CHALLENGE US HEAD ON!
NO! PLEASE
I...
...DON'T WANT TO FIGHT!
!
I WANT THE FIGHTING TO STOP, BUT MASTER AMEENO WOULD NEVER LISTEN TO ME.

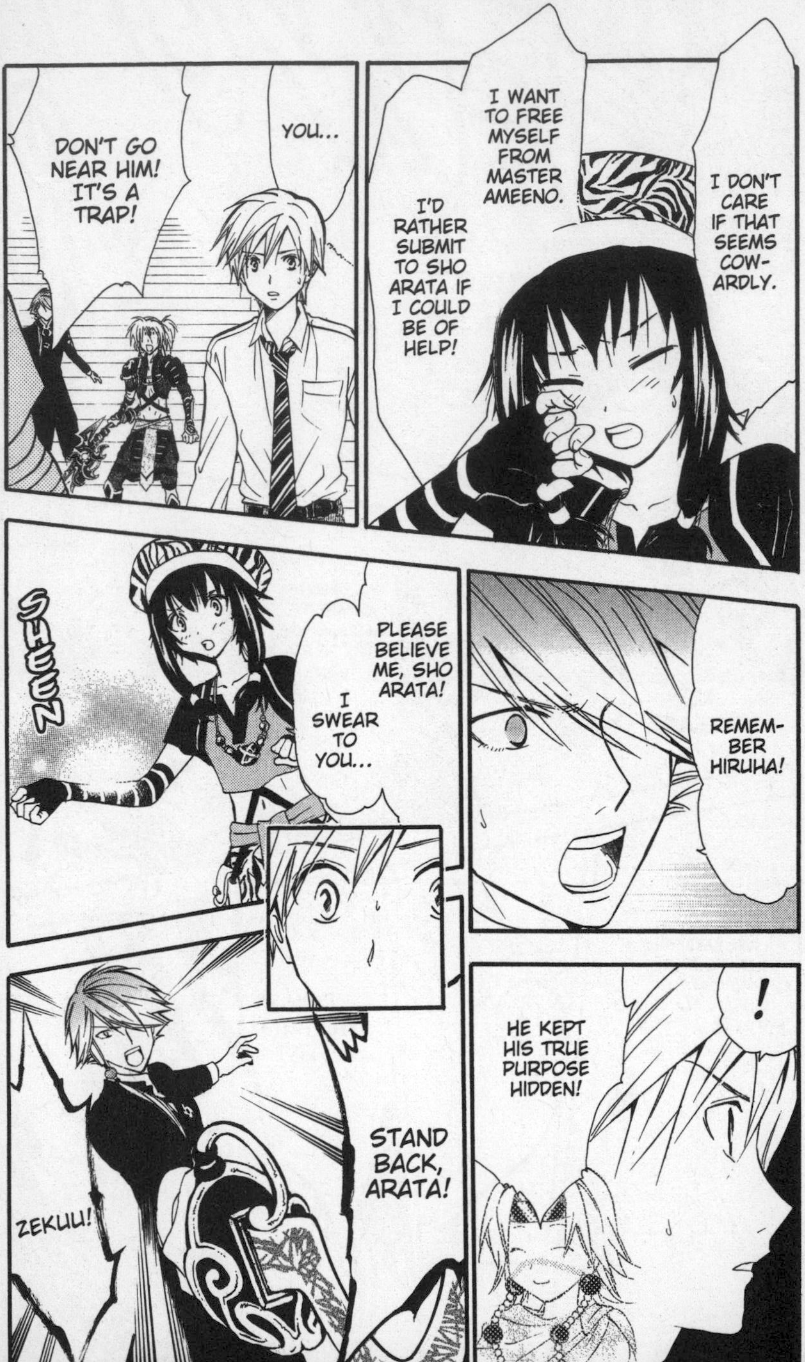
I DON'T CARE IF THAT SEEMS COW-ARDLY.
I WANT TO FREE MYSELF FROM MASTER AMEENO.
I'D RATHER SUBMIT TO SHO ARATA IF I COULD BE OF HELP!
YOU...
DON'T GO NEAR HIM! IT'S A TRAP!
REMEM-BER HIRUHA!
PLEASE BELIEVE ME, SHO ARATA!
I SWEAR TO YOU...
SHEEN
!
HE KEPT HIS TRUE PURPOSE HIDDEN!
STAND BACK, ARATA!
ZEKUU!

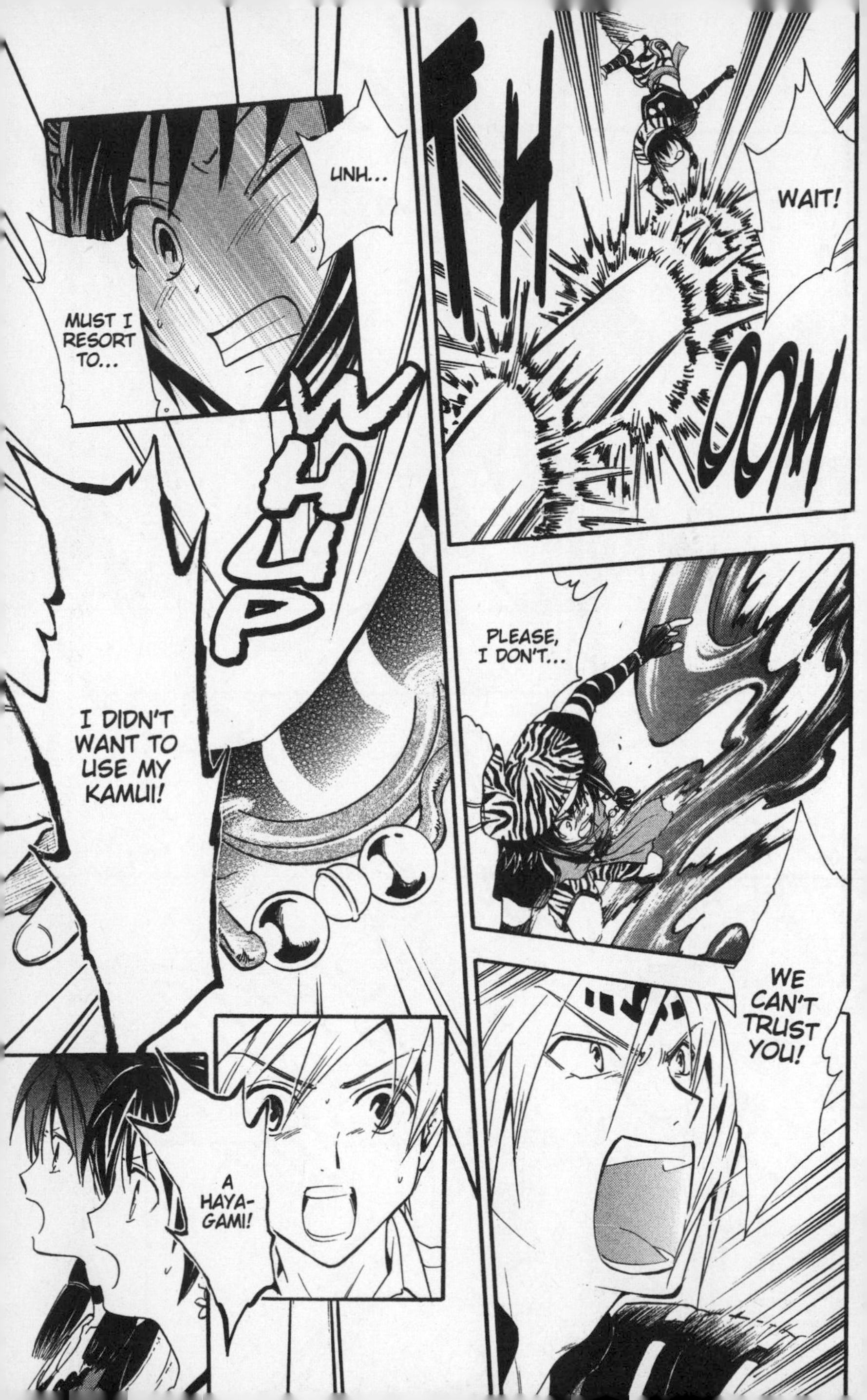
WAIT!
THOOM
UNH…
MUST I RESORT TO…
PLEASE, I DON'T…
WHUP
I DIDN'T WANT TO USE MY KAMUI!
WE CAN'T TRUST YOU!
A HAYA-GAMI!

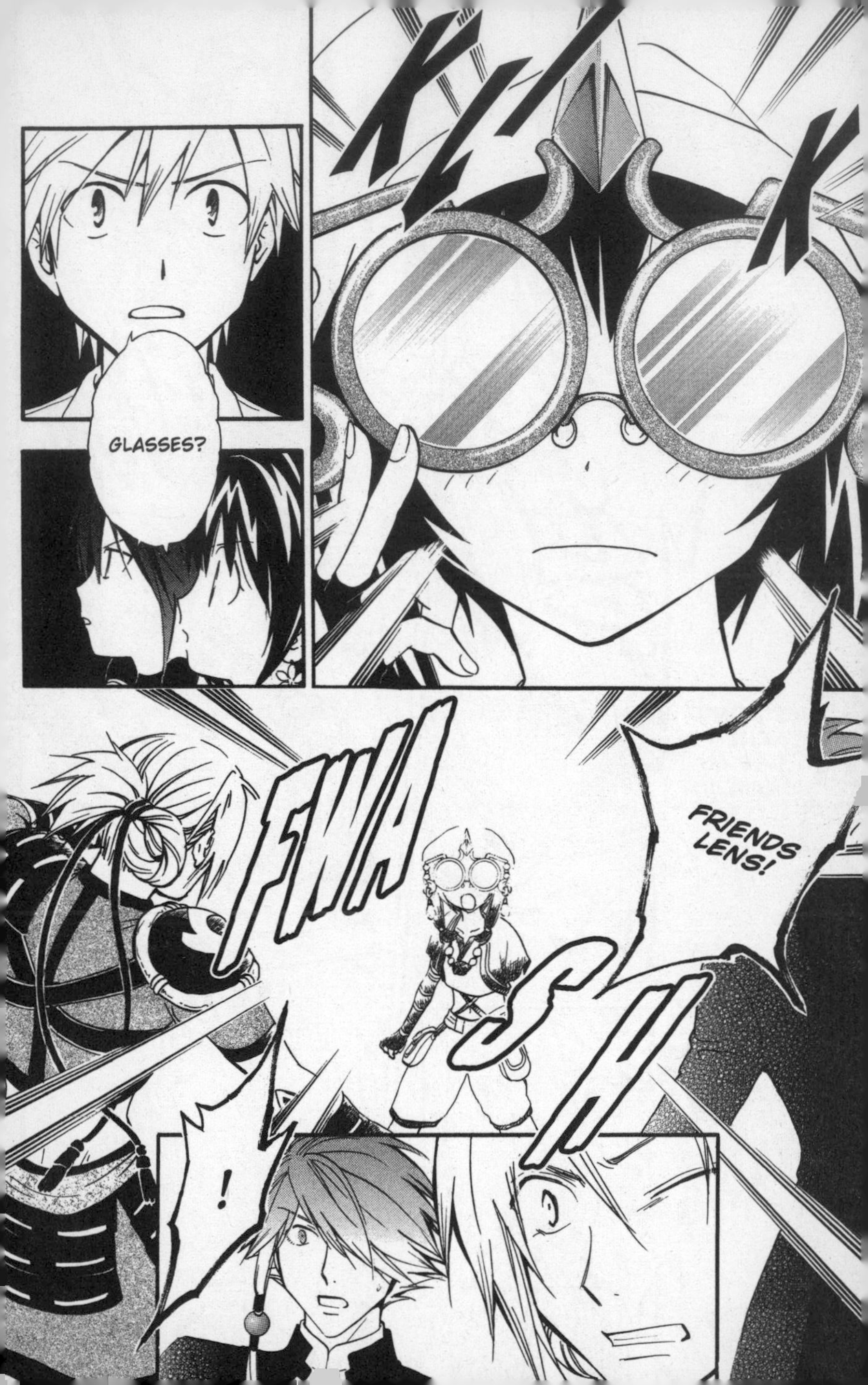
KLIK
GLASSES?
FRIENDS LENS!
FWA
SCH
!

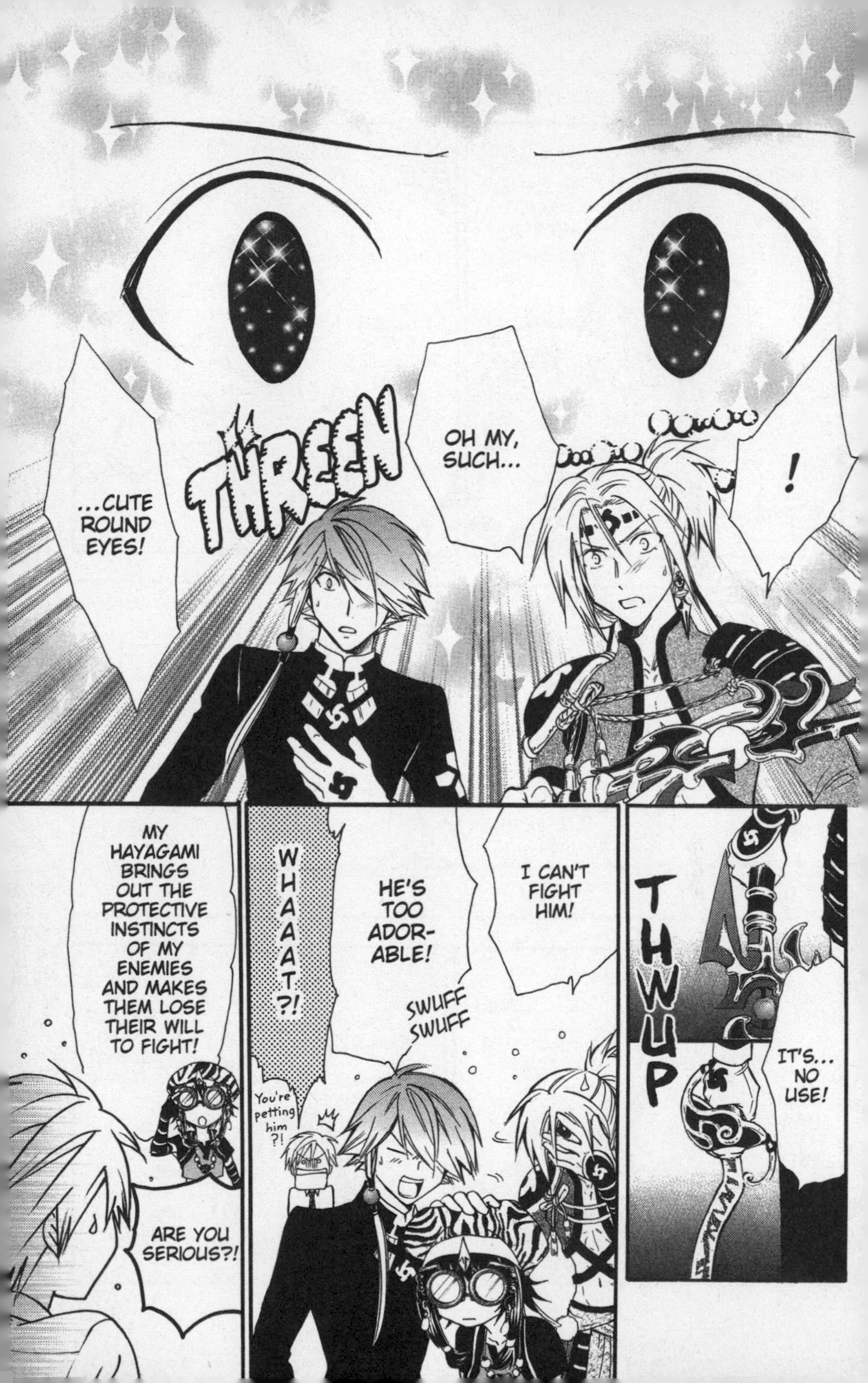
!
OH MY, SUCH...
THREEN
...CUTE ROUND EYES!
THWUP
IT'S... NO USE!
I CAN'T FIGHT HIM!
HE'S TOO ADORABLE!
WHAAAAT?!
SWUFF SWUFF
You're petting him?!
MY HAYAGAMI BRINGS OUT THE PROTECTIVE INSTINCTS OF MY ENEMIES AND MAKES THEM LOSE THEIR WILL TO FIGHT!
ARE YOU SERIOUS?!

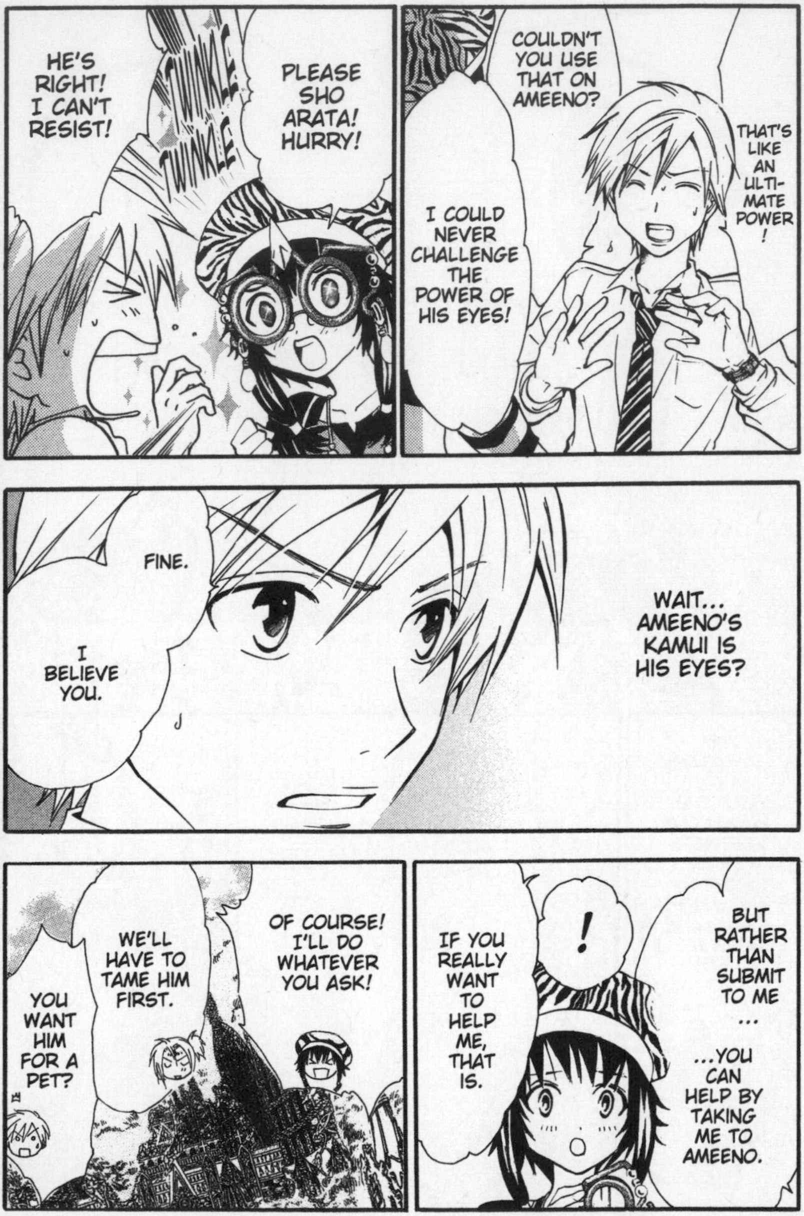
COULDN'T YOU USE THAT ON AMEENO?
THAT'S LIKE AN ULTI-MATE POWER!
I COULD NEVER CHALLENGE THE POWER OF HIS EYES!
PLEASE SHO ARATA! HURRY!
TWINKLE TWINKLE
HE'S RIGHT! I CAN'T RESIST!
WAIT... AMEENO'S KAMUI IS HIS EYES?
FINE.
I BELIEVE YOU.
BUT RATHER THAN SUBMIT TO ME ...
...YOU CAN HELP BY TAKING ME TO AMEENO.
!
IF YOU REALLY WANT TO HELP ME, THAT IS.
OF COURSE! I'LL DO WHATEVER YOU ASK!
WE'LL HAVE TO TAME HIM FIRST.
YOU WANT HIM FOR A PET?

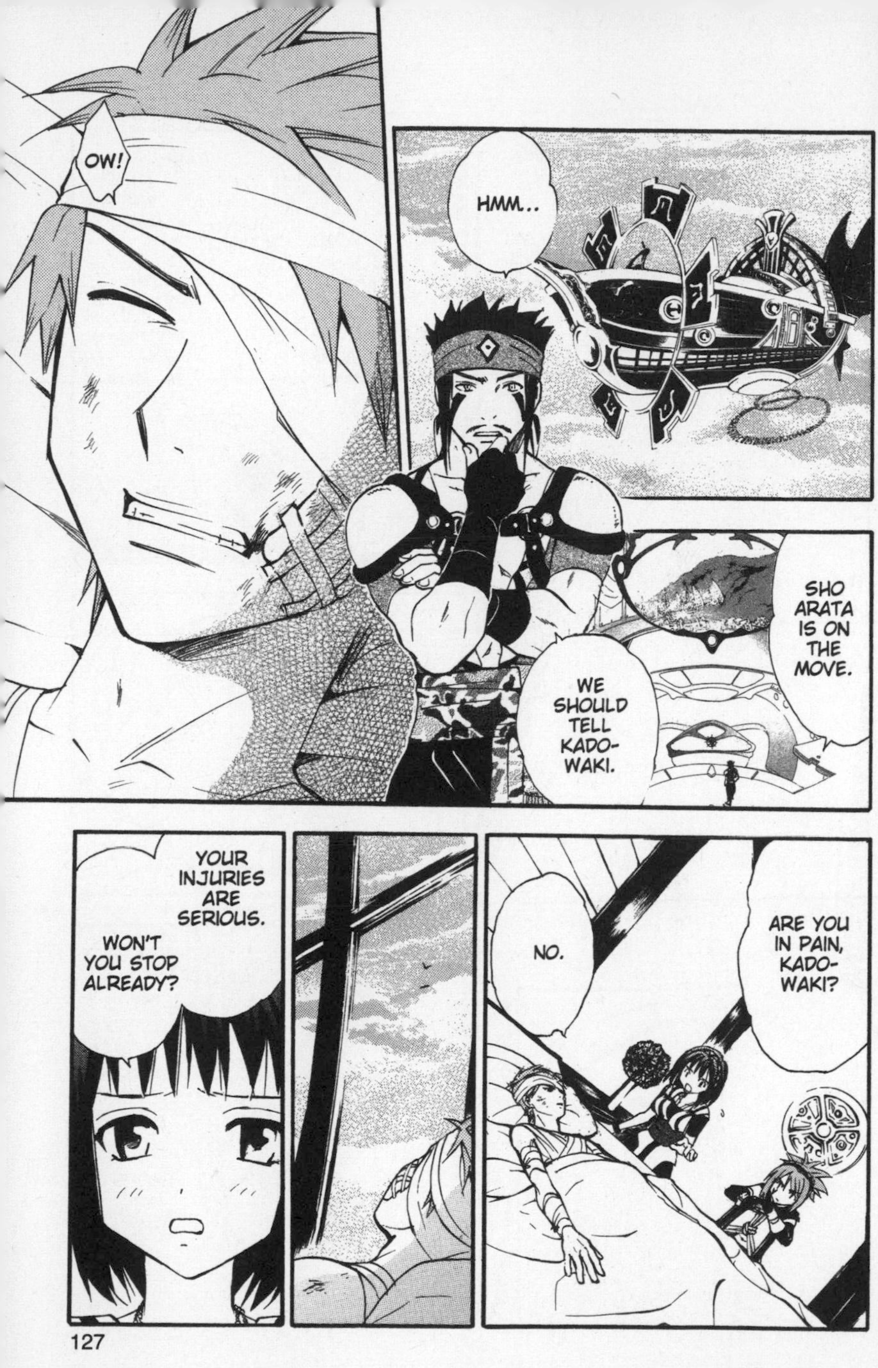
HMM...
SHO ARATA IS ON THE MOVE.
WE SHOULD TELL KADO-WAKI.
OW!
ARE YOU IN PAIN, KADO-WAKI?
NO.
YOUR INJURIES ARE SERIOUS.
WON'T YOU STOP ALREADY?

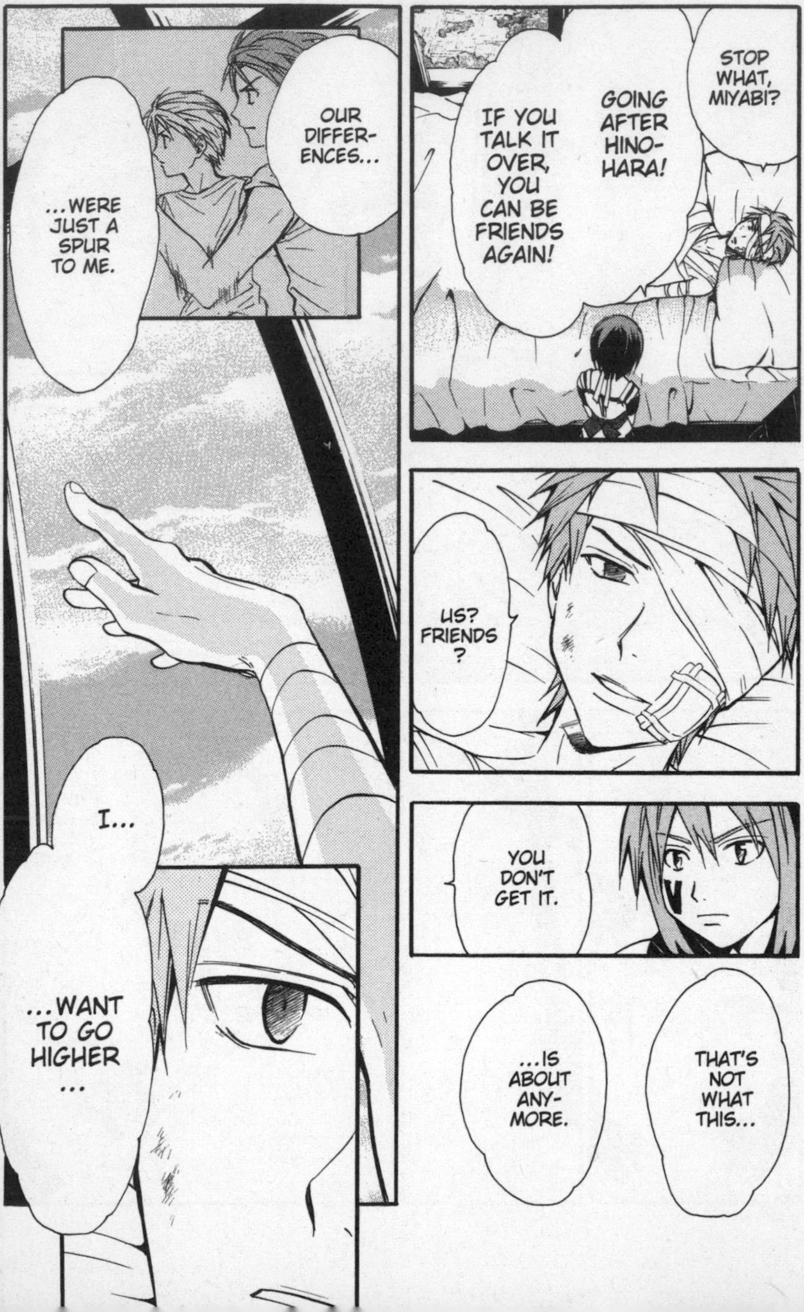
STOP WHAT, MIYABI?
GOING AFTER HINO-HARA!
IF YOU TALK IT OVER, YOU CAN BE FRIENDS AGAIN!
US? FRIENDS?
YOU DON'T GET IT.
THAT'S NOT WHAT THIS...
...IS ABOUT ANY-MORE.
OUR DIFFER-ENCES...
...WERE JUST A SPUR TO ME.
I...
...WANT TO GO HIGHER ...

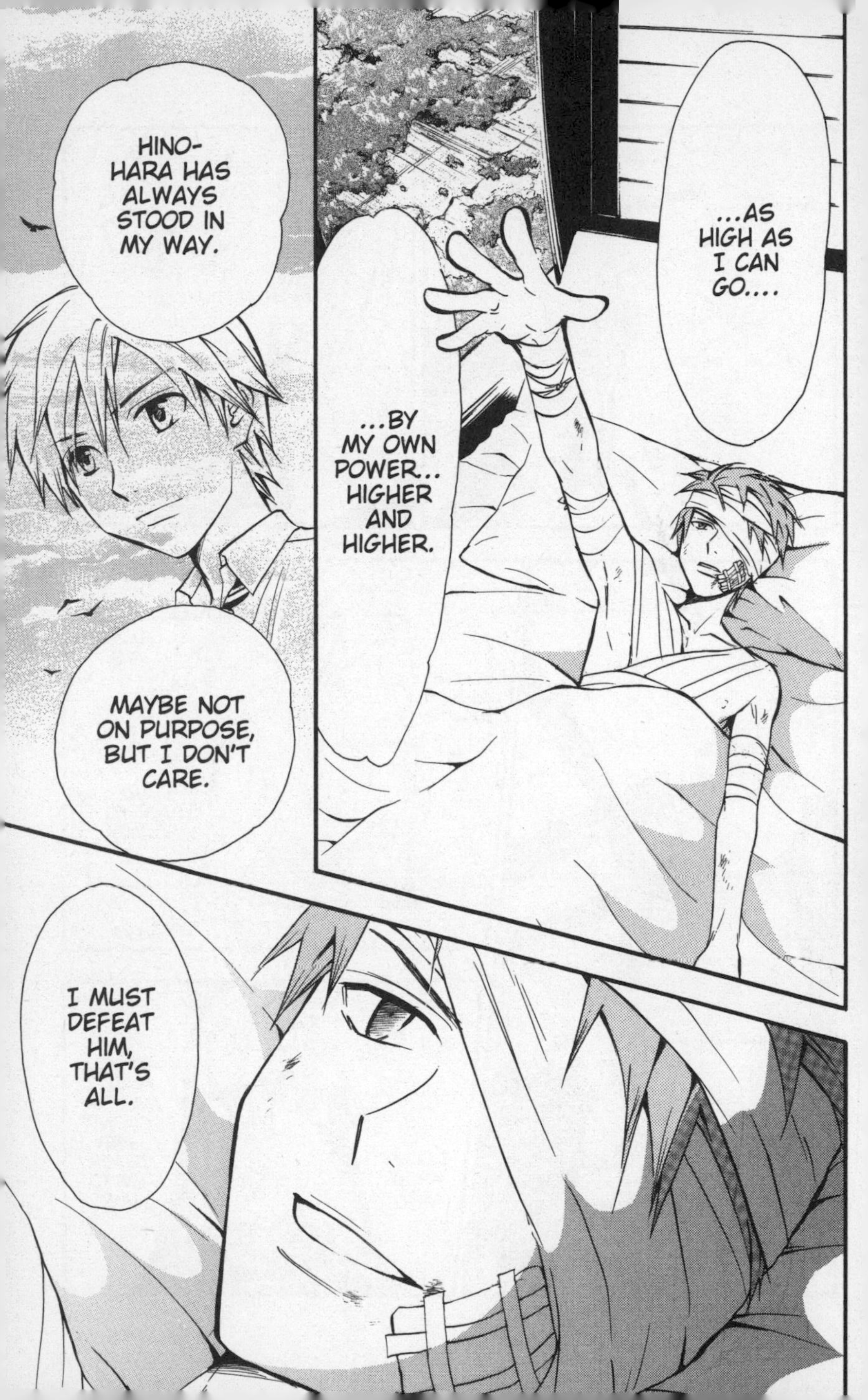
...AS HIGH AS I CAN GO....
...BY MY OWN POWER... HIGHER AND HIGHER.
HINO-HARA HAS ALWAYS STOOD IN MY WAY.
MAYBE NOT ON PURPOSE, BUT I DON'T CARE.
I MUST DEFEAT HIM, THAT'S ALL.

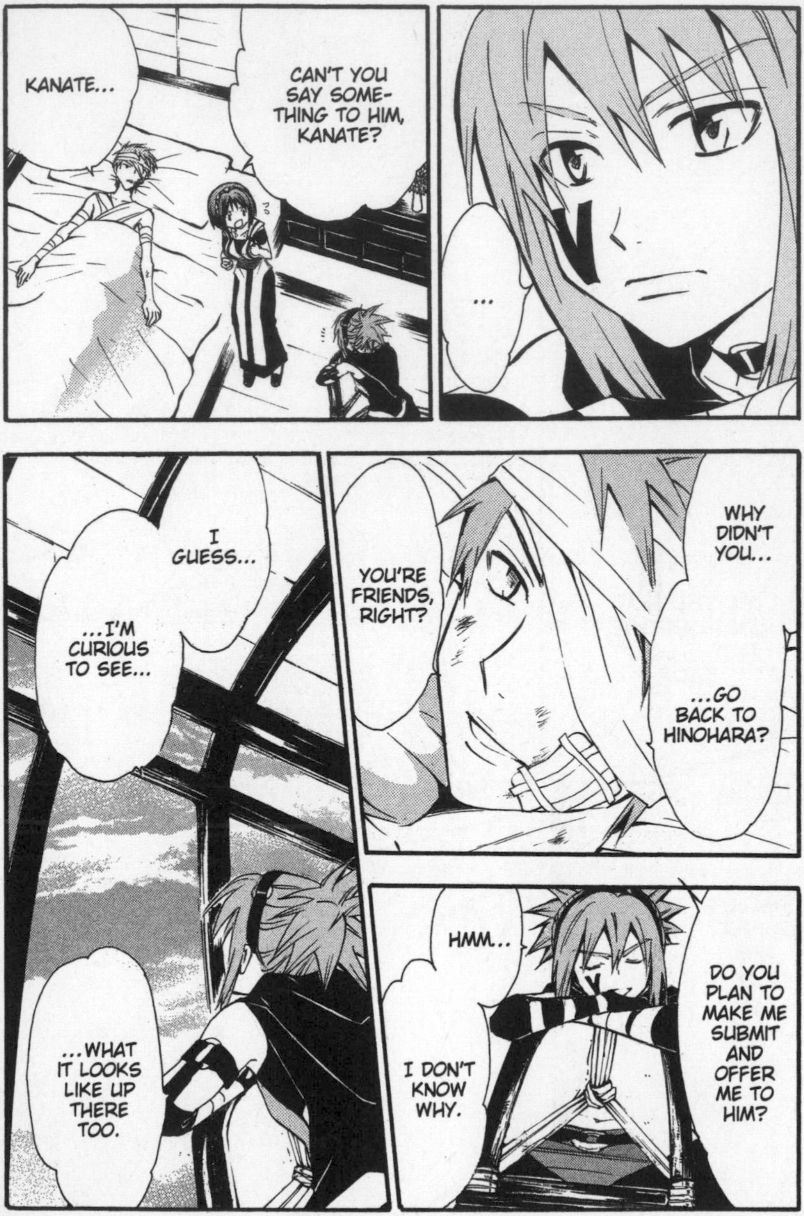
...
CAN'T YOU SAY SOMETHING TO HIM, KANATE?
KANATE...
WHY DIDN'T YOU...
...GO BACK TO HINOHARA?
YOU'RE FRIENDS, RIGHT?
DO YOU PLAN TO MAKE ME SUBMIT AND OFFER ME TO HIM?
HMM...
I DON'T KNOW WHY.
I GUESS...
...I'M CURIOUS TO SEE...
...WHAT IT LOOKS LIKE UP THERE TOO.

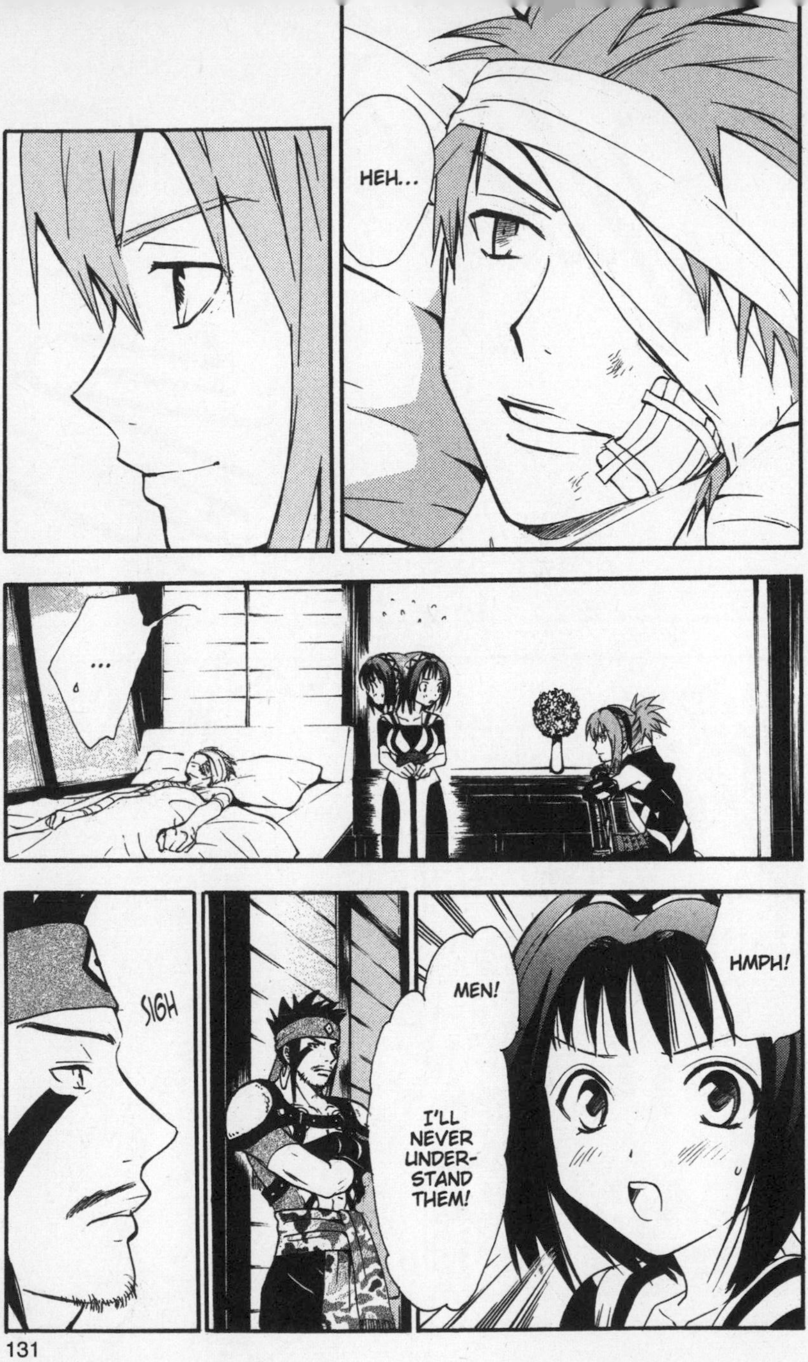
HEH...
...
HMPH!
MEN!
I'LL NEVER UNDER-STAND THEM!
SIGH

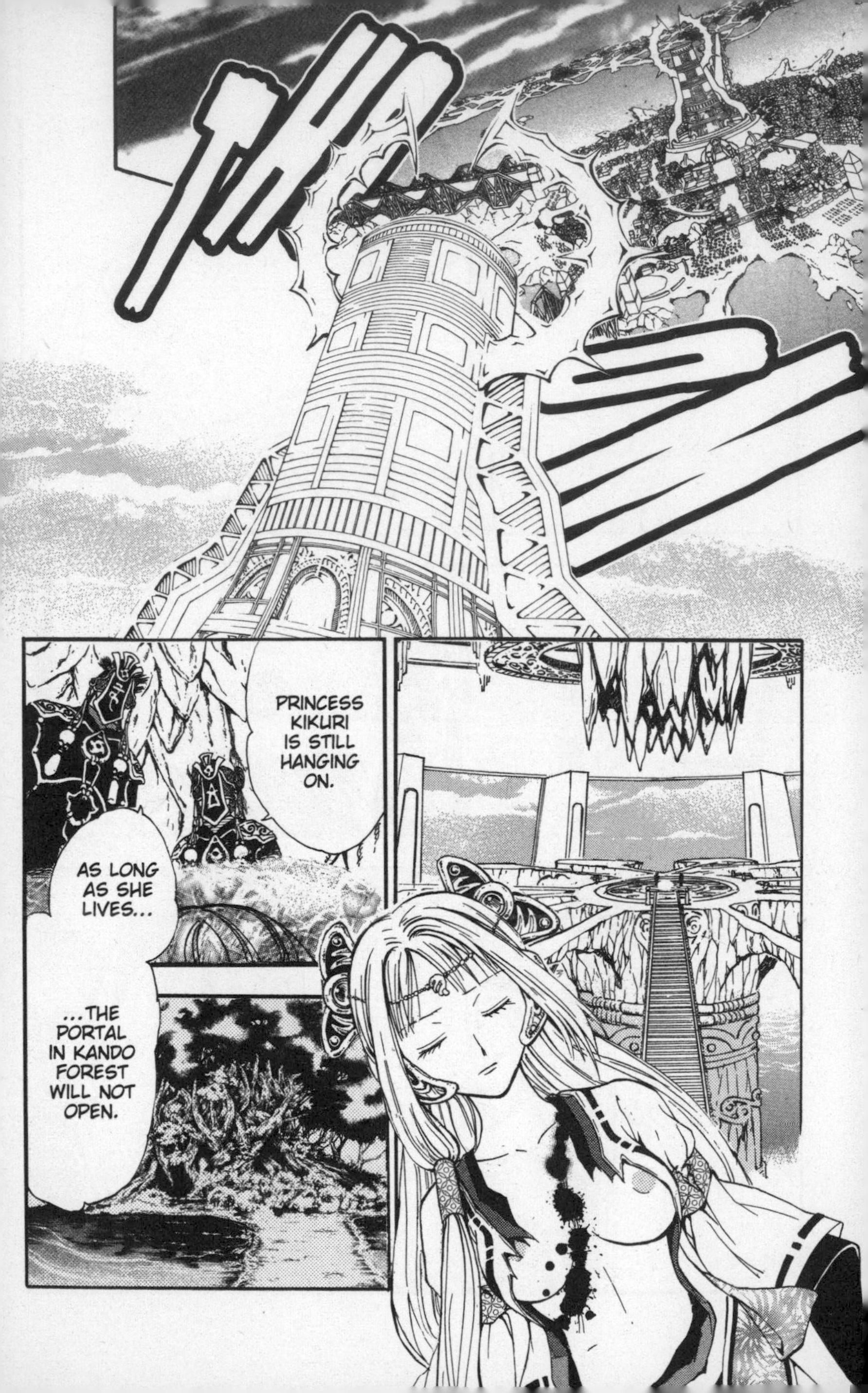
PRINCESS KIKURI IS STILL HANGING ON.
AS LONG AS SHE LIVES...
...THE PORTAL IN KANDO FOREST WILL NOT OPEN.

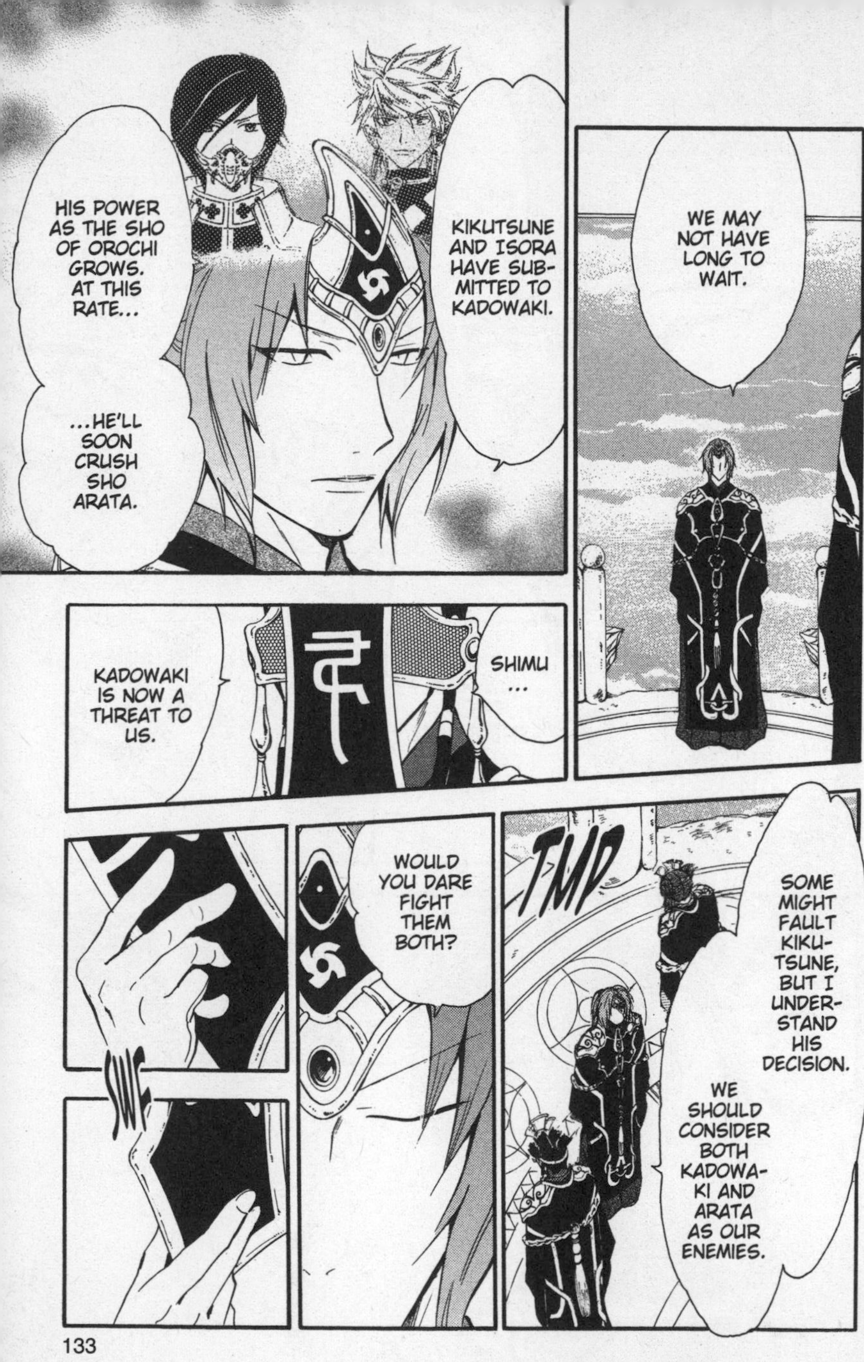
WE MAY NOT HAVE LONG TO WAIT.
KIKUTSUNE AND ISORA HAVE SUBMITTED TO KADOWAKI.
HIS POWER AS THE SHO OF OROCHI GROWS. AT THIS RATE...
...HE'LL SOON CRUSH SHO ARATA.
SHIMU...
KADOWAKI IS NOW A THREAT TO US.
TMP
SOME MIGHT FAULT KIKUTSUNE, BUT I UNDERSTAND HIS DECISION.
WE SHOULD CONSIDER BOTH KADOWAKI AND ARATA AS OUR ENEMIES.
WOULD YOU DARE FIGHT THEM BOTH?
SWF

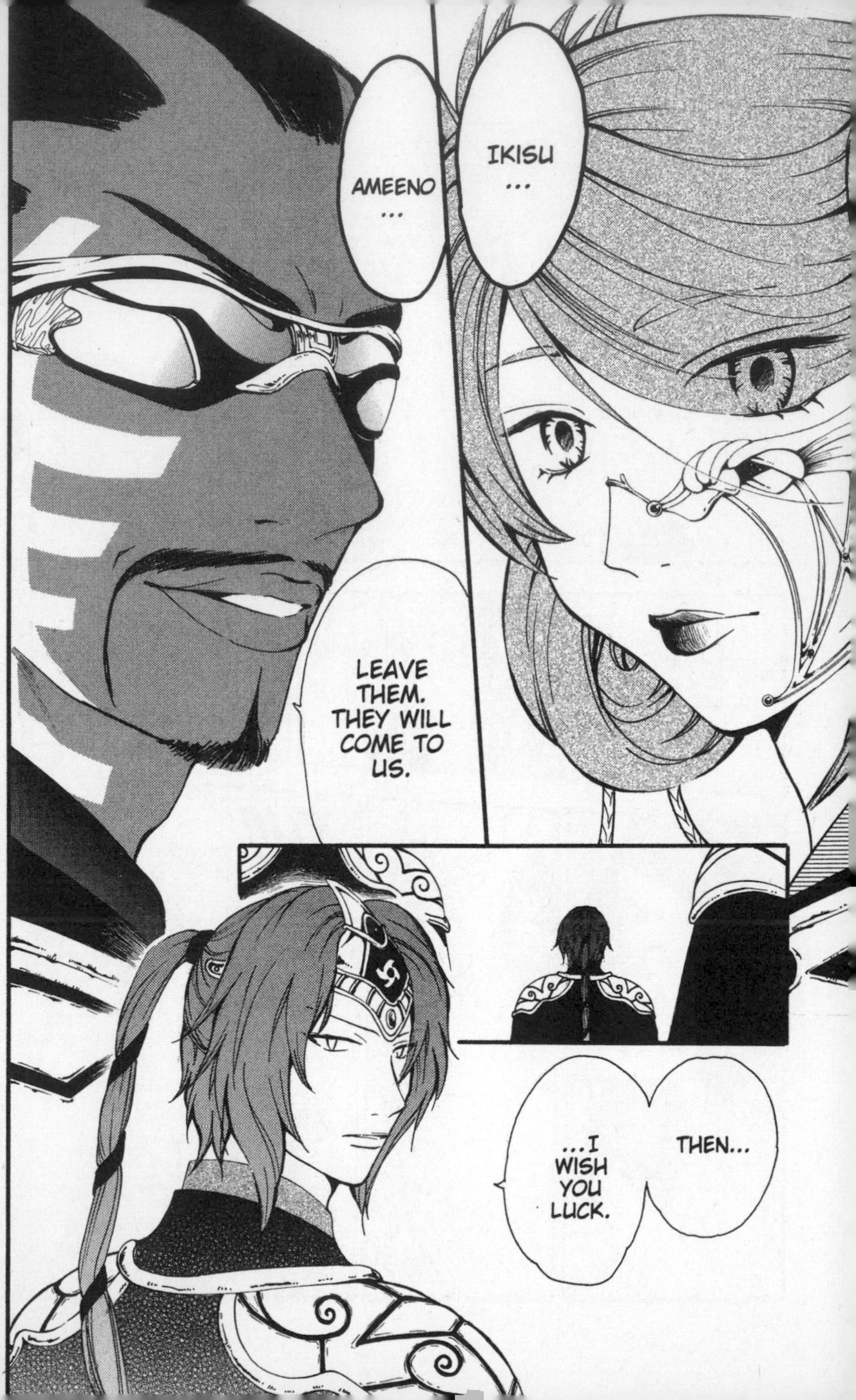
IKISU ...
AMEENO ...
LEAVE THEM. THEY WILL COME TO US.
THEN...
...I WISH YOU LUCK.

CHAPTER 195
THE WATERS OF UBI

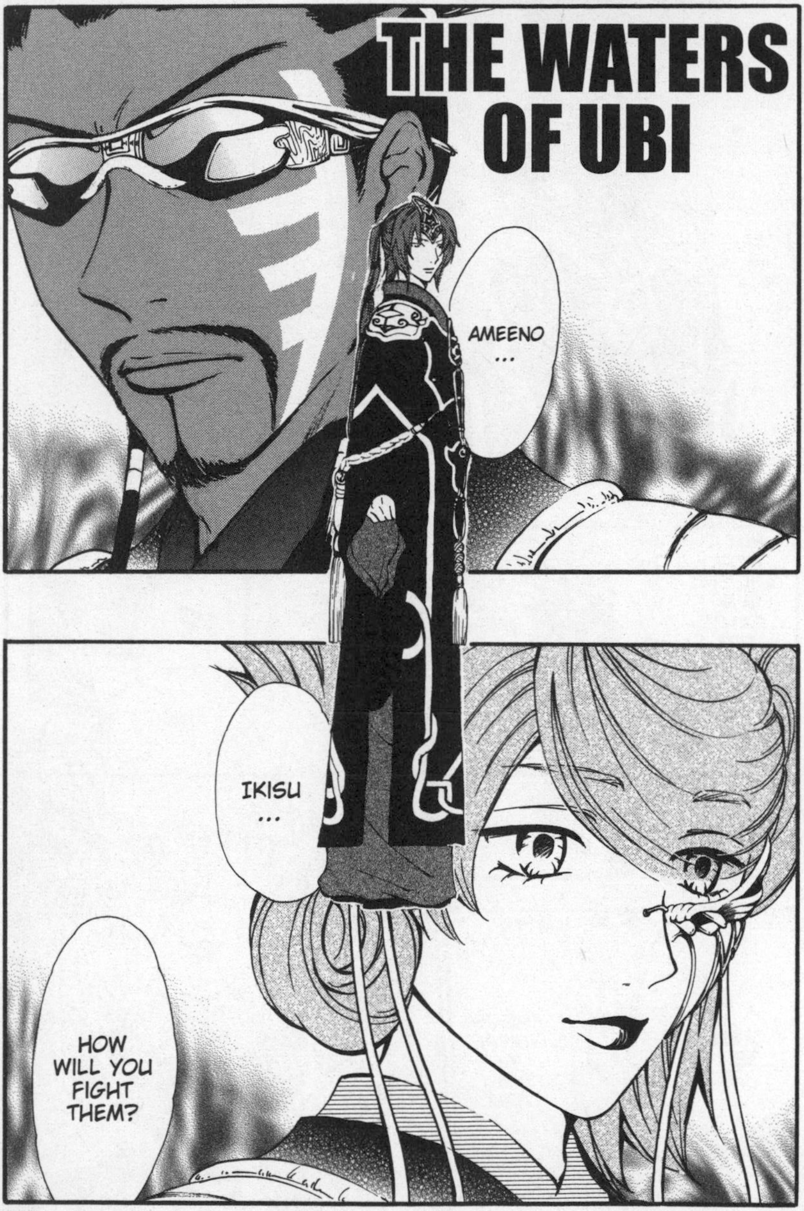
AMEENO ...
IKISU ...
HOW WILL YOU FIGHT THEM?

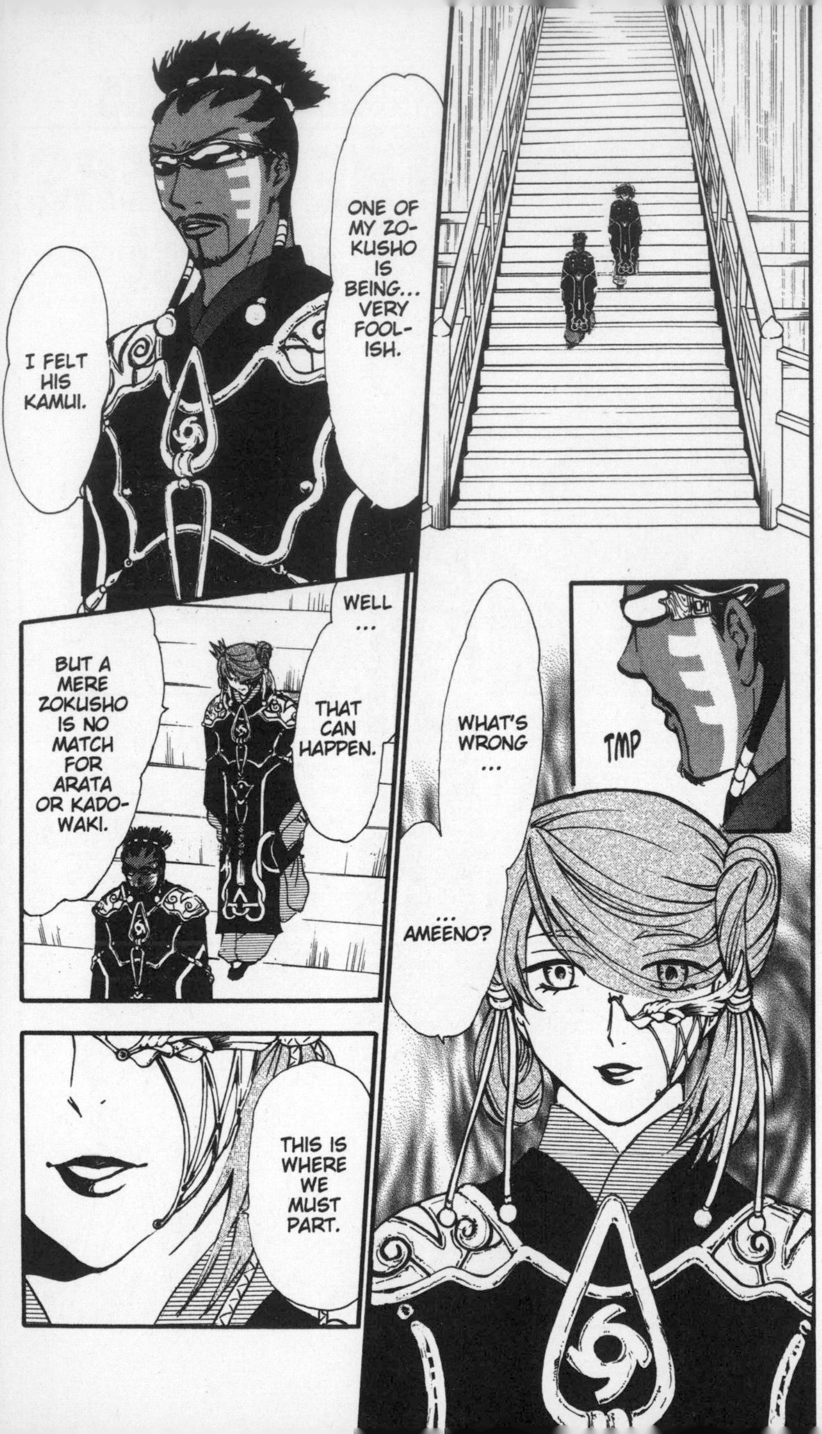
ONE OF MY ZO-KUSHO IS BEING... VERY FOOL-ISH.
I FELT HIS KAMUI.
TMP
WHAT'S WRONG ...
... AMEENO?
WELL ...
THAT CAN HAPPEN.
BUT A MERE ZOKUSHO IS NO MATCH FOR ARATA OR KADO-WAKI.
THIS IS WHERE WE MUST PART.

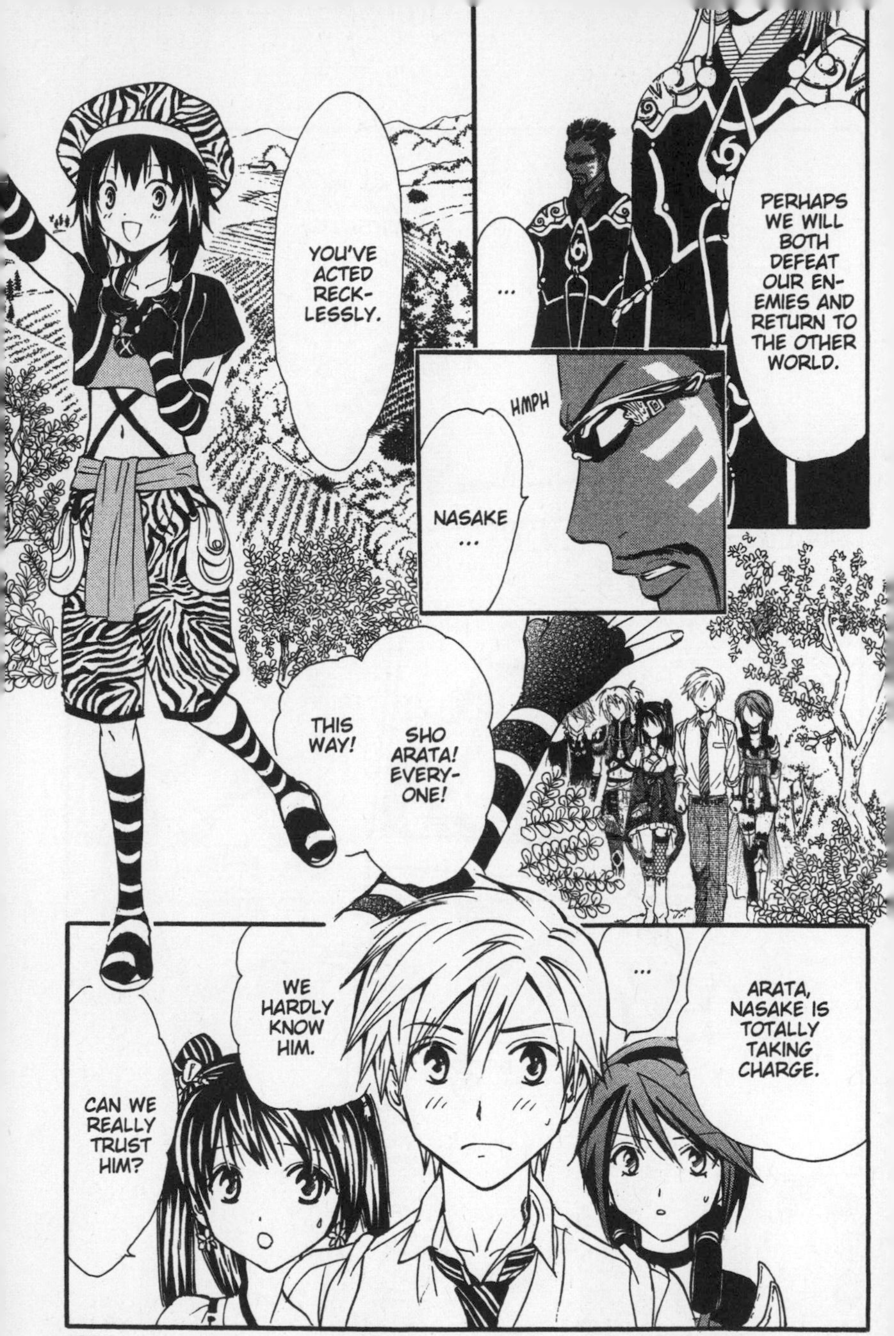
PERHAPS WE WILL BOTH DEFEAT OUR ENEMIES AND RETURN TO THE OTHER WORLD.
...
YOU'VE ACTED RECKLESSLY.
HMPH
NASAKE ...
SHO ARATA! EVERYONE!
THIS WAY!
ARATA, NASAKE IS TOTALLY TAKING CHARGE.
...
WE HARDLY KNOW HIM.
CAN WE REALLY TRUST HIM?

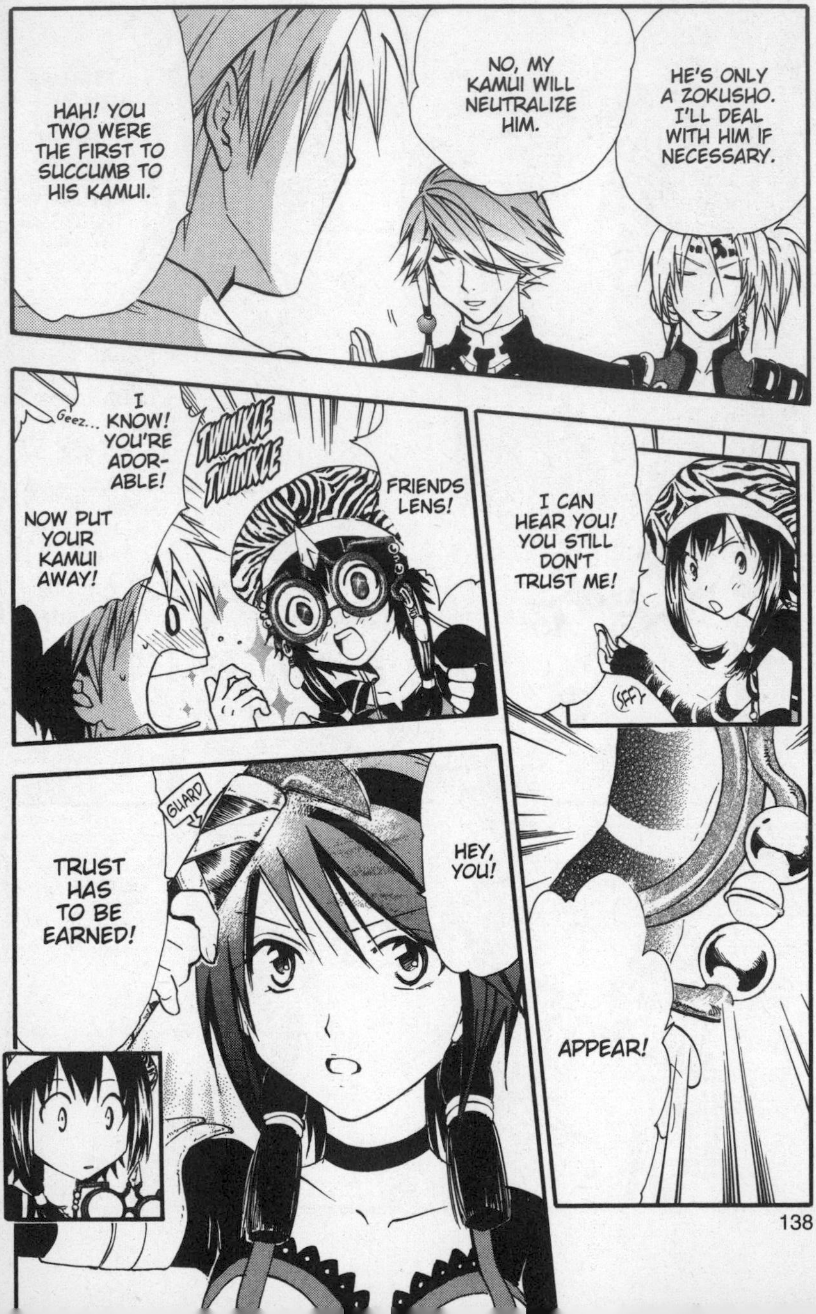
HE'S ONLY A ZOKUSHO. I'LL DEAL WITH HIM IF NECESSARY.
NO, MY KAMUI WILL NEUTRALIZE HIM.
HAH! YOU TWO WERE THE FIRST TO SUCCUMB TO HIS KAMUI.
I CAN HEAR YOU! YOU STILL DON'T TRUST ME!
SFFY
FRIENDS LENS!
TWINKLE TWINKLE
I KNOW! YOU'RE ADORABLE!
Geez...
NOW PUT YOUR KAMUI AWAY!
APPEAR!
HEY, YOU!
GUARD
TRUST HAS TO BE EARNED!

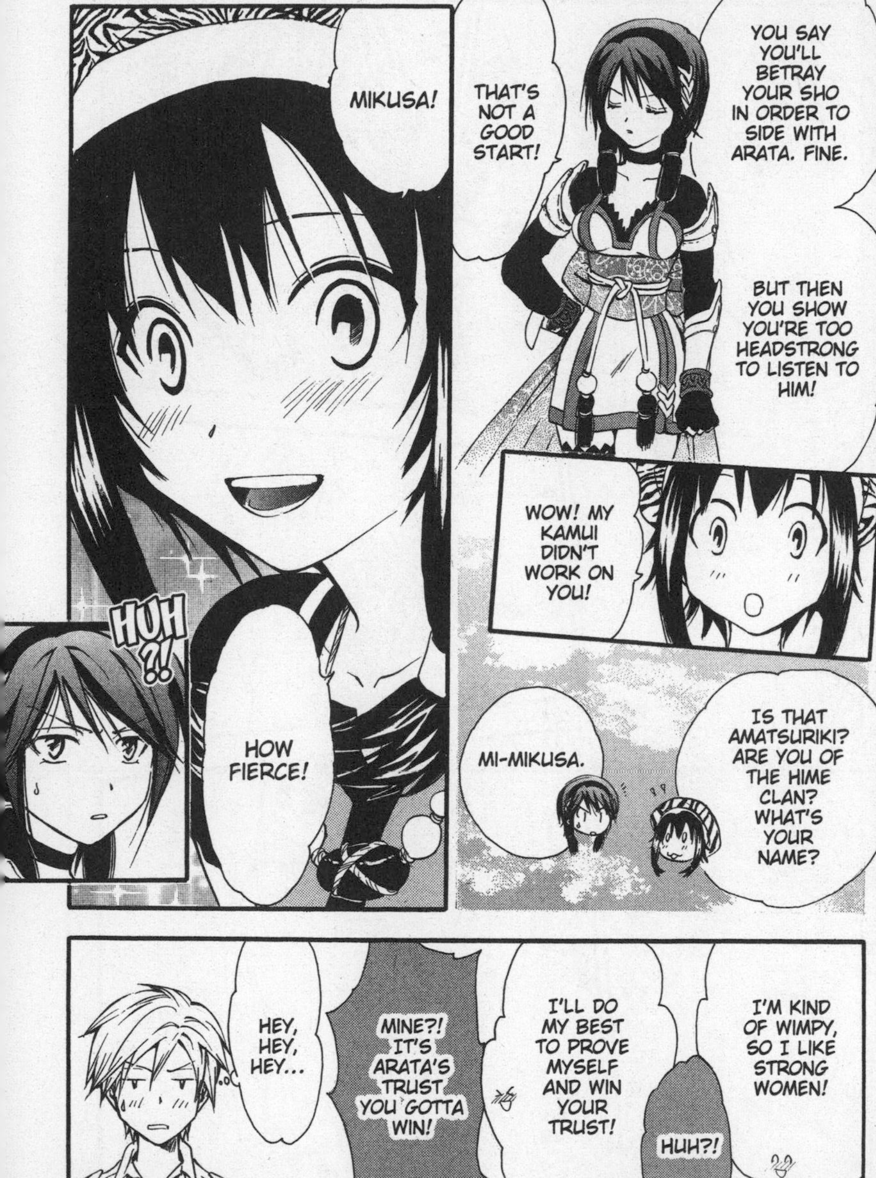
YOU SAY YOU'LL BETRAY YOUR SHO IN ORDER TO SIDE WITH ARATA. FINE.
BUT THEN YOU SHOW YOU'RE TOO HEADSTRONG TO LISTEN TO HIM!
THAT'S NOT A GOOD START!
WOW! MY KAMUI DIDN'T WORK ON YOU!
IS THAT AMATSURIKI? ARE YOU OF THE HIME CLAN? WHAT'S YOUR NAME?
MI-MIKUSA.
MIKUSA!
HOW FIERCE!
HUH ?!
I'M KIND OF WIMPY, SO I LIKE STRONG WOMEN!
HUH?!
I'LL DO MY BEST TO PROVE MYSELF AND WIN YOUR TRUST!
MINE?! IT'S ARATA'S TRUST YOU GOTTA WIN!
HEY, HEY, HEY...

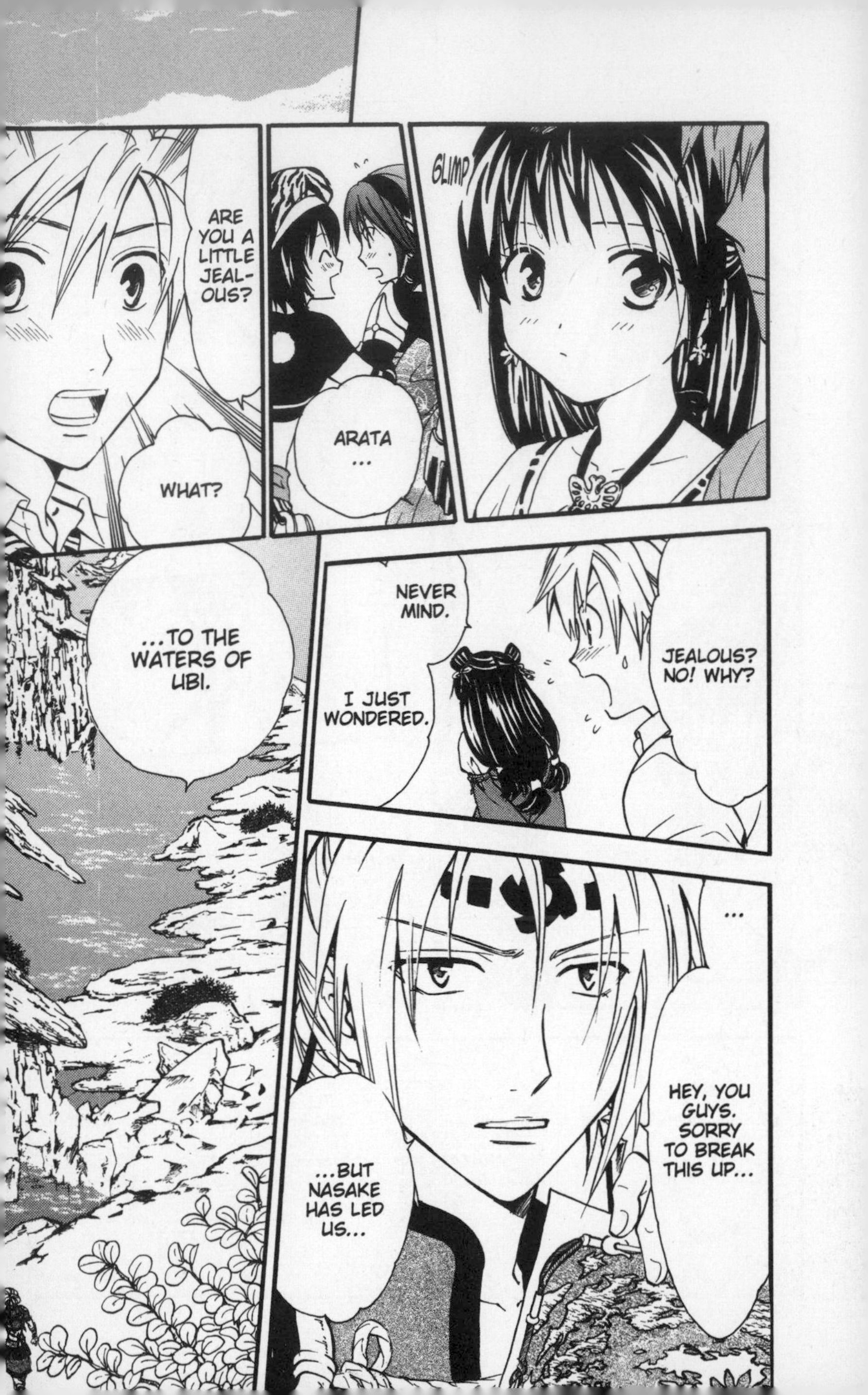
GLIMP
ARATA ...
ARE YOU A LITTLE JEAL-OUS?
WHAT?
JEALOUS? NO! WHY?
NEVER MIND.
I JUST WONDERED.
...
HEY, YOU GUYS. SORRY TO BREAK THIS UP...
...BUT NASAKE HAS LED US...
...TO THE WATERS OF UBI.

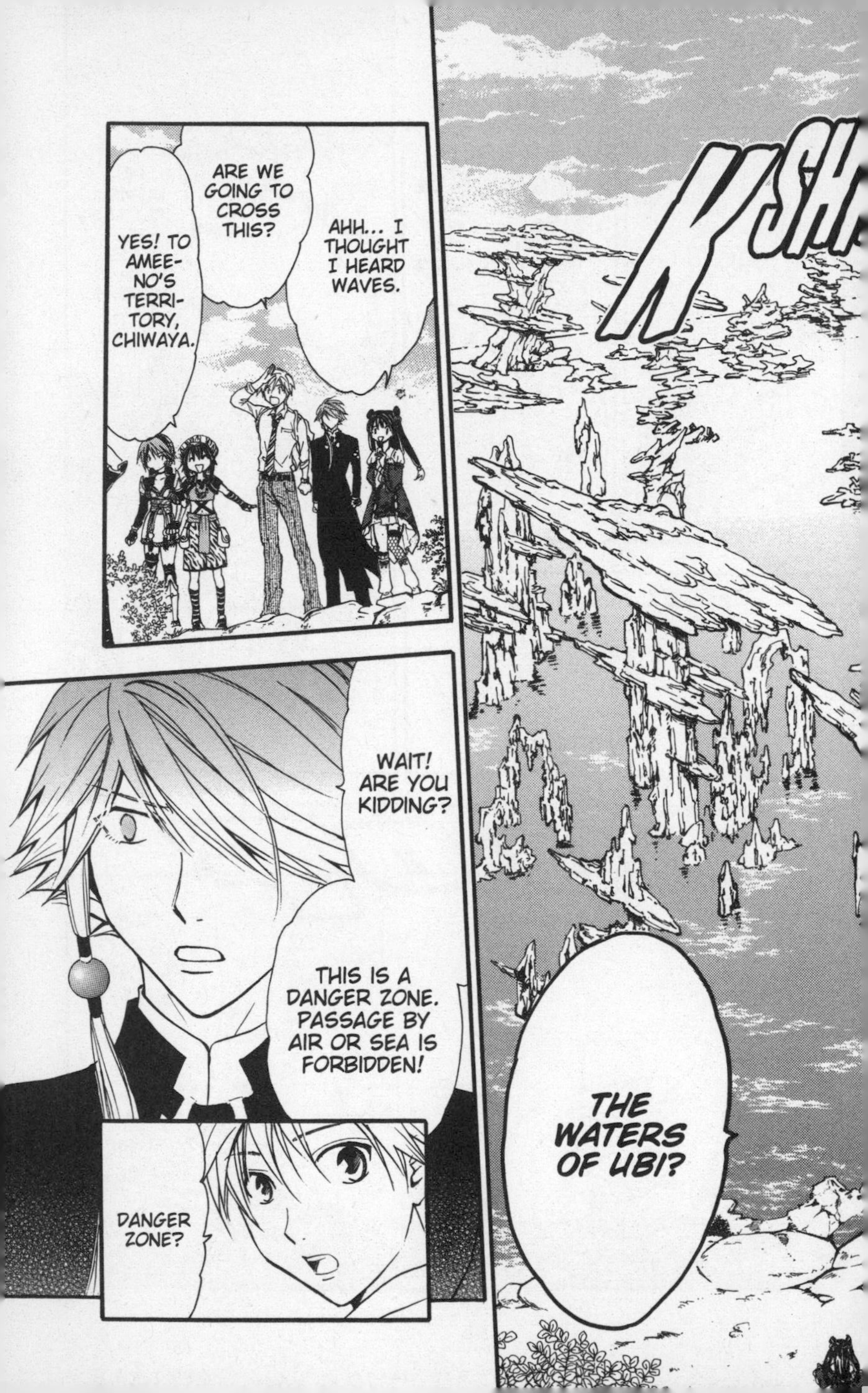
KSH
THE WATERS OF UBI?
AHH... I THOUGHT I HEARD WAVES.
ARE WE GOING TO CROSS THIS?
YES! TO AMEE-NO'S TERRI-TORY, CHIWAYA.
WAIT! ARE YOU KIDDING?
THIS IS A DANGER ZONE. PASSAGE BY AIR OR SEA IS FORBIDDEN!
DANGER ZONE?

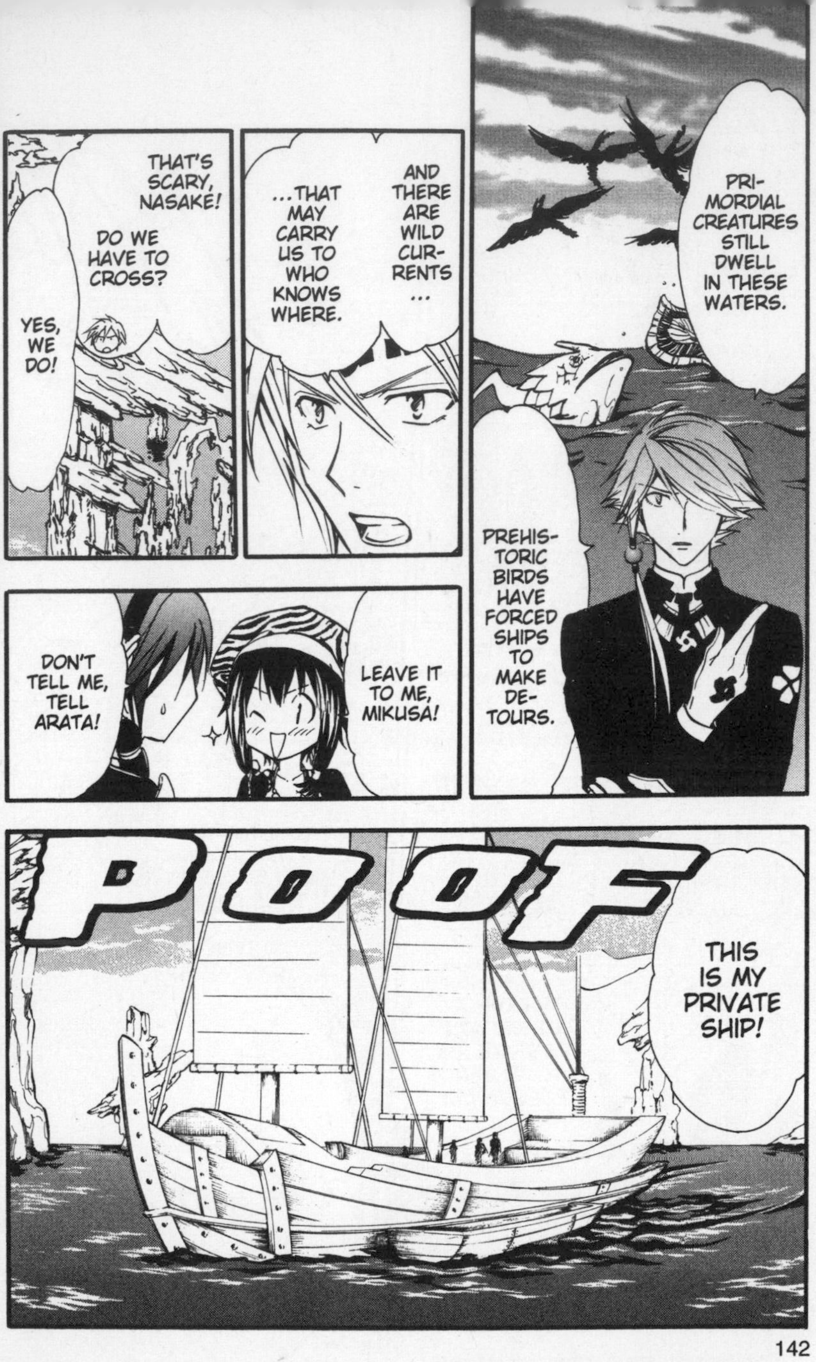
PRIMORDIAL CREATURES STILL DWELL IN THESE WATERS.
PREHISTORIC BIRDS HAVE FORCED SHIPS TO MAKE DETOURS.
AND THERE ARE WILD CURRENTS...
...THAT MAY CARRY US TO WHO KNOWS WHERE.
THAT'S SCARY, NASAKE!
DO WE HAVE TO CROSS?
YES, WE DO!
LEAVE IT TO ME, MIKUSA!
DON'T TELL ME, TELL ARATA!
POOF
THIS IS MY PRIVATE SHIP!

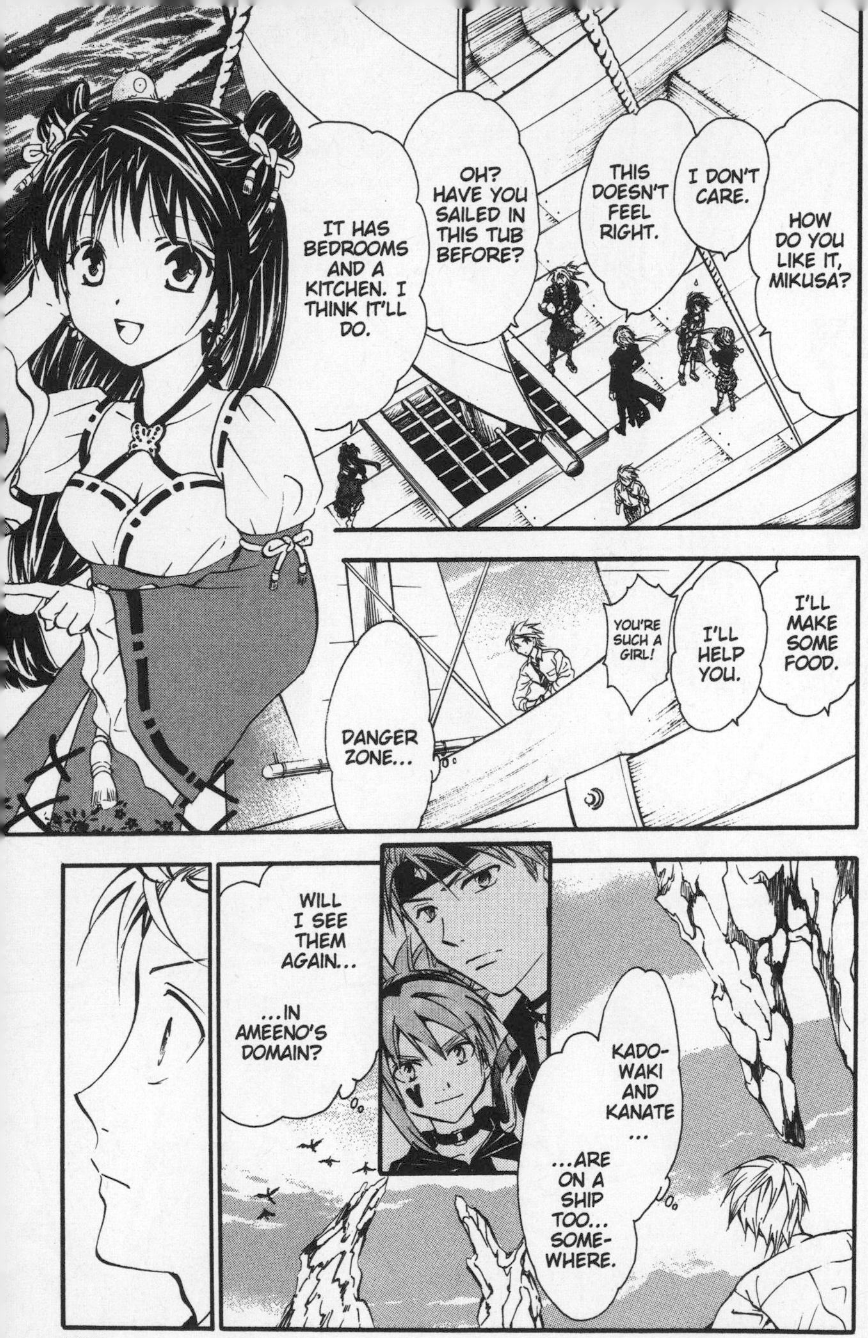
HOW DO YOU LIKE IT, MIKUSA?
I DON'T CARE.
THIS DOESN'T FEEL RIGHT.
OH? HAVE YOU SAILED IN THIS TUB BEFORE?
IT HAS BEDROOMS AND A KITCHEN. I THINK IT'LL DO.
I'LL MAKE SOME FOOD.
I'LL HELP YOU.
YOU'RE SUCH A GIRL!
DANGER ZONE...
KADO-WAKI AND KANATE ...
...ARE ON A SHIP TOO... SOME-WHERE.
WILL I SEE THEM AGAIN...
...IN AMEENO'S DOMAIN?

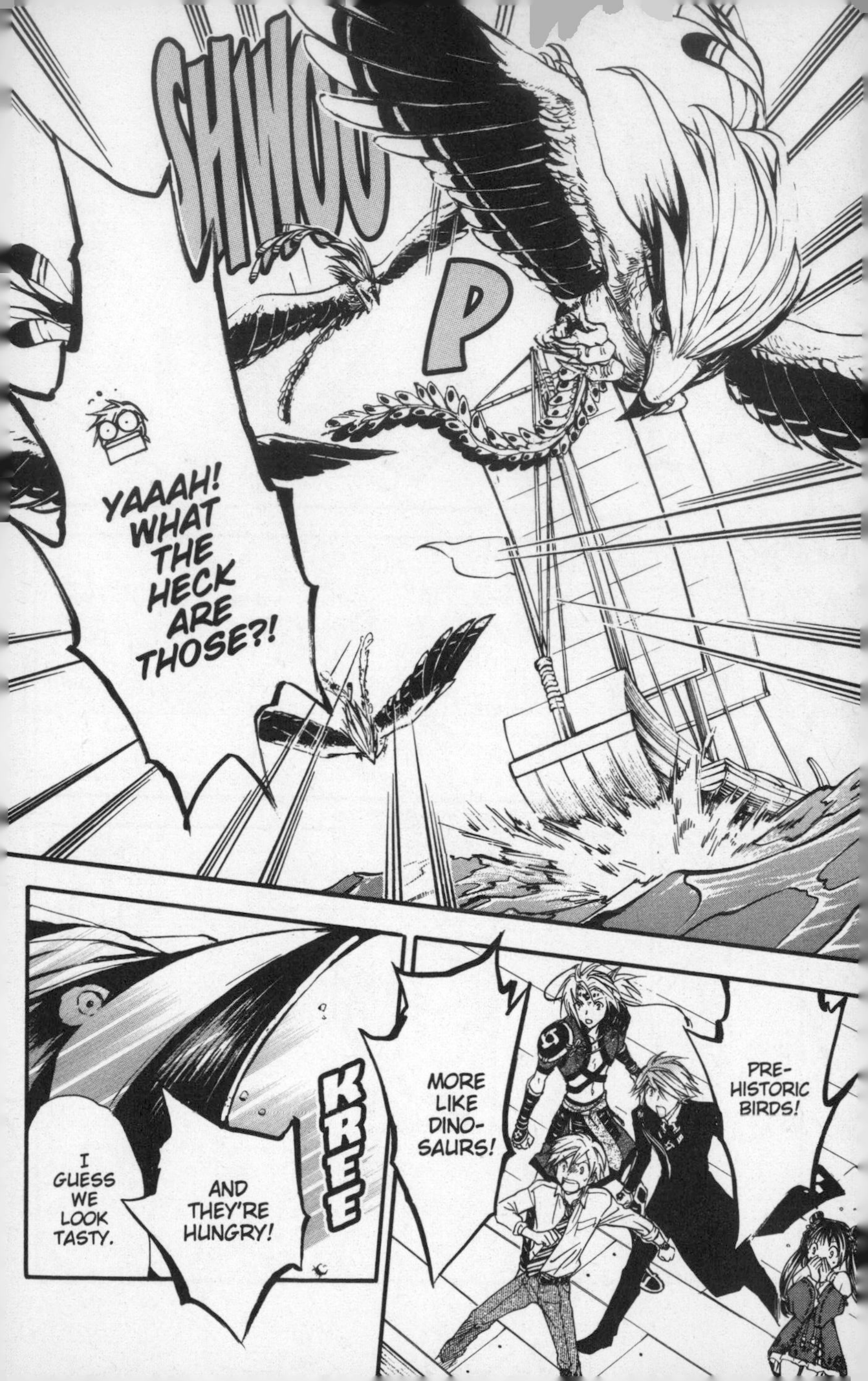
SHWOOP
YAAAH! WHAT THE HECK ARE THOSE?!
PRE-HISTORIC BIRDS!
MORE LIKE DINO-SAURS!
KREE
AND THEY'RE HUNGRY!
I GUESS WE LOOK TASTY.

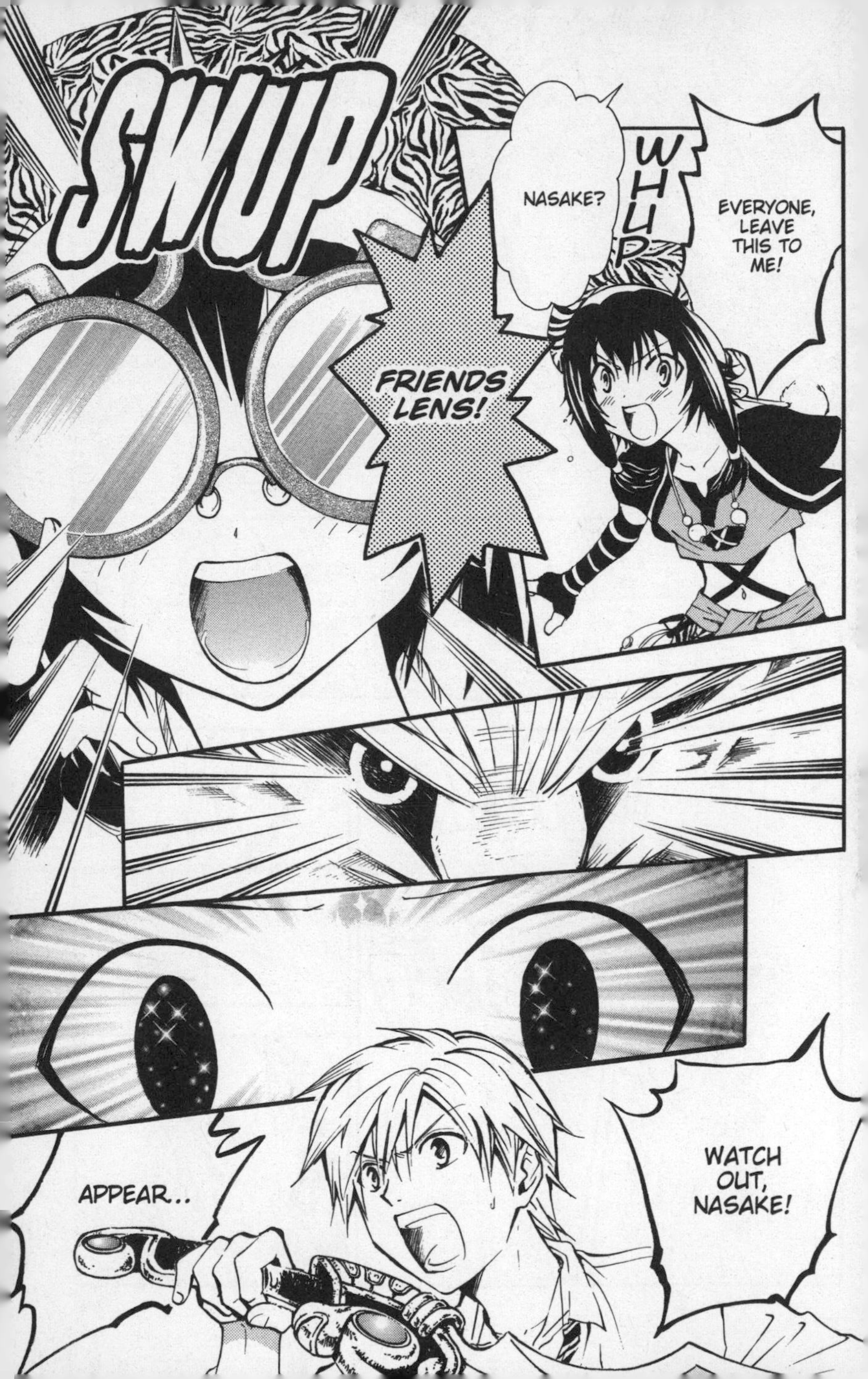
EVERYONE, LEAVE THIS TO ME!
WHUP
NASAKE?
SWUP
FRIENDS LENS!
WATCH OUT, NASAKE!
APPEAR..

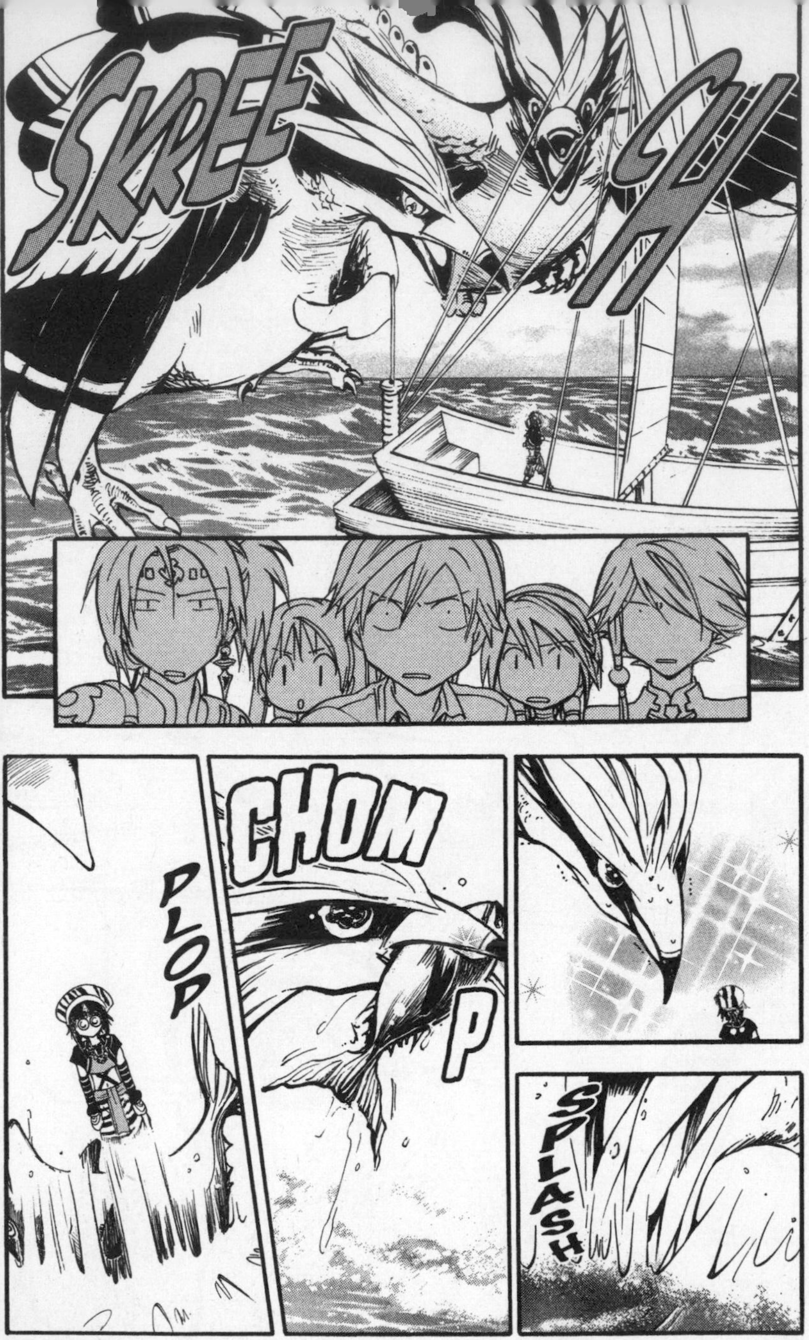
SKREEECH
SPLASH
CHOMP
PLOP

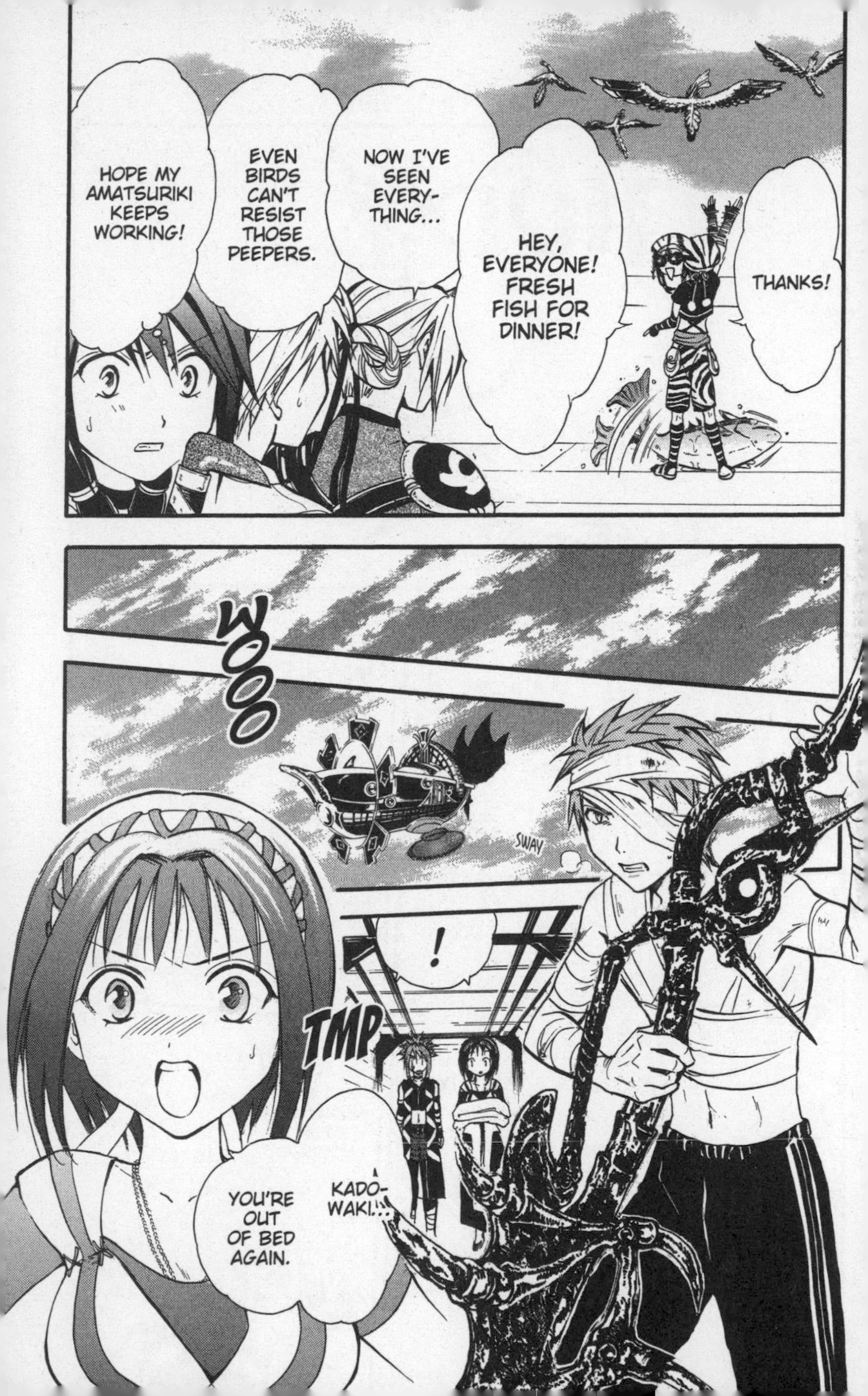
THANKS!
HEY, EVERYONE! FRESH FISH FOR DINNER!
NOW I'VE SEEN EVERY-THING...
EVEN BIRDS CAN'T RESIST THOSE PEEPERS.
HOPE MY AMATSURIKI KEEPS WORKING!
WOOOO
SWAY
!
TMP
KADO-WAKI...
YOU'RE OUT OF BED AGAIN.

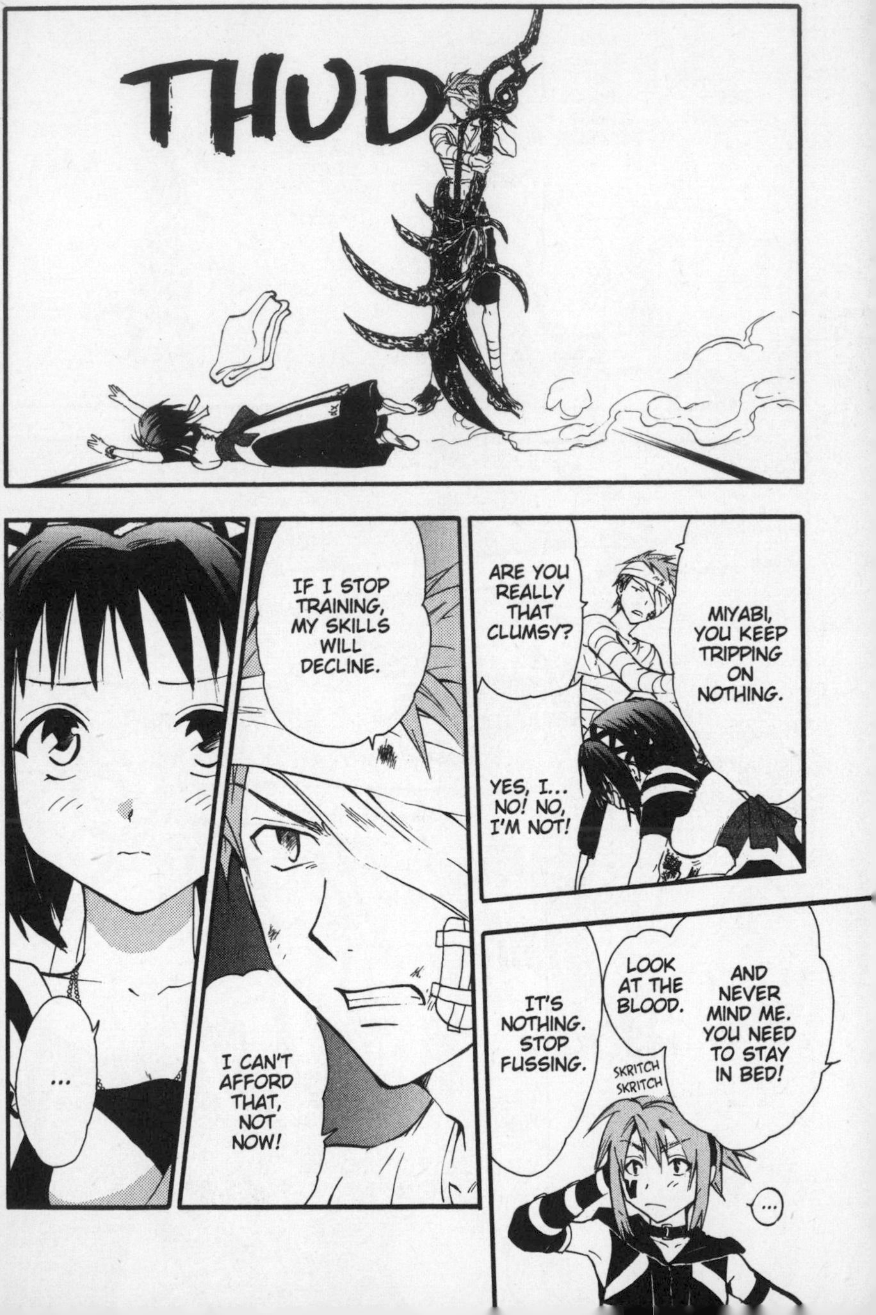
THUD
MIYABI, YOU KEEP TRIPPING ON NOTHING.
ARE YOU REALLY THAT CLUMSY?
YES, I... NO! NO, I'M NOT!
AND NEVER MIND ME. YOU NEED TO STAY IN BED!
LOOK AT THE BLOOD.
...
SKRITCH SKRITCH
IT'S NOTHING. STOP FUSSING.
IF I STOP TRAINING, MY SKILLS WILL DECLINE.
I CAN'T AFFORD THAT, NOT NOW!
...

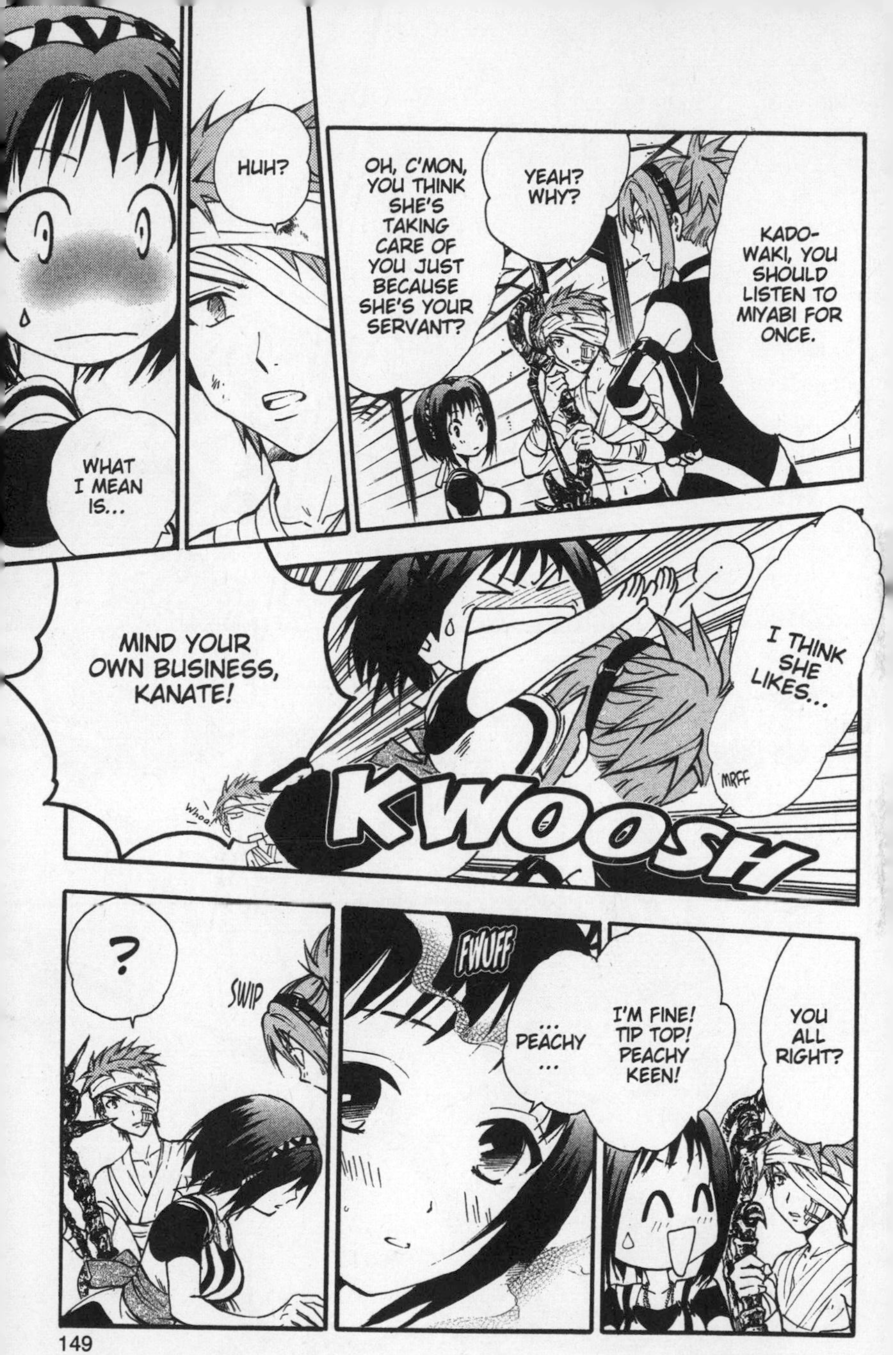
KADO-WAKI, YOU SHOULD LISTEN TO MIYABI FOR ONCE.
YEAH? WHY?
OH, C'MON, YOU THINK SHE'S TAKING CARE OF YOU JUST BECAUSE SHE'S YOUR SERVANT?
HUH?
WHAT I MEAN IS...
I THINK SHE LIKES...
MRFF
KWOOSH
MIND YOUR OWN BUSINESS, KANATE!
Whoa!
YOU ALL RIGHT?
I'M FINE! TIP TOP! PEACHY KEEN!
...PEACHY...
FWUFF
SWIP
?

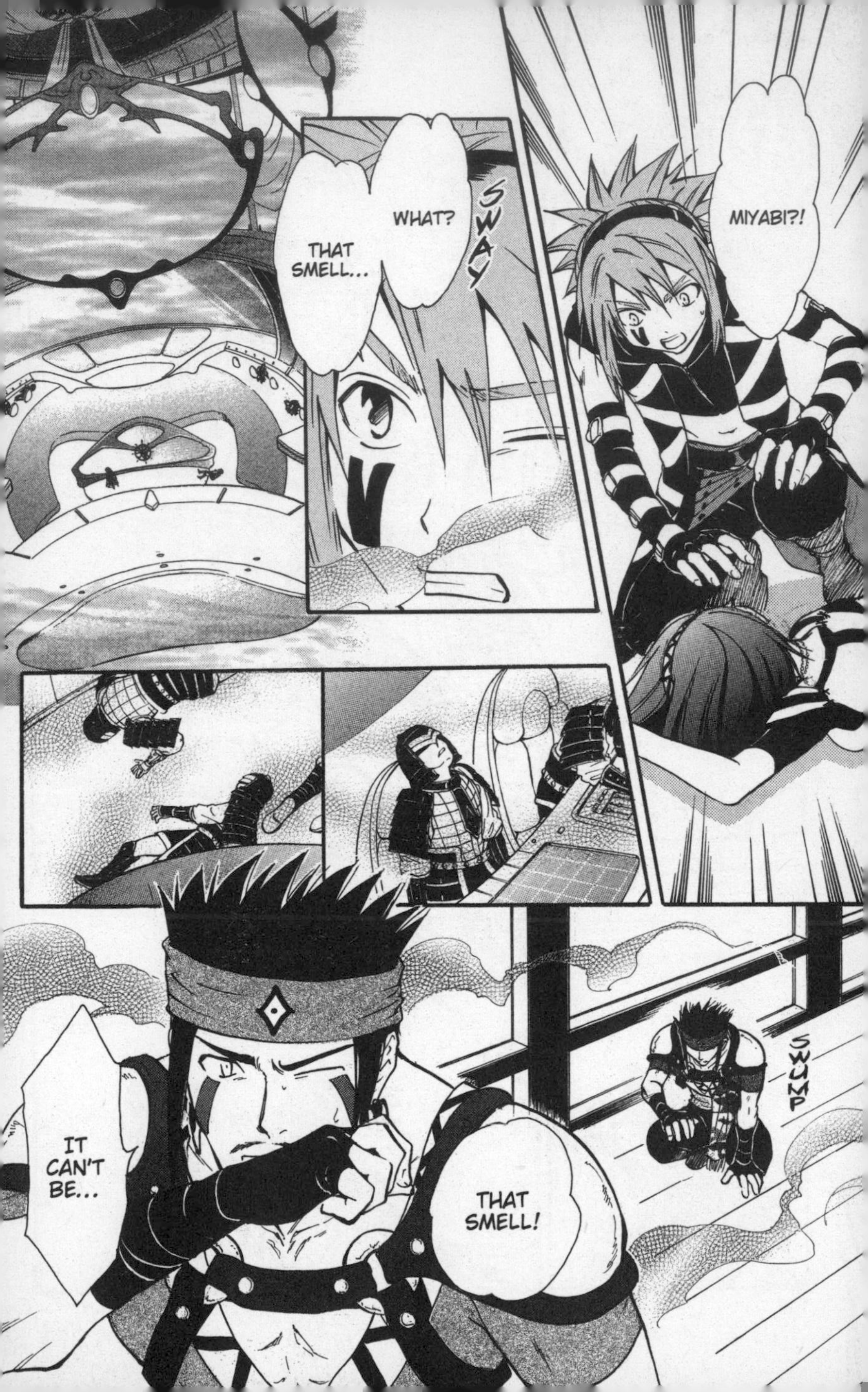
MIYABI?!
SWAY
WHAT?
THAT SMELL...
SWUMP
IT CAN'T BE...
THAT SMELL!

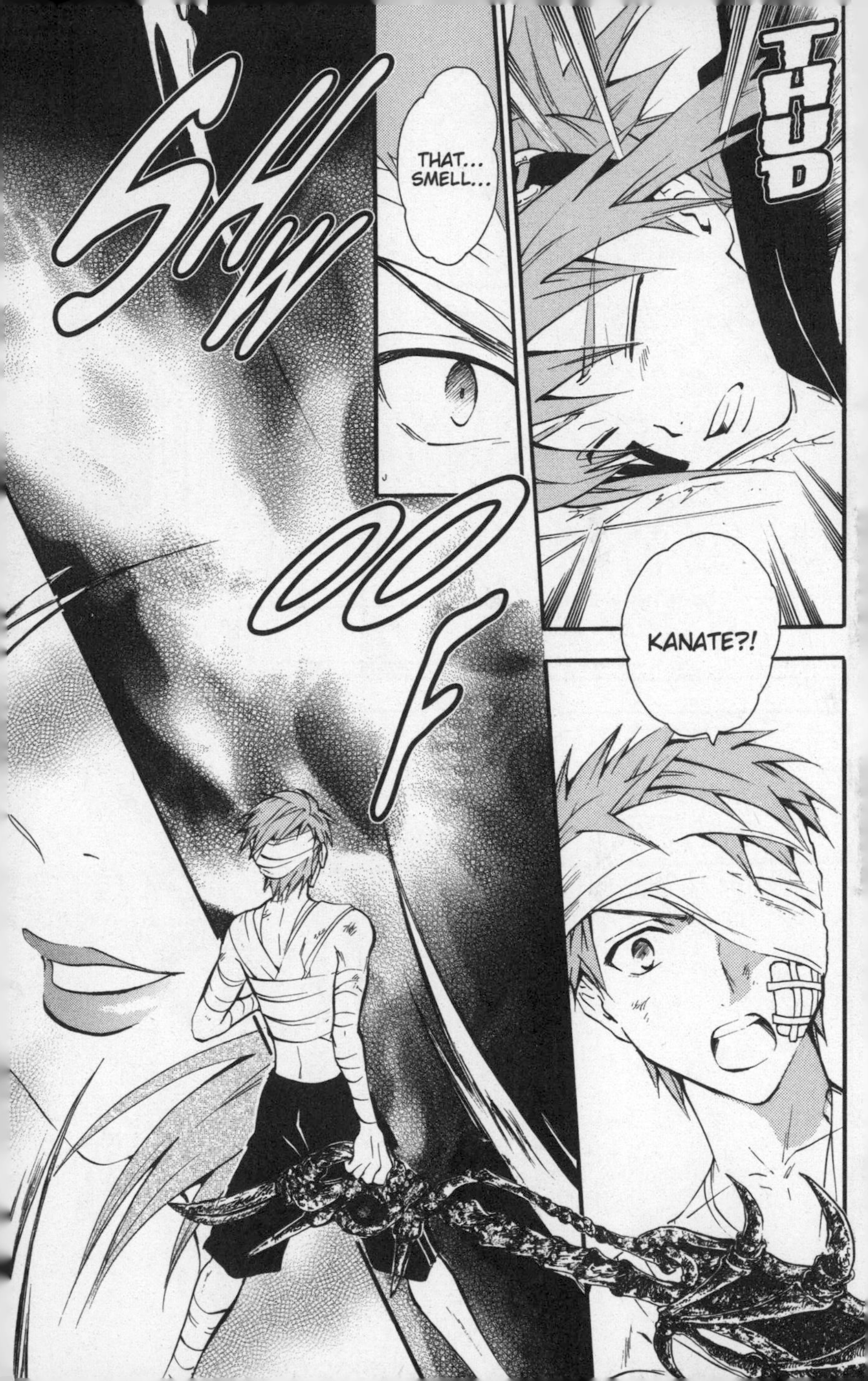
THUD
THAT... SMELL...
KANATE?!
SHWOOF

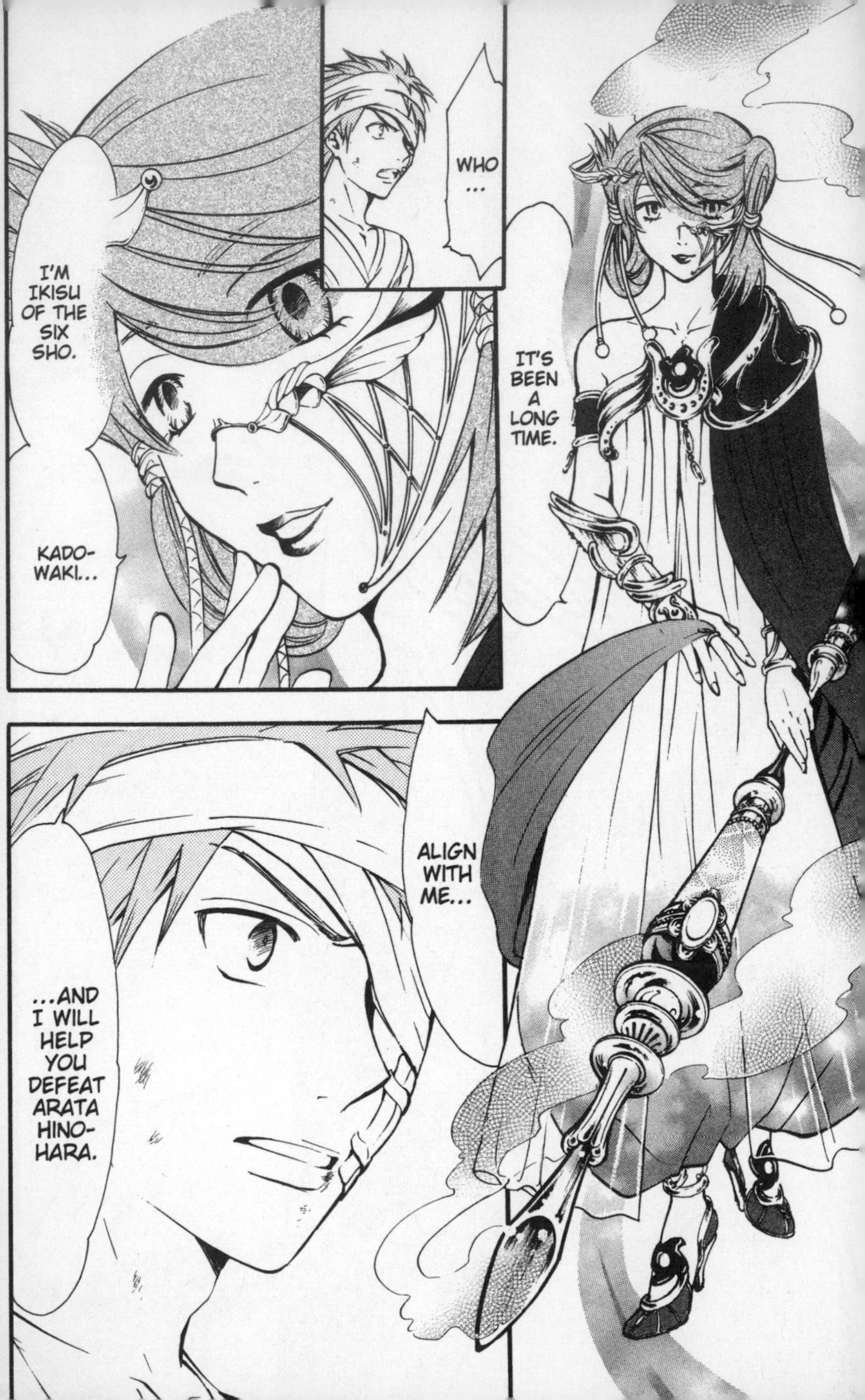
IT'S BEEN A LONG TIME.
WHO ...
I'M IKISU OF THE SIX SHO.
KADO-WAKI...
ALIGN WITH ME...
...AND I WILL HELP YOU DEFEAT ARATA HINO-HARA.

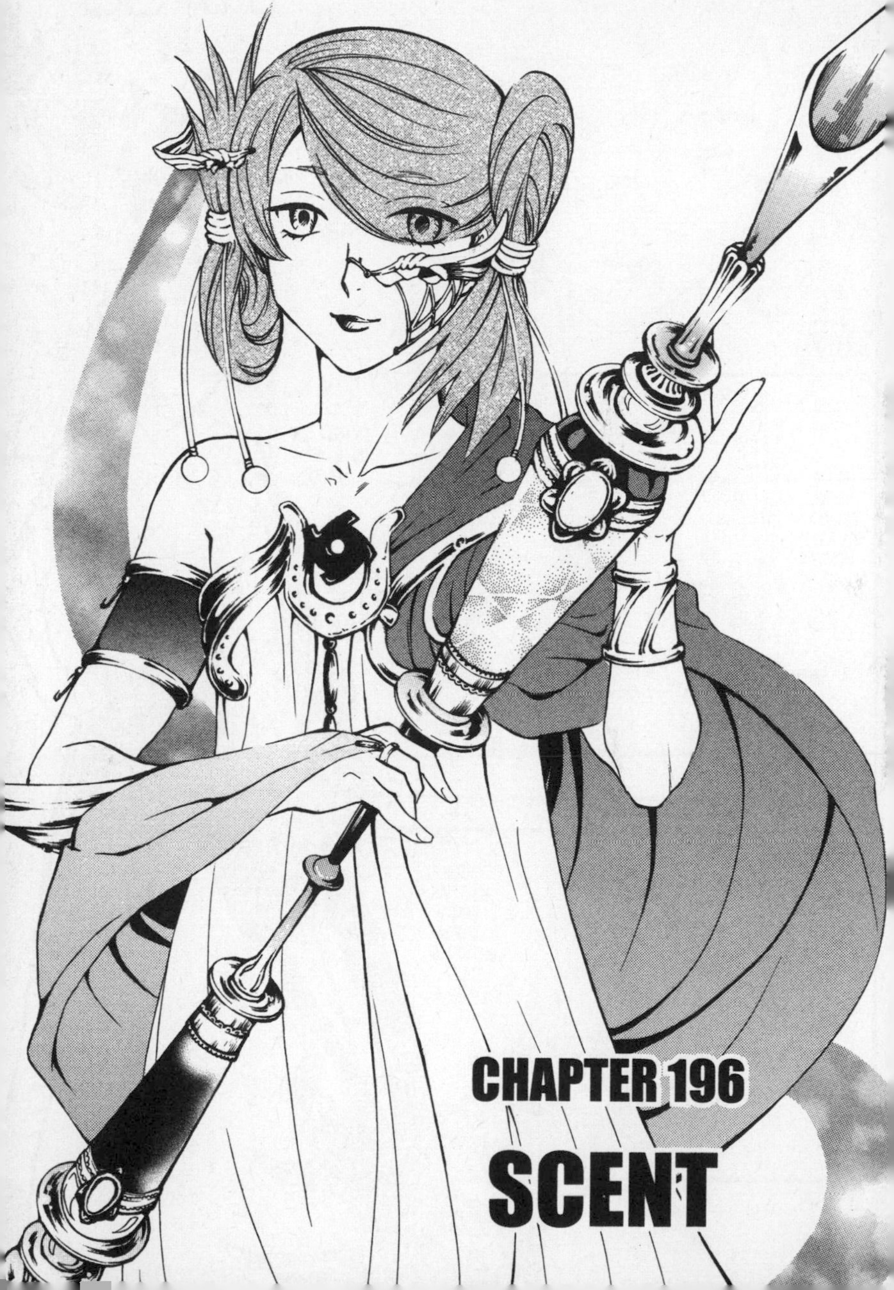
CHAPTER 196
SCENT

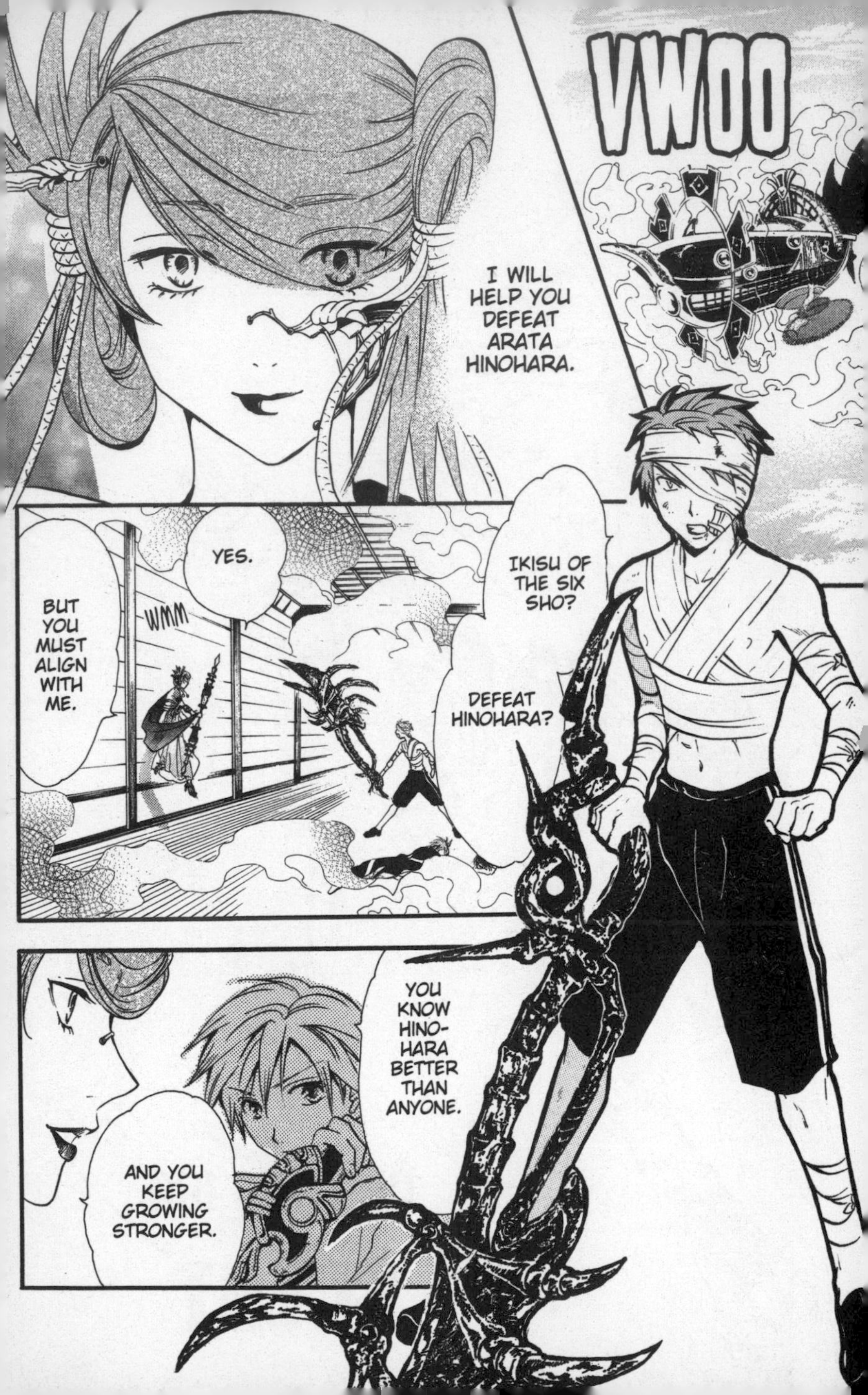
VWOO
I WILL HELP YOU DEFEAT ARATA HINOHARA.
IKISU OF THE SIX SHO?
DEFEAT HINOHARA?
YES.
WMM
BUT YOU MUST ALIGN WITH ME.
YOU KNOW HINO-HARA BETTER THAN ANYONE.
AND YOU KEEP GROWING STRONGER.

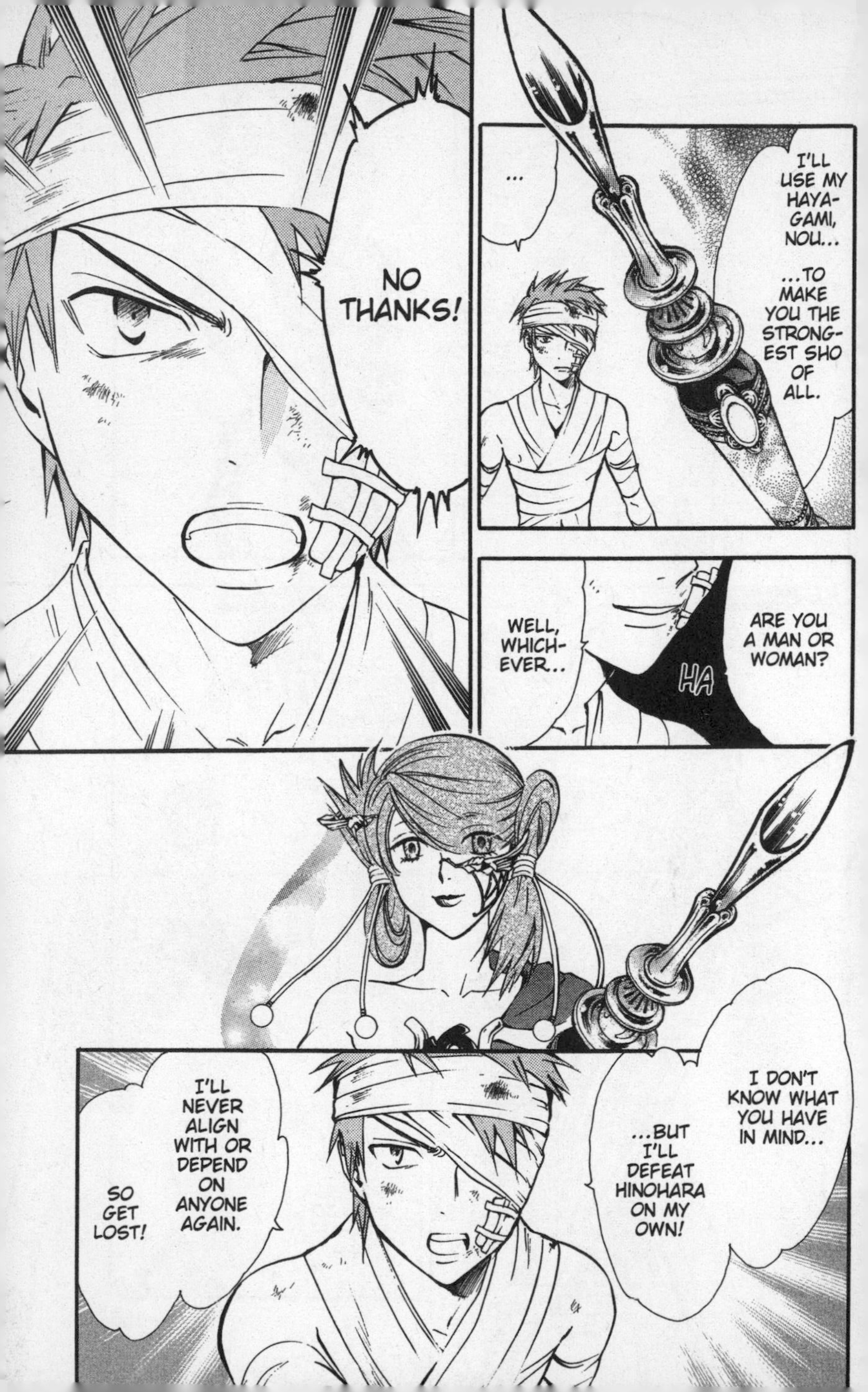
I'LL USE MY HAYA-GAMI, NOU...
...TO MAKE YOU THE STRONG-EST SHO OF ALL.
...
ARE YOU A MAN OR WOMAN?
HA
WELL, WHICH-EVER...
NO THANKS!
I DON'T KNOW WHAT YOU HAVE IN MIND...
...BUT I'LL DEFEAT HINOHARA ON MY OWN!
I'LL NEVER ALIGN WITH OR DEPEND ON ANYONE AGAIN.
SO GET LOST!

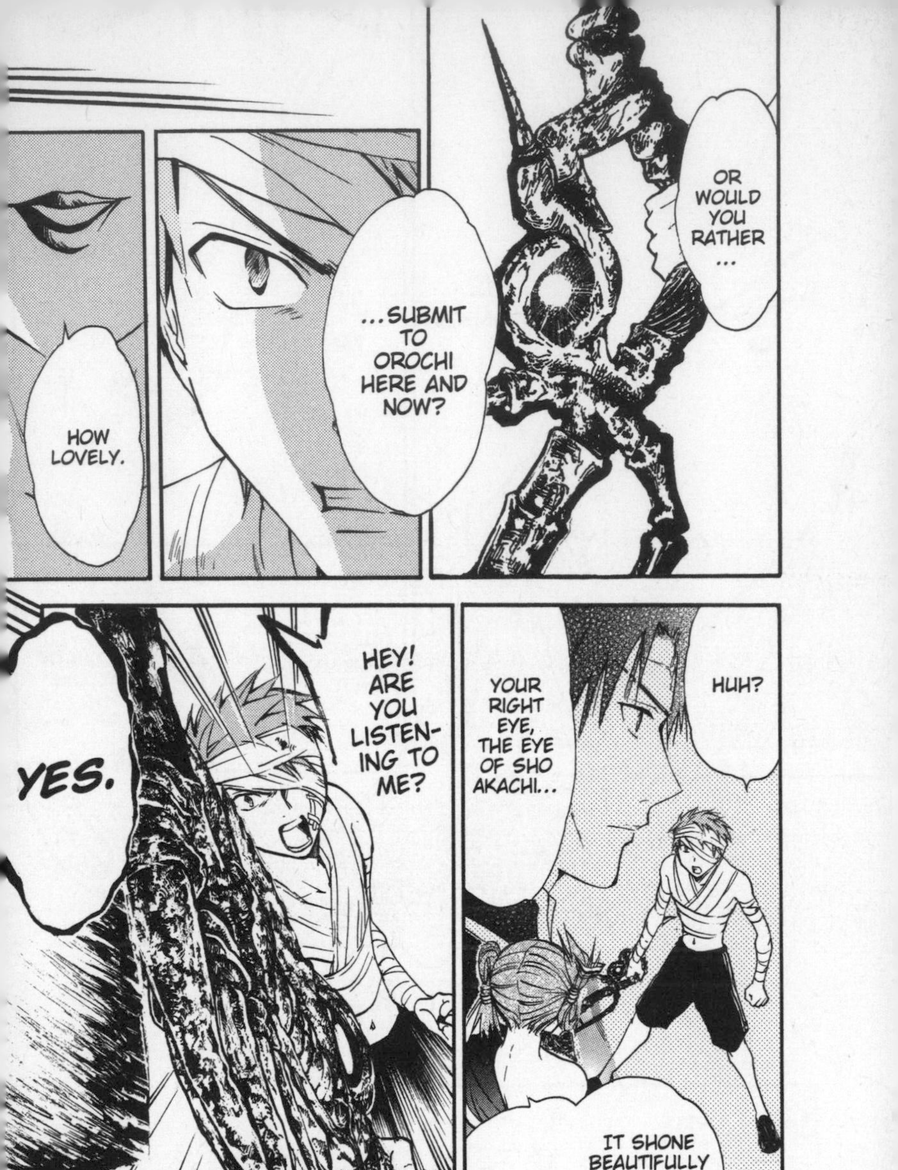
OR WOULD YOU RATHER ...
...SUBMIT TO OROCHI HERE AND NOW?
HOW LOVELY.
HUH?
YOUR RIGHT EYE, THE EYE OF SHO AKACHI...
IT SHONE BEAUTIFULLY FROM HIS FACE AS WELL.
SO YOU WANT TO BE LIKE HIM?
HEY! ARE YOU LISTENING TO ME?
YES.

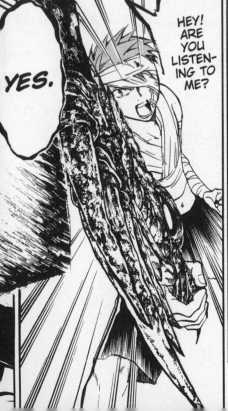

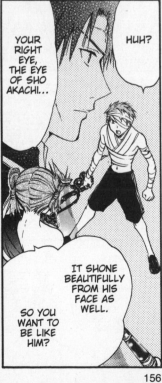

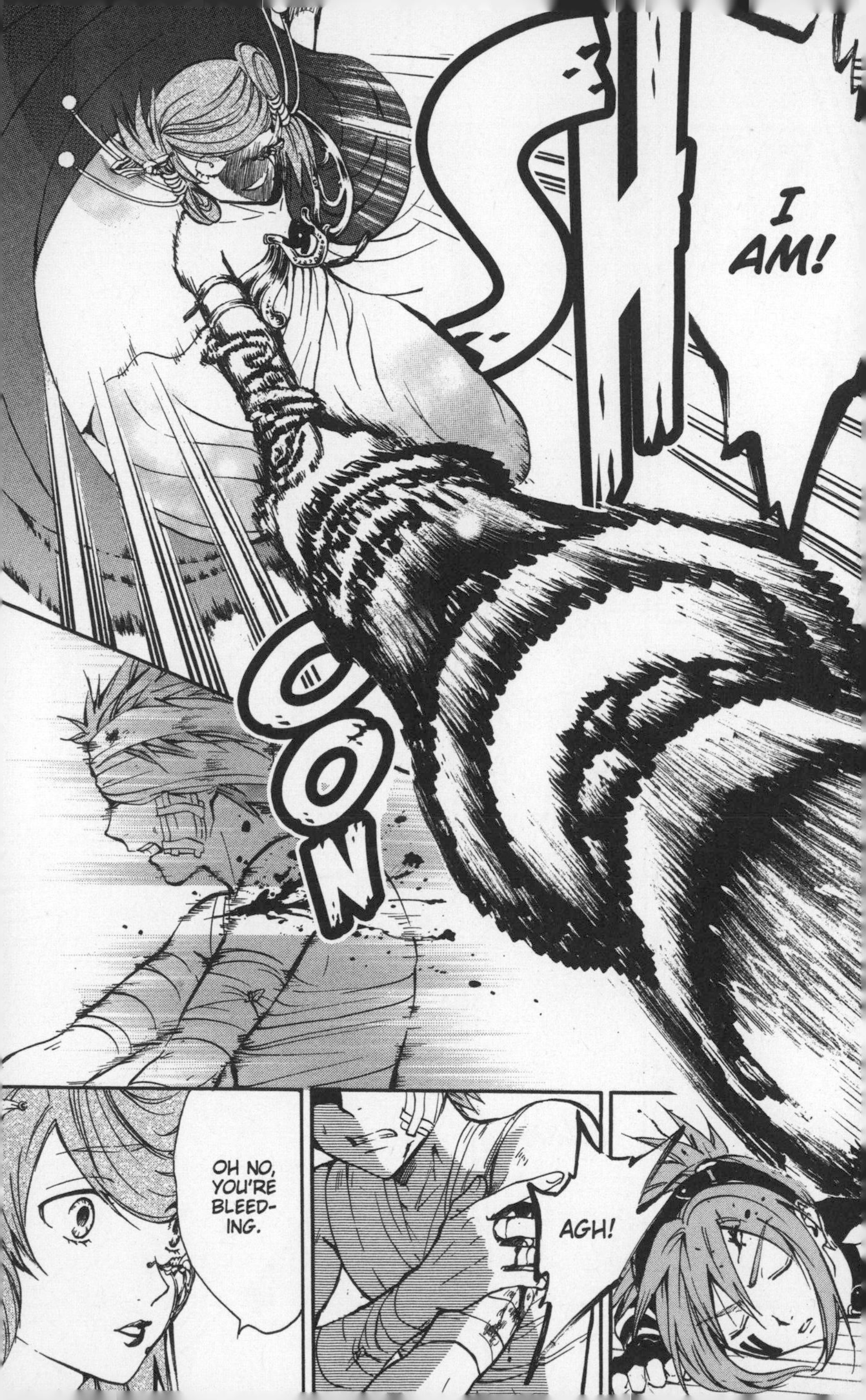
I AM!
AGH!
OH NO, YOU'RE BLEED-ING.

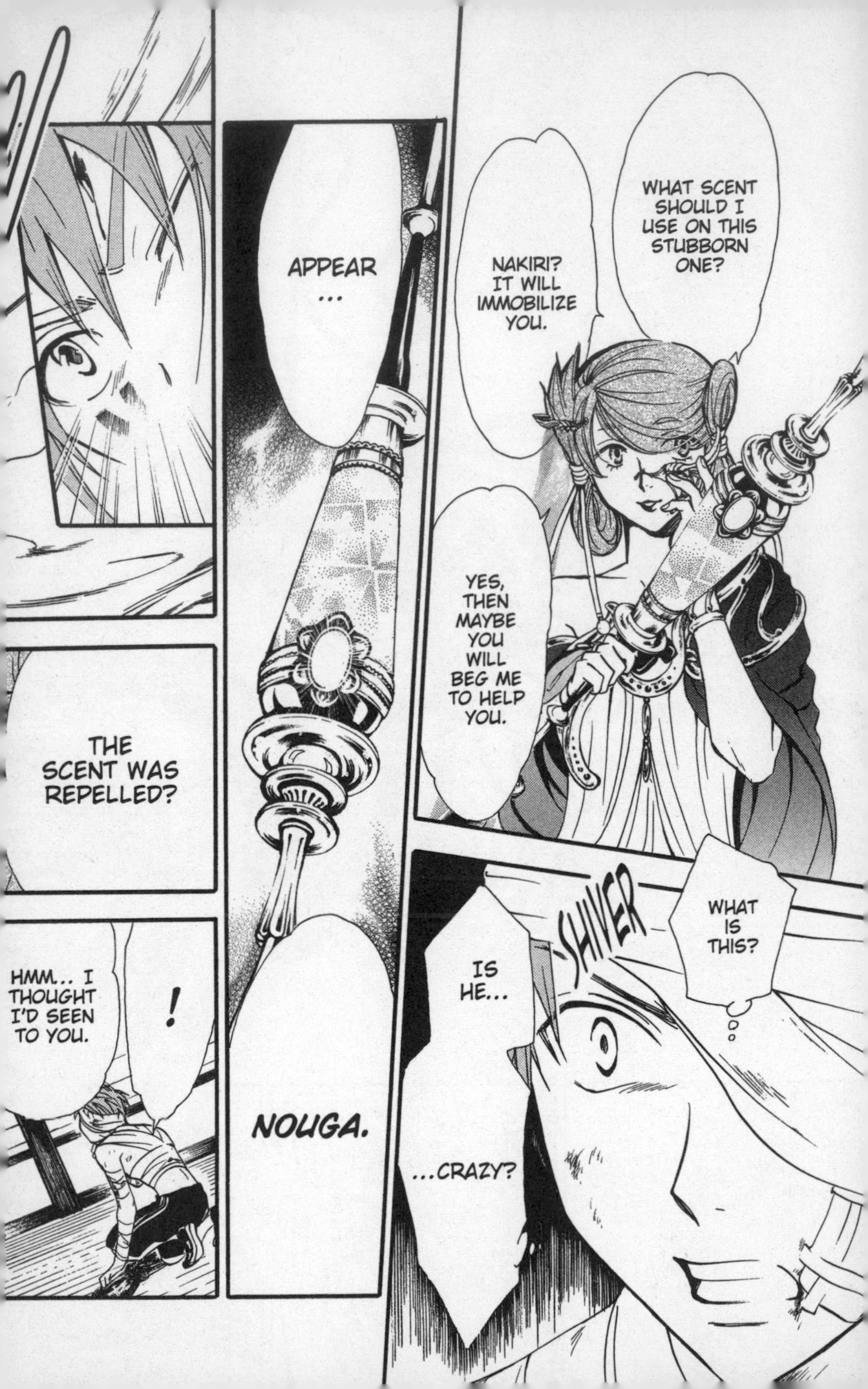
WHAT SCENT SHOULD I USE ON THIS STUBBORN ONE?
NAKIRI? IT WILL IMMOBILIZE YOU.
YES, THEN MAYBE YOU WILL BEG ME TO HELP YOU.
WHAT IS THIS?
SHIVER
IS HE...
...CRAZY?
APPEAR ...
NOUGA.
THE SCENT WAS REPELLED?
!
HMM... I THOUGHT I'D SEEN TO YOU.

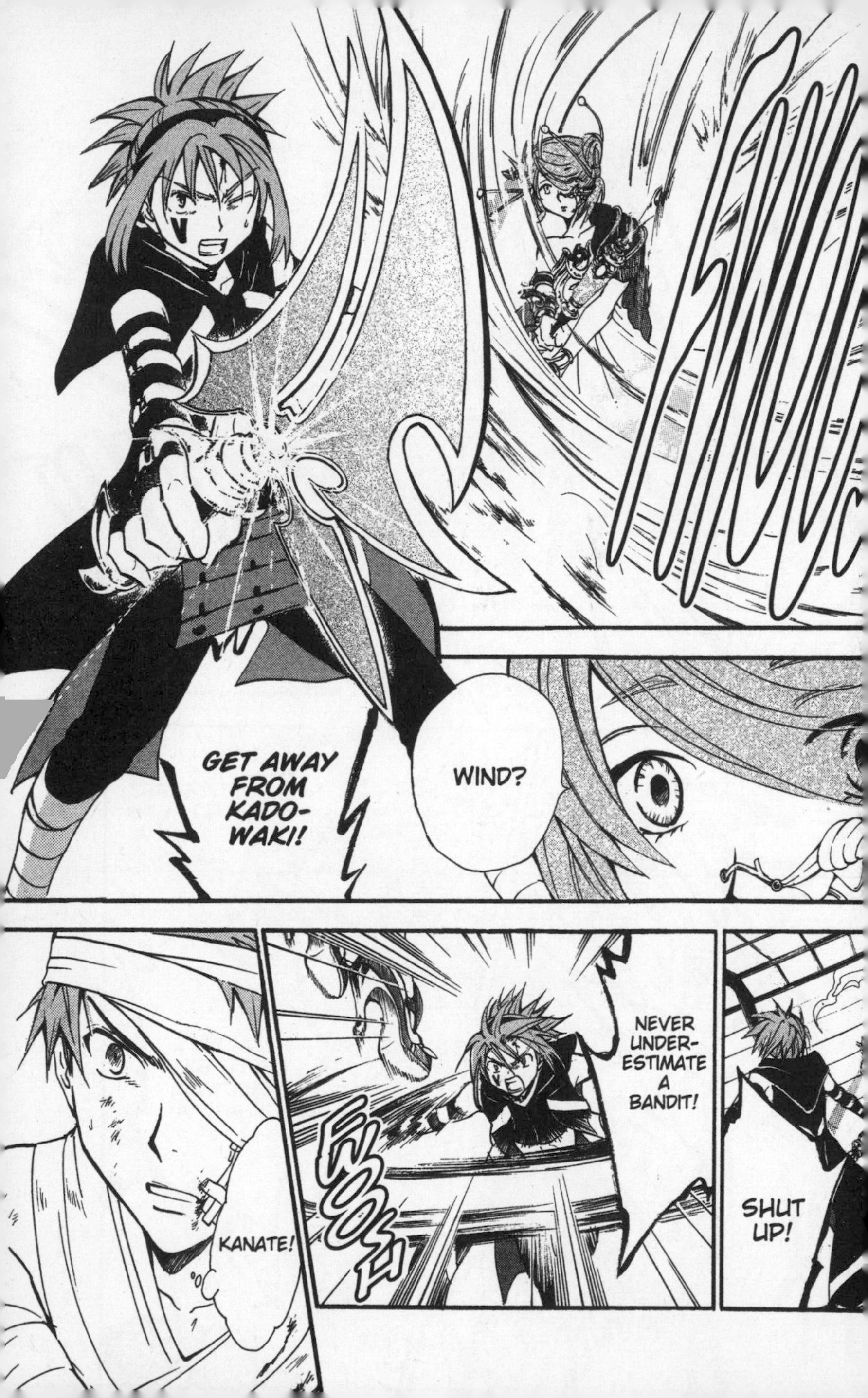
WIND?
GET AWAY FROM KADO-WAKI!
SHUT UP!
NEVER UNDER-ESTIMATE A BANDIT!
FWOOSH
KANATE!

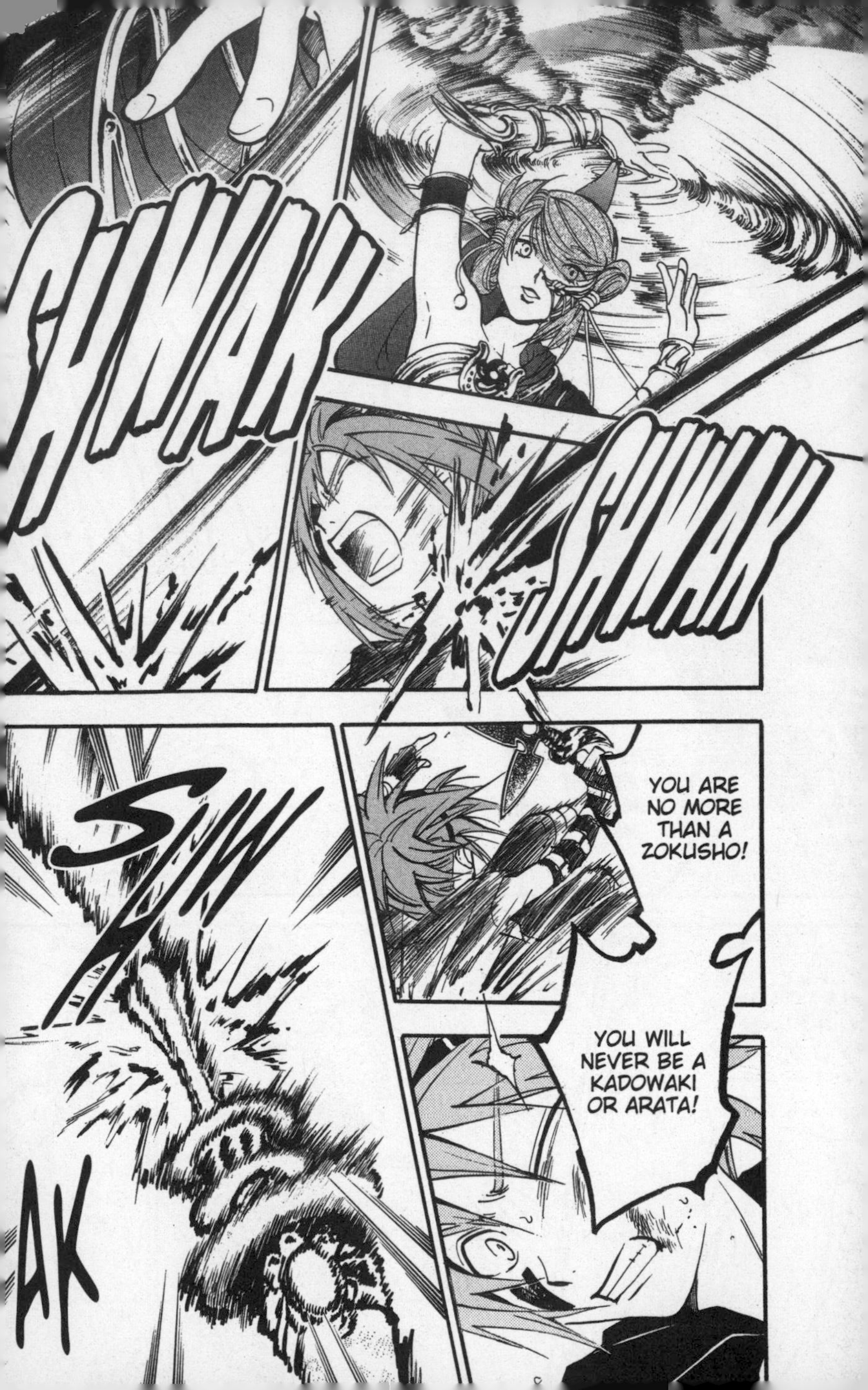
CHWAK
CHWAK
YOU ARE NO MORE THAN A ZOKUSHO!
YOU WILL NEVER BE A KADOWAKI OR ARATA!

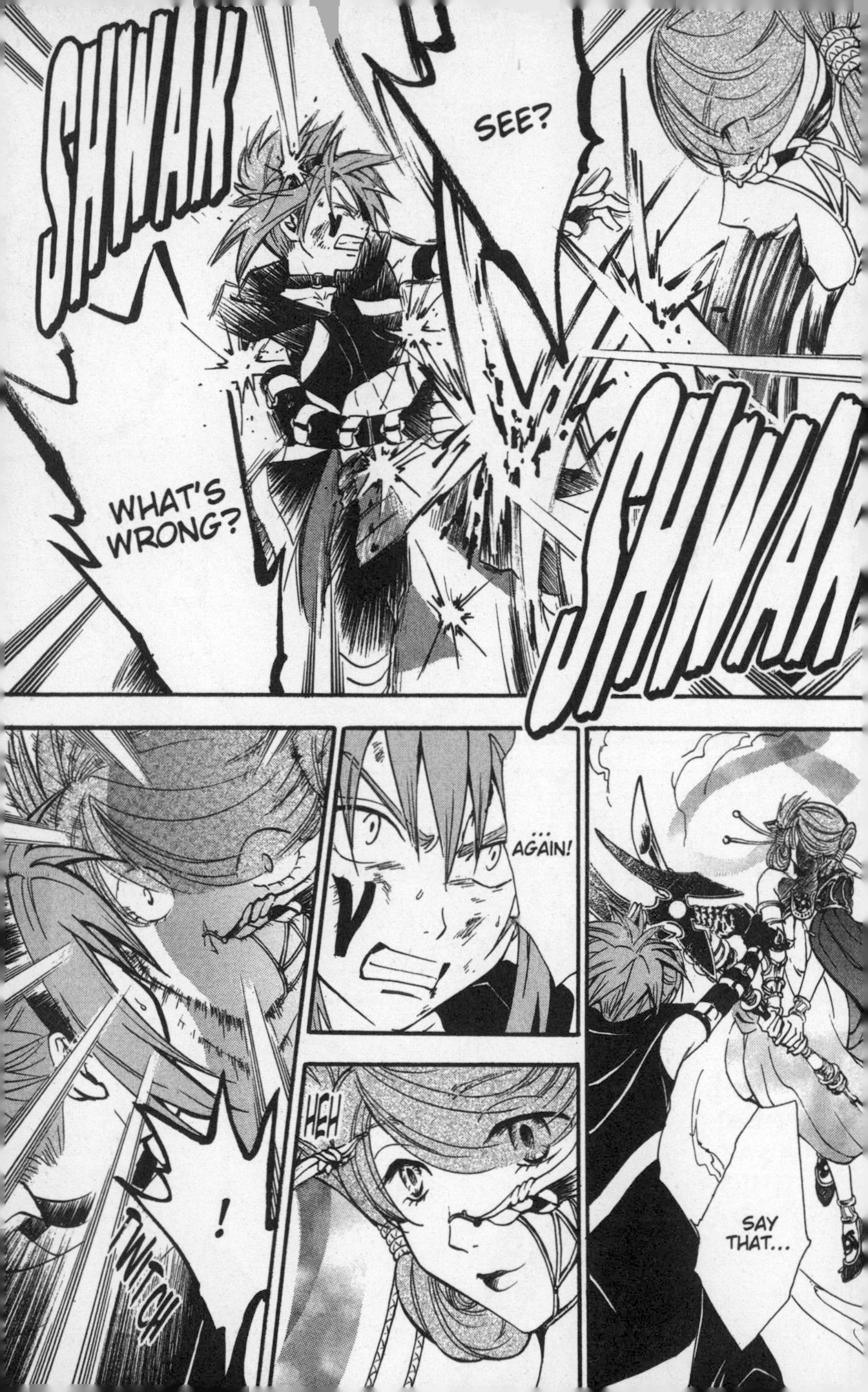
SEE?
SHWAK
SHWAK
WHAT'S WRONG?
SAY THAT...
... AGAIN!
HEH
!
TWITCH

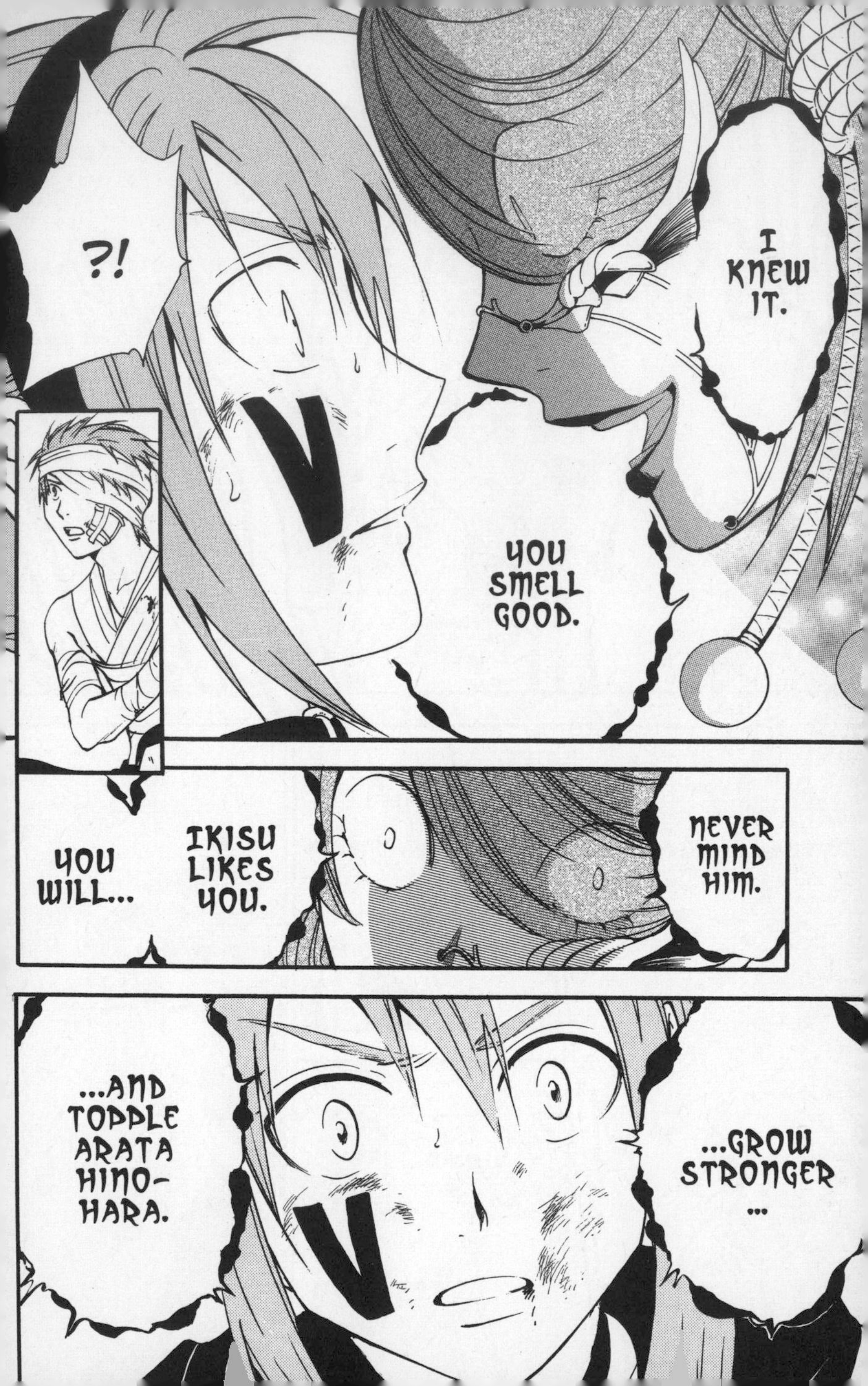
I KNEW IT.
YOU SMELL GOOD.
?!
NEVER MIND HIM.
IKISU LIKES YOU.
YOU WILL...
...GROW STRONGER ...
...AND TOPPLE ARATA HINO-HARA.

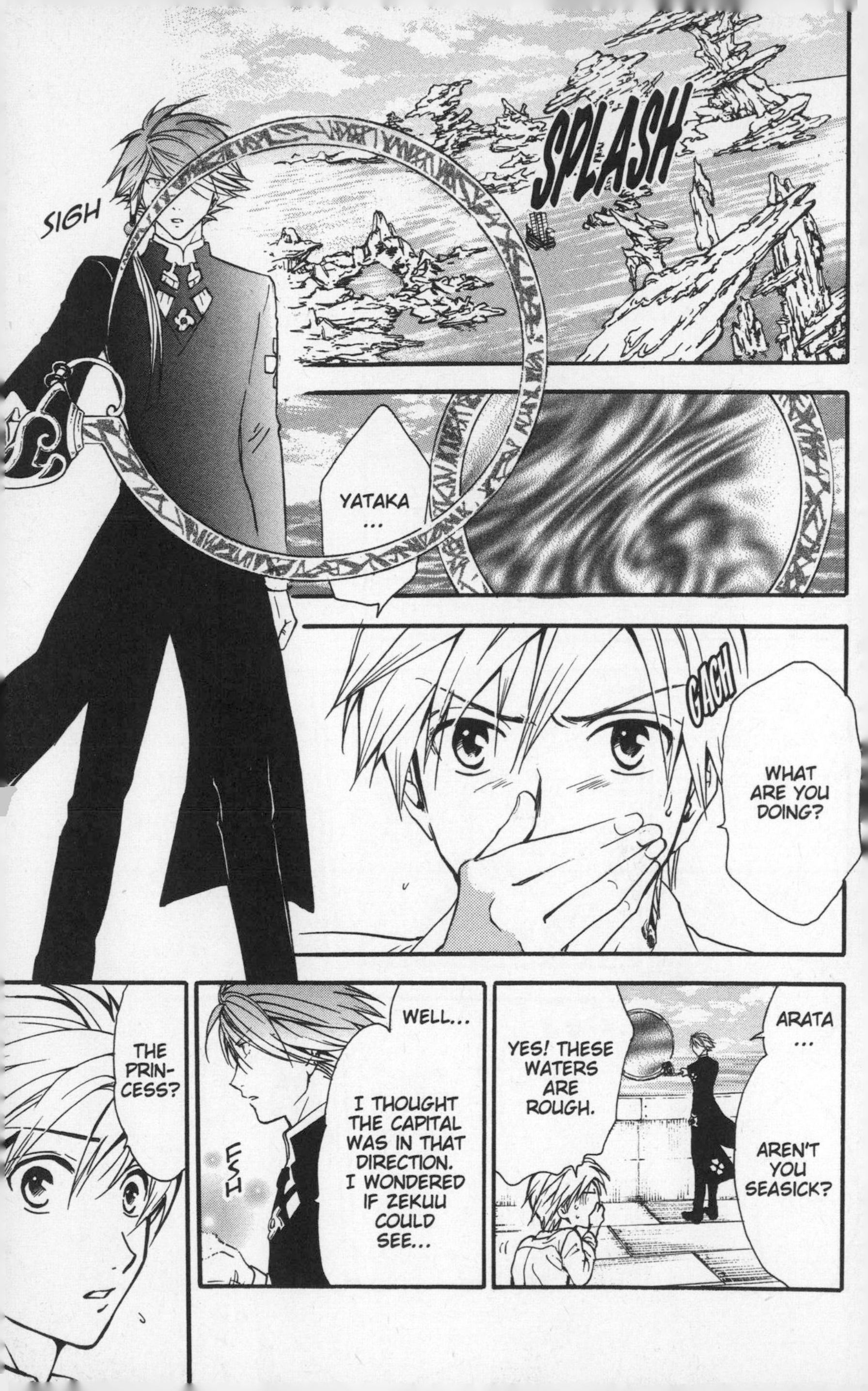
SPLASH
YATAKA...
CACH
WHAT ARE YOU DOING?
SIGH
ARATA...
AREN'T YOU SEASICK?
YES! THESE WATERS ARE ROUGH.
WELL...
I THOUGHT THE CAPITAL WAS IN THAT DIRECTION. I WONDERED IF ZEKUU COULD SEE...
FSH
THE PRIN-CESS?

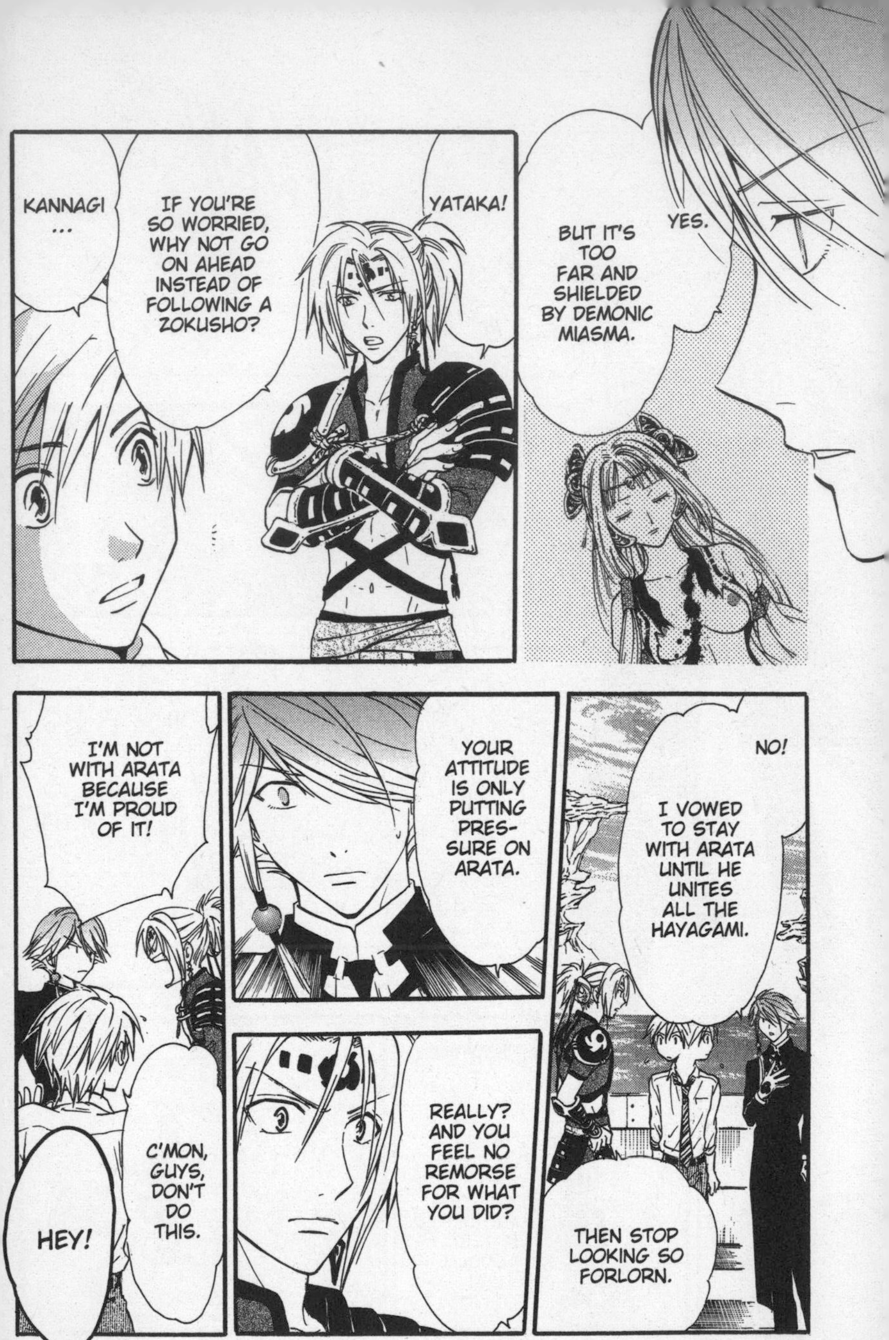
YES.
BUT IT'S TOO FAR AND SHIELDED BY DEMONIC MIASMA.
YATAKA!
IF YOU'RE SO WORRIED, WHY NOT GO ON AHEAD INSTEAD OF FOLLOWING A ZOKUSHO?
KANNAGI ...
NO!
I VOWED TO STAY WITH ARATA UNTIL HE UNITES ALL THE HAYAGAMI.
THEN STOP LOOKING SO FORLORN.
YOUR ATTITUDE IS ONLY PUTTING PRES-SURE ON ARATA.
REALLY? AND YOU FEEL NO REMORSE FOR WHAT YOU DID?
I'M NOT WITH ARATA BECAUSE I'M PROUD OF IT!
C'MON, GUYS, DON'T DO THIS.
HEY!

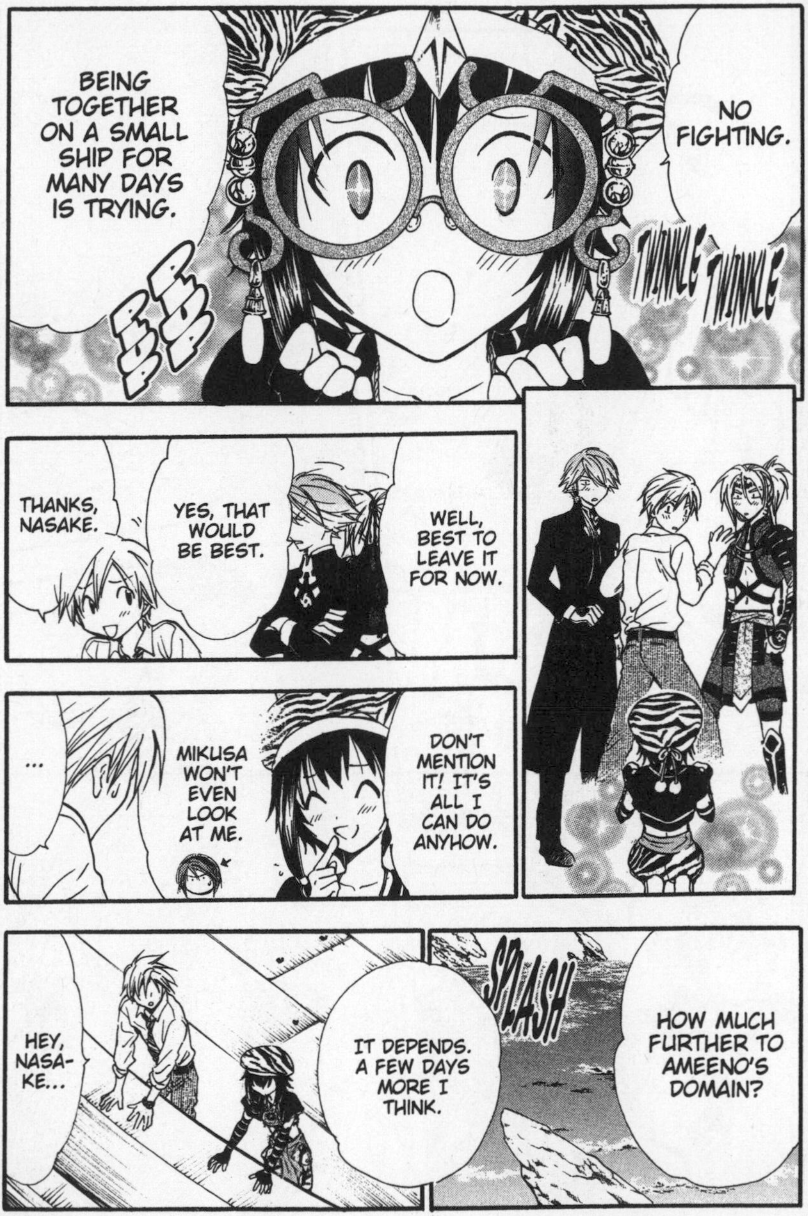
NO FIGHTING.
TWINKLE TWINKLE
BEING TOGETHER ON A SMALL SHIP FOR MANY DAYS IS TRYING.
PUP PUP
WELL, BEST TO LEAVE IT FOR NOW.
YES, THAT WOULD BE BEST.
THANKS, NASAKE.
DON'T MENTION IT! IT'S ALL I CAN DO ANYHOW.
MIKUSA WON'T EVEN LOOK AT ME.
...
SPLASH
HOW MUCH FURTHER TO AMEENO'S DOMAIN?
IT DEPENDS. A FEW DAYS MORE I THINK.
HEY, NASA-KE...

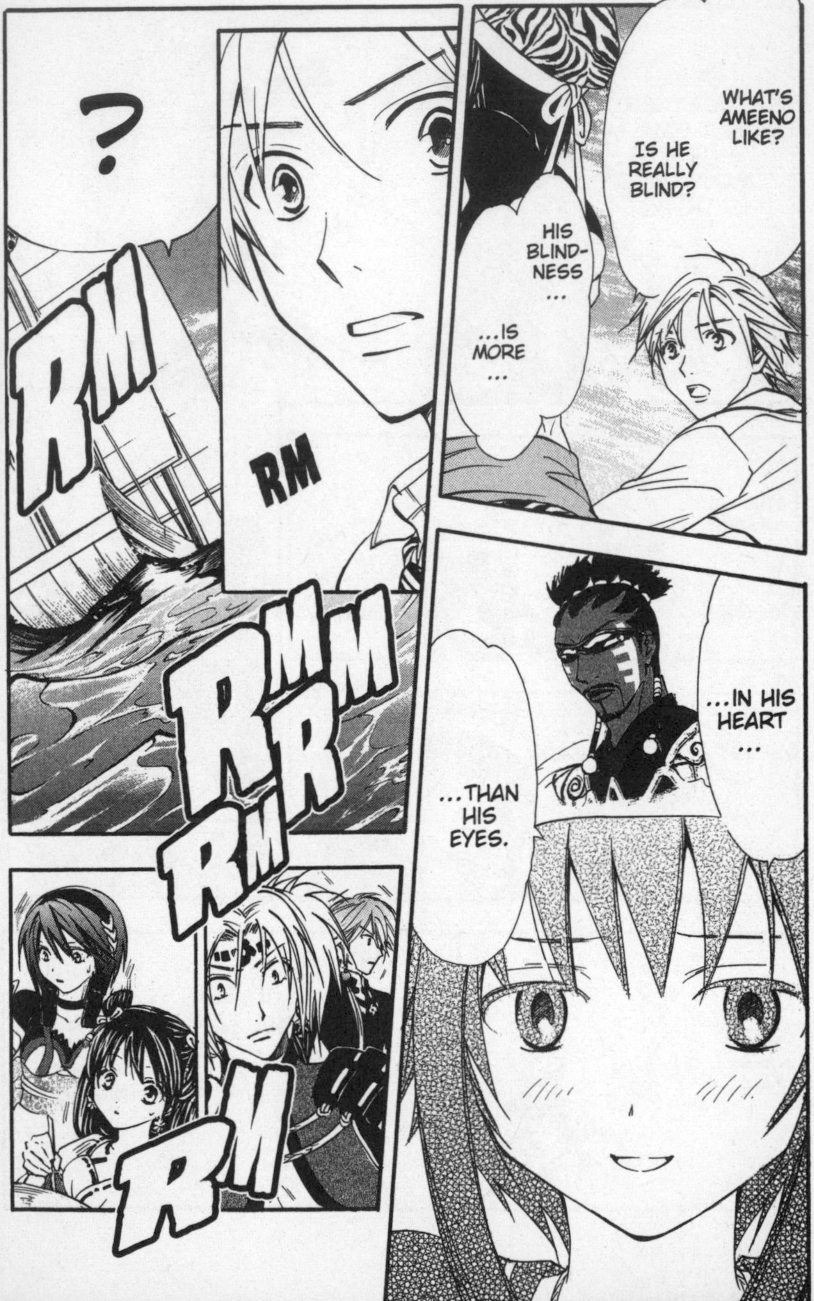
WHAT'S AMEENO LIKE?
IS HE REALLY BLIND?
HIS BLIND- NESS ...
...IS MORE ...
...IN HIS HEART ...
...THAN HIS EYES.
RM
?
RM
RMM
RM
RM
RM

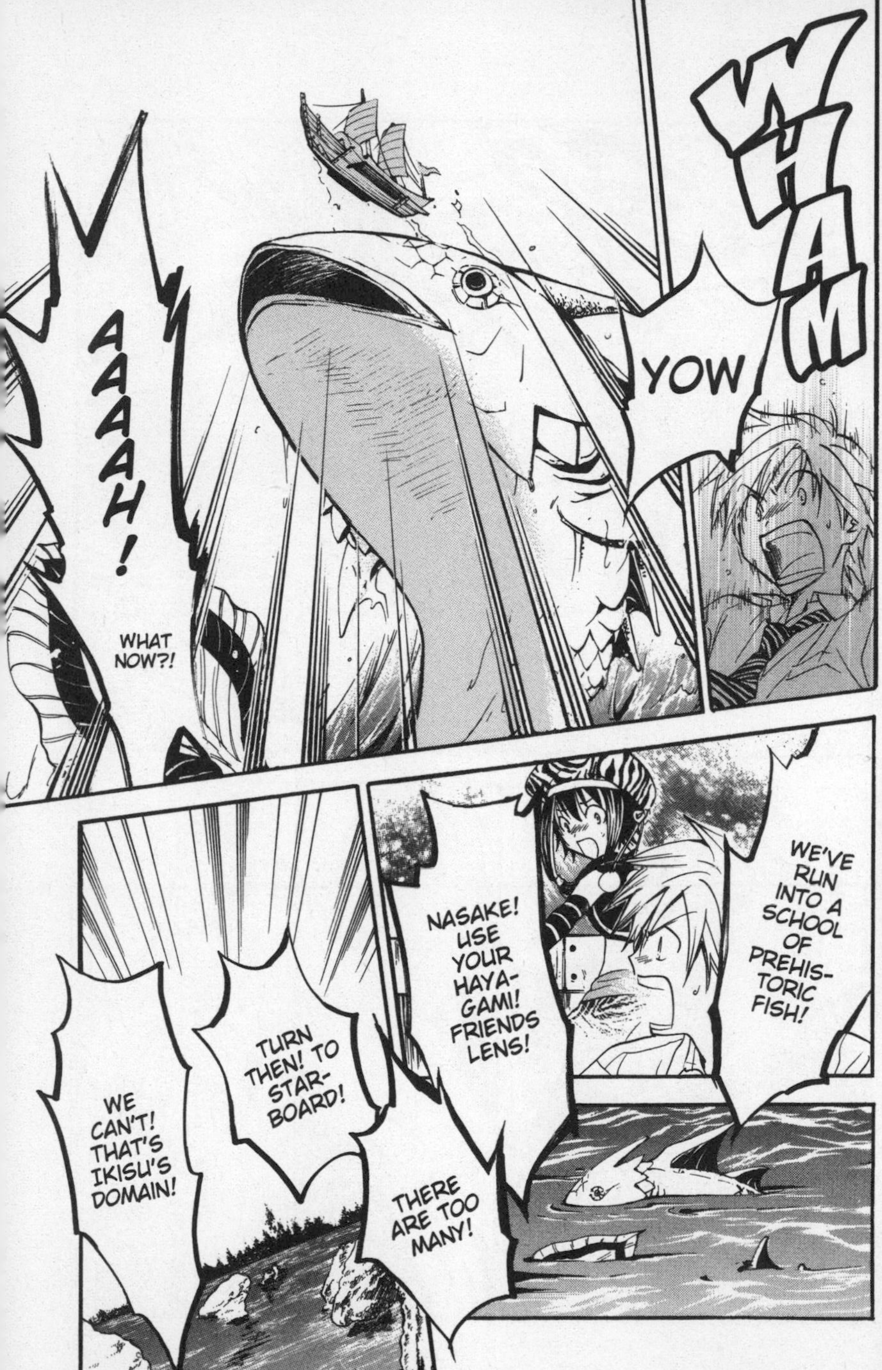
WHAM
YOW
AAAAAH!
WHAT NOW?!
WE'VE RUN INTO A SCHOOL OF PREHIS-TORIC FISH!
NASAKE! USE YOUR HAYA-GAMI! FRIENDS LENS!
THERE ARE TOO MANY!
TURN THEN! TO STAR-BOARD!
WE CAN'T! THAT'S IKISU'S DOMAIN!

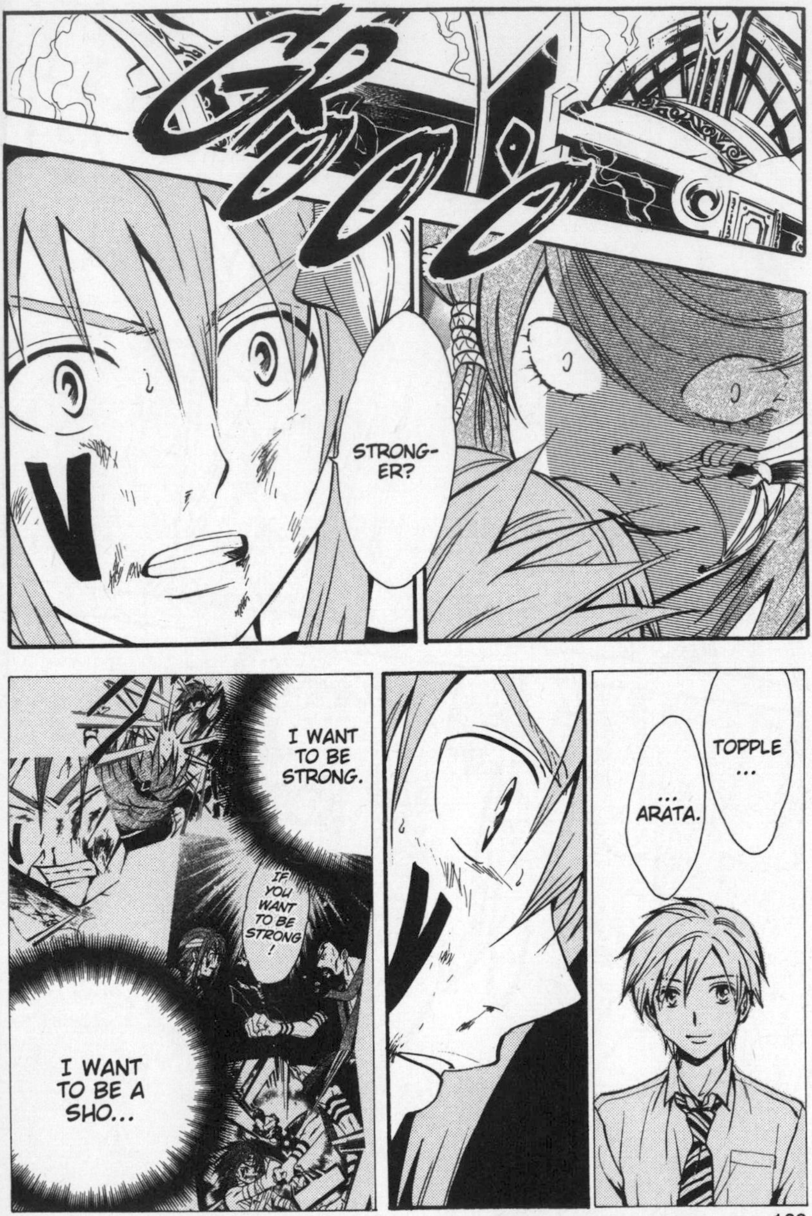
STRONGER?
TOPPLE ...
... ARATA.
I WANT TO BE STRONG.
IF YOU WANT TO BE STRONG!
I WANT TO BE A SHO...

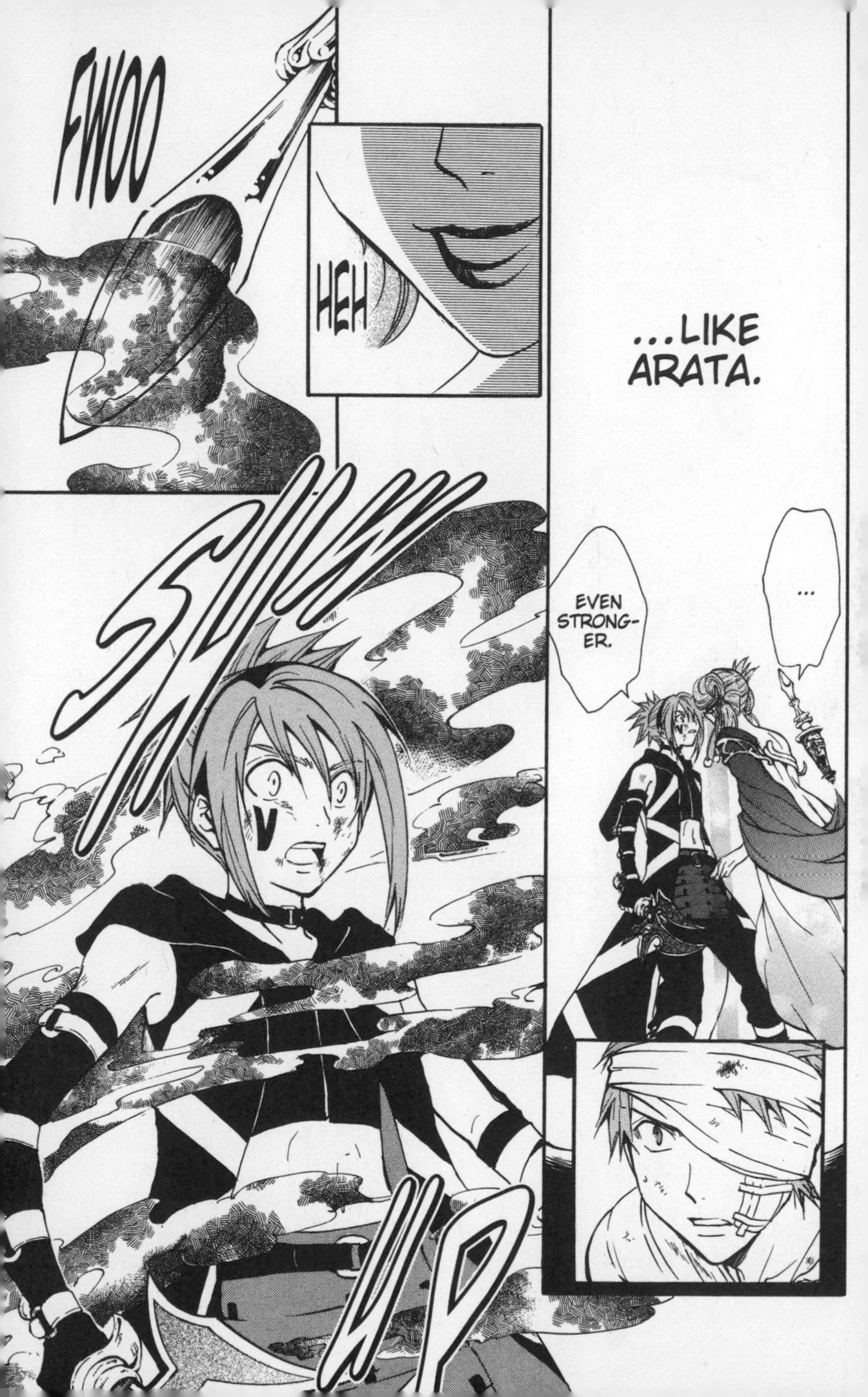
...LIKE ARATA.
...
EVEN STRONG-ER.
HEH
FWOO

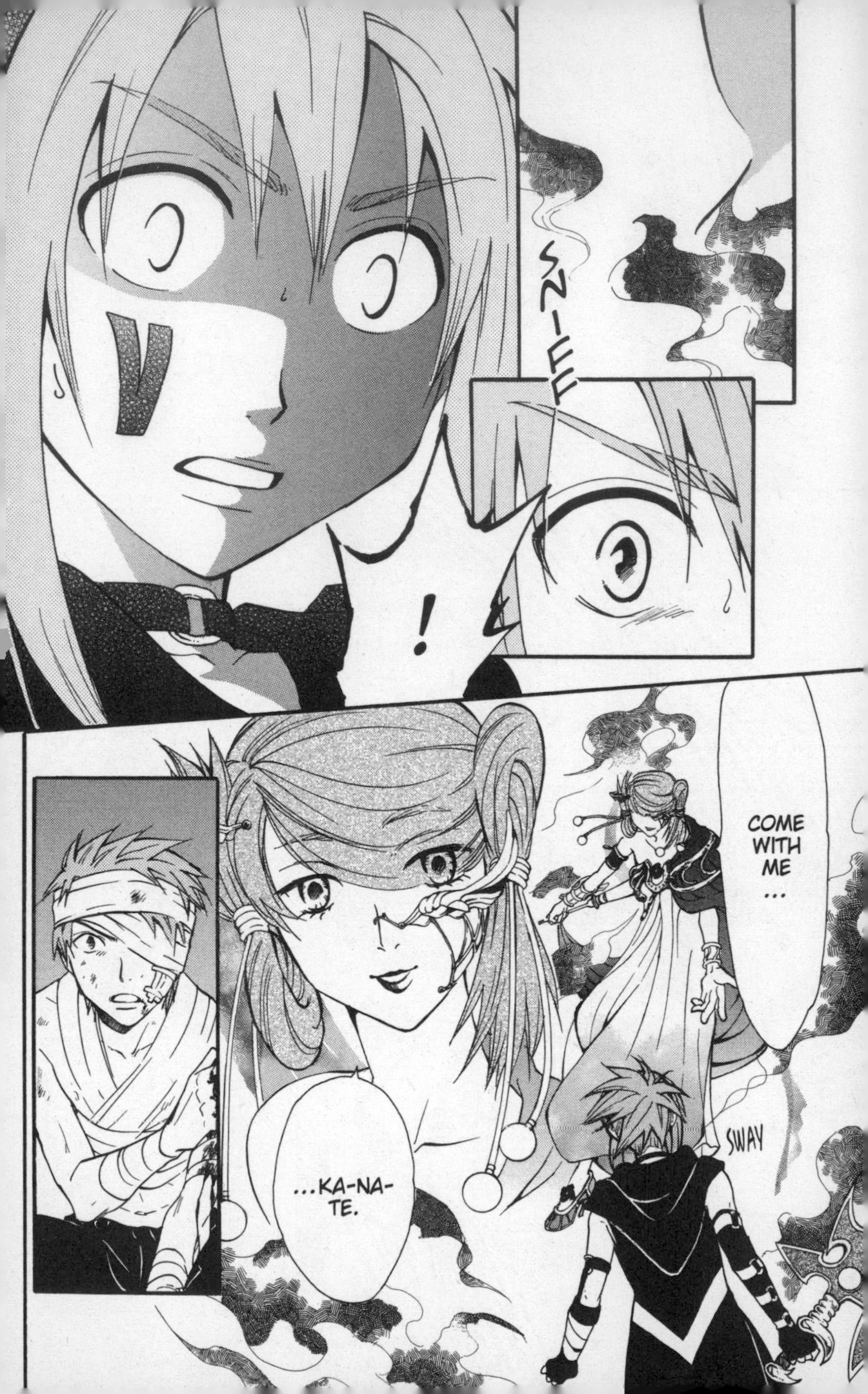
SNIFF
!
COME WITH ME ...
SWAY
...KA-NA-TE.

CHAPTER 197
IKISU'S ISLAND

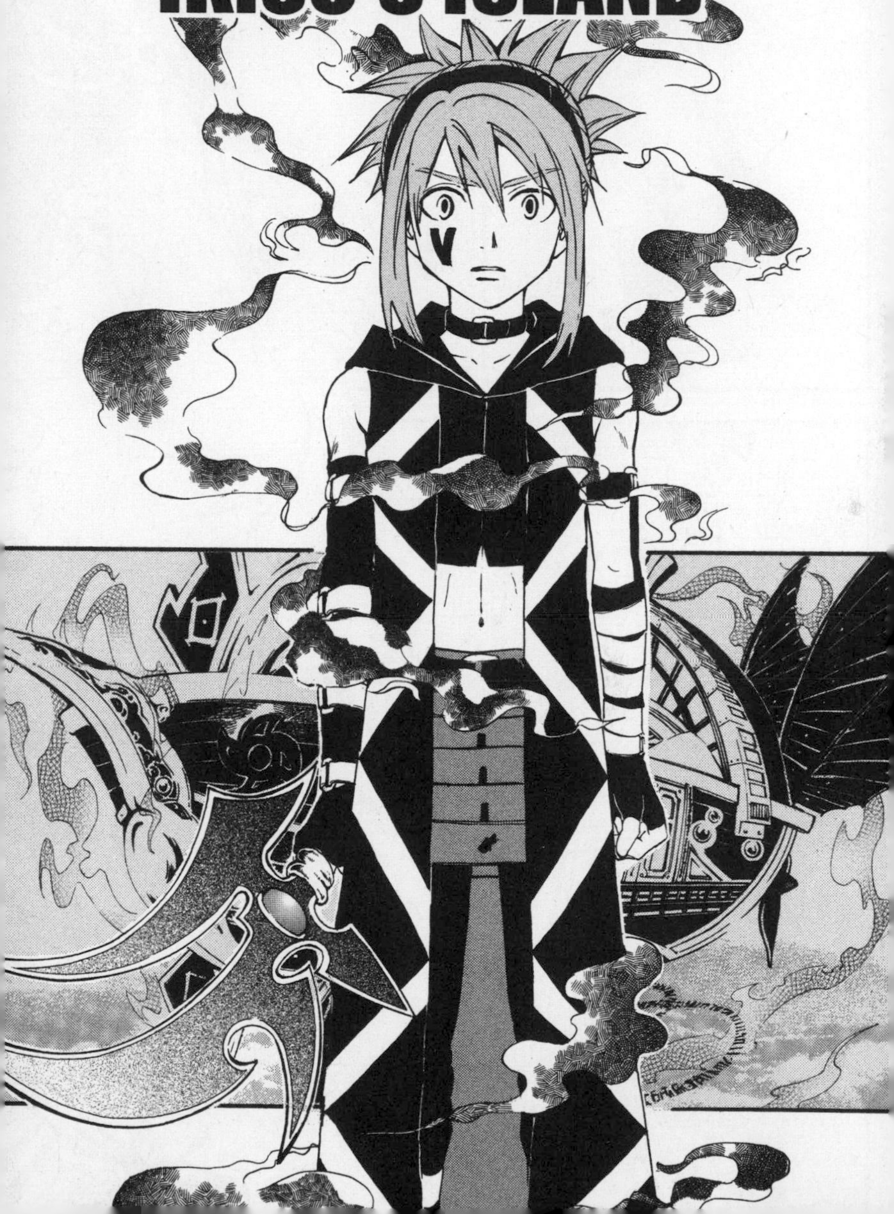

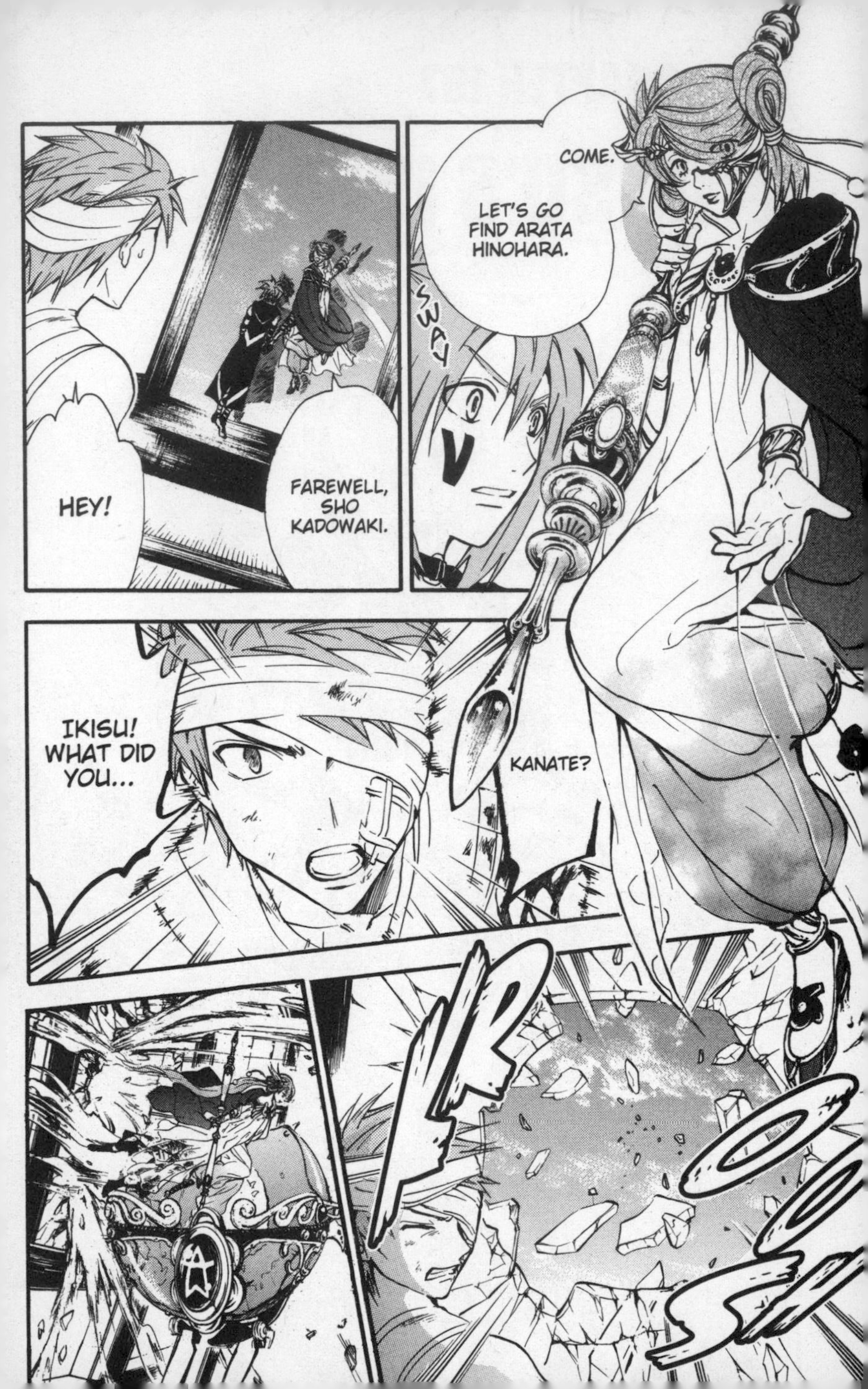
COME.
LET'S GO FIND ARATA HINOHARA.
SWAY
FAREWELL, SHO KADOWAKI.
HEY!
KANATE?
IKISU! WHAT DID YOU...

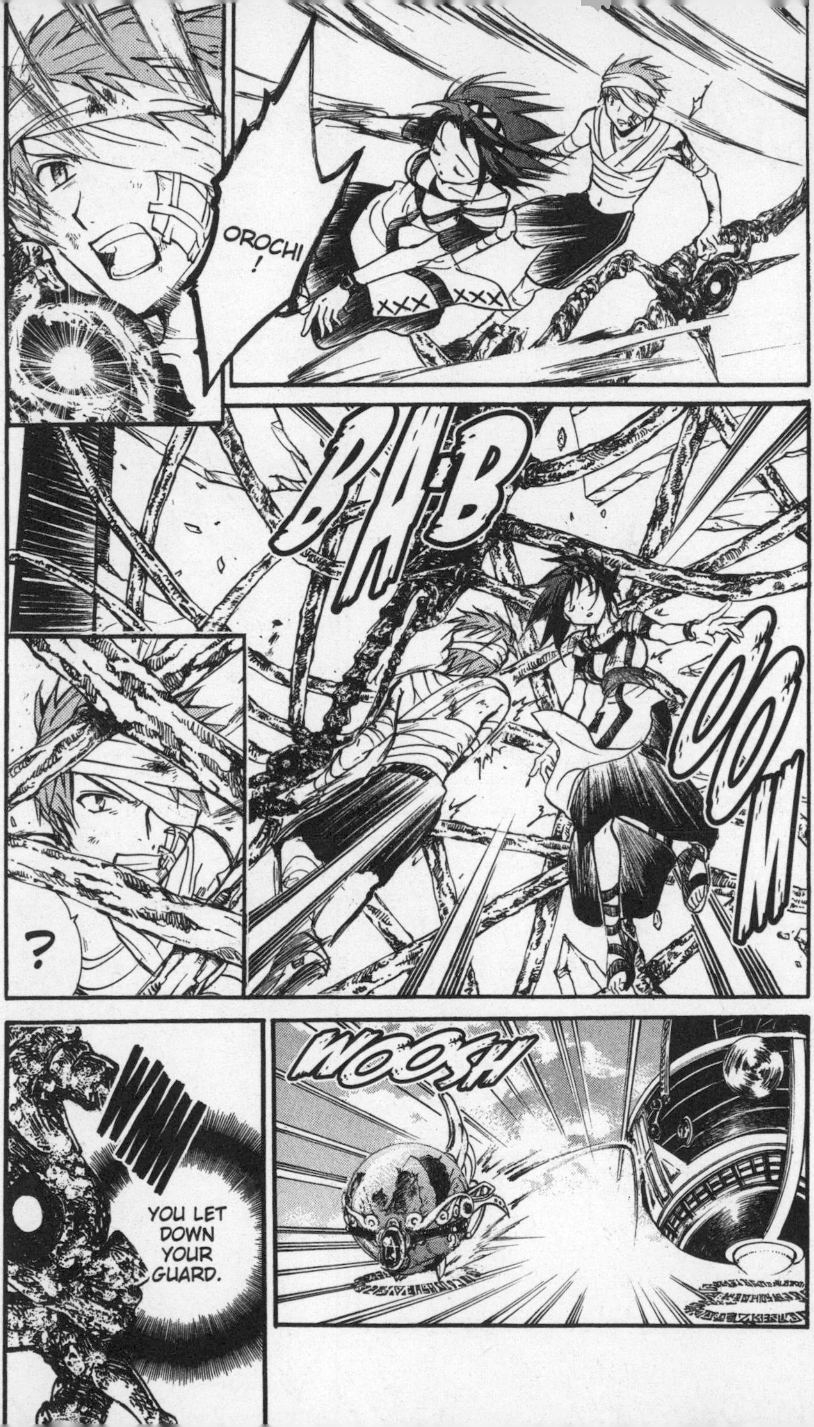
OROCHI!
BA-B
OOOM
?
WOOSH
YOU LET DOWN YOUR GUARD.

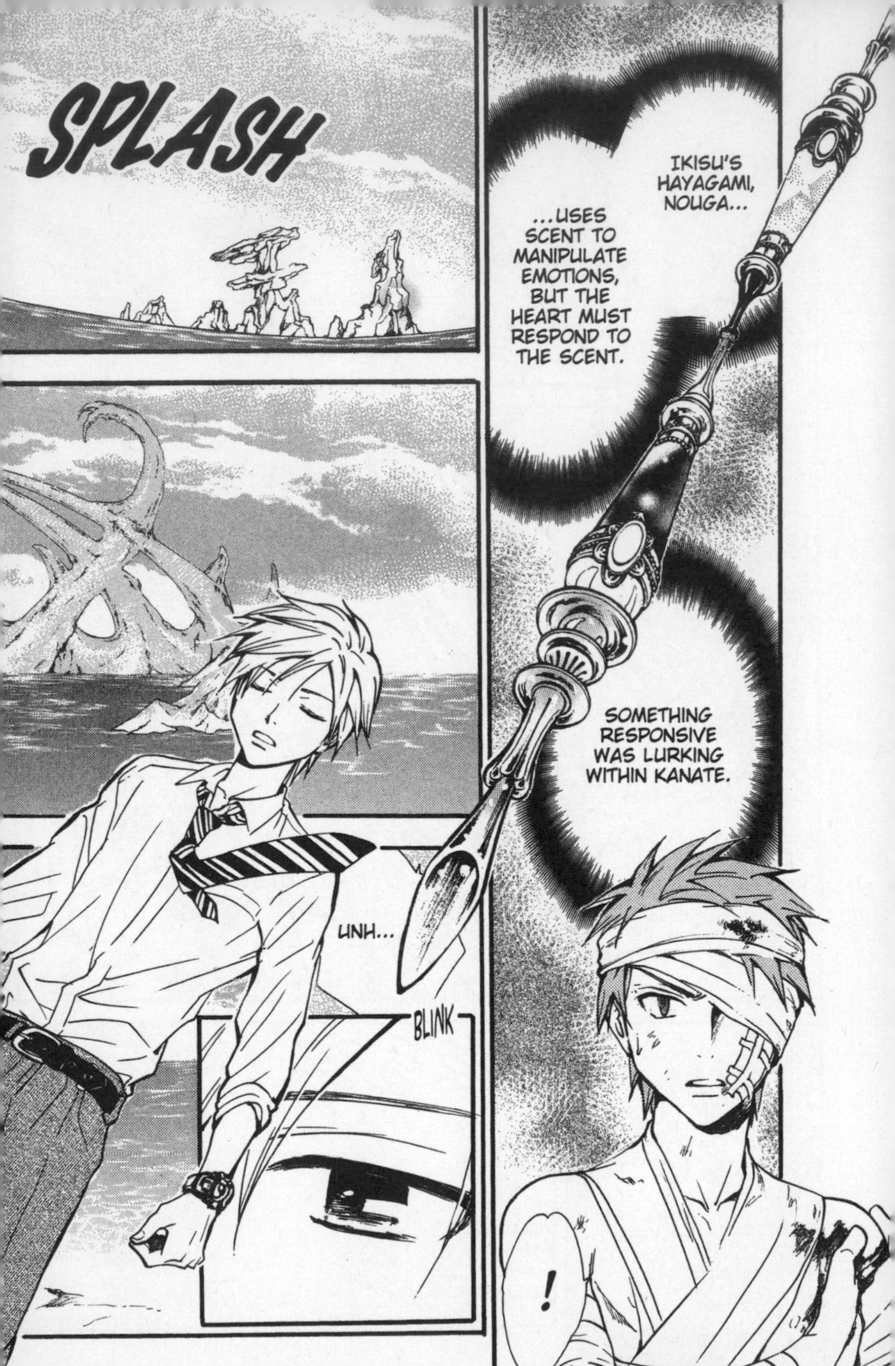

IKISU'S HAYAGAMI, NOUGA...
...USES SCENT TO MANIPULATE EMOTIONS, BUT THE HEART MUST RESPOND TO THE SCENT.
SOMETHING RESPONSIVE WAS LURKING WITHIN KANATE.
!
SPLASH
UNH...
BLINK

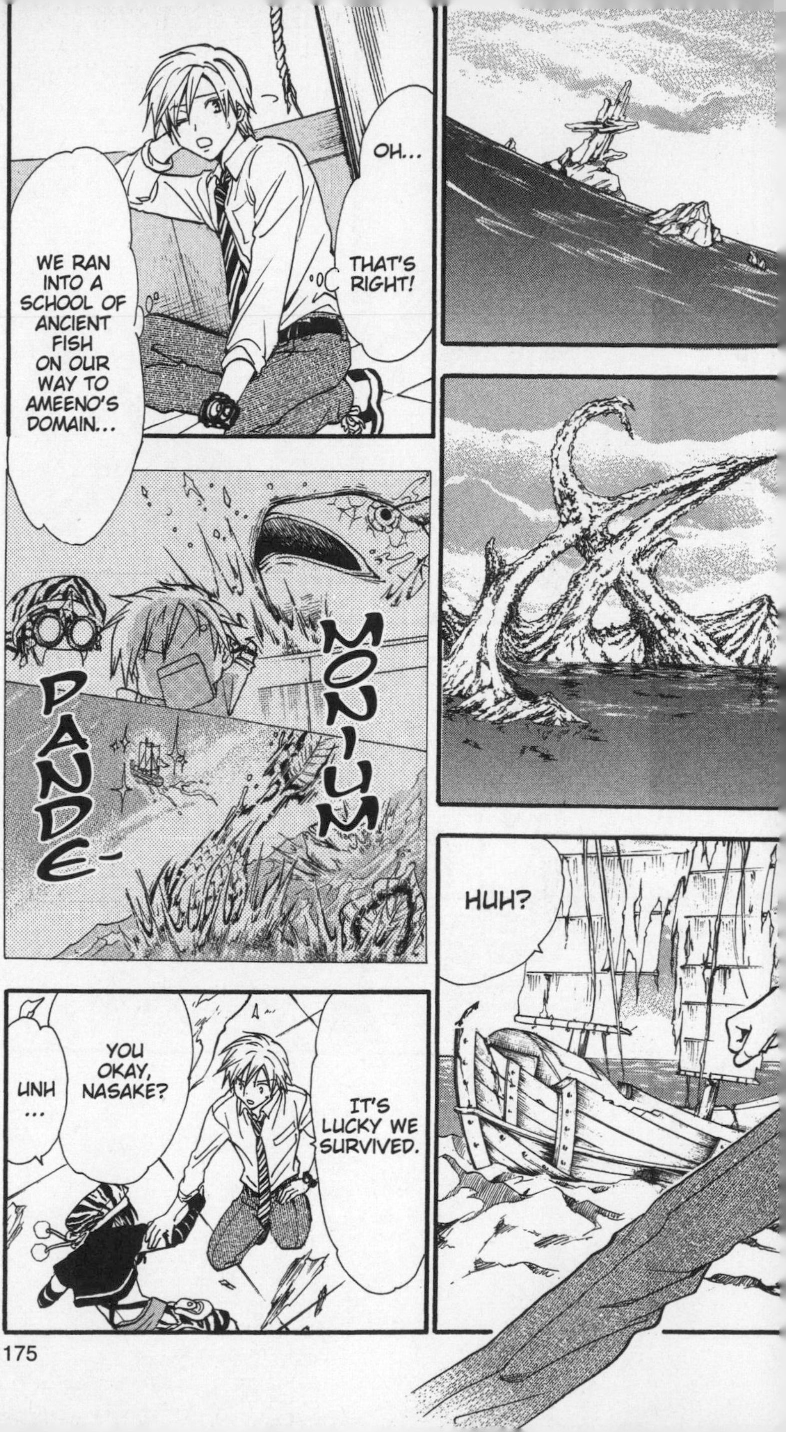
OH...
THAT'S RIGHT!
WE RAN INTO A SCHOOL OF ANCIENT FISH ON OUR WAY TO AMEENO'S DOMAIN...
PANDE-MONIUM
HUH?
IT'S LUCKY WE SURVIVED.
YOU OKAY, NASAKE?
UNH...

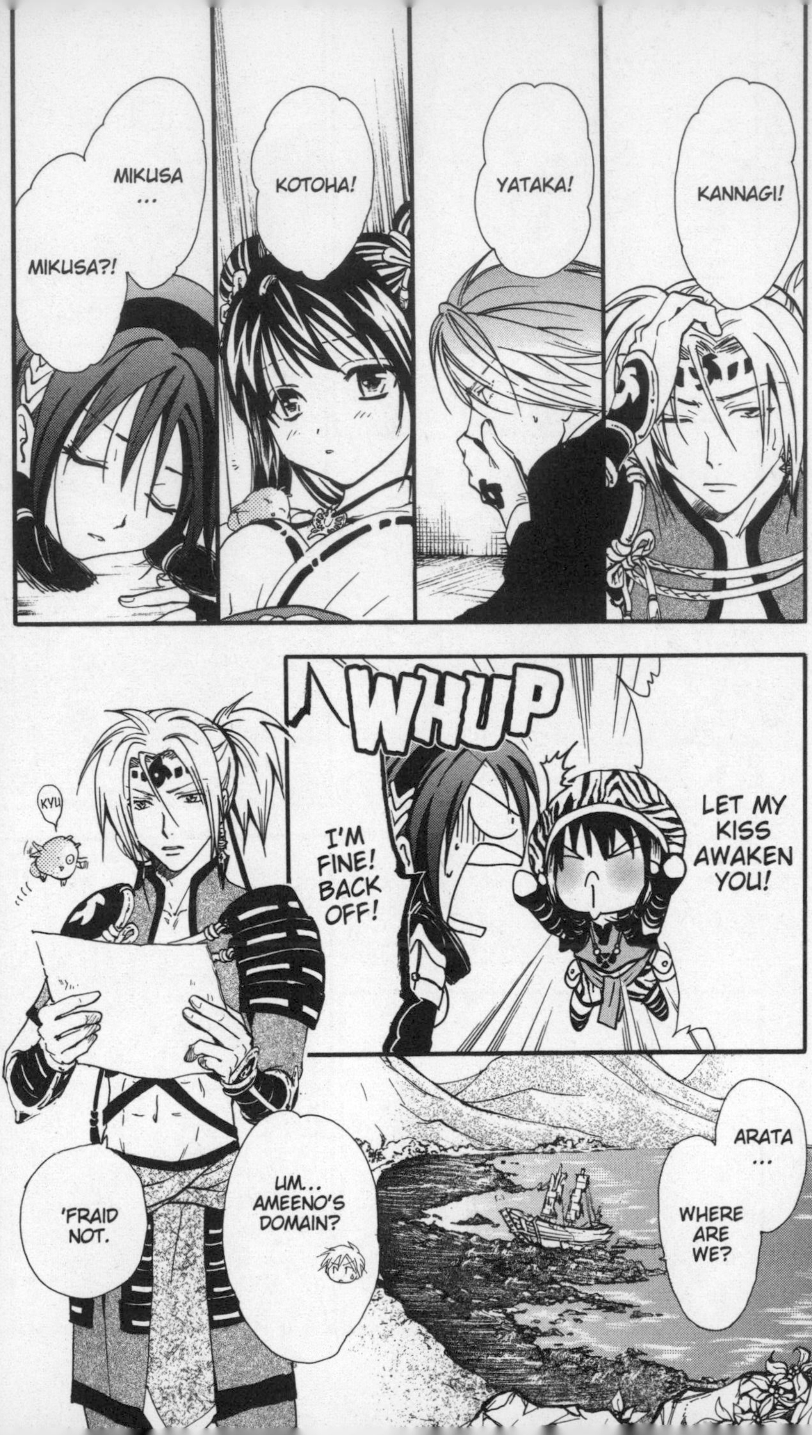
KANNAGI!
YATAKA!
KOTOHA!
MIKUSA ...
MIKUSA?!
WHUP
LET MY KISS AWAKEN YOU!
I'M FINE! BACK OFF!
KYU
ARATA ... WHERE ARE WE?
UM... AMEENO'S DOMAIN?
'FRAID NOT.

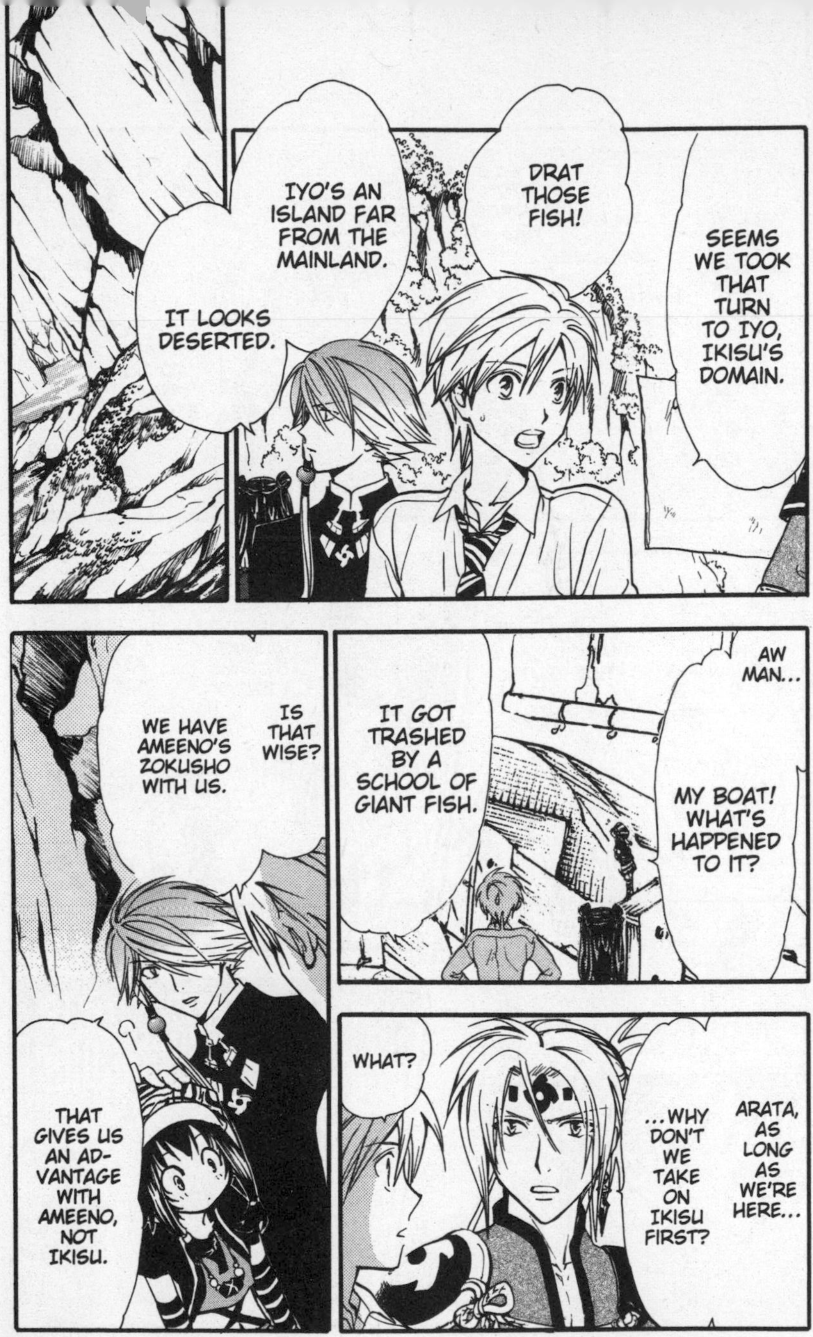

SEEMS WE TOOK THAT TURN TO IYO, IKISU'S DOMAIN.
DRAT THOSE FISH!
IYO'S AN ISLAND FAR FROM THE MAINLAND.
IT LOOKS DESERTED.
AW MAN...
MY BOAT! WHAT'S HAPPENED TO IT?
IT GOT TRASHED BY A SCHOOL OF GIANT FISH.
ARATA, AS LONG AS WE'RE HERE...
...WHY DON'T WE TAKE ON IKISU FIRST?
WHAT?
IS THAT WISE?
WE HAVE AMEENO'S ZOKUSHO WITH US.
THAT GIVES US AN ADVANTAGE WITH AMEENO, NOT IKISU.

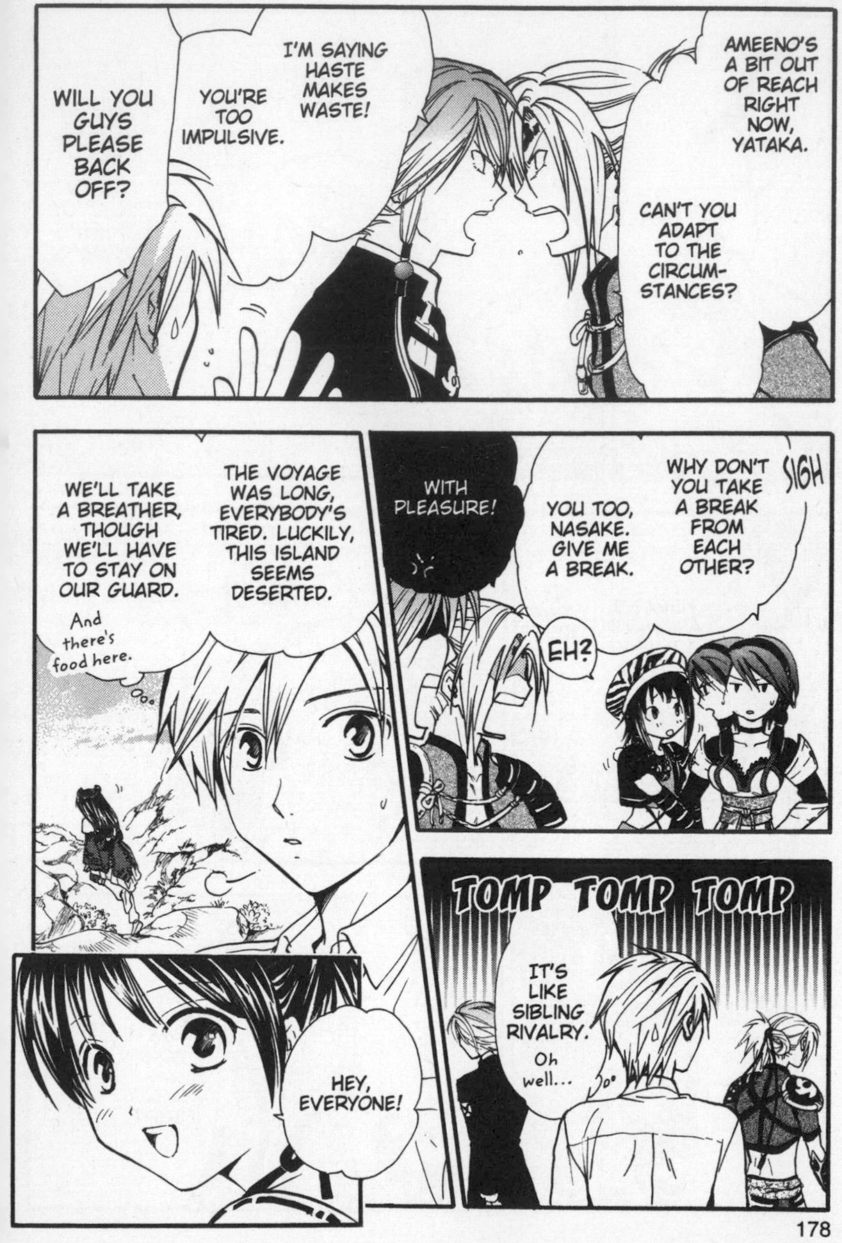
AMEENO'S A BIT OUT OF REACH RIGHT NOW, YATAKA.
CAN'T YOU ADAPT TO THE CIRCUM-STANCES?
I'M SAYING HASTE MAKES WASTE!
YOU'RE TOO IMPULSIVE.
WILL YOU GUYS PLEASE BACK OFF?
SIGH
WHY DON'T YOU TAKE A BREAK FROM EACH OTHER?
YOU TOO, NASAKE. GIVE ME A BREAK.
WITH PLEASURE!
EH?
TOMP TOMP TOMP
IT'S LIKE SIBLING RIVALRY.
Oh well...
THE VOYAGE WAS LONG, EVERYBODY'S TIRED. LUCKILY, THIS ISLAND SEEMS DESERTED.
WE'LL TAKE A BREATHER, THOUGH WE'LL HAVE TO STAY ON OUR GUARD.
And there's food here.
HEY, EVERYONE!

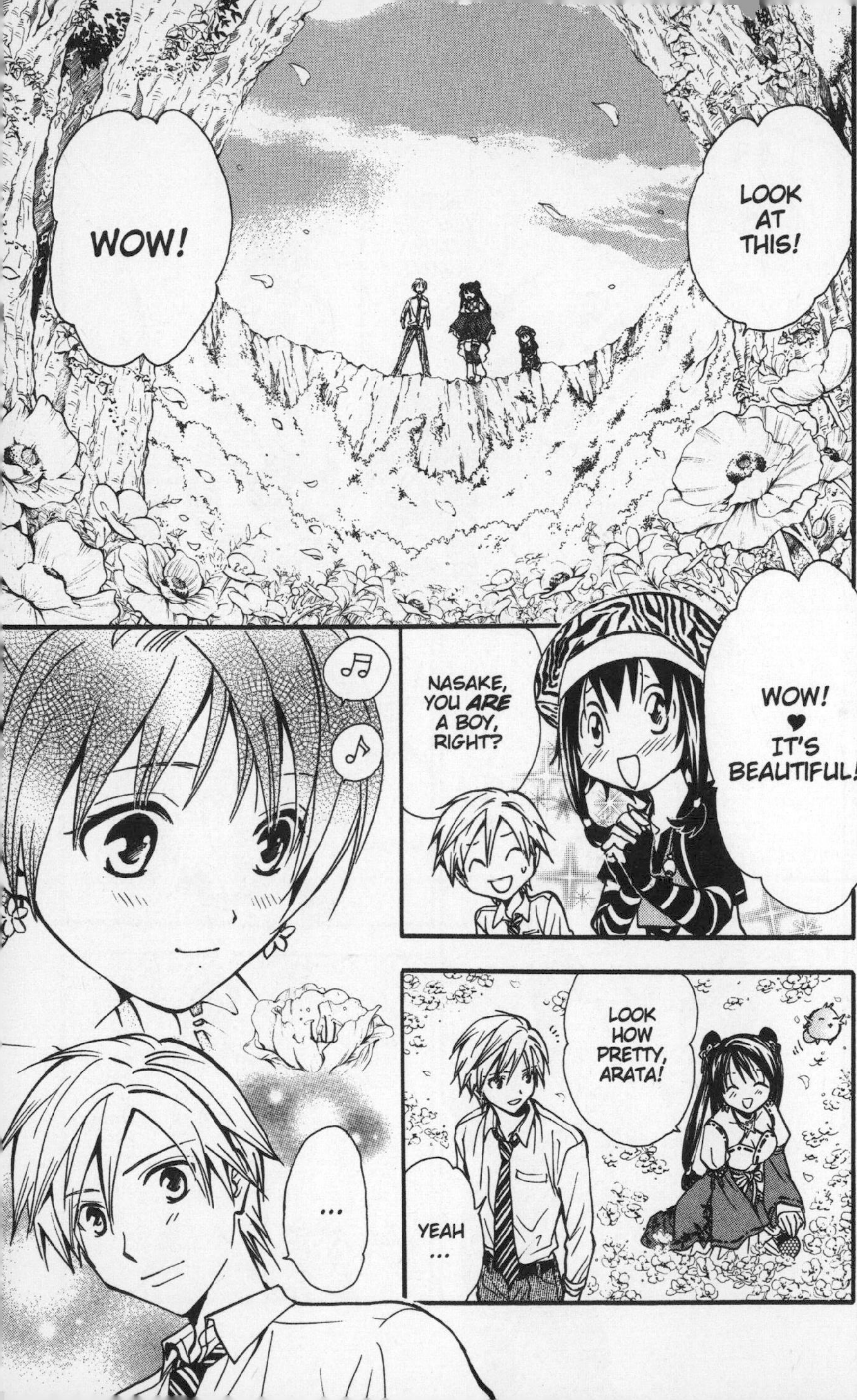
LOOK AT THIS!
WOW!
WOW! ♥ IT'S BEAUTIFUL!
NASAKE, YOU *ARE* A BOY, RIGHT?
LOOK HOW PRETTY, ARATA!
YEAH ...
...

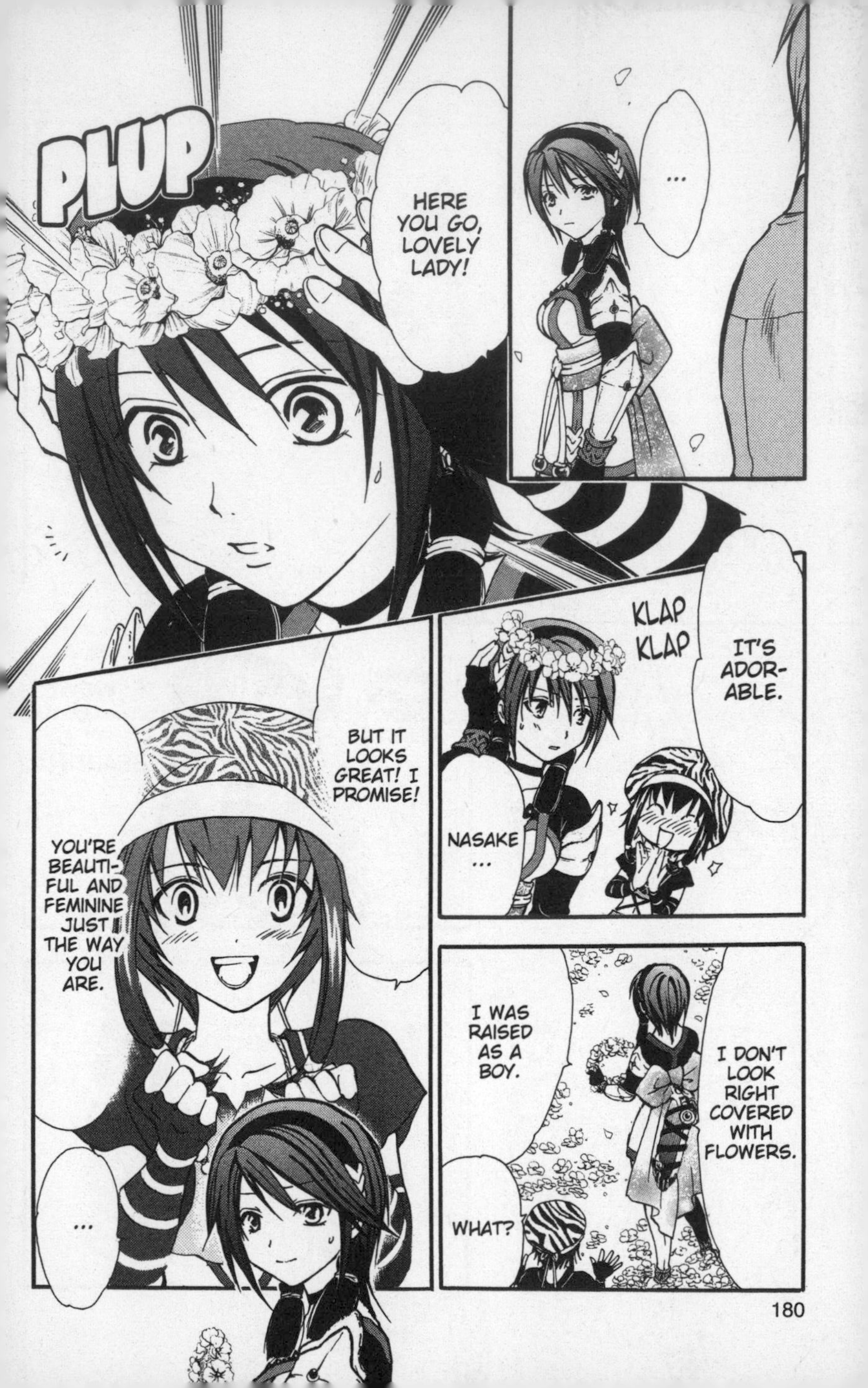
...
PLUP
HERE YOU GO, LOVELY LADY!
IT'S ADORABLE.
KLAP KLAP
NASAKE...
I WAS RAISED AS A BOY.
I DON'T LOOK RIGHT COVERED WITH FLOWERS.
WHAT?
BUT IT LOOKS GREAT! I PROMISE!
YOU'RE BEAUTIFUL AND FEMININE JUST THE WAY YOU ARE.
...

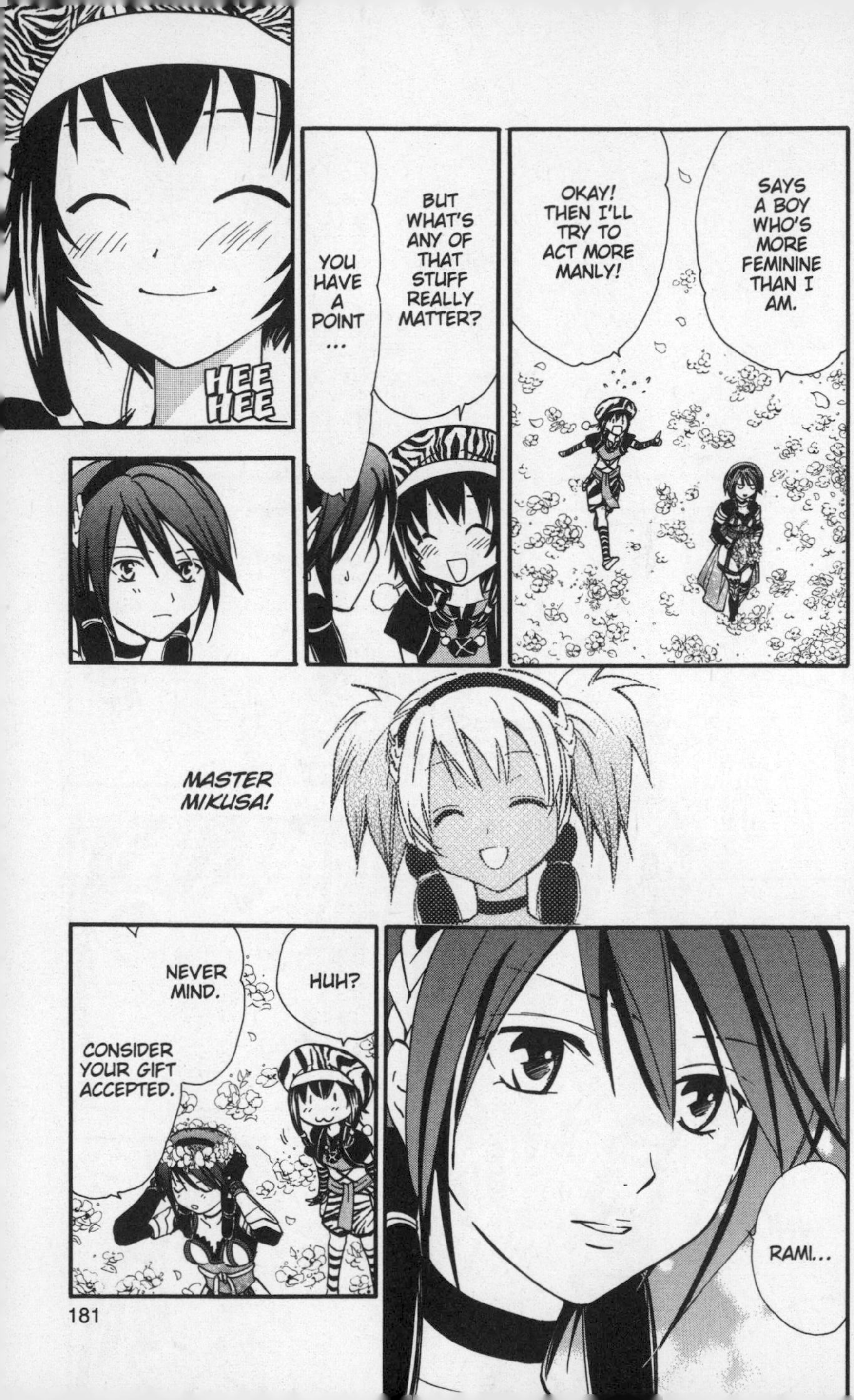
SAYS A BOY WHO'S MORE FEMININE THAN I AM.
OKAY! THEN I'LL TRY TO ACT MORE MANLY!
BUT WHAT'S ANY OF THAT STUFF REALLY MATTER?
YOU HAVE A POINT ...
HEE HEE
MASTER MIKUSA!
RAMI...
HUH?
NEVER MIND.
CONSIDER YOUR GIFT ACCEPTED.

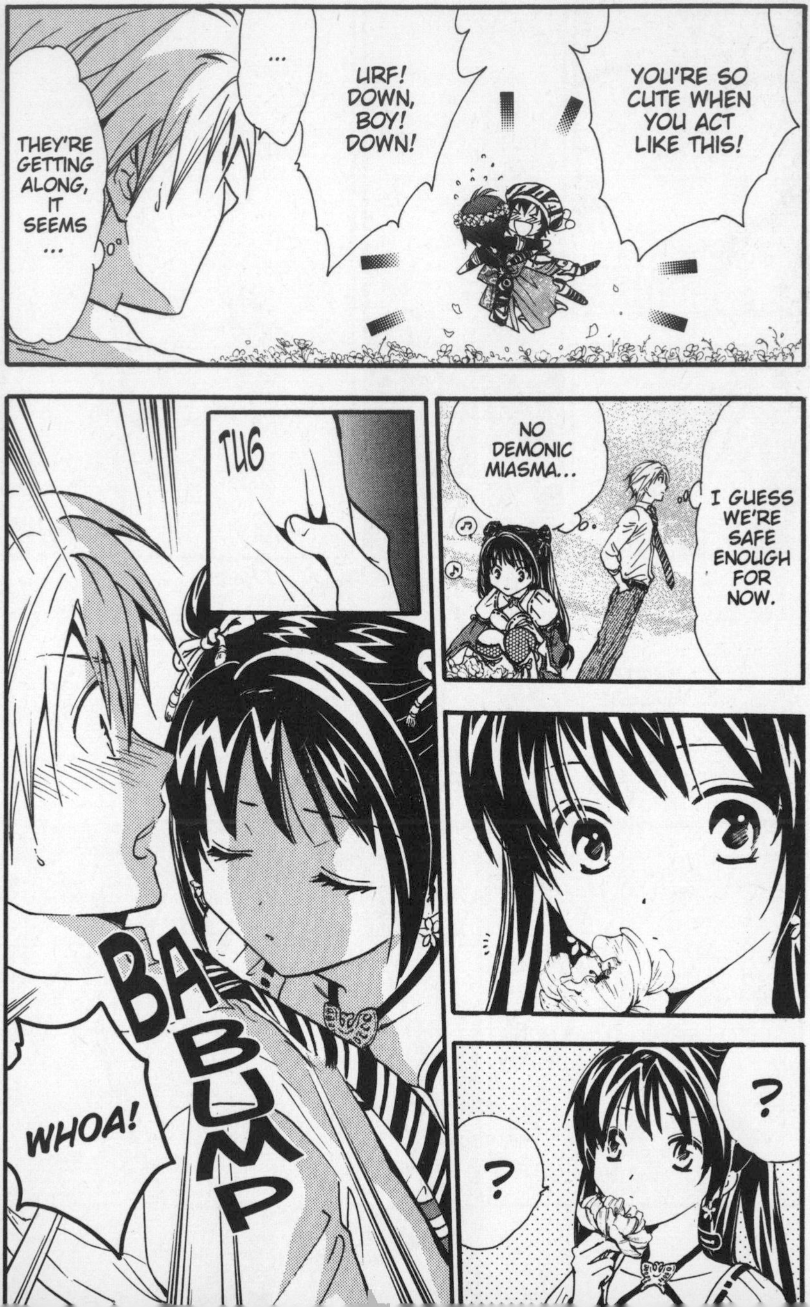
YOU'RE SO CUTE WHEN YOU ACT LIKE THIS!
URF! DOWN, BOY! DOWN!
...
THEY'RE GETTING ALONG, IT SEEMS...
I GUESS WE'RE SAFE ENOUGH FOR NOW.
NO DEMONIC MIASMA...
?
?
TUG
BA-BUMP
WHOA!

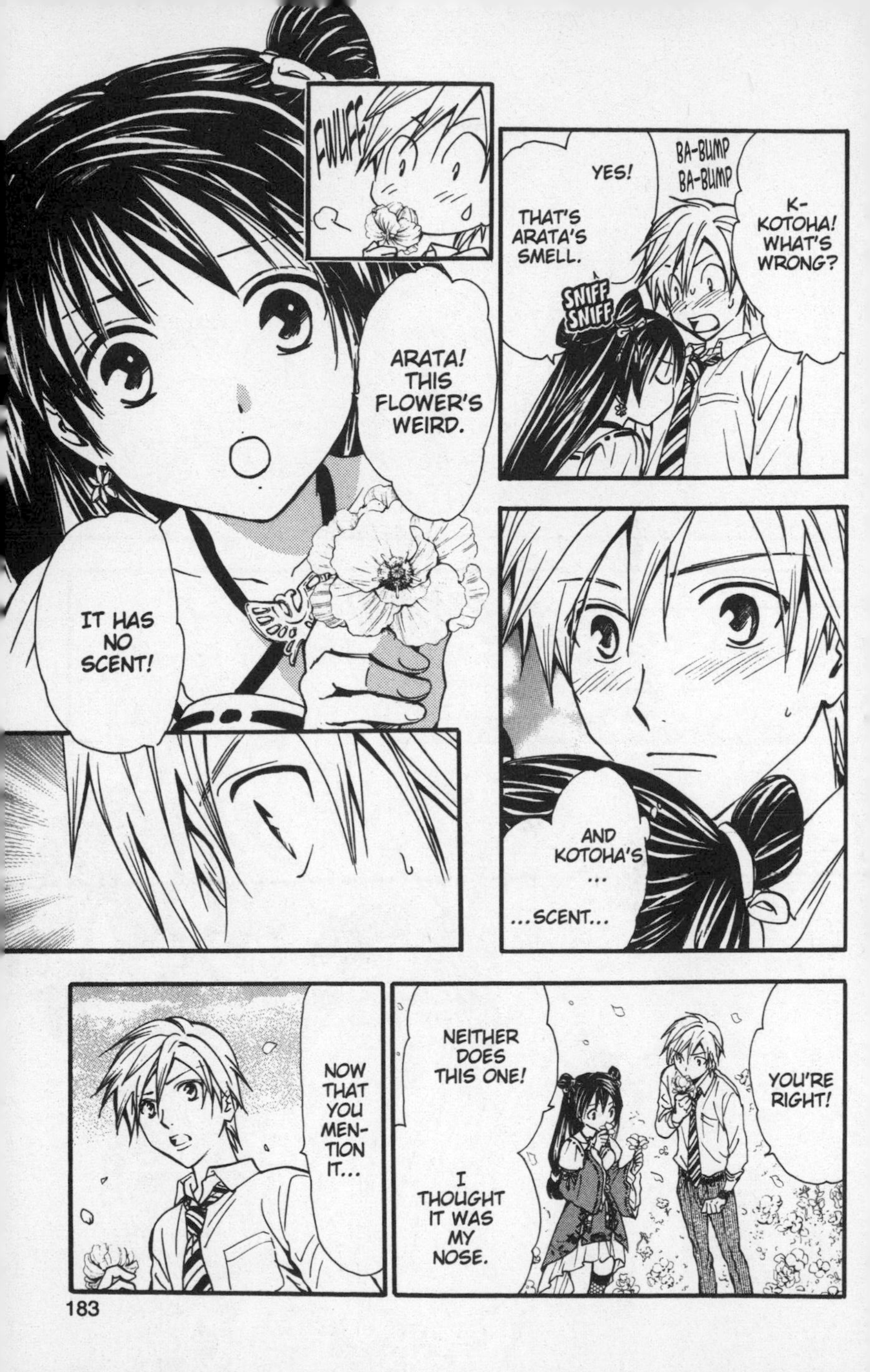
K-KOTOHA! WHAT'S WRONG?
BA-BUMP BA-BUMP
YES!
THAT'S ARATA'S SMELL.
SNIFF SNIFF
AND KOTOHA'S ...
...SCENT...
FWUFF
ARATA! THIS FLOWER'S WEIRD.
IT HAS NO SCENT!
YOU'RE RIGHT!
NEITHER DOES THIS ONE!
I THOUGHT IT WAS MY NOSE.
NOW THAT YOU MEN-TION IT...

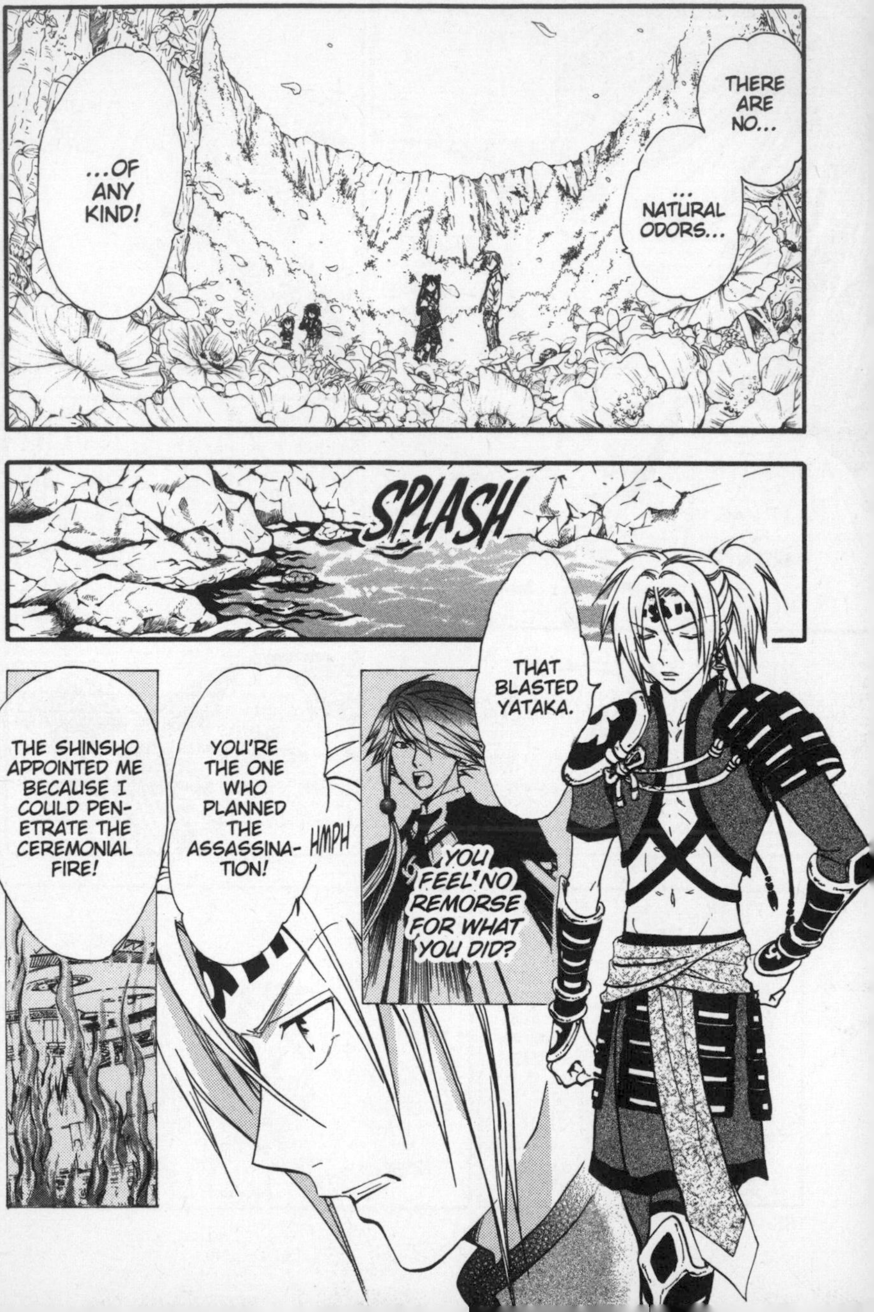
THERE ARE NO...
...NATURAL ODORS...
...OF ANY KIND!
SPLASH
THAT BLASTED YATAKA.
YOU FEEL NO REMORSE FOR WHAT YOU DID?
HMPH
YOU'RE THE ONE WHO PLANNED THE ASSASSINA-TION!
THE SHINSHO APPOINTED ME BECAUSE I COULD PEN-ETRATE THE CEREMONIAL FIRE!

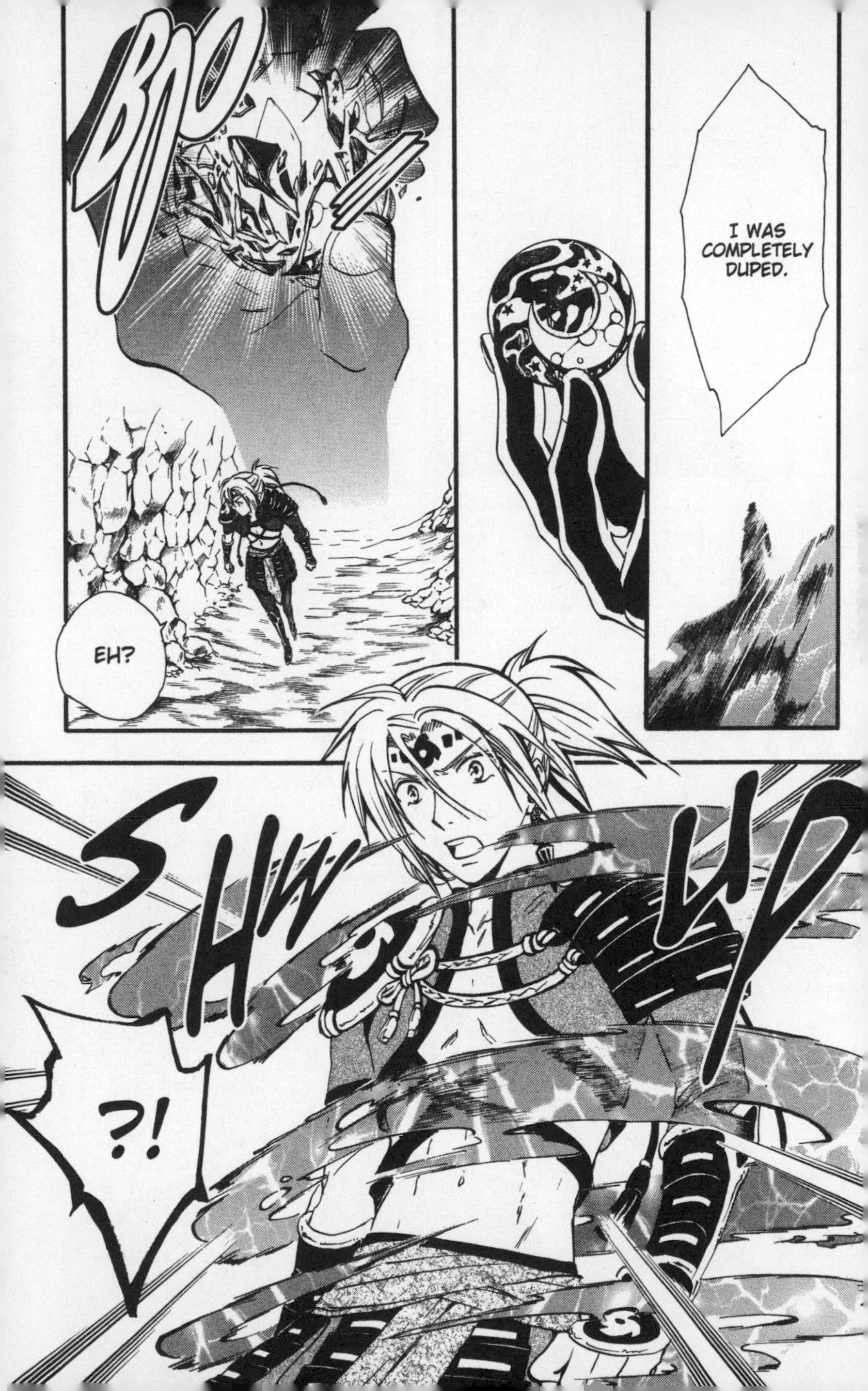
I WAS COMPLETELY DUPED.
BOOM
EH?
SHWUP
?!

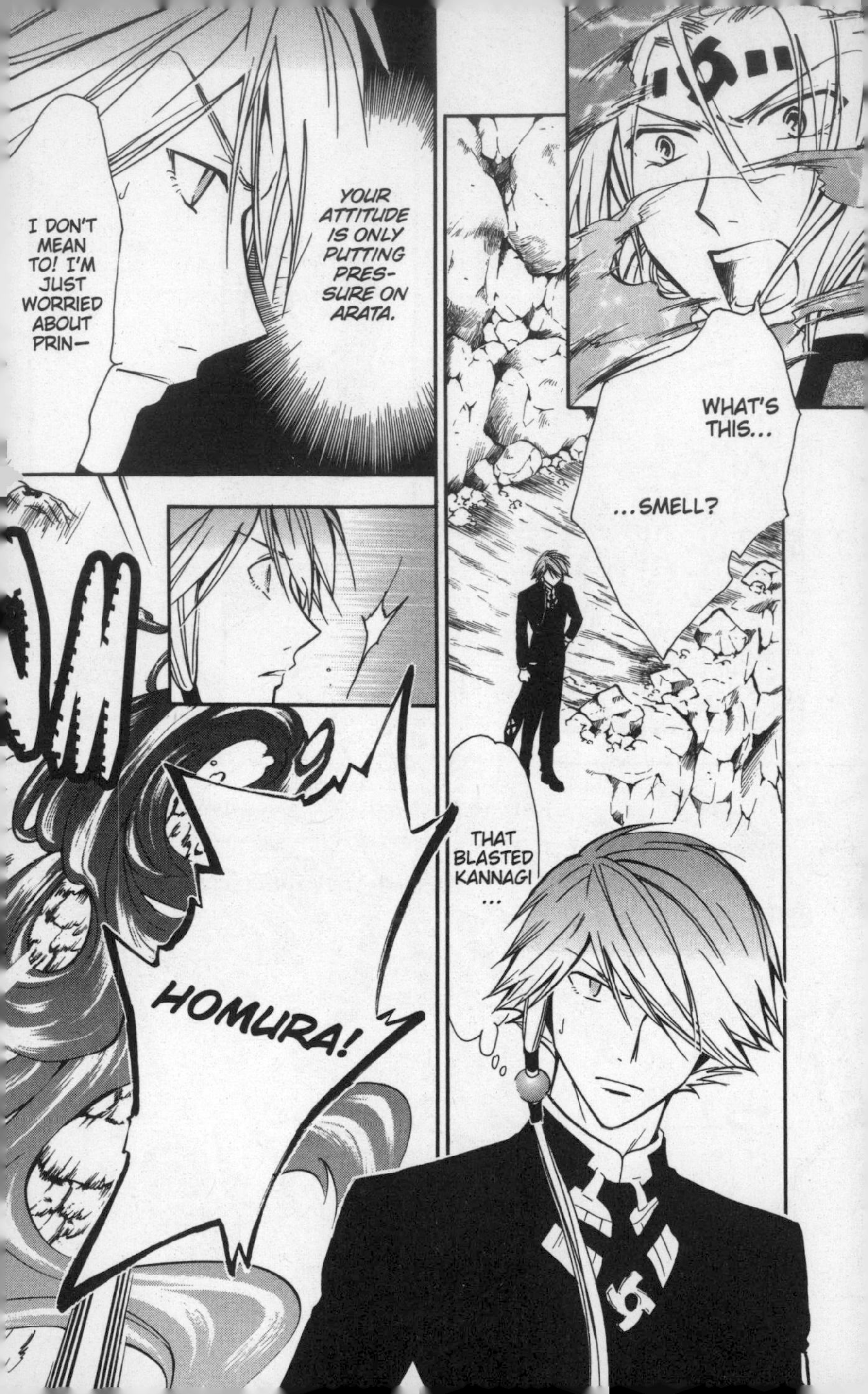
WHAT'S THIS...
...SMELL?
THAT BLASTED KANNAGI...
YOUR ATTITUDE IS ONLY PUTTING PRESSURE ON ARATA.
I DON'T MEAN TO! I'M JUST WORRIED ABOUT PRIN—
HOMURA!

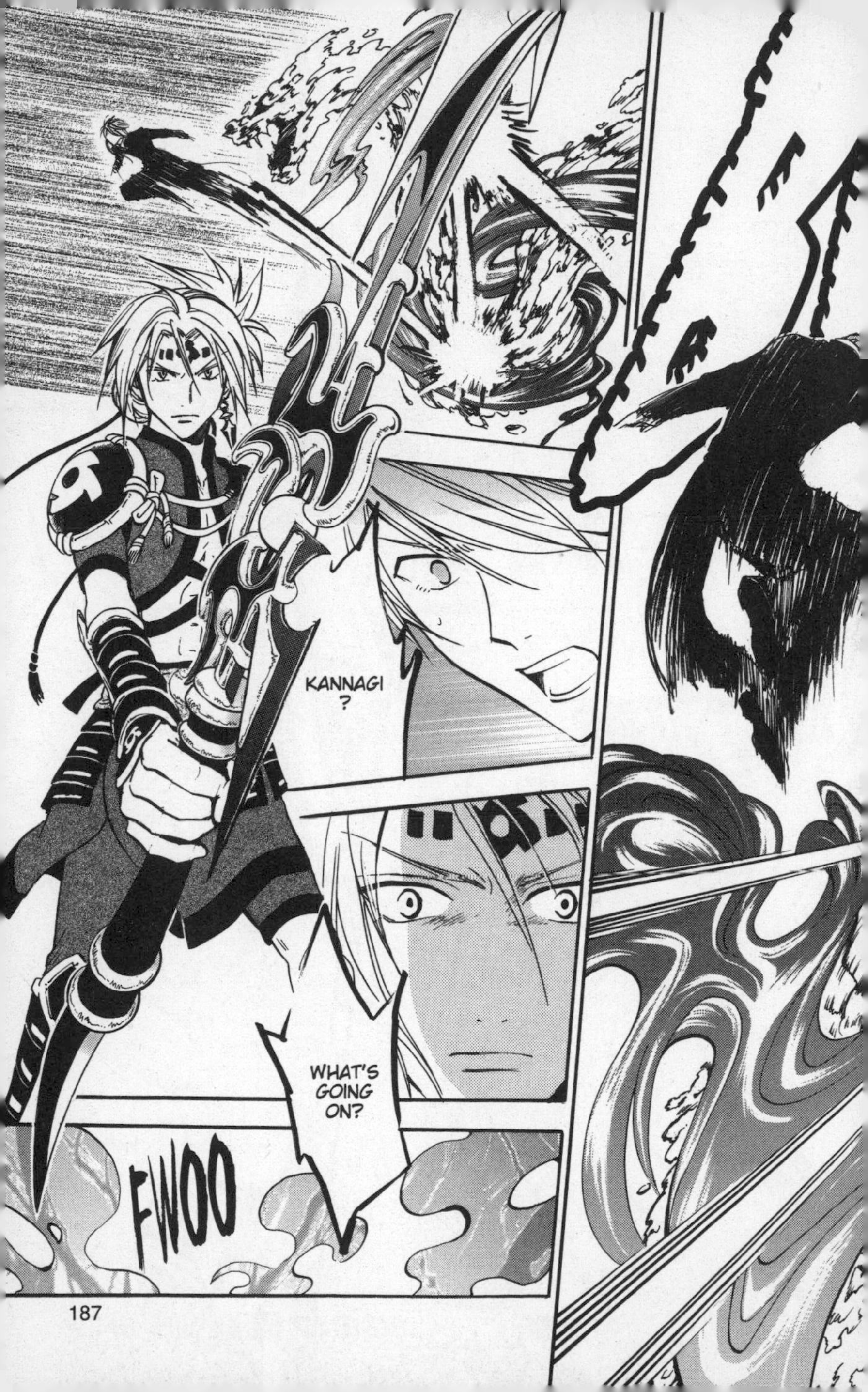
KANNAGI
?
WHAT'S GOING ON?
FWOO

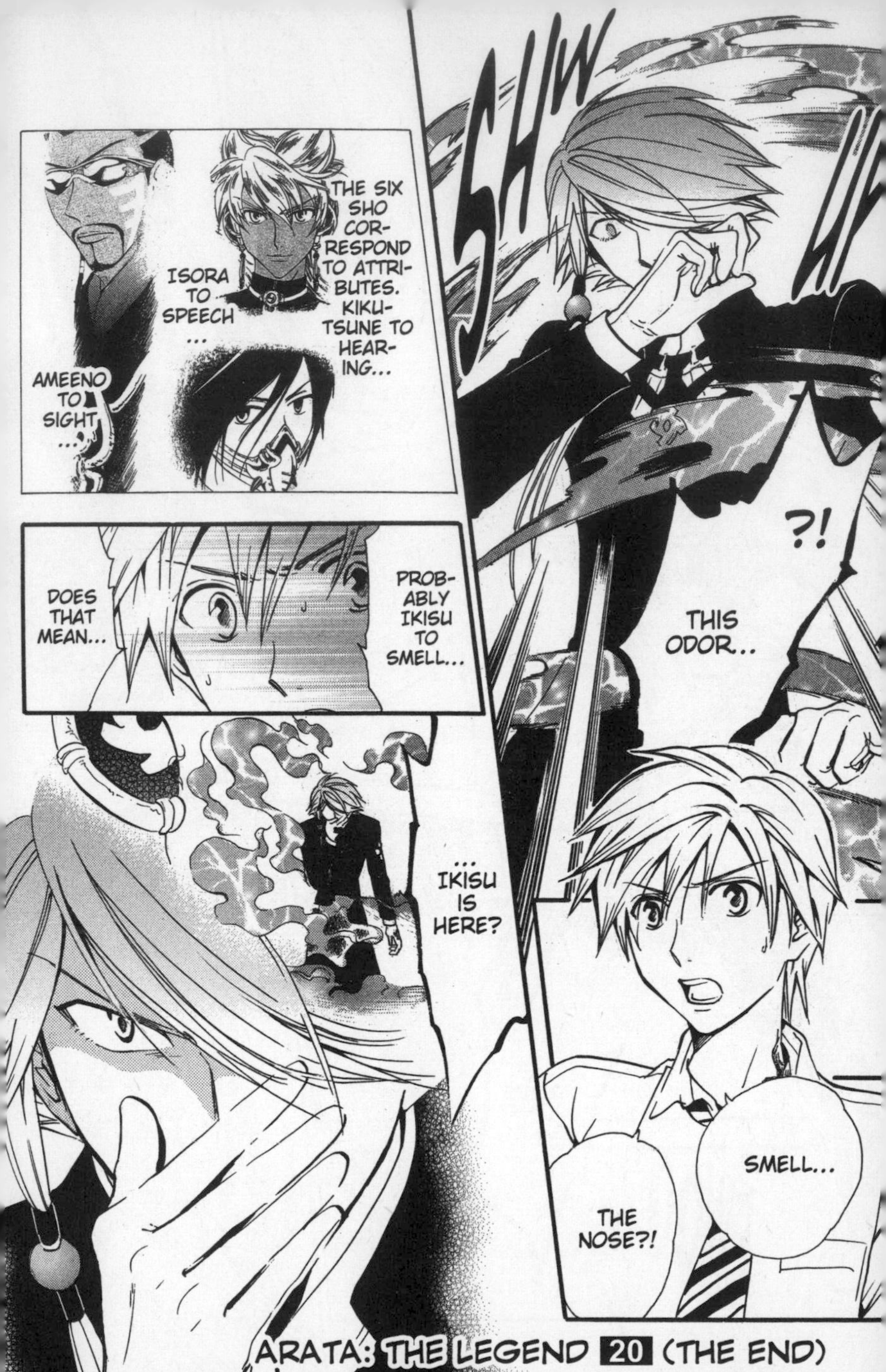
SHW
?!
THIS ODOR...
SMELL...
THE NOSE?!
THE SIX SHO CORRESPOND TO ATTRIBUTES. KIKUTSUNE TO HEARING...
ISORA TO SPEECH...
AMEENO TO SIGHT...
PROBABLY IKISU TO SMELL...
DOES THAT MEAN...
...IKISU IS HERE?

ARATA: THE LEGEND 20 (THE END)

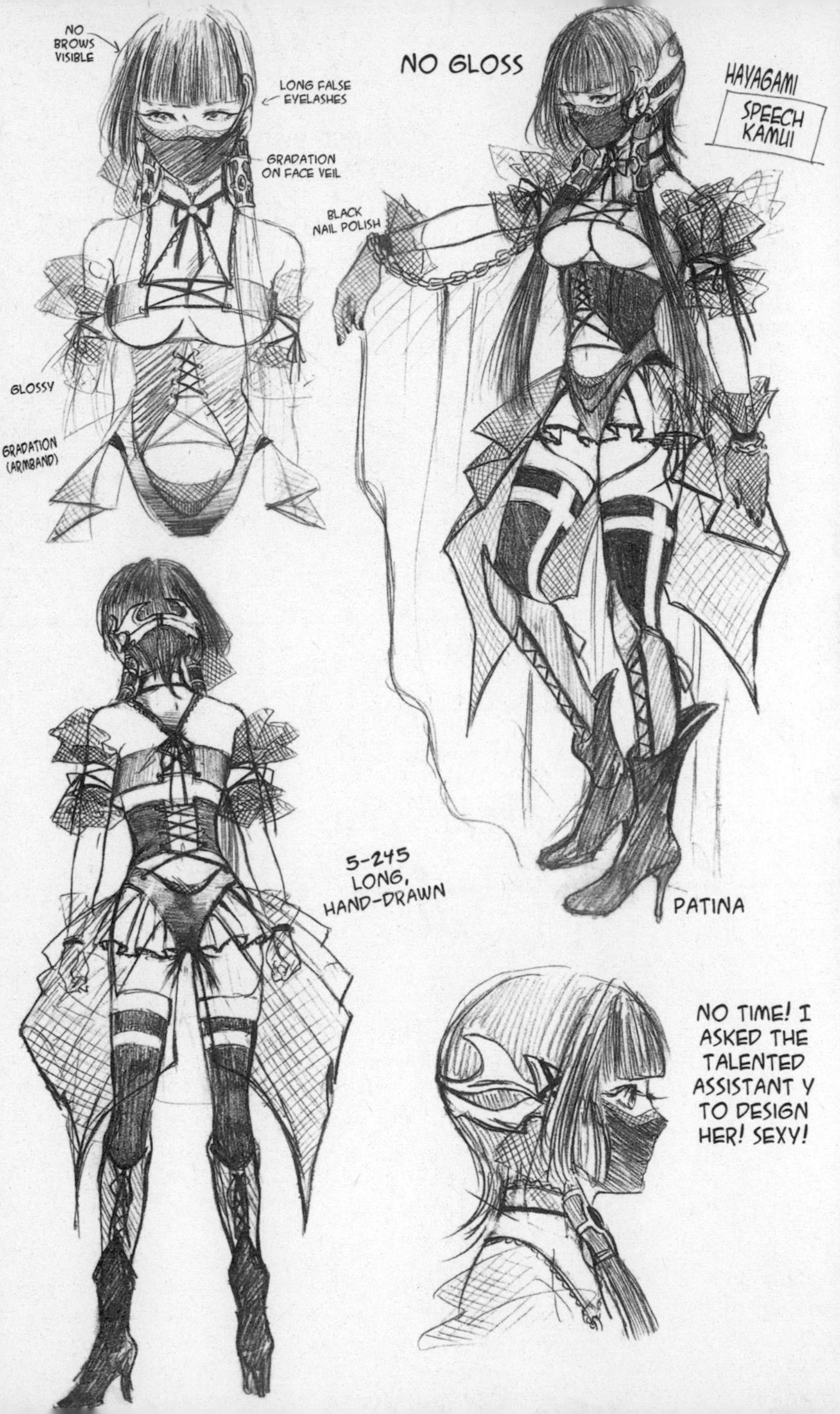
NO BROWS VISIBLE
LONG FALSE EYELASHES
GRADATION ON FACE VEIL
GLOSSY
GRADATION (ARMBAND)
NO GLOSS
HAYAGAMI
SPEECH KAMUI
BLACK NAIL POLISH
PATINA
5-245 LONG, HAND-DRAWN
NO TIME! I ASKED THE TALENTED ASSISTANT Y TO DESIGN HER! SEXY!

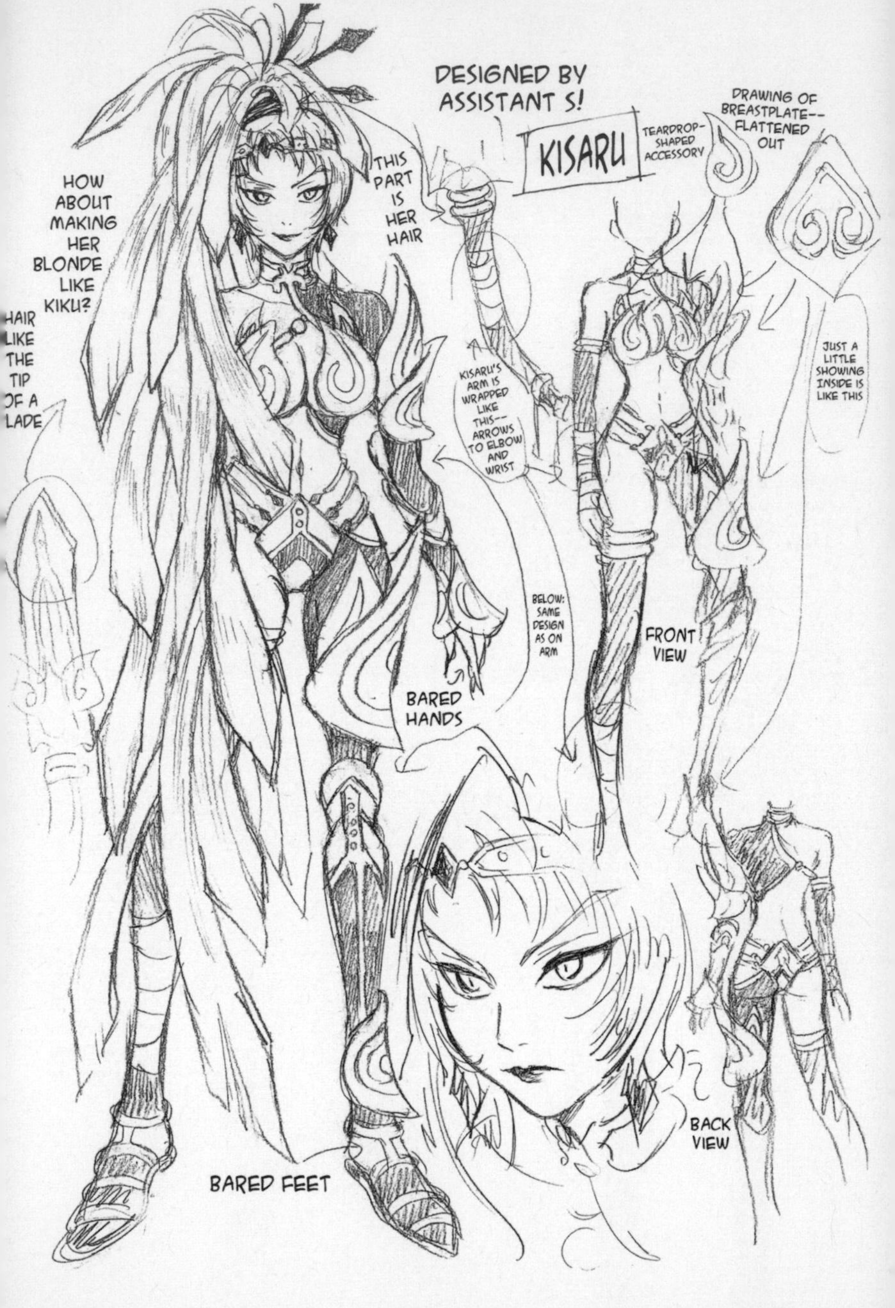
DESIGNED BY ASSISTANT S!
KISARU
TEARDROP-SHAPED ACCESSORY
DRAWING OF BREASTPLATE--FLATTENED OUT
THIS PART IS HER HAIR
HOW ABOUT MAKING HER BLONDE LIKE KIKU?
HAIR LIKE THE TIP OF A LADE
KISARU'S ARM IS WRAPPED LIKE THIS--ARROWS TO ELBOW AND WRIST
JUST A LITTLE SHOWING INSIDE IS LIKE THIS
BELOW: SAME DESIGN AS ON ARM
FRONT VIEW
BARED HANDS
BACK VIEW
BARED FEET

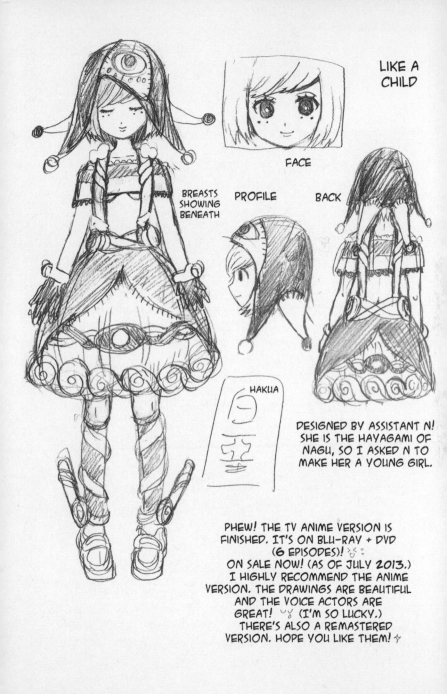

LIKE A CHILD

FACE

BREASTS SHOWING BENEATH

PROFILE

BACK

HAKUA

DESIGNED BY ASSISTANT N! SHE IS THE HAYAGAMI OF NAGU, SO I ASKED N TO MAKE HER A YOUNG GIRL.

PHEW! THE TV ANIME VERSION IS FINISHED. IT'S ON BLU-RAY + DVD (6 EPISODES)! ⸝⸝
ON SALE NOW! (AS OF JULY 2013.)
I HIGHLY RECOMMEND THE ANIME VERSION. THE DRAWINGS ARE BEAUTIFUL AND THE VOICE ACTORS ARE GREAT! ⸝⸝ (I'M SO LUCKY.)
THERE'S ALSO A REMASTERED VERSION. HOPE YOU LIKE THEM! ✦

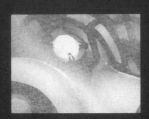

I'm happy to say that *Arata Kangatari* is now in its 20th volume!
I'm so grateful to all of you! Thank you very much!

I've been a manga artist for a long time, but this is the longest-running series I've done.

The story is past its halfway point, but there are lots more episodes left. I'm going to do my best to keep the action and suspense going, so please continue to support the story.

By the way, I've redone the series from volume 1, and a slightly different "remastered" comic with color illustrations, and two volumes combined into one, is now on sale!

If you'd like to see what is different about it, please pick up a copy. Hereafter, it'll be a first (?) in this industry with two simultaneous, but different *Arata Kangatari* versions.

—YUU WATASE—

AUTHOR BIO

Born March 5 in Osaka, Yuu Watase debuted in the *Shôjo Comic* manga anthology in 1989. She won the 43rd Shogakukan Manga Award with *Ceres: Celestial Legend*. One of her most famous works is *Fushigi Yûgi*, a series that has inspired the prequel *Fushigi Yûgi: Genbu Kaiden*. In 2008, *Arata: The Legend* started serialization in *Shonen Sunday*.

ARATA: THE LEGEND

Volume 20
Shonen Sunday Edition

Story and Art by YUU WATASE

ARATA KANGATARI Vol. 20
by Yuu WATASE
© 2009 Yuu WATASE
All rights reserved.
Original Japanese edition published by SHOGAKUKAN.
English translation rights in the United States of America, Canada, the United
Kingdom and Ireland arranged with SHOGAKUKAN.

English Adaptation: Lance Caselman
Translation: JN Productions
Touch-up Art & Lettering: Rina Mapa
Design: Veronica Casson
Editor: Gary Leach

Printed in the U.S.A.

Published by VIZ Media, LLC
P.O. Box 77010
San Francisco, CA 94107

10 9 8 7 6 5 4 3 2 1
First printing, December 2014

www.viz.com

WWW.SHONENSUNDAY.COM

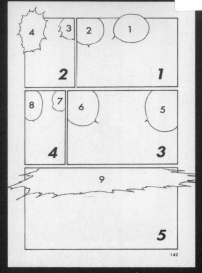

← Follow the action this way.

THIS IS THE LAST PAGE

Arata: The Legend has been printed in the original Japanese format in order to preserve the orientation of the original artwork.

Please turn it around and begin reading from right to left. Unlike English, Japanese is read right to left, so Japanese comics are read in reverse order from the way English comics are typically read. Have fun with it!